Maria-Josep Cuenca and Liesbeth Degand (Eds.)
Discourse Markers in Interaction

Trends in Linguistics
Studies and Monographs

Editors
Chiara Gianollo
Daniël Van Olmen

Editorial Board
Walter Bisang
Tine Breban
Volker Gast
Hans Henrich Hock
Karen Lahousse
Natalia Levshina
Caterina Mauri
Heiko Narrog
Salvador Pons
Niina Ning Zhang
Amir Zeldes

Editor responsible for this volume
Daniël Van Olmen

Volume 376

Discourse Markers in Interaction

From Production to Comprehension

Edited by
Maria-Josep Cuenca and Liesbeth Degand

DE GRUYTER
MOUTON

ISBN 978-3-11-163179-0
e-ISBN (PDF) 978-3-11-079035-1
e-ISBN (EPUB) 978-3-11-079054-2
ISSN 1861-4302

Library of Congress Control Number: 2022936818

Bibliographic information published by the Deutsche Nationalbibliothek
The Deutsche Nationalbibliothek lists this publication in the Deutsche Nationalbibliografie;
detailed bibliographic data are available on the Internet at http://dnb.dnb.de.

© 2024 Walter de Gruyter GmbH, Berlin/Boston
This volume is text- and page-identical with the hardback published in 2022.
Typesetting: Integra Software Services Pvt. Ltd.

www.degruyter.com

Contents

Maria-Josep Cuenca and Liesbeth Degand
1 Discourse markers in interaction: Introduction —— 1

Óscar Loureda, Inés Recio Fernández, Adriana Cruz and Martha Rudka
2 Principles of Discourse Marking: An experimental approach of general and contrastive perspectives —— 17

Joanna Blochowiak and Cristina Grisot
3 New perspectives on *car* and *parce que*: Is it about subjectivity, reasoning or speakers? —— 45

Sandrine Zufferey, Ekaterina Tskhovrebova, Mathis Wetzel and Pascal Gygax
4 Individual differences in the ability to master connectives: The importance of exposure to print —— 69

Mathis Wetzel, Sandrine Zufferey and Pascal Gygax
5 Do non-native readers rely on connectives? The processing of coherence relations in L2 —— 89

Zoé Broisson and Liesbeth Degand
6 How egocentric is discourse marker use? Investigating the impact of speaker orientation and cognitive load on discourse marker production —— 121

Ruiqi Li, Liesbeth Allein, Damien Sileo and Marie-Francine Moens
7 When do discourse markers affect computational sentence understanding? —— 159

Darinka Verdonik
8 Discourse markers and dialogue act annotation for computational dialogue systems —— 191

Maria-Josep Cuenca
9 Translating discourse markers: Implicitation and explicitation strategies —— 215

Mira Ariel
10 Processing polyfunctional discourse markers: Making sense of Hebrew
    harey —— 247

Index —— 277

Maria-Josep Cuenca and Liesbeth Degand
1 Discourse markers in interaction: Introduction

1 An interactive perspective on discourse markers

In any kind of human communication, be it written, spoken or signed, formal or informal, computer-mediated or not, Discourse Markers (henceforth DMs) are part of the game. This ubiquitousness informs us of a crucial inherent aspect of human language. Yet, despite an impressive quantity of work starting in the early 1980s, the linguistic description of DMs remains scattered, first and foremost because it is a very heterogeneous linguistic category, fulfilling many different functions in discourse (for an overview, see, among others, Blühdorn, Foolen & Loureda 2017, Degand, Cornillie & Pietrandrea 2013, Fischer 2016, Maschler & Schiffrin 2015). Many different studies have tried to tackle this categorial heterogeneity or DMs' well-established multifunctionality across a variety of genres and interactive contexts (e.g. Abuzcki 2014, Crible 2018, Maschler 1997, Kyratzis & Ervin-Tripp 1999) as well as cross-linguistically (e.g. Aijmer 2007, Aijmer & Simon-Vandenbegen 2006, Andersen, Brizuela, Dupuy & Gonnerman 1999, Cuenca 2007, Degand, Broisson, Crible & Grzech 2022, Gabarro-López 2017, Nølke 2007).

While many of these studies aim at getting a firmer grip on understanding the inherent properties of DMs as a linguistic category, other researchers take DMs as a starting point to gain insight into other aspects of human communication. As Zufferey et al. (this volume, chapter 4) point out, "as connectives' usage lies at the interface between lexical, syntactic and discursive skills, they raise specific challenges within each of these domains." This explains why the production and processing of DMs involves complex form-function mappings which affect several areas of language use and analysis, such as second language learning, first language acquisition, translation, reading and writing processes, (interactive) speech planning and processing. This has led to a 'confusing patchwork of interesting yet conflicting approaches' (Crible 2017: 100), which we take as the sign of an exciting and evolving domain of research.

To gain further insight into this complex linguistic category, more systematic work is needed on the production and on the interpretation of DMs in a variety of situational settings, resorting to different methodological approaches (see, e.g., Crible 2017, Fischer 2014). Thus, looking at **how** we use DMs is a crucial step in finding out **why** we use them in certain situations and under certain conditions, but also when we do not, i.e. when DMs are left implicit (cf. Asr & Demberg 2012,

Taboada 2009, Zufferey 2016). Specifically, the procedural and applied linguistics approach to DMs, both from a production and a comprehension perspective, need further research in an area that has traditionally been analyzed from a more theoretical and descriptive perspective. For instance, research is still in its initial steps as for the double face of DMs, namely as traces of the speaker's production difficulties accounting for their "potentially disfluent functions" (Crible 2018: 51) and as signals intentionally used by the speaker to facilitate the addressee's interpretation of the discourse.

To make progress on these questions, the production and comprehension perspectives must be combined more systematically. By analyzing how DMs are used or left implicit it is possible to assess the impact of discourse marking on both discourse production and processing. Similarly, by taking into account how the presence of DMs affects the addressee's discourse comprehension, we will get better insight into the underlying cognitive and functional principles of (interactive) language production.

2 Structure and contributions

With this aim in mind, the present volume consists of an introductory paper and nine chapters reporting on research about the role that DMs play in language production and comprehension from an experimental or corpus-based perspective. The five first chapters after the introduction are more experimental in nature. Chapters 7 and 8 explore aspects of DMs use for computational language processing. The two last chapters are corpus-based studies.

The first part of the volume includes papers that address DM comprehension through reading experiments in Chapter 2 (*Principles of discourse marking: An experimental approach of general and contrastive perspectives* by Loureda, Recio, Cruz and Rudka) and in Chapter 3 (*The mapping between the subjective-objective divide and French causal connectives: Is it about the relation, the connectives or the speakers?* by Blochowiak and Grisot). In Chapter 4 (*Individual differences in the ability to master connectives: The importance of exposure to print* by Zufferey, Tskhovrebova, Wetzel and Gygax) and in Chapter 5 (*Do non-native readers rely on connectives? The processing of coherence relations in L2* by Wetzel, Zufferey and Gygax) a similar methodological approach is taken but it is applied to advanced first and second language acquisition, respectively. A speech production perspective is adopted in Chapter 6 (*How egocentric is Discourse Marker use? Investigating the impact of speaker orientation and cognitive load on Discourse Marker produc-*

tion by Broisson and Degand) investigating the impact of different situational settings on DM use.

Chapters 7 (*When Do Discourse Markers Affect Computational Sentence Understanding?* by Li, Allein, Sileao and Moens) and 8 (*Strategies of discourse markers use within dialogue acts* by Verdonik) propose a computational perspective investigating the role of DMs in dialog systems and natural language processing, respectively.

The volume closes with two corpus-based studies. Chapter 9 (*Translating discourse markers: Implicitation and explicitation strategies* by Cuenca) sets out how and when DMs are translated in academic writing, while Chapter 10 (*Processing polyfunctional discourse markers: Making sense of Hebrew* harey by Ariel) illustrates how polyfunctional DMs may provide specific processing instructions.

In Chapter 2, **Loureda, Recio, Cruz and Rudka** ("Principles of discourse marking: An experimental approach of general and contrastive perspectives") describe the results of several untimed eye-tracking reading experiments. The experiments share an analogous design with two independent variables testing the presence or absence of a discourse particle. The markers tested, including both connective DMs and modal markers, were mostly Spanish connectives and scalar particles (namely, *sin embargo* 'however', *a pesar de ello* 'despite that', *por tanto* 'therefore', *por ello* 'thus', *es decir* 'that is', *primero. . . segundo* 'firstly. . . secondly. . . .'; *también* 'also', *hasta* 'even', *incluso* 'even'). The English connective *therefore* and the German modal particle *sogar* 'even' are also the focus of some experiments. The over-all analysis of the data, which include total reading time, first-pass reading time and the re-reading time of utterances and utterance segments, is a solid basis to formulate three Cognitive Principles of Discourse Marking accounting for how discourse particles affect utterance processing.

First Principle of Discourse Marking. The introduction of a discourse particle into a given utterance modifies the processing strategy of the utterance in relation to a corresponding unmarked utterance.

Second Principle of Discourse Marking. The introduction of a discourse particle into a given utterance sets as its maximum processing costs those of the corresponding unmarked utterance.

Third Principle of Discourse Marking. The introduction of a discourse particle into a given utterance immediately sets as the upper limit of the processing efforts of the segment in which it is integrated those of the corresponding unmarked segment.

As a corollary of the first and second principles, Loureda et al. formulate an additional generalization:

> *Corollary of the First and Second Principle of Discourse Marking* (optimal control of reanalysis). A discourse particle regulates the reanalysis of a first assumption in such a way that additional cognitive effort is excluded in the total processing of the marked utterance with respect to the corresponding unmarked utterance.

The *Cognitive Principles of Discourse Marking* predict four common instructions conveyed by discourse particles that explain how they affect discourse processing and also the different types of instructions they encode. The instructions shared by discourse particles are the following:
- establishing new routes to access information (First Principle)
- constraining the processing of semantically more complex information (Second Principle)
- regulating reanalysis in utterance interpretation (Corollary of the First and Second Principle),
- facilitating the immediate integration of the discourse segment directly affected by the discourse particle (Third Principle).

In addition, from a cross-linguistic perspective, the principles provide a frame that sets the variation ranges for the impact of equivalent discourse particles between languages regarding discourse processing.

Blochowiak and Grisot, in Chapter 3 ("The mapping between the subjective-objective divide and French causal connectives: Is it about the relation, the connectives or the speakers?"), present an experimental research on differences in performance according to age groups. Their results challenge a long-standing assumption as for two 'synonym' French causal DMs corresponding to *because*: that *car* is preferred to express subjective causal relations, whereas *parce que* can convey either objective or subjective relations. The authors discuss the results of two experiments designed to assess the explicit preferences for the use of *car* and *parce que* with two different groups of participants as for age: an offline evaluation experiment with university students (aged 20–25) and a crowdsourcing experiment with other native speakers (aged 20–70). The design of the experiments and their results can be related to four hypotheses, three about the use of *car* and *parce que* to express subjective and objective causal relations (the classic hypothesis, the novel hypothesis and the complex subjectivity hypothesis) and one about the participants (the sample-related hypothesis).
1. According to the *classic hypothesis*, *car* is considered a prototypical marker of subjective causal relations, while *parce que* fits both subjective and objective causal relations.

2. Contrary to the classic hypothesis, the *novel hypothesis* predicts that *car* is no longer a prototypical marker of subjective causal relations and becomes interchangeable with *parce que* in the case of both subjective and objective causal relations.
3. The *complex subjectivity hypothesis* predicts that, regarding causal relations, subjectivity is in general more complex than objectivity.
4. The *sample-related hypothesis* predicts that the behaviour of participants recruited among students will be unlike the behaviour of participants recruited among the larger population of speakers of French.

The analysis suggests that the use of the two causal connectives to express subjective and objective relations not only depends on the connective or the relation conveyed but also on the speakers' educational background, reasoning skills and age. The results of the experiments show that *car* has gained ground over *parce que* in expressing objective relations. This implies that, despite the decline of *car* in oral speech, written French is undergoing a change towards greater interchangeability between the two causal connectives, or even a switch towards the objectivization of *car*. The presence of *car* is increasing in written press, SMS and chats, and its use is becoming similar to that of *parce que* in the case of participants between 20 and 60 years old. Only the older group age (60–70) verifies the classic hypothesis, according to which *car* is a prototypical marker for subjective causal relations.

Beyond challenging 'well-established' knowledge, the research has also important methodological consequences, as formulated in the sample-related hypothesis. Older participants behaved differently from younger ones. Moreover, university students behaved differently from a comparable age group with respect to dealing with complex inferences. These observations highlight the importance of choosing the category of participants in experimental studies and how this selection may introduce an important bias in the conclusions derived from any research.

In Chapter 4 ("Individual differences in the ability to master connectives: The importance of exposure to print"), **Zufferey, Tskhovrebova, Wetzel and Gygax** report on a series of experiments designed to investigate individual differences in the mastery of connectives by using tasks such as acceptability judgements and fill-in-the-blank exercises. The experiments were designed to compare the results across three different groups of participants, namely, native adult speakers, native teenagers and second language learners.

One general conclusion is that exposure to print is a strong predictor of linguistic and cognitive skills as for the use of connectives. In all groups, exposure to print is an important factor to predict and assess the ability to handle connectives from the written mode, especially among adults. Other relevant factors are the overall frequency of the marker and its cognitive complexity. According to the degree of exposure to print, native adult speakers exhibit variable levels of competence, mainly affecting the use of less frequent connectives. As for native teenagers, individual variation is strongly dependent on education level, which is also linked to exposure to print. Finally, second language learners show a lower effect of connective frequency, since, as already observed by Crewe (1990), learners usually rely on a small subset of connectives that they overuse while expanding their repertoire, and the subset is not always linked to frequency.

The research makes important theoretical and methodological contributions. First, these kinds of experiments are usually performed with university students, which certainly biases the results. The fact that the same experiments are compared among three different groups (adults, teenagers and second language learners) gives a wider picture of a very complex reality. Second, how to identify factors such as exposure to print is far from simple. The authors use an indirect method, the Author Recognition Test (Stanovich & West 1989), and point out that, although it has advantages as compared to self-assessment, it needs adaptation according to the population group. Third, many experimental studies rely on highly frequent markers, whereas markers that are typical of the written mode, infrequent in speech, remain less explored. Finally, studies regarding L2 learners are usually based on the analysis of natural productions in corpus data (e.g. Granger & Tyson, 1996; Tapper, 2005), whereas the experimental perspective (e.g. Degand & Sanders, 1999; Zufferey et al., 2015) remains under-represented.

"Do non-native readers rely on connectives? The processing of coherence relations in L2" (Chapter 5), by **Wetzel, Zufferey and Gygax**, further develops the experimental research comparing natives and second language learners. The chapter tests the extent to which L2-readers rely on discourse connectives when processing a sentence and whether their reading fluency is affected by missing or misleading connectives. The general hypothesis is that the information conveyed by connectives is less salient when reading in a second language, because non-native readers rely more on lexical propositional information than on functional cues. The authors report on two experiments in which self-paced reading times of native and non-native readers of French for causal and concessive sentences were measured. Experiment 1 tests how missing connectives affect online processing by presenting the examples with or without a correct connective. Experiment 2 explores how inappropriate connectives affect online processing by presenting the same examples with a correct or with an incorrect connective.

The analysis suggests that, independently of language group, (i) all readers tend to read implicitly marked sentences more slowly than explicitly marked ones, and (ii) the reading of native and non-native speakers is affected by the complexity of the coherence relation, which indicates that processing in L2 follows the same general principles as in L1. In contrast, the reading fluency of non-native readers, even if they are generally able to efficiently retrieve the meaning of connectives, is less affected by incorrect connectives than is the case of native readers, thus confirming the hypothesis that non-native readers rely less on connectives than native readers.

Broisson and Degand, in Chapter 6 ("How egocentric is Discourse Marker use? Investigating the impact of speaker orientation and cognitive load on Discourse Marker production"), adopt a production in interaction approach to the use of DMs. On the basis of an elicitated data set, they test the impact on the use of DMs of two variables: the hearer vs. speaker orientation (i.e., allocentric vs. egocentric) and the cognitive load. Speaker orientation was manipulated as follows: In the allocentric task, two participants had to jointly assemble a tangram puzzle (dialogic task). In the egocentric task, all participants had to retell themselves the instructions to the puzzle they had solved (or had attempted to solve) in the first task, using verbal cues only (monologic task). Cognitive load was manipulated in the allocentric task by the addition or not of a dual task (word identification) and in the egocentric task by giving access or not to a memory aid during the retelling task. The data collected were compiled as a corpus containing 36 French oral texts, amounting to a little less than three hours of speech, which were transcribed, annotated for DMs, and analyzed.

The research questions addressed were two:
1. What is the impact of allocentric vs. egocentric speaker orientation on DM production?
2. What is the impact of cognitive load on DM production, especially in the allocentric condition?

The results show that speakers in the egocentric context used a more restricted set of highly frequent DM types characterized by their high degree of polysemy. In contrast, in the allocentric context, speakers use more and more diversified markers, that are less polysemous. More speaker-oriented DMs operate as 'frames' that structure the temporality of discourse, are used as fillers or serve as markers of self-monitored adaptations or repair of speech content (ideational and sequential domains). More hearer-oriented DMs, on the other hand, operate mainly in the interpersonal domain (speaker-hearer management DMs, but also concessive-contrastive, specification or reformulation markers). Cognitive load, however, did not bring about major differences in the density, diversity or polysemy of the DMs. DMs were not produced more frequently but less diversely under a higher mental load.

Broisson and Degand's analysis opens a novel research avenue on the study of DMs. Most studies on DMs are marked by a strong hearer-oriented bias, since DM are considered as expressions that provide instructions for the hearer and contribute to the utterance's relevance (allocentric view). Broisson and Degand's conclusions challenge this assumption by taking into account the contributions of researchers who argue that speakers produce language as if it was intended for themselves in the first place and only under certain conditions adapt it to their addressee (e.g. Bard et al., 2000; Dell & Brown, 1991, Horton & Keysar, 1996; Keysar et al., 1998, 2000; Roßnagel, 2000; Vogels et al. 2020). Their results point to the conclusion that the speaker-oriented and hearer-oriented functions of DMs seem to co-exist and competitively weigh in the decisions that determine use in context to ultimately benefit both interlocutors. An egocentric behavior privileges the use of more economical DMs in terms of processing, such as underspecified DMs. Conversely, an allocentric behavior leads to the use of fewer polysemous and more monosemous DMs, which indicates that speakers do indeed take their hearers' processing cost into account using more specific DMs that are easier to interpret in context.

In Chapter 7 ("When Do Discourse Markers Affect Computational Sentence Understanding?"), **Li, Allein, Sileo and Moens** introduce the perspective of computational models for language processing. The authors explore the effect of discourse connectives on various sentence embedding computational models and how it differs from human sentence processing in the case of connectives. The study of the effects of connectives in computation processing is a relatively new area of study (e.g. Chen, Chu, and Gimpel 2019, Nie, Bennett, and Goodman 2019, Sileo et al. 2019, 2020). Four research questions allow to test the accuracy of sentence embedding computation models:
1. Do sentence embedding models adequately capture the meaning of sentences containing a discourse connective?
2. How well do sentence embedding models deal with different connective types?
3. What is the effect of discourse connective removal on sentence embeddings?
4. If a connective is replaced with another connective, how much does this affect the sentence embedding?

The comparative analysis sheds light on the extent to which sentence embedding models make use of connective information and pinpoint the strengths and weaknesses of current models. The specific results offer other interesting aspects. The type of relation (e.g., sequential, additive, adversative and so on) has an effect on the processing of the relations both with and without a connective. In general terms, sequential connectives were the easiest to handle, whereas adversative connectives were difficult for computational sentiment analysis and additive ones for order-sensitive tasks. Omitting and switching connectives usually have a negative influence on computational language understanding. Interestingly, the richer knowledge of discourse connectives a computation system has, the more negative effect the inappropriate connectives has on them. The analysis uncovers relevant differences between machine and human processing of coherence relations conveyed by connectives. Humans infer inter-sentential relations without connectives more accurately than current sentence embedding models. In contrast with sentence embedding models, the presence of connectives promotes reading continuity and reduces the time that humans need in sentence processing, but this does not necessarily have any effect on reading comprehension accuracy. As for computation systems, the dependence on the use of correct discourse markers for sentence processing is larger than for humans. Therefore, the presence and appropriate use of connectives are a positive incentive for sentence embedding models processing and significantly reduces the error rate in subsequent computational tasks.

Chapter 8 ("Discourse markers and dialogue act annotation for computational dialogue systems") by **Verdonik** deals with DM annotation for computational systems. The general problem explored is how to determine when a DM is a dialogue act on its own or it is integrated in a dialogue act including the following utterance. Dialogue acts are minimal units of interaction that express the speaker's intention. This concept, directly linked to speech-act theory, has been explored in theories related to computational work in building dialogue systems, i.e., systems where a computer communicates with humans by speaking. The author explores this notion and how dialogue acts and DMs are treated in several generic schemes, namely, DAMSL (Allen & Core 1997), SWBD-DAMSL (Jurafsky et al. 1997), AMI (AMI 2005), ISO 24617-2 (2012) and DART (Weisser 2016, 2019).

Considering the contributions of these approaches and taking into account real data, Verdonik presents a corpus study of Slovene casual conversation from a TV show. The analysis allows us to identify several criteria to distinguish DM which are separate dialogue acts, which are prosodic (pauses and intonation fall, emphasis in pronunciation), syntactic (DM derived from imperatives and other procedural units) or combinatory (clusters with a specific illocutionary force). Her contribution highlights the difficulty in segmenting and annotating spoken data, a crucial task to improve computational dialogue systems.

In Chapter 9 ("Translating discourse markers: Implicitation and explicitation strategies"), **Cuenca** describes the strategies and specific techniques used to translate DMs used as text connectives. The study specifically zooms in on the factors favouring implicitation strategies (i.e. the omission of a DM or its substitution by a more general one) and explicitation strategies (i.e. the addition or specification of a DM) as clues to both the production and the interpretation process involved in the use of a DM. As procedural discourse units, connectives are translated differently from content-words. When translating a DM, the translator takes into account the whole context of use, which can expand much farther than in the case of other linguistic expressions. The process of translating a DM implies the comprehension of its meaning and intended effects when produced and a second-level production process by which the translator proposes a linguistic form that transfers both the denotation and the connotation of its relational meaning.

In the chapter, the strategies for translating text connectives (inter-sentential DMs) are identified and illustrated by analyzing a parallel one directional corpus including Catalan articles and their English translation published in a History journal. The results of the analysis can be linked to the three research questions addressed in this chapter:

1. *Which are the strategies for translating DMs linking at the inter-sentential level?* In written academic texts, DMs linking independent sentences tend to be translated literally (or almost literally), but implicitation and explicitation strategies are also significant, especially when compared with other types of dynamic translation.
2. *Which factors (either syntactic or semantic/pragmatic) account for the implicitation or explicitation of a DM?* The crucial factors to implicitate and explicitate are not only syntactic (scope, combination and collocation) and semantic (meaning of the marker and domain), but are also bound to the differences between the two languages involved and the translation process itself.
3. *How can translation help uncover cross-linguistic differences in DMs use and processing?* The analysis of translated texts uncovers cross-linguistic differences related to the lack of direct counterparts or differences as for paradigmatic relations, frequency of use of a DM and stylistic preferences.

Methodologically, the approach adopted by Cuenca is in line with Becher's (2011a, 2011b) analysis since all the connective DMs found in both the source and the translated texts are analyzed. The manual identification of all the markers broadens the picture with respect to some of the previous contributions to DM implicitation or explicitation, which analyze one DM or a pre-defined group of markers. The multifactorial analysis shows the complexity of the processes underlying decision making in the translation of DMs. It is relevant to understand why and how inter-sentential DMs are used in discourse production and comprehension, and contributes to explain how implicit and explicit coherence relations interplay cross-linguistically.

The last chapter, by **Ariel** ("Processing polyfunctional discourse markers: Making sense of Hebrew *harey*), is a corpus-based study of the polyfunctional DM *harey* ('hereby, after all'), which has developed two apparently contradictory procedural meanings. From an original deictic meaning ('here is') *harey* has developed two main uses as a DM: cataphoric and anaphoric. Cataphoric *harey* introduces new information into the discourse. Anaphoric *harey* confers an immediately accessible and unchallengeable status on a piece of new information. The research question is how the two meanings of *harey* are interpreted and achieve relevance in context. The detailed analysis is based on two corpora: the spoken Haifa corpus (with 87 usable *harey* tokens) and the written heTenTen corpus (with 268 relevant tokens of *harey* and its variants out of a random sample of 300 tokens).

Fine-grained contextual analysis allows to distinguish three different discourse functions within the cataphoric use, those which modify new information, and three different discourse functions within the anaphoric use, those with mark the information as already accessible to the addressee. The different procedural uses go hand in hand with different syntactic constraints on positioning and scope, different semantic substitution possibilities, and different pragmatic preferences in terms of written vs. spoken mode, frequency of use and dominant vs. non-dominant discourse status. It is the combination of these different syntactic, semantic and pragmatic features that enables the addressee to reliably distinguish the anaphoric and the cataphoric uses of *harey*. In diachronic terms, this variety of uses can be traced back to small, motivational steps that have been shown to develop from deictic elements, as demonstrated previously by Heine and Kuteva (2002).

3 Research questions and general contribution

As we have pointed out in the panoramic review of the chapters in this volume, they all have a strong empirical basis, making a consistent use of experimentally verified data and/or corpus data. The data come from different languages, namely: Catalan (Cuenca), English (Li et al., Cuenca, Loureda et al.), French (Blochowiak & Grisot, Broisson & Degand, Zufferey et al., Wetzel et al.), German (Loureda et al.), Hebrew (Ariel), Slovene (Verdonik) and Spanish (Loureda et al.).

Each of the contributions to the volume addresses at least one of the following **research questions**:
1. *Are DMs a trace of the speaker's production difficulties and/or a signal to facilitate the addressee's comprehension?*
   The chapters by Loureda et al., Zufferey et al., Broisson and Degand, and Ariel focus on how the presence of DMs facilitates discourse comprehension as cues for inferences. More precisely, the studies show that addressees benefit from the presence of DMs to establish specific discourse relational meanings, even when these meanings may be fairly complex. In addition, Broisson and Degand

show that speakers may also use DMs for themselves, in a "speaker-oriented" way, when they do not need to consider the addressee's perspective.

2. *How does the presence or absence of DMs affect the discourse processing, in humans and in computers?*
The papers by Loureda et al., Zufferey et al., Wetzel et al. and Blochowiak and Grisot tackle the effects of the presence or absence of DM in discourse processing experimentally. They disentangle how DMs, especially connectives, influence online and offline reading processes, thus providing better understanding of the semantic and pragmatic aspects involved in DM processing. A complementary perspective is that adopted in Li et al.'s and Verdonik's papers, which develop the question from a computational perspective, and also Cuenca's contribution, which explores it from the point of view of translation (explicitation and implicitation translation strategies), thus laying bare indirectly how the presence of DMs may lead to different interpretations.

3. *Under what contextual circumstances (both linguistic and extralinguistic) do DMs affect language comprehension?*
The papers by Loureda et al., Blochowiak and Grisot, Broisson and Degand, Li et al., Cuenca, and Ariel single out several linguistic and contextual circumstances affecting DMs processing, such as the type of relation expressed by a DM, syntactic constraints or style. Broisson and Degand also consider pragmatic variables (speaker or hearer orientation and cognitive load). The paper by Blochowiak and Grisot considers the variables of age and exposure to social media. Similarly, the paper by Zufferey et al. explores exposure to print as a relevant factor.

4. *Does individual or group variation affect the use and processing of DMs (e.g. age, native vs. non-native, expertise)?* Specifically,
   a. Do younger and older people exhibit differences as for the use of DMs?
   This is a factor tested by Zufferey et al. and by Blochowiak and Grisot, showing that age does indeed play a role in understanding DMs because semantic (lexical) knowledge of DMs varies with age.
   b. How do second language learners understand and use DMs?
   This is a variable explored in Zufferey et al.'s paper and it is the topic of Wetzel et al.'s contribution, showing that second language processing of DMs evolves with language proficiency.
   c. How do translators interpret and transfer DMs?
   This is the focus of Cuenca's chapter, who shows that adding or omitting DMs in the translation process follow for a variety of factors, which are semantic and syntactic in nature, but can also be idiosyncratic or related to the translation process itself.

5. Can processes of grammaticalization or semantic change lay bare the (linguistic and cognitive) mechanisms involved in the interactional use of DMs?
Two papers, Blochowiak and Grisot's and Ariel's, include as one of their main aims to observe dynamic processes of change related to interactional uses of DMs.

The overview of the different chapters and the research questions addressed in this volume demonstrate its specific focus, namely the role that Discourse Markers play in the production and comprehension of discourse. The combination of experimental, computational and corpus-based studies give insight in the ways DMs are processed in written discourse and spoken interaction and how perspectives of advanced first and second language acquisition, computational or translation applications may provide deeper insight into the use of this ubiquitous, yet evasive linguistic category. This volume is a further step in describing **how** we use Discourse Markers in order to better understand out **why** speakers and writers make massive use of a linguistic category that has been described as syntactically optional, yet appears to be communicatively essential.

References

Abuczki, Agnes. 2014. On the disambiguation of multifunctional discourse markers in multimodal interaction. *Journal on Multimodal User Interfaces* 8(2). 121–134. doi:10.1007/s12193-013-0136-x.

Allen, James & Mark Core. 1997. *Draft of DAMSL: Dialog act markup in several layers*. Available at: https://www.cs.rochester.edu/research/cisd/resources/damsl/RevisedManual/.

AMI. 2005. *Guidelines for Dialogue Act and Addressee Annotation* Version 1.0. Available at: http://groups.inf.ed.ac.uk/ami/corpus/Guidelines/dialogue_acts_manual_1.0.pdf.

Andersen, Elaine S., Maquela Brizuela, Beatrice Dupuy & Laura Gonnerman. 1999. Cross-linguistic evidence for the early acquisition of discourse markers as register variables. *Journal of Pragmatics* 31(10). 1339–1351. doi: 10.1016/S0378-2166(98)00108-8.

Aijmer, Karin. 2007. Translating discourse particles: A case of complex translation. In Gunilla Anderman & Margaret Rogers (eds.) *Incorporating Corpora: The Linguist and the Translator*, 95–116. Bristol, Blue Ridge Summit: Multilingual Matters. https://doi.org/10.21832/9781853599873-009

Aijmer, Karin & Anne-Marie Simon-Vandenbergen (eds.). 2006. *Pragmatic markers in contrast*. (Studies in Pragmatics 2). Amsterdam, Boston, London: Elsevier. http://public.eblib.com/EBLPublic/PublicView.do?ptiID=648983 (10 September, 2013).

Asr, Fatimah, T. & Vera Demberg. 2012. Implicitness of discourse relations. *24th International Conference on Computational Linguistics – Proceedings of COLING 2012: Technical Papers*. 2669–2684.

Bard, Ellen Gurman, Anne H. Anderson, Catherine Sotillo, Matthew Aylett, Gwyneth Doherty-Sneddon & Alison Newlands. 2000. Controlling the intelligibility of referring expressions in dialogue. *Journal of Memory and Language* 42(1). 1–22. doi: 10.1006/jmla.1999.2667

Becher, Viktor. 2011a. When and why do translators add connectives? *Target* 23(1). 26–47.

Becher, Viktor. 2011b. *Explicitation and implicitation in translation. A corpus-based study of English-German and German-English translations of business texts.* PhD dissertation, University of Hamburg.

Blühdorn, Hardarik, Ad Foolen & Oscar Loureda. 2017. Diskursmarker: Begriffsgeschichte – Theorie – Beschreibung Ein bibliographischer Überblick. In Hardarik Blühdorn, Arnulf Deppermann, Henrike Helmer & Thomas Spranz-Fogasy (eds.), *Diskursmarker im Deutschen Reflexionen und Analysen*, 7–47. Göttingen: Verlag für Gesprächsforschung. http://verlag-gespraechsforschung.de/2017/bluehdorn.html (5 July, 2017).

Chen, Mingda, Zewei Chu & Kevin Gimpel. 2019. Evaluation benchmarks and learning criteria for discourse-aware sentence representations. *Proceedings of the 2019 Conference on Empirical Methods in Natural Language Processing and the 9th International Joint Conference on Natural Language Processing.* 649–662.

Crewe, William J. 1990. The illogic of logical connectives. *ELT Journal* 44. 316–325.

Crible, Ludivine. 2017. Towards an operational category of discourse markers: A definition and its model. In Chiara Fedriani & Andrea Sanso (eds.), *Discourse Markers, Pragmatic Markers and Modal Particles: New Perspectives*, 101–126. Amsterdam: John Benjamins.

Crible, Ludivine. 2018. *Discourse Markers and (Dis)Fluency. Forms and Functions across Languages and Registers.* Amsterdam: John Benjamins.

Cuenca, Maria Josep. (ed.). 2007. *Catalan Journal of Linguistics* 6. Special issue on "Contrastive Perspectives on Discourse Markers".

Degand, Liesbeth, Zoé Broisson, Ludivine Crible & Karolina Grzech. 2022. Cross-linguistic variation in spoken discourse markers: Distribution, functions, and domains. In Elizabeth Peterson, Turo Hiltunen & Joseph Kern (eds.), *Discourse-Pragmatic Variation and Change: Theory, Innovations, Contact*, 83–103. Cambridge: Cambridge University Press.

Degand, Liesbeth, Bert Cornillie & Paola Pietrandrea. 2013. *Discourse Markers and Modal Particles: Categorization and description.* (Pragmatics & Beyond New Series 234). Amsterdam & Philadelphia: John Benjamins Publishing.

Degand, Liesbeth & Ted Sanders. 2002. The Impact of Relational Markers on Expository Text Comprehension in L1 and L2. *Reading and Writing* 15. 739–57.

Dell, Gary S & Paula M Brown. 1991. Mechanisms for listener-adaptation in language production Limiting the role of the "model of the listener". In Donna Jo Napoli & Judy Anne Kegl (eds.), *Bridges between psychology and linguistics*, 105–129. New York: Academic Press.

Fischer, Kerstin. 2014. Discourse Markers. In Klaus P. Schneider & Anne Barron (eds.), *Pragmatics of Discourse,* 271–294. (Handbooks of Pragmatics Vol. 3). Boston: De Gruyter Mouton.

Fischer, Kerstin (ed.). 2006. *Approaches to discourse particles.* (Studies in Pragmatics 1). Bingley, UK: Emerald Group Publishing.

Gabarró-López, Sílvia. 2019. When the meaning of same is not restricted to likeness: A preliminary study from the perspective of discourse relational devices in two sign languages. *Discours. Revue de Linguistique, Psycholinguistique et Informatique. A Journal of Linguistics, Psycholinguistics and Computational Linguistics* 24 (October). https://doi.org/10.4000/discours.10053.

Granger, Sylviane & Stephanie Tyson. 1996. Connector usage in the English essay writing of native and non-native EFL speakers of English. *World Englishes* 15. 17–27.

Heine, Bernd & Tania Kuteva. 2002. *World lexicon of grammaticalization*. Cambridge: Cambridge University Press.

Horton, William S. & Boaz Keysar. 1996. When do speakers take into account common ground? *Cognition* 59(1). 91–117. doi:10.1016/0010-0277(96)81418-1.

ISO 24617-2. 2012. *ISO DIS 24617-2 Language resource management – Semantic annotation framework* (SemAF), Part 2: Dialogue acts, Geneva.

Jurafsky, Dan, Shriberg, Elizabeth & Debra Biasca. 1997. *Switchboard SWBD-DAMSL shallow-discourse-function annotation*. Coders manual, draft 13. University of Colorado at Boulder & +SRI International. Available at: https://web.stanford.edu/~jurafsky/ws97/manual.august1.html.

Keysar, Boaz, Dale J. Barr & William S. Horton. 1998. The egocentric basis of language use insights from a processing approach. *Current Directions in Psychological Science* 7(2). 46–49. doi: 10.1111/1467-8721.ep13175613.

Keysar, Boaz, Dale J. Barr, Jennifer A. Balin & Jason S. Brauner. 2000. Taking perspective in conversation: the role of mutual knowledge in comprehension. *Psychological Science* 11(1). 32–38. doi: 10.1111/1467-9280.00211.

Kyratzis, Amy & Susan Ervin-Tripp. 1999. The development of discourse markers in peer interaction. *Journal of Pragmatics*. 31(10). 1321–1338. https://doi.org/10.1016/S0378-2166(98)00107-6.

Maschler, Yael. 1997. Discourse markers at frame shifts in israeli hebrew talk-in-interaction. *Pragmatics. Quarterly Publication of the International Pragmatics Association (IPrA)* 7(2). 183–211. https://doi.org/10.1075/prag.7.2.04mas.

Maschler, Yael & Deborah Schiffrin. 2015. Discourse markers: language, meaning, and context. In Deborah Tannen, Heidi Ehernberger Hamilton & Deborah Schiffrin (eds.), *The Handbook of Discourse Analysis*. 2nd ed, 189–221. Hoboken, NJ: John Wiley & Sons.

Nie, Allen, Erin D. Bennett & Noah D. Goodman. 2019. DisSent: Learning sentence representations from explicit discourse relations. *Proceedings of the 57th Annual Meeting of the Association for Computational Linguistics*. 4497–4510.

Nølke, Henning. 2007. Connectors in a Cross-Linguistic Perspective. *Languages in Contrast* 7(2). 167–83.

Roβnagel, Christian. 2000. Cognitive load and perspective-taking: applying the automatic-controlled distinction to verbal communication. *European Journal of Social Psychology* 30 (3): 429–445. doi:10.1002/(SICI)1099-0992(200005/06)30:3<429::AID-EJSP3>3.0.CO;2-V.

Sileo, Damien, Tim Van de Cruys, Camille Pradel & Philippe Muller. 2019. Mining discourse markers for unsupervised sentence representation learning. *Proceedings of the 2019 Conference of the North American Chapter of the Association for Computational Linguistics: Human Language Technologies*. 3477–3486.

Sileo, Damien, Tim Van de Cruys, Camille Pradel & Philippe Muller. 2020. DiscSense: Automated semantic analysis of discourse markers. *Proceedings of the 12th Language Resources and Evaluation Conference*. 991–999.

Stanovich, Keith E. & Richard F. West. 1989. Exposure to print and orthographic processing. *Reading Research Quarterly* 24(4). 402–433.

Taboada, Maite. 2009. Implicit and explicit coherence relations. In Jan Renkema (ed.), *Discourse, of course,* 125–138. Amsterdam: John Benjamins.

Tapper, Marie. 2005. Connectives in advanced Swedish EFL learners' written English–preliminary results. *The Department of English: Working Papers in English Linguistics* 5. 116–144.

Vogels, Jorrig, David M. Howcroft, Elli Tourtouri & Vera Demberg. 2020. How speakers adapt object descriptions to listeners under load. *Language, Cognition and Neuroscience* 35(1). 78–92. doi:10.1080/23273798.2019.1648839.

Weisser, Martin 2016. DART – The dialogue annotation and research tool. *Corpus Linguistics and Linguistic Theory*, 12(2). 355–388.

Weisser, Martin 2019. *The DART Taxonomy v. 3*. Available at: http://martinweisser.org/DART_scheme.html.

Zufferey, Sandrine. 2016. Discourse connectives across languages: factors influencing their explicit or implicit translation. *Languages in Contrast* 16(2). 264–279.

Zufferey, Sandrine, Willem Mak, Liesbeth Degand & Ted Sanders. 2015. Advanced learners' comprehension of discourse connectives: The role of L1 transfer across on-line and off-line tasks. *Second Language Research* 31. 389–411.

Óscar Loureda, Inés Recio Fernández, Adriana Cruz
and Martha Rudka

2 Principles of Discourse Marking: An experimental approach of general and contrastive perspectives

Abstract: On the basis of experimental eye tracking studies, this contribution outlines the cognitive principles predicting the effects of the presence of discourse particles for utterance processing. Data show that, compared with non-marked utterances, discourse particles activate four instructions linked to basic cognitive processes, namely: building a new access route to information (First Principle), constraining processing effort of semantically more complex information (Second Principle), optimizing the initial access to a communicated assumption and constrain the need for reanalysis (Corollary of the First and Second Principles) and facilitating the immediate discursive integration of the upcoming segments (Third Principle). The value of principles is twofold: (i) they allow one to further define functionally the category of discourse particles, by excluding related expressions, which are, however, substantially different (sentential adverbs); and (ii) they allow one to compare processing patterns between different languages.

Keywords: discourse particles, procedural meaning, discourse marking, eye tracking

1 General theoretical considerations

Because of their high sensitivity to contextual factors and their different morphological, syntactic and semantic properties across languages, discourse particles (DPs) pose a theoretical and descriptive challenge for general and for contrastive pragmatics (Aijmer 2007; Cuenca 2007; Loureda et al. 2019, among others). There are still divergences in basic aspects related to DPs such as their denomination,

---

Note: *Dedicated to José Portolés, with our affection and admiration.*

Óscar Loureda, Heidelberg University, oscar.loureda@uni-heidelberg.de
Inés Recio Fernández, Heidelberg University, ines.recio@hcla.uni-heidelberg.de
Adriana Cruz, Heidelberg University, adriana.cruz@uni-heidelberg.de
Martha Rudka, Heidelberg University, martha.rudka@uni-heidelberg.de

https://doi.org/10.1515/9783110790351-002

their specific features and the extent of DPs as a functional class. Despite these debates, there is remarkable consensus about their main function in communication: DPs *mark* discourses guiding inference retrieval according to their morphosyntactic, semantic and syntactic properties (Fraser 1999; Schiffrin 1994; Martín Zorraquino and Portolés Lázaro 1999; Portolés Lázaro [1998] 2001; Fischer 2006; Portolés Lázaro, Sáinz González and Murillo Ornat 2021, among others). The functional category of DPs encompasses expressions with argumentative functions (e.g., *however, therefore, furthermore*), expressions acting at the formulative level (e.g., *that is*), information-structuring expressions (e.g., *even, also*) and conversational units (e.g., *listen, hey*), besides modal particles (e.g., *right, without a doubt*).[1]

The ability of DPs to constrain the access to a given context rests upon an essentially cognitive notion of verbal communication in which a speaker produces a stimulus that is decoded by the interlocutor and anchored in a context to

---

[1] This chapter also presents the results of experiments on some sentential adverbs (Sp. *supuestamente* 'allegedly', *posiblemente* 'possibly', *lamentablemente* 'regrettably'). These studies were performed to check whether or not sentential adverbs exhibit similar cognitive patterns as the other units tested, which are traditionally included among the DPs, in order to provide experimental evidence on a still open debate. There are arguments for and against considering sentential adverbs as a type of DPs. Four arguments in favor are given in Martín Zorraquino (2010: § 7):
– DPs and sentential adverbs coincide in certain formal properties: they can appear in a peripheral position in relation to the sentential predication and they are invariable expressions;
– they may introduce certain pragmatic values in utterances, such as the propositional attitude or illocutionary force;
– they do not modify the truth conditions of the communicated assumption;
– they behave differently depending on whether they are used within the sentence or peripherally.

Against these arguments, it is often adduced that sentential adverbs have a core conceptual meaning, which substantially differentiates them from DPs, in which any remaining conceptual meaning is subordinated to their procedural meaning (Nicolle 1998, 2015; Wilson 2011): for instance, in the Spanish modal particle *sin duda* 'no doubt', the conceptual value of the noun *doubt* is increasingly less transparent and always "embedded" (de Saussure 2011: 58) in the instructional meaning. By contrast, the lexical content of sentential adverbs is highly transparent and seems to determine their pragmatic value. As a result, the meaning of many sentential adverbs is predictable from the qualifying adjectives from which they originate, since they are the product of a morphological process of derivation.

Against the idea that adverbs such as *sincerely* have a conceptual meaning when they function within the sentence and an instructional meaning when they are employed at the extra-sentential margins, it is argued that the possible differences between such adverbs employed within or outside the sentence are rather due to the nature of their syntactic position: "the comprehension of these adverbs is not the result of their properties alone, but also of the combination of a given syntactic and discursive position, and a meaning that is compatible with that position" (Portolés Lázaro 2014: § 4.2).

derive the assumption. Such contextual anchoring implies inferential computations and is aimed at obtaining the most *relevant* assumption from the utterance, i.e., the strongest cognitive effects at the lowest cognitive effort (Sperber and Wilson [1986] 1995; Blakemore 1987, 2002; Portolés Lázaro [1998] 2001). Since DPs constrain access to contexts to obtain the most relevant contextual effects, it can be theoretically assumed that they have an extraordinary communicative value. These assumptions have been experimentally tested in a series of experiments carried out across different languages (Spanish, English, German, and Italian), with the aim of finding correlations between formal properties of DPs and their cognitive processing (§ 2).

In order to explain the function of DPs, a distinction between *conceptual meaning* and *procedural meaning* is assumed (Blakemore 1987, 2002). Conceptual meaning comprises information about the propositional content of utterances, while procedural meaning comprises information about how conceptual meaning has to be processed and how inferential computations must be performed[2] (Blakemore 1987, 2002; Wilson and Sperber 1993; Escandell-Vidal and Leonetti 2011; Escandell-Vidal 2017; Portolés Lázaro, Sáinz González and Murillo Ornat 2021). The semantics of DPs is essentially procedural. As a result, DPs do not primarily generate representations of reality and they require conceptual meaning to act upon. In (1):

(1) David is vegetarian. **Therefore**, he doesn't eat ham.

Therefore is not accessible to consciousness (Carston 2002: 321–322), but encodes causal instructions on how mental representations (*David is vegetarian* and *he doesn't eat ham*) should be combined to generate contextual effects. The resulting discourse relation must be adjusted to the context in order to add new communicative material to the stored assumptions. This is performed either by activating an immediately adjustable assumption (as in (1)) or, if necessary, by creating an *ad hoc* assumption (Beaver and Zeevat 2007).

---

2 Diane Blakemore (1987, 2002) initially drew the distinction between conceptual-meaning expressions (mainly nouns, verbs, adjectives, and adverbs) and procedural-meaning items, which correspond to other non-lexical word classes. This division has been recently revised, leading to an alternative solution (Nicolle 1998, 2015; Pons Bordería 1998; Hansen 2006; Fischer 2006): both types of meaning can co-occur in a given linguistic unit. They are thus non-exclusive. This means that the distinction between procedural and conceptual meaning does not correspond directly to two types of expressions (grammatical and lexical). All language utterances encode instructions in some way at different levels of meaning (Escandell-Vidal and Leonetti 2011). If the conceptual and procedural information coexist in the same word, they must be arranged hierarchically (Nicolle 1998, 2015; Pons Bordería and Loureda 2018).

Procedural meaning is a semantic property common to all DPs, regardless of the language. The combinatorial and morphological requirements are not common to all DPs, which is why they cannot be integrated into traditional syntactic or grammatical categories (Carter and McCarthy 2006: 208–235). DPs belong to different classes of words as adverbs or adverbial phrases (En. *anyway*, Sp. *sin embargo* 'however', Ge. *nämlich* 'namely'), conjunctions/conjunctive expressions (Sp. *pero* 'but', En. *and*, Ge. *weil* 'because'), interjections (Sp./En. *ah*, Ge. *gell* 'right'); or lexical word classes, such as nouns or verbs, which have reduced their inflection or lost it completely and assume discourse-marking functions in communication (noun forms such as Sp. *tío* 'dude', Ge. *Mensch* 'man'; verbal forms such as Sp. *¿sabes?* or the equivalents En. *you know*, Ge. *weißt du*). For this reason, DPs are better treated as a functional class encompassing a wide range of linguistic expressions that cannot be reduced to a single world class, even less when considered from a cross-linguistic perspective.

From a semantic viewpoint, DPs can fulfill different functions in communication, that have given rise to a number of taxonomies (Sanders, Spooren and Noordman 1993; Martín Zorraquino and Portolés Lázaro 1999, among others). A flexible and straightforward one distinguishes the following categories of DPs (Briz Gómez, Pons Bordería and Portolés Lázaro 2008; Loureda and Acín Villa 2010):

– *modal particles*, which convey the speaker's attitude towards his own discourse;
– *conversational particles*, used by interlocutors for contact-management; and
– *connectives* and *operators*, which organize discourses on an argumentative, formulative, structural or informational level.

Although DPs are defined by their inference-constraining function, their formal properties are not irrelevant. For this reason, broader definitions of DPs consider procedural meaning as an essential semantic criterion and additionally syntactic and morphological features. The syntactic features allow to determine, for example, whether a given DP connects two discourse segments (En. *therefore*, Sp. *por tanto* 'therefore') or whether it operates upon a single segment specifying its relation with the previous co(n)text (Ge. *sogar*, Sp. *incluso*, both equivalent to 'even') (Briz Gómez, Pons Bordería and Portolés Lázaro 2008; Portolés Lázaro [1998] 2001; Fuentes Rodríguez 2009).[3] Morphological features of DPs allow to determine, among others, their distributional mobility. The prepositional origin of

---

3 "Connectives connect semantically and pragmatically a discourse segment with a previous one, or with an easily accessible contextual assumption" (Portolés Lázaro [1998] 2001: 139), translation is ours); argumentative operators, in turn, "condition the discursive potentialities of the discourse segment in which they occur or which they affect, but without relating it with a previous segment"

the Spanish focus operator *hasta* (approx. 'even') restricts its distributional potential and only licenses its uses in a pre-focal position. By contrast, *incluso* ('even'), which stems from an adverb, can be used in pre-focal or post-focal position; morphological features also determine to what extent a DP can accept modifiers. For instance, compared with connecting cues in an initial grammaticalization state, more grammaticalized DPs cannot be modified (En. *particularly for this reason* vs. **particularly therefore*; Sp. *por todo ello* 'due to all that' vs. *por todo tanto '*all therefore') (Portolés Lázaro, Sáinz González and Murillo Ornat 2021).

The theoretical argument that, due to their procedural meaning all DPs constrain inferences in communication (low-level implicatures) and determine the illocutionary force of what is said (high-level implicatures, Wilson and Sperber 1993; Carston 2002) requires empirical verification. Introducing a DP in a given utterance should lead to a modification of the utterance processing pattern, compared with an analogous unmarked utterance. The alternative to this hypothetical assumption would be to claim that, despite their instructional meaning, DPs are superfluous in discourse and do not necessarily determine how mental representations are processed. Since DPs conventionalize information that may not be immediately retrievable in their absence, the first claim seems more plausible. For example, in (2) the use of the argumentative operator En. *on the contrary*, Sp. *al contrario* and Ge. *im Gegenteil* instructs the interlocutor to recover a mental assumption opposite to what is stated in the previous one (Briz Gómez, Pons Bordería and Portolés Lázaro 2008; Cuenca 2020):

(2) EN. *He did not regret his decision*, **on the contrary**.
SP. *No estaba arrepentido de la decisión tomada*, **al contrario**.
GE. *Er hat seine Entscheidung nicht bereut*, **im Gegenteil**.

In (2), the DP conventionally instructs the reader to recover a mental assumption opposite to regretting a decision, for instance, being pleased with it. As a conventional implicature, it cannot be cancelled:

(3) EN. #*He did not regret his decision, on the contrary.* **Although he disliked it.**
SP. #*No estaba arrepentido de la decisión tomada, al contrario.* **Aunque no le gustaba.**
GE. #*Er hat seine Entscheidung nicht bereut, im Gegenteil.* **Obwohl er sie nicht mochte.**

(Portolés Lázaro [1998] 2001: 143). It is possible that the same expression performs both functions depending on the context.

By contrast, in (4) the implicature is not conventionally given and can be cancelled (5) (Portolés Lázaro [1998] 2001: § 5; Blakemore 2002):

(4) EN. *He did not regret his decision.*
SP. *No estaba arrepentido de la decisión tomada.*
GE. *Er hat die Entscheidung nicht bereut.*

(5) EN. *He did not regret the decision he had taken,* **although he disliked it**.
SP. *No estaba arrepentido de la decisión tomada,* **aunque no le gustaba**.
GE. *Er hat die Entscheidung nicht bereut,* **obwohl er sie nicht mochte**.

As a consequence, DPs condition the progress of discourse orienting it towards a given argumentative direction which is more specific than the one given in an utterance where no DP is provided. Theoretical and empirical evidence available so far confirms the hypothesis set out above. DPs condition utterance processing and are, thus, gravitational centers of the construction of discourse. They constrain the access to the specific context and optimize the retrieval of cognitive effects. (Loureda et al. 2021, for Spanish DPs).

On the basis of experimental data from processing studies carried out for different DPs and languages, we have formulated a series of *Cognitive Principles of Discourse Marking* (Loureda et al. 2021). These principles predict a frame within which DPs affect utterance processing, while systematically excluding processing patterns beyond those predictions. The Cognitive Principles of Discourse Marking and their value to describe different types of units in one language or to contrast between different expressions in different languages are presented in detail in § 3, following the methodological description of the experiments in §2.

2 Experiments on discourse particles: Methodology and design

The Cognitive Principles of Discourse Marking have been formulated on the basis of a series of experimental studies carried out in different languages by the DPKog research group at Heidelberg University. They include studies on causal-consecutive connectives, as Spanish *por tanto* 'therefore' (Recio Fernández 2020) and *por ello*[4] 'that is why' (Cuello Ramón 2022), English *therefore*; additive connec-

---

4 *Por ello*, approximately equivalent to En. 'that is why' belongs to the paradigm of causal-consecutive connectives and is less grammaticalized than other connectives within the paradigm

tives, as Spanish *además* and Italian *inoltre* 'furthermore' (Thome 2018), counter-argumentative connectives, as Spanish *sin embargo* 'however' (Nadal 2019; Recio Fernández 2020), *a pesar de ello* 'despite that' (Guillén Jiménez 2021); focus operators, as Spanish *incluso* (Cruz Rubio 2020), *hasta* (Torres Santos 2020) and German *sogar* (Rudka in preparation), all three equivalent to En. 'even'; formulative operators as Spanish *es decir* and *o sea*, both equivalent to 'that is', 'that is to say' (Loureda et al. 2021). These studies tie in with previous experimental studies on the impact of DPs for discourse processing and comprehension. Experimental evidence shows that DPs guide discourse processing, leading to a constraint of the processing effort needed to process utterances compared with implicit discourse (Murray 1997; Sanders and Noordman 2000; Canestrelli, Mak and Sanders 2013 for connectives; Filik, Paterson and Sauermann 2011 for focus operators). In general, explicating a DP in discontinuous relations (e.g., counter-argumentative utterances) reduces processing costs more strongly than in continuous relations (e.g., additive or causal relations). DPs also enhance comprehension to a greater extent for non-experts than for expert readers (van Silfhout, Evers-Vermeul and Sanders 2015, but see Degand and Sanders 2002 for a study with L1 vs L2 readers, where both groups perform likewise and Wetzel, Zufferey and Gygax, this volume, chapter 5). DPs have also been found to exert their processing-guiding effects immediately (Cozijn, Noordman and Vonk 2011; Canestrelli, Mak and Sanders 2013; Mak and Sanders 2013).

All studies considered in this contribution consisted in untimed eye tracking reading experiments and shared an analogous design with two independent variables (1x2 factorial design). Potential confounding variables were controlled for (word frequency and word length, Rayner 2009). Critical stimuli and filler items were combined in a 2:1 ratio. Different stimuli sets were created and distributed in counterbalanced lists (Latin square design) and presented in a pseudo-randomized order (Arunachalam 2013; Loureda et al. 2021).

Given that the common goal of all studies was to confirm the effects of discourse marking, the independent variable tested for was the presence (6a) or absence (6b) of a DP:

(6) a. *John and Mary are vegetarians.* **Therefore**, *they don't eat ham.*
    b. *John and Mary are vegetarians. They don't eat ham.*

---

like *por tanto* 'therefore'. Among the aims of the study performed with *por ello* was finding out whether different degrees of grammaticalization lead to different utterance processing patterns. For a detailed analysis, see Cuello Ramón (2022).

To obtain a comprehensive view on the functioning of DPs, the studies carried out gathered evidence on DPs exhibiting different features and belonging to different languages. Experiments were performed for DPs in English, Spanish and German. From a semantic-functional viewpoint, we considered canonical uses of consecutive and counter-argumentative connectives, as in (7a) – (7b). (En. *therefore*, Sp. *sin embargo* 'however', *a pesar de ello* 'despite that', *por ello* 'that is why', *por tanto* 'therefore'), focus operators (8) (e.g., Sp. *incluso*, Ge. *sogar*, both equivalent to En. 'even'), formulative markers (9) (Sp. *es decir* 'that is to say'), and discourse organizers (10) (Sp. *primero. . . segundo. . .* 'firstly. . .secondly. . .'):

(7) a. EN. *John and Mary are vegetarians.* ***Therefore****, they don't eat ham.*
SP. *Tienen un hotel muy bonito.* ***Por tanto/Por ello****, tienen muchos clientes.*
'They have a very nice hotel. ***Therefore/That is why****, they have a lot of customers.'
b. SP. *Enrique y Marta estudian mucho.* ***Sin embargo/A pesar de ello****, sacan malas notas.*
'Enrique and Marta study hard. ***However/Despite that****, they get bad grades.'

(8) SP. *David y Ana hablan inglés e* ***incluso*** *chino.*
GE. *David und Ana sprechen Englisch und* ***sogar*** *Chinesisch.*
'David and Ana speak English and ***even*** Chinese.'

(9) SP. *Silvia y Paula compran prensa rosa,* ***es decir****, conocen la vida de todos los famosos.*
'Silvia and Paula buy tabloids, ***that is to say***, they know about the lives of any celebrity.'

(10) SP. *Tienes que tomar mucha leche.* ***Primero****, serás más alto y,* ***segundo****, tendrás los huesos más fuertes.*
'You have to drink a lot of milk. ***Firstly***, you will be taller and, ***secondly***, you will have stronger bones.'

Regarding the syntactic level, some of them connect two segments (e.g. (7a) – (7b)), while some DPs do not have a connective function (e.g. (8) – (10)). From a morphological perspective, the studies present data on fully grammaticalized expressions (e.g., Sp. *por tanto* 'therefore', *incluso* 'even', Ge. *sogar* 'even') and less grammaticalized DPs (Sp. *por ello* 'that is why', *a pesar de ello* 'despite that') that still encode combined instructions which are partly procedural and partly anaphoric. Finally, experiments were performed with sentential adverbs –the epistemic adverb *posiblemente* 'possibly', the evaluative adverb *lamentablemente* 'regrettably', and the evidential *supuestamente* 'allegedly'– to check for potential differences between them and canonical DPs in terms of the processing patterns they respectively trigger (see footnote 1 and Loureda et al. 2021 for further details):

(11) **Lamentablemente/Posiblemente/Supuestamente**, *la enfermedad del paciente es muy grave.*
'**Regrettably/Possibly/Allegedly**, the patient's illness is very serious.'

For the evaluation of the results, the experimental stimuli were segmented into three areas of interest (AOIs):[5] (1) the utterance as a whole, which considers all conceptual-meaning words of the utterance (i.e., excluding the DP and the subject area); (2) the segment preceding the DP, and (3) the segment immediately following/hosting the DP.

(12) $_1$[*John and Mary* $_2$[*are vegetarians.*] **Therefore,** $_3$[*they don't eat ham*].]
$_1$[*John and Mary* $_2$[*are vegetarians.*] $_3$[*They don't eat ham*].]

(13) $_1$[***Philip und Boris have*** $_2$[***dogs, cats***] ***and even*** $_3$[***snakes***].]
$_1$[*Philip und Boris have* $_2$[*dogs, cats*] *and* $_3$[*snakes*].]

These three AOIs allow to isolate the behavior of the functional areas affected by the marking process triggered by the DP. This allows to observe how procedural-meaning devices modify processing patterns of conceptual-meaning expressions in relation to analogous unmarked utterances; either considering global processing (area 1) or considering the specific effects of the DP upon the areas more directly affected by the marking process (areas 2 and 3).

Processing times were computed for three parameters, the dependent variables of the studies: *total reading time*, a cumulative parameter amounting to the total time spent on a target area and thus an indicator of global effects. Considering that cognitive processing encompasses the construction of a tentative

---

5 An area of interest is a delimited region for which eye tracking data is collected. In reading studies, areas of interest can be stretches of text, whole sentences, multi-word segments, single words or even single characters or strings of characters (Holmqvist et al. 2011: 187). The areas of interest considered focus on conceptual-meaning regions that lead to the construction of an assumption. The proper nouns in the subject of many of the stimuli were excluded from the analysis since they have a merely denotative value: they are not class names and lack logical input. Thus, they do not contribute to the representation of reality, but are merely identificatory (Loureda et al. 2021).

assumption triggering a specific inferential route and the metapragmatic task of controlling, this initial assumption to readjust it, two further parameters are required that provide more fine-grained information on utterance processing, the *first-pass reading time* and the *re-reading time*. The first-pass reading time amounts to the sum of all fixations on a given area before exiting it either to the right or to the left. This parameter measures the processing effort required to carry out tasks that lead to the construction of an initial assumption in which the decoded information has been contextually enriched and could result in the activation of a specific inferential route. The re-reading time is the sum of all returning fixations to a target area after previously having left it. It measures the time for reanalysis of a given area, during which the initial assumption is reconsidered in order to confirm, modify or delete it. This parameter thus reflects the control of the optimal relevance of the initial assumption (Rayner 2009; Holmqvist et al. 2011; Conklin, Pellicer-Sánchez and Carrol 2018).

Eye movement data were recorded with an SMI eye tracker (temporal resolution 250Hz or 500Hz). Participants were native speakers of the language dealt with in the corresponding experiment and read a series of utterances on a screen silently and at their own pace. They were aged 18 – 40 and had an ongoing or completed university degree. Participants needed between 15 – 20 minutes to complete the study. The data treatment was carried out with linear additive mixed models using *R* software (*R Core Team*, 2018) after prior handling of outliers.[6] The AOIs were treated as fixed effects, while participants and stimuli versions were treated as random effects. Word length of the AOI was treated as a nonlinear effect. Interpretation of the statistical results is based on the effect sizes of the predictive values. Based on theoretical assumptions, differences below 4% are considered trivial effects as they are highly unstable; differences between this minimum threshold and 10% are considered sufficiently stable; and differences over 10% reveal large or very large effects, which are stable and allow a high level of predictability (Loureda et al. 2021).

3 Cognitive Principles of Discourse Marking

The marking effect of DPs is expressed through the *Cognitive Principles of Discourse Marking*. These principles predict how an utterance is processed in certain conditions, while excluding processing patterns beyond those predictions' observable

---

[6] The statistical analysis of the experimental studies has been carried out in collaboration with the consulting team of the *StabLab* at the Institute for Statistics of the University of Munich.

in similar unmarked utterances (Loureda et al. 2021). The Cognitive Principles of Discourse Marking do not delimit a single behavior pattern but establish a range for potential effects when interlocutors process marked utterances, compared to when no DP is provided. This effect ranges, which cover minimum and maximum effects, provide explanatory force to two approaches in pragmatics research.

The first one concerns communication in general and how expressions determine certain processes in a language. In this sense, it would not be expectable that all DPs of one language follow a specific processing pattern, since they present different semantic, syntactic and morphological features. *Semantic features*, since DPs can encode instructions affecting different levels of communication (argumentation, information-structuring, discourse organization, formulation, modalization or contact-management); *syntactic features*, since DPs can connect discourse segments or determine combinatorial possibilities of a single segment; or *morphological*, since processing instructions can be fully grammaticalized, as in Sp. *sin embargo* or its equivalent En. *however*, or only partially, as in Sp. *a pesar de ello* 'despite that', which combines a counter-argumentative and an anaphoric instruction.

The second approach concerns contrastive pragmatics. A central issue is to analyze whether the instructions encoded in expressions from different languages but usually treated as semantic equivalents lead to similar discourse marking patterns, as predicted by the general principles and their effect ranges. Doing so allows to perform interlinguistic comparisons and, particularly, to compare discourse marking strategies in different languages (Aijmer 2007; Degand 2009; Zufferey and Cartoni 2012; Zufferey 2016).

3.1 First Principle of Discourse Marking

If *discourse marking* consists in introducing conditions that guide inferential processing into communication, DPs cannot be considered superfluous or insignificant expressions; on the contrary, by introducing a DP into an utterance, nothing is communicatively equal anymore. This is predicted by the *First Principle of Discourse Marking*, which excludes the possibility that two analogous utterances, a marked and an unmarked one, are processed identically and with the same cognitive effort.

> ***First Principle of Discourse Marking.*** *The introduction of a discourse particle into a given utterance modifies the processing strategy of the utterance in relation to a corresponding unmarked utterance.*

The indicator used for the First Principle is the lexical mean of the total reading time, both in the global area (= the utterance as a whole) and the local areas (= the utterance segments). The lexical mean is an adequate indicator here, because it reflects the time needed to process words with a non-instructional meaning, which are affected by the DP in the marked condition and are more underdetermined in the unmarked condition. The discourse marking effect is shown in Figure 1, where +/–4% indicates the threshold of the differences between conditions (marked and unmarked). The expressions under consideration are grouped according to their semantic functions: argumentative, informational, organizational or formulative. The principle isolates a range of possibilities with a minimum and a maximum limit. The minimum limit reflects a local modification of the functional discourse segment affected by the DP; the maximum limit includes a local effect and the global processing of the utterance.

The First Principle of Discourse Marking establishes a continuum of possibilities to explain the homogeneity and heterogeneity of DPs concerning their properties in a given language. Firstly, the principle isolates the marking effects which arise due to the procedurality of DPs and their impact on utterance processing; but, secondly, the principle also defines a range of possibilities to explain how semantic, syntactic and morphological features of DPs influence processing. Considering the semantic level of the fully grammaticalized expressions in Spanish, only DPs with information-structuring functions (Sp. *incluso* 'even') and causal-consecutive relations (Sp. *por tanto* 'therefore') lead to local effects. This can be explained by the interpretative flexibility common to both structures: for causal relations this is due to the linearity and continuity holding between the adjacent segments that in addition are related causally, which has been found to be smoothly interpreted also in the absence of a DP (Sanders and Noordman 2000; Sanders 2005, among others). For information-structures marked by *incluso* 'even', this is due to the fact that the DP does not impact the semantic-argumentative construction of the utterance, but the informative organization of the constituents to optimally orient the assumption towards the progression of the discourse. The stronger interpretative rigidity of argumentative structures compared with the flexibility of informative structures has been underscored in theoretical and empirical works (Clifton, Bock and Radó 2000; Filik, Paterson and Sauermann 2011). Considering the syntactic and morphological level, no stable differences can be observed between the connectives, which mark a two-place relation (Fraser 1999: 938) and the discourse operators, which mark a one-place operation; nor between the effects of more or less grammaticalized units (Fuentes Rodríguez 2009). It seems that under the observations of the predictions of the First Principle the general marking function of DPs prevails over formal features to describe their impact on utterance interpretation.

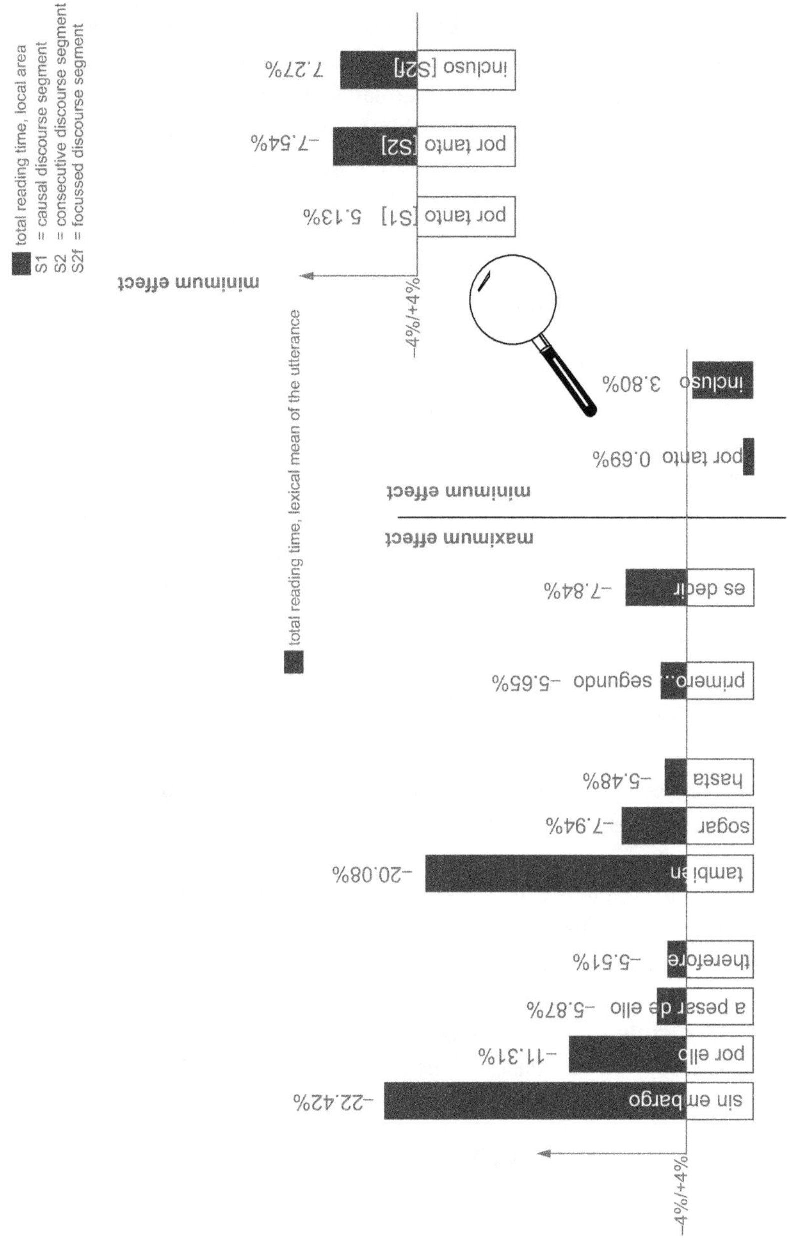

2 Principles of Discourse Marking — 29

Figure 1: Differences in processing of marked and unmarked utterances of the First Principle of Discourse Marking (lexical mean of the utterance, total reading time).

From a cross-linguistic perspective, the principle provides a basis for comparison of the instructions of equivalent expressions belonging to different languages. The impact on processing of the Spanish and German focus operators and the Spanish and English causal connectives is not equivalent in terms of their cognitive effects on utterance processing. Sp. *incluso* 'even' affects utterance processing minimally with a local modification of a discourse segment, which contrasts with the maximum effect of the German DP in the same paradigm Ge. *sogar* 'even' showing the maximum effect with a modification on the global utterance level. Similarly, Spanish *por tanto* 'therefore' exhibits only minimum effects, compared to the maximum effects of the English equivalent connective *therefore*. The specific reasons for the differences between these expressions have to be investigated in further experiments that isolate possible typological and paradigmatic variables. Neither the informative structure, nor the paradigm of focus operators in Spanish and German are identical. However, the principle provides a limit for the contrastive variation, since it defines the space in which the marking effect deploys in different languages. The differences between the expressions across languages occur within that range of possibilities, and not beyond. Thus, all DPs comply to the principle due to their procedural meaning, and present either global or local effects on utterance processing.

3.2 Second Principle of Discourse Marking

The *Second Principle of Discourse Marking* predicts that the introduction of a DP in a given utterance sets as the maximum limit of processing efforts those of a corresponding unmarked utterance. In relation to an unmarked utterance, the modification of the cognitive processing of a marked utterance can theoretically be linked to the conventionalizing role of DPs in communication, whereby they reduce the linguistic under-determinacy of utterances (Wilson 2011; Carston 2002).

> ***Second Principle of Discourse Marking.*** *The introduction of a discourse particle into a given utterance sets as its maximum processing costs those of the corresponding unmarked utterance.*

The theoretical basis of this principle is the fact that utterances are linguistically under-determined. This under-determinacy is compensated by means of inferential computations.[7] As a result, the degree of inferential processing during commu-

---

[7] "An utterance explicitly codes only part of the meaning of the utterance into explicit linguistic material, the rest having to be provided by inferencing" (Sanders and Spooren 2001: 4; Sperber and Wilson [1986] 1995).

nication conditions cognitive processing. A marked utterance leads the interlocutor to activate an inferential route that is more strongly specified than the possibly activated routes of a corresponding unmarked utterance. This effort-constraining effect is linked to the ability of DPs to regulate access to mental representations. DPs introduce additional semantic content into communication, but at the same time reduce the under-determinacy of unmarked utterances establishing conventional routes for utterance processing.

As in the First Principle, the range of effects is established by means of the average processing time for an utterance word and for the functional areas implicated in the discourse marking. The minimum effect corresponds to processing of the marked utterance, which is not slowed down (Figure 2: Sp. *por tanto* 'therefore' and *incluso* 'even'); the maximum effect is reflected by the speeding up of the utterance processing (Figure 2: all other DPs). A slowdown effect of discourse marking is in any case excluded. Introducing a DP into an utterance never leads to an increased processing effort of the utterance compared to an unmarked utterance. DPs control how the discourse segments affected by them are integrated into a semantic schema defined by them. This schema is qualitatively different, more accessible and at the same time communicatively more informative than in unmarked utterances:

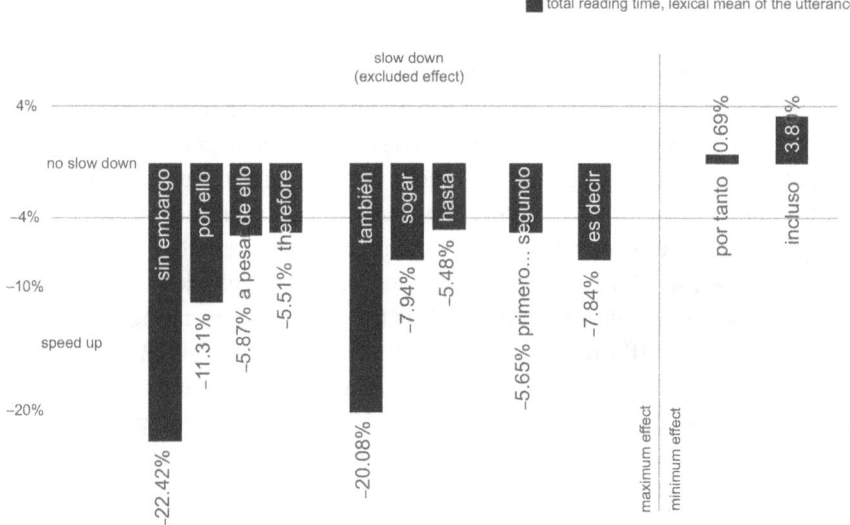

Figure 2: Differences in processing of marked and unmarked utterances of the Second Principle of Discourse Marking (lexical mean of the utterance, total reading time).

Due to the excluded effect, the Second Principle of Discourse Marking allows for a general observation. The Principle delimits the definition of what a DP is and what it probably is not (see footnote 1). In the studies undertaken, the effects of three Spanish sentential adverbs were analyzed: epistemic adverbs (e.g. *posiblemente* 'possibly'), evaluative adverbs (e.g. *lamentablemente* 'regrettably'), and evidentials (e.g. *supuestamente* 'allegedly'). The results show that the effects of these units upon utterance processing is not aligned with the cognitive functioning of DPs. The processing patterns of the sentential adverbs under study cannot be predicted by the Cognitive Principles of Discourse Marking. Utterance-marking by means of a sentential adverb generates a total processing over-effort of approximately 20% (Figure 3).[8] The relative differences in processing of the three utterances are not theoretically relevant, as they lie below the 4%-effect threshold. Therefore, it can be claimed that the three types of modification considered – evidential, modal and evaluative – can be reduced to the same processing operation compared to unmarked utterances.

In sum, the presence of sentential adverbs does modify the processing of utterances as predicted by the First Principle of Discourse Marking. However, the processing pattern does not comply with the range of possibilities given by the Second Principle of Discourse Marking. This observation is considered an indicator that sentential adverbs do not lead to the same processing patterns as procedural-meaning expressions and provide an argument to position sentential adverbs beyond the framework of DPs.

By delimiting a range of possibilities, the Second Principle of Discourse Marking allows to verify whether the semantic, syntactic, and morphological properties of different DPs in a language lead to different processing patterns. As in the First Principle, different syntactic or morphological properties are not clearly determinant for a given processing pattern. The results do not provide distinctive and stable processing patterns, neither for argumentative and informative structures, nor for the comparison between languages. However, common to all structures is their procedurality. It is the procedural meaning which conditions processing effort, rather than the specific features of a DP, which seem secondary in relation to processing costs. From a contrastive point of view, the predominance of the marking function in each language over the specific formal features provides a solid basis for a comparison (*tertium comparationis*) grounded on communicative values.

---

[8] To help confirm or refine this claim further studies in other languages are required in which sentential adverbs and DP present similar semantic differences.

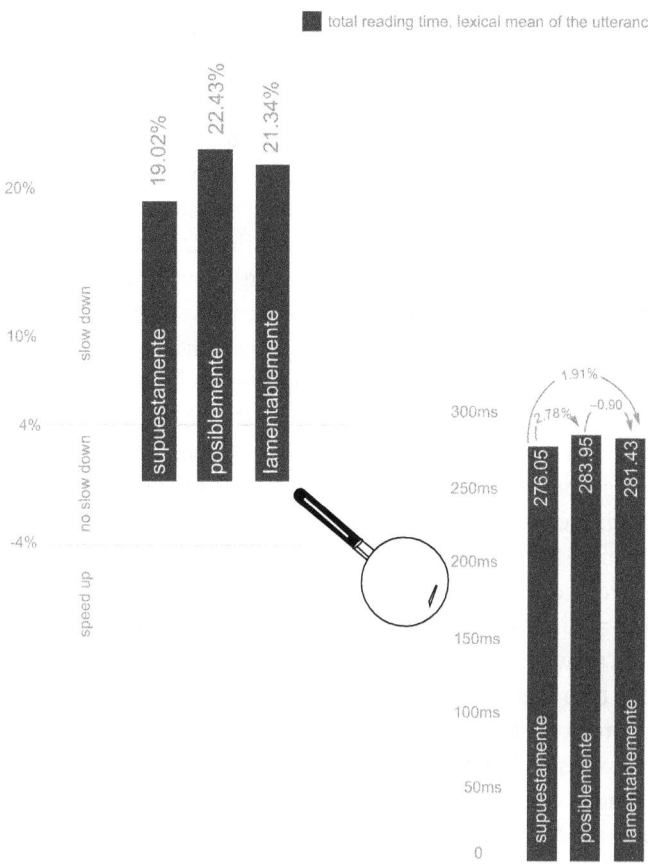

Figure 3: Differences in processing of marked and unmarked utterances of the Second Principle of Discourse Marking of sentential adverbs (lexical mean of the utterance, total reading time).

Regarding grammaticalization processes of DPs, it can be observed that in argumentative relations, less grammaticalized DPs (Sp. *por ello* 'that is why', *a pesar de ello* 'despite that') establish more complex processing patterns (global effects) than more grammaticalized units (Sp. *por tanto* 'therefore'). This is due to the fact that fully grammaticalized DPs are "more procedural" than expressions in earlier stages of the grammaticalization process. Along the grammaticalization process, DPs lose semantic substance and gradually increase their instructional content. Thus, *por ello* 'that is why', as a less grammaticalized expression, still is more anaphoric in nature than the more grammaticalized *por tanto* 'therefore' lacking an anaphoric nature and encoding an autonomous instruction which leads to less complex processing (Recio Fernández 2020).

The First and Second Principles speak for a description of DPs in terms of their procedural-meaning and underscore their role as constraints on relevance (Blakemore 2002) and, subsequently, on cognitive effort. The range of possible effects defined by the principles also ties in with predictions formulated by the Cognitive approach to Coherence Relations (CCR, Sanders, Spooren and Noordman 1993, Sanders 2005). CCR offers a framework to describe, categorize and annotate discourse relations on the basis of cognitive primitives: polarity (negative or positive); basic operation (causality or addition); source of coherence (objective or subjective); and order of the segments (basic or non-basic) (Sanders, Spooren and Noordman 1993; Spooren and Sanders 2008). Since CCR treats discourse relations as cognitive entities, i.e., as resulting mental representations, it operates independently of whether relations are marked by a DP or not.

Like the Cognitive Principles of Discourse Marking, the complexity of the different primitives proposed by CCR and, as a result, the relative complexity of a given discourse relation relies on empirical evidence (Spooren and Sanders 2008; Evers-Vermeul and Sanders 2011, 2019; Hoek et al. 2017; Recio Fernández 2020). More complex relations (e.g., negative compared to positive relations or causality compared to addition) appear later in language acquisition compared with simpler ones, and usually trigger more effortful processing. This complexity effects can be linked to the ranges of effects – minimum or maximum – of a DP for utterance processing predicted by the Cognitive Principles of Discourse Marking. Relating such effect ranges to the description of discourse relations according to the CCR primitives may result in a powerful tool to enrich explanations of the specific behavior triggered by different DPs in communication. Importantly, this applies to cross-linguistic analyses as well, since both the relevance-based Cognitive Principles of Discourse Markers and CCR provide a framework that functions independent of the language at issue.[9]

As inference-constraining devices that reduce linguistic under-determinacy in communication, the effects of DPs can affect discourses in a number of ways, but, in general, they can be observed in two levels: in relation to the discourse segments upon which they act (Third Principle) and in relation to the cognitive

---

9 Applied to the data presented here, converging evidence from both approaches is visible for negative versus positive polarity relations (Figure 2). According to CCR, counter-argumentation is classified as a negative polarity relation and causality as a positive-polarity relation. The higher cognitive complexity of negative polarity relations (Evers-Vermeul and Sanders 2011, among others) connects with the minimum effects of the fully grammaticalized causal connective *por tanto* 'therefore' on utterance processing, versus the maximum effects of *sin embargo* 'however': negative relations are cognitively more complex, so they benefit to a greater extent from the presence of a processing guide (Murray 1997).

operations that they trigger (Third Principle and Corollary of the First and Second Principle see below).

3.3 Third Principle of Discourse Marking

DPs determine how the discourse segments under their scope must be integrated in a semantic schema by specifying how conceptual representations activated from the utterance segments are to be arranged to feed the inferential stage of communication. DPs globally regulate the access to the communicated assumption as a whole (First and Second Principles) and, locally, determine the communicative value of the discourse segments more directly affected by it. This is observed in a more fine-grained way both for the construction of a first assumption and for its reanalysis, when the initial assumption may be revised and contrasted with contextual information to confirm, modify or eliminate a previously entertained assumption to obtain the greatest contextual effects. In communication, the cognitive effort is oriented towards building an assumption, whereby certain operations aim at controlling the quality of such assumption to achieve the strongest possible cognitive effects. DPs constrain inferential computations in both tasks. Primarily, DPs do so by optimally controlling the recovery of a first (tentative) assumption. They assign a specific discourse status to the discourse segment directly affected by them and thereby prevent it from being processed at a greater cognitive effort than the corresponding unmarked segment:

> **Third Principle of Discourse Marking** *(immediate local regulation). The introduction of a discourse particle into a given utterance immediately sets as the upper limit of the processing efforts of the segment in which it is integrated those of the corresponding unmarked segment.*

The indicator of the Third Principle of Discourse Marking is the lexical mean of the conceptual elements during first-pass reading time of the area directly affected by the DP. It reflects the time required during the construction of the first hypothesis of the assumption which serves as a basis for the interlocutor to activate a specific inferential route. The indicator comprises a processing continuum excluding the possibility that a segment affected by the DP is more effortful than an analogous unmarked segment (Figure 4).

The immediate effects of DPs during the recovery of a first assumption adjusts to a frame where the segment more directly affected by them is processed less effortfully than an unmarked segment due to the higher determinacy introduced by the DP. This holds for all DPs under consideration across syntactic and mor-

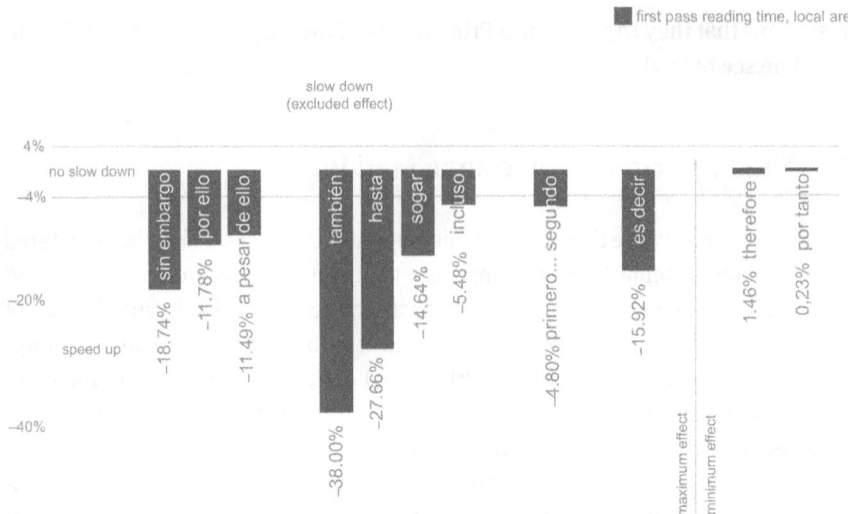

Figure 4: Differences in processing of the local area of marked and unmarked utterances of the Third Principle of Discourse Marking (lexical mean of the local area, first pass reading time).

phological features, across functional paradigms and across languages (Filik, Paterson and Sauermann 2011; Cozijn, Noordman and Vonk 2011; Canestrelli, Mak and Sanders 2013; Loureda et al. 2021).

The specific effect ranges predicted by the Principle, however, supply further information for the description of how DPs function in discourse. A DP can either immediately accelerate the processing of the discourse segment more directly affected by it and thus exhibit maximum effects; or it can constrain the processing effort needed to compute the segment under its direct scope, so that it is not processed more effortfully than an analogous unmarked segment. This equals to the minimum effect and is only visible for the more grammaticalized consecutive connectives Sp. *por tanto* and En. *therefore*. The effect of all other DPs considered deploys at its maximum level. The non-accelerating effect of DPs belonging to the paradigm of causal connection may be linked to several theoretical facts. Firstly, that the human mind is biased towards expecting forward continuous discourse relations, so that markers that break that continuity lead to stronger facilitation effects, as would be the case of counter-argumentative relations signaled by Sp. *sin embargo* 'however' or *a pesar de ello* 'despite that' (Murray 1997); and secondly, that positive polarity relations can be left unsignaled without leading to enhanced processing efforts of the utterance (Fetzer 2018).

The Third Principle adds further arguments for the analysis of DPs in the languages considered and for contrastive comparisons. The exclusion of a slow-down effect in the discourse segment upon which the DP directly acts is common to all expressions regardless of their semantic, syntactic and morphological features and across languages. Therefore, the Third Principle complements the framework of DP-constrained behavior patterns. It facilitates the identification of a function of a DP and the contrastive analysis between analogous communicative structures of different languages.

3.4 Corollary of the First and Second Principles of Discourse Marking

The constraining effects of discourse marking also deploy at the level of utterance reanalysis of an initial assumption. From a theoretical perspective, DPs can guide inferences during the construction of a first assumption triggering a particular inferential route. As a result, a tentative representation is built, which may be reconsidered when being contrasted with accessible contextual information that is confirmed, modified or cancelled to obtain the most relevant cognitive effects. The Corollary of the First and Second Principles of Discourse Marking describes precisely how discourse marking also controls the reanalysis task:

> **Corollary of the First and Second Principle of Discourse Marking** (*optimal control of reanalysis*). *A discourse particle regulates the reanalysis of a first assumption in such a way that additional cognitive effort is excluded in the total processing of the marked utterance with respect to the corresponding unmarked utterance.*

The corollary does not exclude any readjustment pattern of marked utterances, which is why its indicator is relational. The impact of the reanalysis (re-reading time) on the total processing of the utterance (total reading time). The reanalysis can be *positive, negative* or *neutral*: it is positive when it requires less processing effort in a marked utterance than in an analogous unmarked one; it is negative when it requires more processing effort in the marked utterance; and it is neutral if the differences between marked and unmarked utterances are statistically irrelevant. The different reanalysis patterns triggered by DP can be associated to speed-up effects or to no-slow-down effects, but never to a slowdown of the total processing time (Figure 5). Any local readjustment (of the segments affected by the DP), either to the left or to the right of the DP, is carried out in such a way that it does not increase the total processing effort of the utterance, and thus complies with the First and Second Principles.

This confirms the processing-guiding role of DPs: not only do they optimize the task of initial-assumption recovery, but they also limit the reanalysis of such

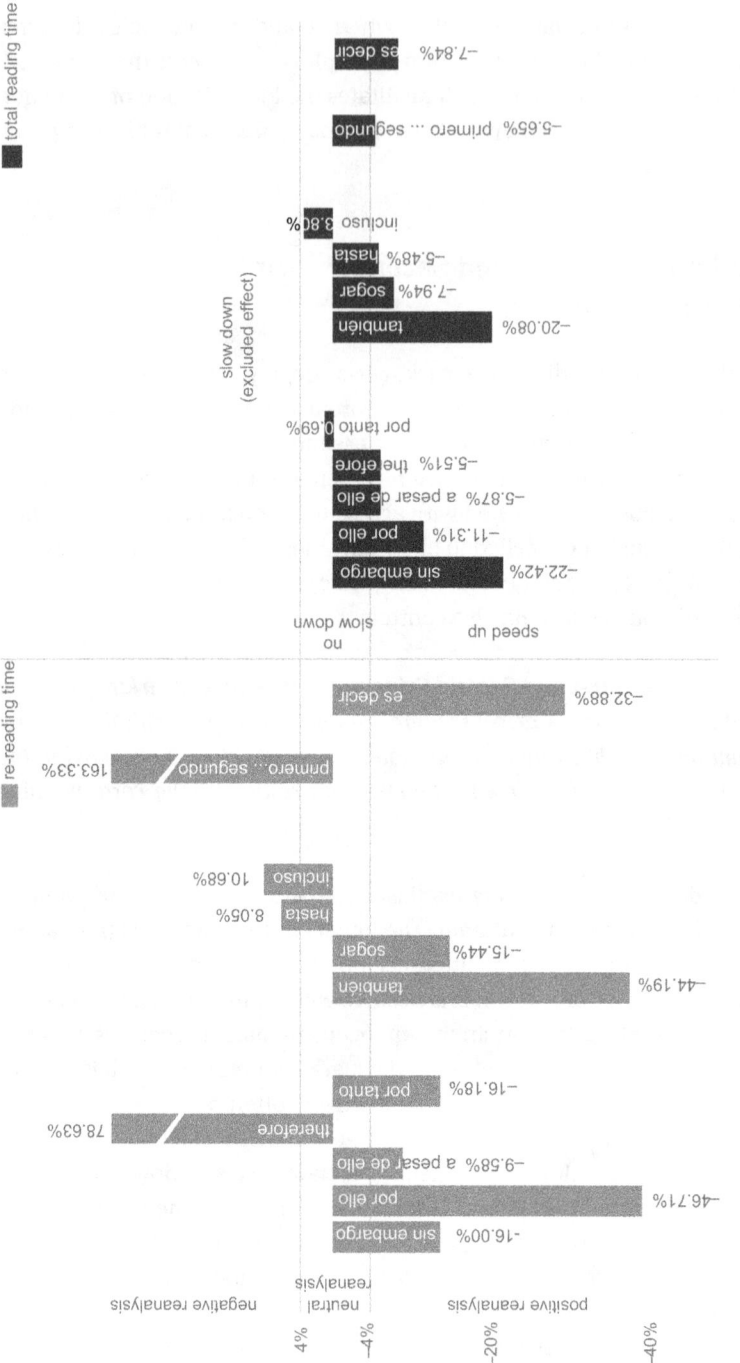

Figure 5: Differences in processing of the local area of marked and unmarked utterances as well as the utterance as a whole of the Third Principle of Discourse Marking (lexical mean of the local area and the utterance; total reading time and re-reading time).

an assumption, activating the optimal interpretative context for the interlocutor to achieve contextual effects.

The corollary theoretically implies that DPs reduce utterance under-determinacy. Unmarked utterances tend to be more effort-demanding, since the interlocutor must solve inferentially the more pronounced implicitness of the communicated assumption. Marked utterances, by contrast, have more encoded information which immediately define constraints for contextual access, both during the recovery of a first assumption and during any possible readjustment. This is seen systematically in our studies for all potential levels of variation linked to the use of one or another DP: languages, grammaticalization stages or functional paradigms. From a contrastive perspective, a range of possibilities is obtained that define a common communicative space, which, beyond the comparison of concrete DPs, establish comparisons of the discourse marking processes.

4 Conclusions

The Cognitive Principles of Discourse Marking set out in this chapter, its predictions in terms of ranges of effects, with an upper and a lower threshold, and the effects that they exclude have been formulated on the basis of experimental processing data. They constitute non-contingent spaces, since DPs compel the interlocutor to perform their rigid instructions. Therefore, the principles are to be taken as a frame to define the universal effects of DPs. At the same time, the principles establish a range of possibilities that allows to further investigate the effects of DPs considering different potential levels of variation: the semantic, the syntactic, the grammaticalization and the inter-linguistic level.

DPs are linguistic resources specialized in guiding inferential processes. As a result, instructions conveyed by DPs condition utterance processing according to the pattern frameworks predicted by the principles:
- *establishing* new routes to access information (First Principle)
- *constraining* the processing of semantically more complex information (Second Principle)
- *reducing* reanalysis in utterance interpretation (Corollary of the First and Second Principle),
- *facilitating* the immediate integration of the discourse segment directly affected by the DP (Third Principle).

The ability of DPs to activate these four processes is linked to the fact that, regardless of their formal features and of linguistic variation, they perform a discourse-marking function enabled by their procedural nature.

The Principles of Discourse Marking also verify the main feature of procedural meaning in any language: its *asymmetry* as to conceptual meaning. This asymmetric relation is evidenced by the ability of DPs, as procedural-meaning expressions, to regulate how conceptual-meaning elements are processed. This regulation is both quantitative and qualitative in nature. From a quantitative viewpoint, conceptual-meaning expressions are processed differently depending on whether they are marked by a DP or not (quantitative regulation, First Principle). From a qualitative viewpoint, such marking involves the optimal control of the processing efforts required to manipulate conceptual representations according to the complex instructions encoded in the DP (Second and Third Principle).

The Cognitive Principles of Discourse Marking allow to define the communicative space in which cognitive processing triggered by discourse marking occurs. They do not predict a single behavior pattern of different DPs in a specific language, but, on the contrary, provide a range of possibilities encompassing the variation that different syntactic, semantic and morphological features of DPs present in discourse. From a contrastive perspective, the principles focus on the communicative function of DPs. They establish a dynamic *tertium comparationis* by means of which different contrastive tasks can be identified. The principles provide information, e.g., for foreign language teachers or translators, on how analogous DPs of different languages may give rise to similar mental representations and trigger similar inferential process. However, the heterogeneity of the DP based on different formal features, different functional paradigms or different typological properties of languages is not irrelevant. It just leads to cognitive patterns predicted within the framework of the common communicative space defined by the principles, as DPs are not considered independently across languages, but in relation to the marking effects they trigger in utterances.

References

Aijmer, Karin. 2007. Translating discourse particles: A case of complex translation. In Gunilla Anderman & Margaret Rogers (eds.), *Incorporating Corpora. Multilingual Matters*, 95–116. Bristol/Blue Ridge Summit: Multilingual Matters.

Arunachalam, Sudha. 2013. Experimental methods for linguists. *Language and Linguistics Compass* 7(4). 221–232.

Beaver, David & Henk Zeevat. 2007. Accommodation. In Gillian Ramchand & Charles Reiss (eds.), *The Oxford Handbook of Linguistic Interfaces*, 503–541. Oxford: Oxford University Press.
Blakemore, Diane. 1987. *Semantic Constraints on Relevance*. Oxford: Blackwell.
Blakemore, Diane. 2002. *Relevance and Linguistic Meaning: The Semantics and Pragmatics of Discourse Markers*. Cambridge: Cambridge University Press.
Briz Gómez, Antonio, Salvador Pons Bordería & José Portolés Lázaro. 2008. *Diccionario de partículas discursivas del español*. http://www.dpde.es (last accessed: May 25, 2021).
Canestrelli, Anneloes, Willem Mak & Ted Sanders. 2013. Causal connectives in discourse processing: How differences in subjectivity are reflected in eye movements. *Language and Cognitive Processes* 28(9). 1394–1413.
Carston, Robyn. 2002. *Thoughts and Utterances: The Pragmatics of Explicit Communication*. Oxford: Blackwell.
Carter, Ronald & Michael McCarthy. 2006. *Cambridge Grammar of English. A comprehensive guide. Spoken and written English. Grammar and usage*. Cambridge: Cambridge University Press.
Clifton, Charles, Jeannine Bock & Janina Radó. 2000. Effects of the focus particle *only* and intrinsic contrast on comprehension of reduced relative clauses. In Alan Kennedy, Ralph Radach, Dieter Heller & Joël Pynte (eds.), *Reading as a Perceptual Process*, 591–619. Amsterdam: Elsevier.
Conklin, Kathy, Ana Pellicer-Sánchez & Gareth Carrol. 2018. *Eye-tracking. A Guide for Applied Linguistic Research*. Cambridge: Cambridge University Press.
Cozijn, Rein, Leo Noordman & Wietzke Vonk. 2011. Propositional integration and world-knowledge inference: Processes in understanding *because* sentences. *Discourse Processes* 48(7). 475–500.
Cruz Rubio, Adriana. 2020. *Processing Patterns of Focusing: An Experimental Study on Pragmatic Scales Triggered by the Spanish Focus Operator* incluso. Heidelberg: Heidelberg University dissertation.
Cuello Ramón, Carlos. 2022. *Psycholinguistic Correlates of Grammaticalization of Discourse Markers: Analysis of a Consecutive Subparadigm through Eye-Tracking*. Heidelberg/Valencia: Heidelberg University/University of Valencia dissertation.
Cuenca, Maria Josep (ed.). 2007. Contrastive perspectives on discourse markers. *Catalan Journal of Linguistics* 6. www.raco.cat/index.php/CatalanJournal/article/view/74207/pdf (last accessed: May 25, 2021).
Cuenca, Maria Josep. 2020. Defective connective constructions: Some cases in Catalan and Spanish. *Corpus Pragmatics* 4. 423–448.
de Saussure, Louis. 2011. On some methodological issues in the conceptual/procedural distinction. In María Victoria Escandell-Vidal, Manuel Leonetti & Aoife Ahern (eds.), *Procedural Meaning: Problems and Perspectives*, 55–79. Leiden: Brill.
Degand, Liesbeth & Ted Sanders. 2002. The impact of relational markers on expository text comprehension in L1 and L2. *Reading and writing* 15(7–8). 739–757.
Degand, Liesbeth. 2009. On describing polysemous discourse markers. What does translation add to the picture. In Stef Slembrouck, Miriam Taverniers & Mieke van Herreweghe (eds.), *From will to well. Studies in Linguistics offered to Anne-Marie Simon-Vandenbergen*, 173–184. Ghent: Academia Press.
Escandell-Vidal, María Victoria & Manuel Leonetti. 2011. On the rigidity of procedural meaning. In María Victoria Escandell-Vidal, Manuel Leonetti & Aoife Ahern (eds.), *Procedural Meaning: Problems and Perspectives*, 81–102. Leiden: Brill.

Escandell-Vidal, María Victoria. 2017. Notes for a restrictive theory of procedural meaning. *Doing Pragmatics Interculturally: Cognitive, Philosophical, and Sociopragmatic Perspectives* 312. 79–95.

Evers-Vermeul, Jacqueline & Ted Sanders. 2019. Subjectivity and causality in discourse and cognition. Evidence from corpus analyses, acquisition and processing. In Óscar Loureda, Inés Recio Fernández, Laura Nadal & Adriana Cruz (eds.), *Empirical Studies of the Construction of Discourse*, 273–298. Amsterdam/Philadelphia: John Benjamins.

Evers-Vermeul, Jaqueline & Ted Sanders. 2011. Discovering domains – On the acquisition of causal connectives. *Journal of Pragmatics* 43(6). 1645–1662.

Fetzer, Anita. 2018. The encoding and signaling of discourse relations in argumentative discourse: Evidence across production formats. In María de los Ángeles Gómez González & John Lachlan Mackenzie (eds.), *The Construction of Discourse as Verbal Interaction*, 13–44. Amsterdam/Philadelphia: John Benjamins.

Filik, Ruth, Kevin Paterson & Antje Sauermann. 2011. The influence of focus on eye movements during reading. In Simon Liversedge, Iain Gilchrist & Stefan Everling (eds.), *The Oxford Handbook of Eye Movements*, 925–941. Oxford: Oxford University Press.

Fischer, Kerstin. 2006. *Approaches to Discourse Particles*. Leiden: Brill.

Fraser, Bruce. 1999. What are discourse markers?. *Journal of Pragmatics* 31(7). 931–952.

Fuentes Rodríguez, Catalina. 2009. *Diccionario de conectores y operadores del español*. Madrid: Arco/Libros.

Guillén Jiménez, Diego. 2021. *Experimental Analysis of the Processing Schemas of Counter-Argumentation and Anaphoric Substitution Signaled by the Spanish Connective* a pesar de ello. Heidelberg: Heidelberg University dissertation.

Hansen, Maj-Britt. 2006. A dynamic polysemy approach to the lexical semantics of discourse markers (with an exemplary analysis of French '*toujours*'). In Kerstin Fischer (ed.), *Approaches to Discourse Particles*, 21–41. Leiden: Brill.

Hoek, Jet, Sandrine Zufferey, Jacqueline Evers-Vermeul & Ted Sanders. 2017. Cognitive complexity and the linguistic marking of coherence relations. A parallel corpus study. *Journal of Pragmatics* 121(2). 113–131.

Holmqvist, Kenneth, Marcus Nyström, Richard Andersson, Richard Dewhurst, Halszka Jarodzka & Joost van de Weijer. 2011. *Eye Tracking: A Comprehensive Guide to Methods and Measures*. Oxford: Oxford University Press.

Loureda, Óscar & Esperanza Acín Villa. 2010. *Los estudios sobre marcadores del discurso en español, hoy*. Madrid: Arco/Libros.

Loureda, Óscar, Adriana Cruz, Inés Recio & Martha Rudka. 2021. *Comunicación, partículas discursivas y pragmática experimental*. Madrid: Arco/Libros.

Loureda, Óscar, Inés Recio, Laura Nadal & Adriana Cruz. 2019. *Empirical Studies of the Construction of Discourse*. Amsterdam/Philadelphia: John Benjamins.

Mak, Willem & Ted Sanders. 2013. The role of causality in discourse processing: Effects of expectation and coherence relations. *Language and Cognitive Processes* 28(9). 1414–1437.

Martín Zorraquino, María Antonia & José Portolés Lázaro. 1999. Los marcadores del discurso. In Ignacio Bosque & Violeta Demonte (eds.), *Gramática descriptiva de la lengua española*, 4051–4213. Madrid: Espasa Calpe.

Martín Zorraquino, María Antonia. 2010. Los marcadores del discurso y su morfología. In Óscar Loureda & Esperanza Acín (eds.), *Los estudios sobre marcadores del discurso en español, hoy*, 93–182. Madrid: Arco/Libros.

Murray, John. 1997. Connectives and narrative text: The role of continuity. *Memory & Cognition* 25(2). 227–236.
Nadal, Laura. 2019. *Lingüística experimental y contraargumentación; un estudio del conector sin embargo en español.* Frankfurt: Peter Lang.
Nicolle, Steve. 1998. A relevance theory perspective on grammaticalization. *Cognitive Linguistics* 9. 1–35.
Nicolle, Steve. 2015. Diachronic change in procedural semantic content. *Nouveaux Cahiers de Linguistique Française* 32. 133–148.
Pons Bordería, Salvador & Óscar Loureda (eds.). 2018. *Discourse Markers in Grammaticalization and Constructionalization: New Issues in the Study of Language Change.* Leiden: Brill.
Pons Bordería, Salvador. 1998. *Conexión y conectores: estudio de su relación en el registro informal de la lengua.* Valencia: University of Valencia.
Portolés Lázaro, José, Eugenia Sáinz González & Silvia Murillo Ornat. 2021. Partículas discursivas e instrucciones de procesamiento. In María Victoria Escandell-Vidal, José Amenós & Aoife Ahern (eds.), *Pragmática*, 284–302. Madrid: Akal.
Portolés Lázaro, José. [1998] 2001. *Marcadores del discurso.* 2nd edition. Barcelona: Ariel.
Portolés Lázaro, José. 2014. Gramática, semántica y discurso en el estudio de los marcadores. In María Marta García Negroni (ed.), *Marcadores del discurso: perspectivas y contraste*, 203–231. Buenos Aires: Santiago Arcos.
R Core Team. 2018. *R: A language and environment for statistical computing.* Wien: R Foundation for Statistical Computing. www.R-project.org (last accessed: May 25, 2021).
Rayner, Keith. 2009. Eye movements and attention in reading, scene perception, and visual search. *The Quarterly Journal of Experimental Psychology* 62(8). 1457–1506.
Recio Fernández, Inés. 2020. *The Impact of Procedural Meaning on Second Language Processing: A Study on Connectives.* Heidelberg: Heidelberg University dissertation.
Rudka, Martha. In preparation. *Informationsstruktur und experimentelle Pragmatik: Verarbeitungsmuster bei der Fokussierung mit Diskurspartikeln im Deutschen.* Heidelberg: Heidelberg University dissertation.
Sanders, Ted & Leo Noordman. 2000. The role of coherence relations and their linguistic markers in text processing. *Discourse Processes* 29(1). 37–60.
Sanders, Ted & Wilbert Spooren. 2001. Text representation as an interface between language and its users. In Ted Sanders, Joost Schilperoord & Wilbert Spooren (eds.), *Text Representation: Linguistic and Psycholinguistic Aspects*, 1–25. Amsterdam/Philadelphia: John Benjamins.
Sanders, Ted, Wilbert Spooren & Leo Noordman. 1993. Coherence relations in a cognitive theory of discourse representation. *Cognitive Linguistics* 4(2). 93–133.
Sanders, Ted. 2005. Coherence, causality and cognitive complexity in discourse. In *Proceedings/Actes SEM-05, First International Symposium on the Exploration and Modelling of Meaning*, 105–114. Toulouse: University of Toulouse-Jean Jaurès.
Schiffrin, Deborah. 1994. *Approaches to Discourse.* Oxford: Blackwell.
Sperber, Dan & Deirdre Wilson. [1986] 1995. *Relevance: Communication and Cognition.* 2nd edition. Oxford: Blackwell.
Spooren, Wilbert & Ted Sanders. 2008. The acquisition of coherence relations: On cognitive complexity in discourse. *Journal of Pragmatics* 40(12). 2003–2026.
Thome, Sarah. 2018. *Additive Konnektoren mit argumentativer Funktion. Eine experimentelle Studie zu sp. además und it. inoltre.* Heidelberg: Heidelberg University master thesis.

Torres Santos, Lourdes. 2020. *The Scalar Focus Operator* hasta: *An Experimental Study on Processing Costs in Spanish*. Heidelberg: Heidelberg University dissertation.

van Silfhout, Gerdineke, Jacqueline Evers-Vermeul & Ted Sanders. 2015. Connectives as processing signals: How students benefit in processing narrative and expository texts. *Discourse Processes* 52(1). 47–76.

Wilson, Deirdre & Dan Sperber. 1993. Linguistic Form and Relevance. *Lingua* 90(1–2). 1–25.

Wilson, Deirdre. 2011. *The Conceptual-Procedural Distinction: Past, Present and Future*. Bingley: Emerald.

Zufferey, Sandrine & Bruno Cartoni. 2012. English and French causal connectives in contrast. *Languages in Contrast* 12(2). 232–250.

Zufferey, Sandrine. 2016. Discourse connectives across languages. Factors influencing their explicit or implicit translation. *Languages in Contrast* 16(2). 264–279.

Joanna Blochowiak and Cristina Grisot

3 New perspectives on *car* and *parce que*: Is it about subjectivity, reasoning or speakers?

Abstract: In contemporary French, the difference between the causal connectives *parce que* and *car* is traditionally related to the prototypical causal relations they are meant to convey. The main claim has been that *car* more frequently conveys subjective relations whereas *parce que* is equally well-suited for both subjective and objective relations. Nevertheless, in the recent years, empirical evidence offered by a number of studies suggests that *car* has gained ground over *parce que* in expressing objective relations too. Despite the decline of *car* in oral speech, its presence is still widely attested in the written press, in SMS and in chats. In this chapter, we present the results of an exploratory study in which we compare how university students aged 19–25 (Experiment 1) and other native speakers, aged 20–70 and recruited via a crowdsourcing platform (Experiment 2), evaluate the acceptability of objective and subjective relations expressed with *car* and *parce que*. Our study reveals significant differences between the two target groups of participants. The results show that the mapping between the subjective-objective divide and the two French causal connectives depends on the type of relation (i.e., subjective relations are overall less acceptable than objective causal relations) and on the connective (i.e., *parce que* does not seem to fit objective and subjective relations equally well, but this applies only to older people). This suggests that the use of the two connectives to express subjective and objective relations may also depend on the speakers' educational background, reasoning skills, and age.

Keywords: causal connectives, subjectivity, reasoning, age groups, French, experimental study

1 Introduction

This chapter addresses the contemporary use of the French causal connective *car* ('because') as opposed to another French causal connective, *parce que* ('because'), from both methodological and theoretical perspectives. The issue with these two

Joanna Blochowiak, Université catholique de Louvain, joanna.blochowiak@uclouvain.be
Cristina Grisot, University of Zürich, cristina.grisot@uzh.ch

https://doi.org/10.1515/9783110790351-003

connectives, which are almost synonyms, is that native speakers of French would intuitively agree that there are differences in the usage of *car* and *parce que*, and various analyses have sought to pinpoint these differences within different theoretical frameworks (Le groupe-λ-1 1975; Moeschler 1987, 2005; Ferrari 1992; Iordanskaja 1993; Debaisieux 2002, 2004; Degand and Pander Maat 2003; Lambrecht et al., 2006; Zufferey 2012). First, it has long been assumed that *car* more frequently conveys subjective relations whereas *parce que* is equally well-suited for both types of relations, i.e. objective and subjective (Iordanskaja 1993; Debaisieux 2002; 2004; Degand & Pander Maat 2003; Lambrecht et al. 2006; Simon & Degand 2007; Fagard & Degand 2008; Degand & Fagard 2012; Zufferey 2012). Second, it has been suggested that *car* is restricted to the written mode and to formal register (Frei 1982/1929; Bentolila 1986; Fagard & Degand 2008; Fagard & Degand 2012; Zufferey 2012). Yet, the extant body of empirical and experimental studies has not reached any clear-cut results that would confirm these claims (see Zufferey et al., 2018 for a recent attempt).

One of the explanations for this difficulty might be that the two causal connectives have undergone – and are still undergoing – semantic change affecting their use (Degand & Fagard 2012). As such, it seems that *car* is currently undergoing certain changes due to new technologies, such as text messaging and the use of social media (Véronis & Guimier de Neef 2006; Blochowiak et al. 2020). For example, Blochowiak et al. (2020) have investigated the frequency of *car* and *parce que* in a journalistic corpus and in a corpus of SMS and have found that the two connectives present a similar frequency. Crucially, this change would result in a lack of differentiation between these two connectives among younger generations. This result is corroborated by evidence in Zufferey (2012), who found that university students accept both connectives equally.

Nevertheless, until recently the participants in most experimental studies have been university students who attend courses in language sciences, linguistics, philosophy of language, or other related disciplines. This is likely to be problematic, since such participants may not be a representative sample of the population of native speakers as far as age and educational background are concerned. Thus, researchers need to consider testing participants across all age groups, as well as from diverse educational backgrounds. A new hypothesis would be that older speakers may accept *car* and may still differentiate between the two causal connectives not only because they were exposed to this connective in their youth but also because they continue to be proportionally the main consumers of written texts, such as (classical) literature and press,[1] and far more so than today's young people.

---

[1] It is important to mention that recent studies (Blochowiak et al. 2020) have found no significant difference between the subjective and the objective uses of the two causal connectives in

For these reasons, in this chapter we have decided to examine the use of *car* vs. *parce que* from a two-fold perspective: (i) with an offline evaluation experiment whose goal is to assess university students' (aged 19–25) explicit preferences vis-à-vis the use of *car* and *parce que*; and (ii) with a crowdsourcing experiment whose goal is to assess the explicit preferences vis-à-vis the use of *car* and *parce que* in a larger pool of native speakers aged 20–70.

This chapter is structured as follows. The next Section examines the current state of research on French causal connectives (in 2.1.) and discusses how they express subjective and objective causal relations (in 2.2). Section 3 presents our experimental investigation into this issue, namely the hypotheses of our experiments (in 3.1); the offline experiment with university students (in 3.2); and the crowdsourcing experiment with all age groups (in 3.3). A general discussion of the results follows in Section 4. Finally, Section 5 provides a conclusion with a summary of the chapter's results.

2 Current state of research

2.1 The connectives *car* and *parce que*: A change of paradigm?

For some years now, the causal connectives *car* and *parce que* have attracted the attention of researchers, who have discussed them from various perspectives not only in French (Le groupe-λ-l 1975; Ducrot 1983; Roulet et al. 1985; Iordanskaja 1993; Nølke 1995; Bentolila 1986; Bertin 1997; Moeschler 2003) but also in other languages too (see Pasch 1983 for the German markers *denn* and *weil*; and Van Belle 1989 for the Dutch markers *doordat* and *omdat*). Based on the different syntactic and semantic properties of these connectives, as well as their informational status (new information for *car* vs. old for *parce que*), the Groupe-λ-l proposed that *parce que* is a propositional operator (i.e., it links two propositions into one complex proposition) whereas *car* is a speech act marker (i.e., it links two speech acts) (see also Ariel, this volume, chapter 10). These observations reflect the cognitive approach proposed more recently by Sweetser (1990) for the English *because*, in which she distinguishes between three different domains of use: content (1), epistemic (2), and speech act domain (3):

---

corpora with contemporary journalistic texts (e.g., *Le Monde* in the year 2012). This does not preclude the possibility that there might be differences between the two connectives in a corpus with older journalistic texts (e.g., from the '70s–'80s, when the older population from our study acquired the use of *car* and *parce que*).

(1) *John got angry because Max insulted him.*

(2) *Mary is at home, because her bike is in front of her house.*

(3) *Are you free this evening? Because there is a nice movie.*

In the content domain, *because* conveys a causal relation between eventualities occurring in the world (the event of Max's insulting of John caused the event of John's getting angry). In the epistemic domain, *because* serves to provide evidence (the presence of the bike) for a speaker's opinion or belief (Mary's presence at home). In the speech act domain, *because* provides a justification for the use of a speech act such as a question. Content relations are considered to be objective because they refer to external, factual reality (causal relations between eventualities which are often independent of the speaker); the relations conveyed in the epistemic and speech act domains, on the other hand, are claimed to be subjective as they refer to speakers' internal reality, providing justification for their opinions, beliefs, or actions (cf. Sanders & Spooren 2015).

It is well established that these domains of use are associated with two types of causal relations: the content domain pairs with objective causal relations, while the epistemic and speech act domains couple with subjective causal relations (Pander Maat and Degand 2001; Pit 2003; Stukker and Sanders 2012). In the light of this distinction in terms of causal relations, *car* is considered a prototypical marker of subjective relations whereas *parce que* functions as a more polyvalent connective suited equally well for any type of relation, whether objective or subjective (Iordanskaja 1993; Debaisieux 2002, 2004; Degand and Pander Maat 2003; Lambrecht et al. 2006; Simon and Degand 2007; Fagard and Degand 2008; Degand and Fagard 2012; Zufferey 2012). Furthermore, some researchers have proposed that the use of *car* in contemporary French is limited to high register, especially in (formal) writing such as newspaper articles (Zufferey 2012; Zufferey et al. 2018). *Car* is certainly far less attested in oral speech (Degand and Fagard 2012), and some studies have claimed that *car* has almost totally disappeared in contemporary oral speech, with its use in written texts also declining (Frei 1982/1929; Bentolila 1986; Fagard and Degand 2008; Zufferey 2012).

However, recent studies indicate that this picture may no longer be accurate. For instance, Nazarenko (2000) has reported that *car* can also be used to express objective relations, and Zufferey et al. (2018: 100) have cast doubt on the subjective nature of *car*:

> In French 'car' is not strongly associated with subjective relations, which implies that French-speaking readers do not use 'car' to infer the presence of a subjective relation during reading,

an observation that is in line with the fact that in corpus data 'car' is not strongly associated with subjective relations, and that participants do not have a strong tendency to choose it for subjective relations.

Zufferey (2012) had already reported that the younger population of French native speakers use the two connectives as interchangeable for many objective and subjective causal relations in writing. In the same vein, in an annotation study of journalistic and SMS texts Blochowiak et al. (2020) found that the French connective *car* is not predominantly used to express subjectivity but is, in fact, employed to convey the message in a more objective way. As it turns out, a similar observation had been made previously by Véronis and Guimier de Neef (2006), who identified a frequent use of *car* in chats. Since these two modes of communication (SMS and chats) are typically associated with low register, *car* cannot be restricted to high register only.

The current state of research outlined so far reveals two hypotheses regarding the use of *car* and *parce que* in expressing objective and subjective causal relations. The first is the **classic hypothesis**, according to which *car* is considered a prototypical marker of subjective causal relations while *parce que* serves both subjective and objective causal relations equally well (Iordanskaja 1993; Debaisieux 2002; 2004; Degand and Pander Maat 2003; Lambrecht et al. 2006; Simon & Degand 2007; Fagard & Degand 2008; Degand and Fagard 2012; Zufferey 2012). The second is the **novel hypothesis**, according to which *car* is no longer a prototypical marker of subjective causal relations and becomes interchangeable with *parce que* in the case of both subjective and objective causal relations (Nazarenko 2000; Zufferey et al. 2018; Blochowiak et al. 2020).

2.2 The complexity of subjective causal relations

Objective and subjective causal relations differ in their complexity. Objective relations are considered to be simpler, as they refer to a causal relation which links two eventualities (events, states, or other types of eventualities), as is the case for example in (4) whereby John's getting angry is caused by Max having insulted him. As such, this type of relation is dyadic, i.e. it involves only two relata.

(4) *John got angry because Max insulted him.*
   CAUSE (e1, e2), where: e1 = Max insulted John, e2 = John got angry

Subjective causal relations are more complex in at least three ways. First, they relate to reasons of beliefs, opinions, suppositions, (un)certainty, etc., involving *ipso facto* a subject of these cognitive states, sometimes called *subject of consciousness* (Sanders & Spooren 2015). Even though this type of relation is tagged in many frameworks as causal, the very nature of this relation is epistemic, and is therefore better referred to as reason: the speaker (or subject of consciousness) s has a reason r to hold that p (Blochowiak 2014; Blochowiak et al. 2020). Therefore, a subjective causal relation denotes the triadic relation REASON because it ties three relata. The type of reason behind a given epistemic state may vary, as it can come from different sources: for instance, hearsay or testimony, illustrated in (5); more or less direct perception, illustrated in (6); or inferential, illustrated in (7).

(5) *Hearsay type of reason*
  a. Joe believes that Mary is at home because the housekeeper told him.
  b. REASON (s, r, p), where: s = Joe, r = the housekeeper told Joe that Mary is home, p = Mary is home

(6) *Perception type of reason*
  a. Joe is sure that Mary is at home because he saw her on the balcony.
  b. REASON (s, r, p), where: s = Joe, r = Joe saw Mary on the balcony, p = Mary is home

(7) *Inferential type of reason*
  a. Joe is sure that Mary is at home, because her car is parked in front of her house.
  b. REASON (s, r, p), where: s = Joe, r = Joe inferred that Mary was at home based on the fact that her car was in the parking spot, p = Mary is home

Another degree of complexity in subjective causal relations is specifically linked to one of these types of reason, namely the inferential one. Indeed, it is more complex than the others, since it involves a reasoning that the speaker needs to perform using his or her world knowledge (Cozijn et al. 2011; Blochowiak 2014, 2017). In particular, the speaker concludes that Mary is at home on the basis of his or her background knowledge, according to which if people are at home their cars are parked nearby, combined with the fact that Mary's car is parked in front of her house. The general rule works as a major premise (usually not explicitly mentioned), the second segment of *because* as a minor premise, and the first segment of *because* as the conclusion, as presented schematically in (8).

(8) Reasoning behind the inferential type of reason (abductive kind)
   a. Major premise: *If people are at home, their cars are parked nearby*
   b. Minor premise: *Mary's car is parked in front of her house*
   c. Conclusion: *Mary is at home*

This type of reasoning is enthymemic, as not all steps are explicit. Moreover, in non-monotonic logic this particular type of example is considered as abductive (the minor premise refers to the consequent of the conditional), while in classical logic this corresponds to the *affirmation of the consequent* fallacy.

Finally, the third complexity involved in subjective relations also applies to the inferential (abductive) type, given that their formulation can be left implicit, as in (9), or made explicit by means of various epistemic markers, as in (10).[2]

(9) *Mary is at home, because her car is parked in front of her house.*

(10) *Joe believes/thinks/supposes that Mary is at home, because her car is parked in front of her house.*

The use of the epistemic markers provides facilitated access to the subjective relation, since it clearly indicates that the relation expressed is constructed by a speaker (subject of consciousness) who refers to his or her mental states. In terms of Fauconnier's mental space theory, the treatment of subjective relations sets up a mental space containing the speaker's beliefs, opinions, thoughts, etc. (cf. Fauconnier 1994; Sweetser and Fauconnier 1996; Kleijn et al. 2021). If the speaker's involvement in the construction of the subjective relation is overtly marked with an epistemic marker, the fact that a subjective mental space has been generated is immediately obvious. However, when the speaker's involvement is attenuated or absent, access to such a subjective mental space is more difficult. Experimental studies confirm these observations: participants have more difficulty in processing subjective causal relations when they are left implicit than when they are overtly marked with an epistemic marker (Traxler et al. 1997a; Traxler et al. 1997b; Canestrelli et al. 2013; Kleijn et al. 2021).

Based on such findings, we can formulate a **complex subjectivity hypothesis** according to which subjectivity, as expressed with subjective causal relations, is in general more complex than objectivity, as expressed with objective causal

---

[2] It should be noted that the presence of an epistemic marker can lead to different interpretations due to scope ambiguities: *[Joe believes that Mary is at home] because [the lights are on]* or *Joe believes that [Mary is at home because the lights are on]* (see Blochowiak 2010 for a more detailed analysis of different interpretations, depending on various embedding contexts).

relations. This complexity applies especially to inferential subjective relations because they correspond to reasoning that is usually based on some unspoken premises that comprehenders have to retrieve from their background knowledge. This difficulty is compounded by the fact that the subjective relations can be left implicit, requiring further effort on the comprehender's part to recover them.

3 Experimental investigation

A large majority of empirical work on connectives and other linguistic phenomena is carried out on student populations. As already mentioned, this practice may impose a limitation, as students represent a particular sample of the society characterized as WEIRD (Western, Educated, Industrialized, Rich, and Democratic). Studies that have examined a wide range of experimental work, mainly in psychology, have demonstrated that the behaviour of participants from such narrow samples is quite specific; thus, the results of experiments involving them cannot, and should not, be generalised to the entire population (Henrich et al. 2010). The aim of this chapter is not to resolve this problem in its entirety, but rather to propose a small-scale exploratory comparison between student participants and non-student participants, the latter sought out via a crowdsourcing experiment, in order to observe whether studies on language should also seek more variation in the choice of population. For this purpose, we formulate a **sample-related hypothesis**, according to which the behaviour of participants recruited among students will be different from the behaviour of participants recruited among the general population of speakers of French.

3.1 Predictions

Below we summarise the hypotheses formulated in Section 2 and provide the predictions (about the concrete measures performed during the experiment), which follow from them with a view to testing them experimentally by way of an acceptability task.

The classic hypothesis claims that *car* is considered a prototypical marker of subjective causal relations, while *parce que* fits subjective and objective causal relations equally well. Its ensuing predictions are: first, we would expect higher scores given to sentences with subjective *car* than those with objective *car*; and second, we would expect similar scores given to sentences with subjective *parce que* and those with objective *parce que*.

The novel hypothesis claims that *car* is no longer a prototypical marker of subjective causal relations and has become interchangeable with *parce que* in the case of both subjective and objective causal relations. Its ensuing predictions are: first, we would expect similar scores given to sentences with subjective *car* and those with objective *car*; and second, we would expect similar scores given to sentences with subjective *parce que* and those with objective *parce que*.

The complex subjectivity hypothesis claims that subjective causal relations are more complex than objective relations, regardless of the connective used. Its ensuing prediction is that we would expect lower scores given to sentences expressing subjective causal relations than those given to sentences expressing objective relations.

The sample-related hypothesis refers to the fact that researchers frequently recruit their participants among students, who may not correspond to a representative sample of the speaking population, given that they are usually young and highly educated. Its ensuing prediction is that we would expect different results in Experiment 1, which is focused on university students, and in Experiment 2, which is based on a larger pool of native speakers. First, by their age, students widely use SMS and chats, in which both connectives occur with a similar frequency (as shown in corpora studies). Thus, the prediction is that young participants do not distinguish between the two connectives anymore while older participants still maintain this distinction, mainly because their use of SMS and chats is less pronounced. Second, as students receive broad education training, they should develop good reasoning skills. Thus, they are expected to process particularly well subjective relations, which are inferential (abductive) in our study and therefore require a higher aptitude for addressing inferential patterns (see also Zufferey et al., this volume, chapter 4).

3.2 Off-line experiment with university students

3.2.1 Methodology

Participants in this experiment were 26 second- and third-year students from the Faculty of Humanities (19 females, mean age: 21.73, range 19–25). Their participation in the experiment was part of their attendance of a course in linguistics, and they were not paid for their participation.

In order to investigate how each connective (*car* vs. *parce que*) and the type of relation (subjective vs. objective) influence the participants' acceptability of sentences with *car* or with *parce que*, we carried out a within-group 2x2 offline evaluation experiment (see Appendix for the items). In other words, each connective occurred under each relation, thus both connectives appeared at an equal number of times in each condition. Each participant read items in all four experimental conditions. 16 experimental items were built: 8 expressing an objective relation, as in (11), and 8 expressing a subjective relation, as in (12). All the items conveying subjective relations assumed the inferential (abductive) type without an epistemic marker, while all the items conveying objective relations referred to causality as it occurs in the physical world. As such, by their construction, the items were clearly identifiable as subjective (as they express inferential abductive relations) or as objective (since they express causality in the physical world). The items were double checked by the authors and another non-academic French native speaker.

(11) Robert s'est fâché très fort **car/parce que** Valentin l'a insulté.
 'Robert got very angry because Valentin insulted him.'

(12) Monique est à la maison **car/parce que** son vélo est devant chez elle.
 'Monique is at home, because her bike is in front of her house.'

The experiment was carried out using the paper-and-pen technique. Given the face-to-face format of the experiment, no verification items were used in this experiment. Participants were told that they would receive a series of sentences, each of them in two variants: one with the connective *car* and one with the connective *parce que*. Participants saw the experimental items in a random order. They were asked to rate on a sheet of paper their acceptability of each variant, on a 5-point Likert scale, where 1 corresponds to sentences with the lowest acceptability and 5 to sentences with the highest acceptability. They were allowed to give the same score to both variants of the same sentence if they wanted to.

Due to a printing problem, one of the items expressing an objective relation had to be discarded from the analysis. Further analysis was carried out on 650 data points, resulting from the 26 participants' reading of 15 experimental items.

To analyse the data, we constructed logistic mixed-effects models, which allow to include both participants and items as random factors in all analyses. To build the logistic mixed-effects models we used the R software (R Development Core Team, 2010). Models were tested using the clmm() function of the *ordinal* package of R, and model comparisons were assessed using the anova() function, which uses likelihood ratio tests to assess the goodness of fit in two competing models. Following Field et al. (2014), we built the models by moving from the simplest model, which only encompasses items and participants as random factors, to the one of interest, which incorporates the connective and the relation expressed, as well as their interaction, as fixed factors.

Adding the connective as a fixed factor to the simplest model did not improve the model (LR=0.022, df= 1, p = .881). Likewise, adding the relation and the connective as fixed factors, as well as their interaction, to the simplest model, also did not improve the model (LR = 1.467, df = 3, p = .689). This final model showed that there was no statistically significant difference in participants' acceptability scores among the two connectives: mean=2.16 for *car*, mean=2.15 for *parce que* (β=0.018, SE=0.197, p= .924), or between the two relations: mean=2.20, SE=.044 for objective relations, mean=2.13 for subjective relations (β=−0.117, SE=0.190, p= .536). In addition, the interaction between connective and relation was not found significant: mean=2.19 for *car* objective, mean=2.14 for *car* subjective, mean=2.20 for *parce que* objective and mean=2.11 for *parce que* subjective (β=−0.773, SE=0.268, p= .773) (Figure 1).

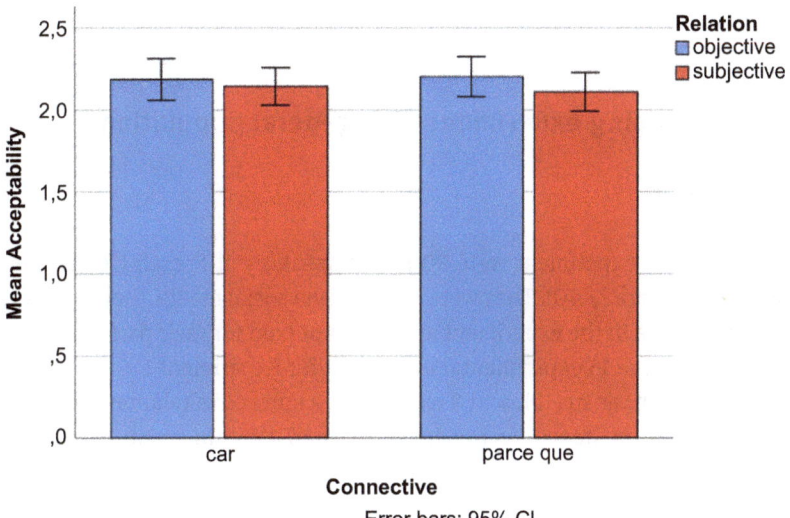

Figure 1: Mean Acceptability Score for the Connectives *Car* and *Parce que* Across Two Types of Causal Relations in Experiment 1.

3.2.2 Results

The results show that the participants – all being university students – judge causal sentences with *car* and *parce que* as equally acceptable. This result is anticipated according to the *novel* hypothesis, which predicts that young participants should give similar scores to sentences with *car* and those with *parce que*, because they are exposed not only to *parce que* but also to *car*. Indeed, it was found that *car* is as frequent as *parce que* not only in the recent written press (e.g., *Le Monde* in 2012) but also in SMS and chats (Véronis & Guimmier de Neef, 2006;

Blochowiak et al. 2020). As for the interaction between the type of connective and the relation expressed, our results are not in accordance with the *complexity hypothesis* as university students yield similar scores to sentences with *subjective car* and to sentences with *subjective parce que*.

The question which remains open is whether these hypotheses are confirmed with data from older participants and whether the results for university students (19–25 years old) are replicable in this age group too. To address this question, we carried out a second experiment, with the same design and material, but using the crowdsourcing technique. This experiment draws on the *sample-related* hypothesis, which predicts differences among young students and non-student participants, as well as between young and less young participants. We present Experiment 2 in the next section.

3.3 Crowdsourcing experiment with general population

3.3.1 Methodology

Participants in this experiment were 90 native speakers of French (76 females, mean age: 37.08, range 22–70). They were recruited via social media, they explicitly agreed to participate in the experiment and were not paid for their participation.

We used the same 16 experimental items built for Experiment 1: 8 expressing an objective relation, as in (13), and 8 expressing a subjective relation, as in (14) (see Appendix 1 for the items). As previously, we had a within-group 2x2 design, thus both connectives appeared at an equal number of times in each condition. Each participant read items in all four experimental conditions. We also created 20 verification items, having the same structure (segment 1, connective, segment 2), using the connectives *et* ('and'), as in (15), and *sinon* ('otherwise'), as in (16). The sentences with *sinon* were used to control whether participants read for comprehension, as they should be rated as "incorrect".

(13) Robert s'est fâché très fort **car/parce que** Valentin l'a insulté sans raison.
'Robert got very angry because Valentin insulted him for no reason.'

(14) Monique est à la maison **car/parce que** son vélo est devant chez elle.
'Monique is at home because her bike is in front of her house.'

(15) Patrick a oublié de mettre de l'essence **et** sa voiture s'est arrêtée au beau milieu de la route.
'Patrick forgot to put petrol in his car and it stopped in the middle of the road.'

(16) Le front de Danny est très chaud **sinon** sa mère a pris sa température.
'Danny's forehead is very hot otherwise his mother has taken his temperature.'

This was a crowdsourcing experiment and was distributed using the Qualtrics software. Participants were told that they would take part in a survey about discourse connectives. Their task was to read a series of sentences, which contained connectives such as *parce que*, *car* or *sinon*, and to rate them on a 6-point Likert scale, where 0 corresponds to an incorrect sentence, 1 to a sentence with a low acceptability and 6 to a sentence with a very high acceptability.[3] The total of 52 sentences (16 for each connective and 20 fillers) were distributed in 13 blocks and were shown in a random order.

Among the 90 participants, 3 were discarded because they did not finish the task and 5 others because they accepted more than 50% of the sentences with *sinon*. Further analysis was carried out on 2619 data points, resulting from the 82 participants.

As in Experiment 1, the results were analysed by means of logistic mixed-effects models. We built the models by moving from the simplest model to the one of interest. In particular, we first tested a model that only encompasses items and participants as random factors (i.e., random intercepts). We then compared this model to one including the connective as a fixed factor, and one that incorporates the connective and the relation expressed, as well as their interaction, as fixed factors. Finally, we compared this last model with one that incorporates the connective, the relation expressed and the participants' age, as well as their interaction, as fixed factors. To incorporate participants' age in the analysis, we formed the following age groups: 20–30, 31–40, 41–50, 51–60 and 61–70 years old.

3.3.2 Results

Adding the connective as a fixed factor to the simplest model, which only includes items and participants as random effects, improved the simplest model (LR = 4.382, df = 1, p = .036). Adding the connective and its interaction with relation as a fixed factor to the previous model further improved the model's fit (LR = 54.623,

---

[3] The difference in the acceptability scale between Experiment 1 (5-point Likert scale) and Experiment 2 (6-point Likert scale) comes from the fact that in Experiment 2 we included verification items. These were ungrammatical sentences, for which the zero score had to be used. In addition, in Qualtrics, for the answer to be registered, participants had to move the slider. As such, all items with *sinon* would receive a zero score while all items with *car* and *parce que* were, in fact, judged on a 5-point scale.

df = 2, p < .001). Finally, adding age to the model, which already contains the connective, the type of relation and their interaction, further improved the model's fit (LR = 47.45, df = 16, p < .001). According to this model, there is a significant main effect of the connective, a significant main effect of the relation (but no significant effect of age) and several significant interactions between connective and relation, as well as connective, relation and age (Figure 2).

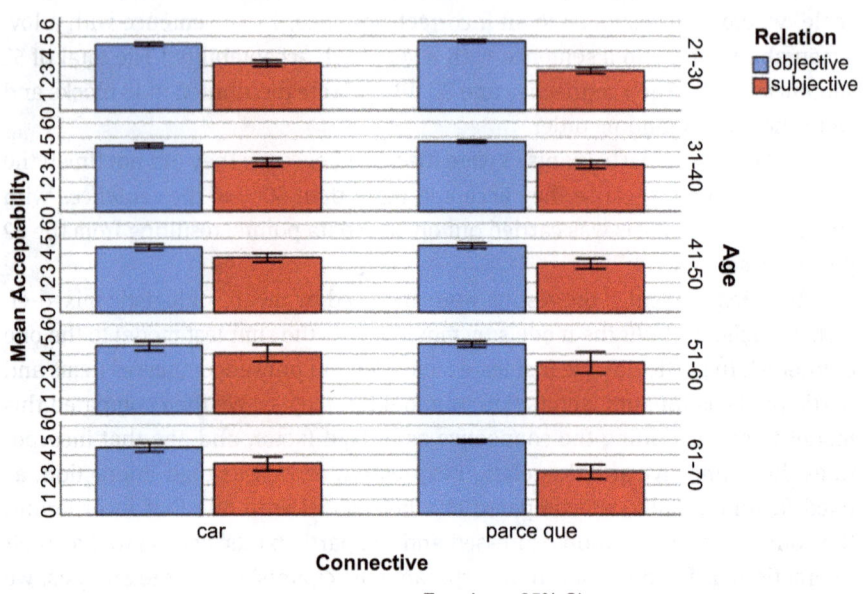

Figure 2: Mean Acceptability Score for the Connectives *Car* and *Parce que* Across Two Types of Causal Relations in five Groups of Age in Experiment 2.

First, the model shows that, in general, the connective *parce que* (mean=3.83) receives lower scores than *car* (mean=3.91) (β=0.431, SE=0.212, p= .042). Second, subjective relations (mean=3.17) receive lower scores than objective relations (mean=4.56) (β=–2.152, SE=0.383, p< .001). Third, there is no significant main effect of age. Precisely, the differences among the groups of age established are not statistically significant: compared to the group of 21–30, the 31–40, 41–50, 51–60 and 61–70 age groups have similar acceptability scores (β=0.234, SE=0.373, p=0.529; β=0.001, SE=0.442, p= .997; β=0.375, SE=0.746, p= .614 and, respectively, β=0.734, SE=0.611, p= .229). Fourth, the significant interaction between connective and relation reveals that the subjective use of *parce que* (mean=2.99) receives lower scores than the subjective use of *car* (mean=3.36) (β=–1.035, SE=0.266, p< .001). In fact, the interaction between connective, relation and age shows that it is the 61–70 age group that yields lower scores to the subjective *parce que* (mean=2.87) than to the subjective *car* (mean=4.52) (β=−1.647, SE=0.839, p= .049) while the other groups yield similar scores (p>.05 for the 31–40, 41–50 and 51–60 groups of age).

To compare the results of this experiment with those from Experiment 1 on university students (age 19–25), we focused our analysis on the age group 20–25 consisting of 9 participants. In a similar vein, we built the models by moving from the simplest model to the one of interest. Adding the connective as a fixed factor to the simplest model, which only includes items and participants as random effects, improved the simplest model (LR = 6.898, df = 1, p = .008). Adding the connective and its interaction with relation as fixed factors to the previous model further improved the model's fit (LR = 33.571, df = 2, p < .001). According to this model, participants present similar acceptability scores to sentences with *car* (mean=3.99) compared to *parce que* (mean=3.63) (β=0.018, SE=0.427, p= .965). We also found that participants yield lower acceptability scores to subjective relations (mean=2.95) than to objective relations (mean=4.66) (β=−2.504, SE=0.437, p< .001). In addition, they demonstrate a tendency to give lower acceptability scores to sentences with subjective *parce que* (mean=2.57) than to sentences with subjective *car* (mean=3.33) (Figure 3)). However, this difference is not statistically significant (β=−0.949, SE=0.525, p>.05).

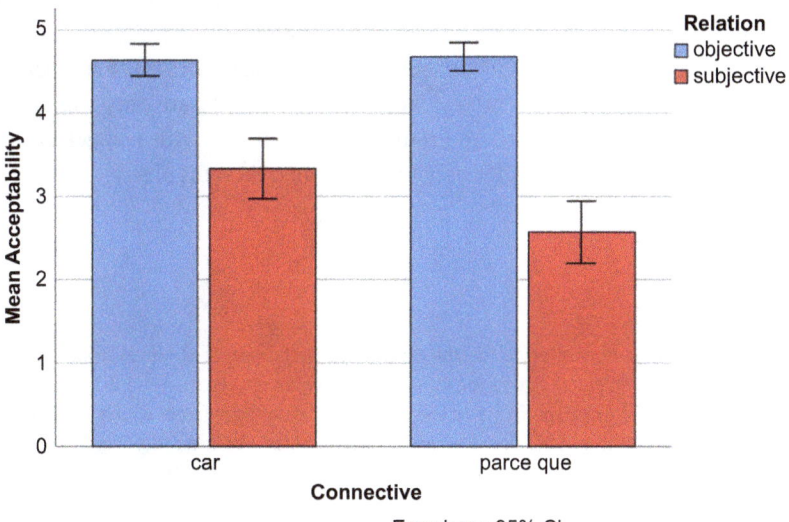

Figure 3: Mean values in the four conditions for the 20–25.

Experiment 2 thus confirms the prediction in the **complex subjectivity hypothesis**, as we observe that subjective relations receive lower scores than objective relations across all five age groups. Furthermore, the **classic hypothesis** is confirmed only for 61–70 age group, who give lower scores to the subjective *parce que* than to the subjective *car*. In other words, the other age groups yield similar scores to both the subjective *parce que* and the subjective *car*. In fact, this behaviour is the one predicted in the **novel hypothesis**.

4 Discussion

In this chapter, we have presented two experiments on the French causal connectives *parce que* and *car*, with the aim of exploring a widely attested assumption concerning their meaning and use (namely that *car* is subjective) in two different groups of participants: university students (aged 19–25) and other native speakers (aged 20–70). For these experiments, we formulated one hypothesis regarding the participants (the **sample-related hypothesis**) and three hypotheses regarding the use of *car* and *parce que* as means of expressing subjective and objective causal relations (the **classic hypothesis**, the **novel hypothesis**[4] and the **complex subjectivity hypothesis**).

The results of our experiments partly support the sample-related hypothesis, according to which university students (studying language-related disciplines) may behave differently from a wider pool of native speakers in a similar age group when it comes to the use of causal connectives and/or the treatment of subjective and objective causal relations. The results from Experiment 1 are only similar to those found for the comparable age group in Experiment 2 with respect to the use of *car* and *parce que*, and differ only vis-à-vis the treatment of subjective and objective relations.

---

[4] As observed by an anonymous reviewer, the differences in the results obtained from the various extant studies – which gave rise to the classic and novel hypotheses – are intriguing. One potential explanation could be the fact that the target periods of time (from which the corpus data have been collected) might be too wide-ranging and diverse. For example, Simon and Degand's (2007) corpus of spoken data includes data collected since 1987 until the time of the study. As for their corpus of written data, it was composed of novels and travel stories written between 1990 and 2007. In contrast, Blochowiak et al. (2020) analysed a journalistic corpus dated in 2012, while Cougnon's (2015) corpus of SMS was initiated in 2010. Therefore, if one analyses the use and frequency of *car* and *parce que* in such wide-ranging periods of time, they may arrive at different results. Further research should target shorter spans of time and investigate in a systematic way the use and frequency of these connectives in each period, as well as in each type of stylistic register in both the written and the oral mode.

Regarding the first point, the 20- to 25-year-old group provide similar acceptability scores in both experiments to the sentences with the connectives *car* and *parce que*. In addition, in neither of the two groups (students vs. the 20- to 25-year-old group) is the interaction between the connective and the relation found to be significant. In other words, this age range does not differentiate between the two connectives. As far as the second point is concerned, the 20- to 25-year-old group in Experiment 2 yield lower scores for subjective relations than for objective ones. In contrast, the group of university students present similar scores for both types of relations. One possible explanation for this relates to the complexity of subjective causal relations: university students may be more apt in dealing with complex inferential patterns, like those involved in subjective causality, especially in its inferential abductive form. This would probably be due to the fact that academic work substantially contributes to the development of this kind of skill. Another possible explanation is task-related, as Experiment 1 was pen-and-paper while the second one was a remote crowdsourcing survey. For this reason, in the second experiment verification questions were included to identify those participants who could accomplish the task without paying too much attention. Finally, the results may also reflect the fact that the number of participants from this age group in Experiment 1 and 2 was not well balanced. Further research should target specifically this age group and document the educational and social background of the participants (e.g., at what age their institutional education ended, what studies they pursued, at what age their professional activity started, what is their professional activity, their reading habits, etc.), because these factors may shed some more light on their language and communication skills.

By contrast, the complex subjectivity hypothesis is validated by the results in Experiment 2, in which all tested age groups (20–30, 31–40, 41–50, 51–60, 61–70) provide lower scores to subjective relations than to objective ones. This confirms the assumption that subjective causal relations in which the epistemic marker is absent are inherently harder to deal with than objective relations, whereby there is no additional epistemic layer to be inferred.

Our experimental study also addressed the classic and the novel hypotheses on the use of the connectives *car* and *parce que*. The results of Experiment 2 reveal that the classic hypothesis, according to which *car* is a prototypical marker of subjective causal relations, is only confirmed for one age group: that of participants 60- to 70-year-old, who present higher scores with subjective *car* than with subjective *parce que*. The remaining age groups do not show any preference for either connective with respect to expressing subjective relations.

Experiment 2 does not confirm the high polyvalency of the connective *parce que*, assumed in the classic hypothesis, with the exception of the 60–70 age group. In particular, we have found a main effect of the connective, according to which participants yield lower scores with *parce que* than with *car*, regardless of the type of causal relation expressed (although this effect is reversed for the 60–70 age group, as stated above). Furthermore, this effect is absent for the 20–25 age group and for the university students, who provide similar scores for both connectives. In other words, this result seems to validate the novel hypothesis, which assumes that *car* is no longer a prototypical marker of subjective causal relations and has instead become interchangeable with *parce que* in the case of both subjective and objective causal relations. Specifically, we have found that both university students in Experiment 1 and the 20–30, 31–40, 41–50 and 51–60 age groups in Experiment 2 present similar scores with *car* and *parce que*.

These results raise the question as to how the meaning of *car* evolved from a diachronic point of view. Recent studies and our own results have jointly shown that *car* is perceived to convey the causal content in a more objective way than initially thought (and assumed in the classic hypothesis) (Nazarenko 2000; Zufferey et al. 2018; Blochowiak et al. 2020). The question that arises is whether the objectivisation of *car* balances the use of the two connectives, which thus become fully interchangeable, or whether the objectivisation of *car* will completely reverse the paradigm (i.e., *car* will become the prototypical connective for objective relations). At this stage, our results point to the first possibility because we have found that younger speakers accept both connectives equally. The age group for whom this change seems absent is the 60–70 group, since they preferred subjective relations expressed with *car*. As such, the differences among the various age groups analysed may also bring into light an effect of ageing in the usage of these connectives.[5] This should be further investigated in a separate study.

Overall, our experiments reveal the significance of carefully choosing the type of participants recruited in experimental studies. First, university students behave differently from a comparable age group vis-à-vis complex inferences, although the two groups show similar preferences with respect to the use of the two causal connectives tested. Second, it is important to test a wide range of age groups (from younger to older speakers), as this may unveil a longitudinal evolution in the use of discourse connectives, whose usage has been influenced by the massive use of social media.

---

5 We are thankful to an anonymous reviewer for this suggestion.

5 Conclusion

The two experiments presented in this chapter provide evidence for two main conclusions. The first concerns a change of paradigm concerning the meaning and use of the causal connectives *parce que* and *car*. On the one hand, we demonstrate that the preferences in the older group age (60–70) verify the classic hypothesis, according to which *car* is a prototypical marker for subjective causal relations. On the other hand, we show that the participants' behaviour across all other age groups (20–60), including students, validates the novel hypothesis, according to which *car* and *parce que* suit both types of relations equally well. These results suggest that contemporary French is currently undergoing a change towards greater interchangeability between the two causal connectives, or even a switch towards the objectivisation of *car* (Nazarenko 2000; Zufferey, et al. 2018; Blochowiak et al. 2020). This trend may be due to the massive use of social media by younger and also older populations, in which we observe a revival of the use of *car* that was previously claimed to be in decline (Véronis & Guimier de Neef 2006; Blochowiak et al. 2020).

The second conclusion that follows from this chapter relates to the population tested. Our exploratory investigation into this issue indicates that recruiting exclusively students as a repository of participants for studies of language is likely biased. Our experiments show that the results collected from student participants are not similar to the results collected from participants in a similar age group but recruited from the larger population. In particular, students turn out to be more skilled in understanding epistemic (inferential abductive) relations, which require more advanced reasoning skills. Even though this comparison is only tentative, it should alert researchers to the need to test larger populations when it comes to language experiments.

Appendix: List of items in Experiment 1 and 2

Objective (causal) items

IT01

Janine s'est couchée de bonne heure parce que/car sa journée était fatigante. Elle devait rendre un rapport au directeur.

IT02

Les autoroutes sont impraticables parce que/car la neige est tombée toute la nuit. Fort heureusement c'était le weekend.

IT03

Robert s'est fâché très fort parce que/car Valentin l'a insulté sans raison. Les deux hommes ne s'aimaient déjà pas avant.

IT04

Les poissons sont revenus en nombre parce que/car le lac a été assaini. Les autorités vont nettoyer tous les lacs du pays.

IT05

L'eau potable a été contaminée parce que/car le fleuve a inondé le village. Les habitants étaient ravitaillés par les camions citernes.

IT06

Michel a eu une amende parce que/car sa voiture était mal garée. C'était sa deuxième amende ce mois-ci.

IT07

Véronique est heureuse parce que/car sa sœur lui a rendu visite avec les enfants. Elles habitent très loin l'une de l'autre.

IT08

Il y a eu de grands embouteillages sur la route parce que/car les vacances ont commencé. Les enfants se réjouissent d'arriver à la mer.

Subjective (inferential abductive) items

IT09

Il a fait froid cette nuit parce que/car les géraniums ont gelé sur le balcon. L'hiver n'est plus très loin.

IT10

Il y a des mites dans l'armoire de Marie parce que/car tous ses pulls ont des trous. Marie doit maintenant s'acheter de nouveaux pulls.

IT11

Les plantes n'ont pas eu assez d'eau parce que/car les feuilles sont toutes fanées. Il faudra bien les arroser pour qu'elles revivent.

IT12

Monique est à la maison parce que/car son vélo est devant chez elle. Il est attaché avec un cadenas.

IT13

Les voisins sont chez eux parce que/car la lumière est allumée au salon. Ils regardent un film d'horreur.

IT14

Justine n'est pas encore partie du travail parce que/car son veston est sur la chaise. Elle attend son amie Anne-Claire.

IT15

Il a beaucoup plu ce dernier temps parce que/car les champs sont pleins d'eau. Les agriculteurs ne sont pas très contents.

IT16

Le sac est très lourd parce que/car Max n'arrive pas à le prendre. Le sac contient des cailloux pour le jardin.

References

Ariel, Mira. this volume. Processing polyfunctional discourse markers: Making sense of Hebrew *harey*.

Bentolila, Fernand. 1986. *Car* en français écrit. *La Linguistique*. 95–115.

Bertin, Annie. 1997. *L'expression de la cause en ancien français*. Vol. 219. Genève: Librairie Droz.

Blochowiak, Joanna. 2010. Some formal properties of causal and inferential 'because'in different embedding contexts. *Generative Grammar in Geneva* 6. 191–202.

Blochowiak, Joanna. 2014. *A theoretical approach to the quest for understanding. Semantics and pragmatics of whys and becauses*. Genève: Université de Genève dissertation.

Blochowiak, Joanna. 2017. Connectives: Order, Causality and Beyond. In Joanna Blochowiak, Cristina Grisot, Stephanie Durrleman-Tame, & Christopher Laenzlinger (eds.), *Formal Models in the Study of Language*, 181–197. Cham: Springer.

Blochowiak, Joanna, Cristina Grisot & Liesbeth Degand. 2020. What type of subjectivity lies behind French causal connectives? A corpus-based comparative investigation of *car* and *parce que*. *Glossa: A Journal of General Linguistics* 5(1). 1–36.

Canestrelli, Anneloes R., Willem M. Mak & Ted JM Sanders. 2013. Causal connectives in discourse processing: How differences in subjectivity are reflected in eye movements. *Language and Cognitive Processes* 28(9). 1394–1413.

Cozijn, Reinier, Leo GM Noordman & Wietske Vonk. 2011. Propositional integration and world-knowledge inference: Processes in understanding because sentences. *Discourse Processes* 48(7). 475–500.

Debaisieux, Jeanne-Marie. 2002. *Le fonctionnement de parce que en français contemporain: étude quantitative*. Tübingen: Gunter Narr Verlag.

Debaisieux, Jeanne-Marie. 2004. Les conjonctions de subordination: mots de grammaire ou mots du discours? Le cas de *parce que*. *Revue de Sémantique et Pragmatique* 15–16. 51–67.

Degand, Liesbeth & Benjamin Fagard. 2012. Competing connectives in the causal domain: French car and parce que. *Journal of Pragmatics* 44(2). 154–168.

Degand, Liesbeth & Henk Pander Maat. 2003. A contrastive study of Dutch and French causal connectives on the Speaker Involvement Scale. *LOT Occasional Series* 1. 175–199.

Ducrot, Oswald. 1983. Opérateurs argumentatifs et visée argumentative. *Cahiers de Linguistique Française* 5. 7–36.

Fagard, Benjamin & Degand, Liesbeth. 2008. La fortune des mots: grandeur et décadence de 'car'. In H. Durand & B. Laks (eds.), Congrès Mondial de Linguistique Française, 211–223. Paris: Institut de Linguistique Française. DOI: https://doi.org/10.1051/cmlf08213.

Fauconnier, Gilles. 1994. *Mental spaces: Aspects of meaning construction in natural language*. Cambridge: Cambridge University Press.

Ferrari, Angela. 1992. Encore à propos de parce que, à la lumière des structures linguistiques de la séquence causale. *Cahiers de Linguistique Française* 13. 183–214.

Field, Andrew, Jeremy Miles & Zoë Field. 2014. *Discovering Statistics Using R*. 2nd edn. New York: SAGE Publications.

Frei, Henri. 1982. *La Grammaire des Fautes*. Genève: Slatkine Publishers.

Henrich, Joseph, Steven J. Heine & Ara Norenzayan. 2010. The weirdest people in the world? *Behavioral and Brain Sciences* 33(2–3). 61–83.

Iordanskaja, Lidija. 1993. Pour une description lexicographique des conjonctions du français contemporain. *Le Français Moderne* 2. 159–190.

Kleijn, Suzanne, Willem M. Mak & Ted JM Sanders. 2021. Causality, subjectivity and mental spaces: Insights from on-line discourse processing. *Cognitive Linguistics* 1(32). 35–65.

Lambrecht, Knud, Julia Bordeaux & Robert Reichle. 2006. Cognitive constraints on assertion scope. The case of spoken French parce que. In Chiyo Nishida & Jean-Pierre Y. Montreuil (eds.), *New Perspectives on Romance Linguistics: Morphology, syntax, semantics and pragmatics*. Vol. 275, 143–154. Amsterdam/Philadelphia: John Benjamins.

Le Groupe λ-l. 1975. Car, parce que, puisque. *Revue Romane*.

Maat, Henk Pander & Liesbeth Degand. 2001. Scaling causal relations and connectives in terms of speaker involvement. *Cognitive Linguistics* 12(3). 211–246.

Moeschler, Jacques. 1987. Trois emplois de parce que en conversation. *Cahiers de Linguistique Française* 8. 97–110.

Moeschler, Jacques. 2005. Connecteurs pragmatiques, inférences directionnelles et représentations mentales. *Cahiers Chronos* 12. 35–50.

Nazarenko, Adeline. 2000. *La cause et son expression en français*. Paris: Ophrys.

Nølke, Henning. 1995. Contrastive and argumentative linguistic analysis of the French connectors' donc'and'car'. *Leuvense Bijdragen* 84(3). 313–328.

Pasch, Renate. 1983. Die Kausalkonjunktionen da, denn und weil: drei Konjunktionen-drei lexikalische Klassen. *Deutsch Als Fremdsprache* 20(6). 332–337.

Pit, Mirna. 2003. *How to express yourself with a causal connective: subjectivity and causal connectives in Dutch, German and French*. Amsterdam: Rodopi.

Roulet, Eddy, Antoine, Auchlin & Jacques Moeschler. 1985. *L'articulation du discours en français contemporain*. Berne: Peter Lang.

Sanders, Ted JM & Wilbert PM Spooren. 2015. Causality and subjectivity in discourse: The meaning and use of causal connectives in spontaneous conversation, chat interactions and written text. *Linguistics* 53(1). 53–92.

Simon, Anne Catherine & Liesbeth Degand. 2007. Connecteurs de causalité, implication du locuteur et profils prosodiques: le cas de car et de parce que. *Journal of French Language Studies* 17(3). 323.

Stukker, Ninke & Ted Sanders. 2012. Subjectivity and prototype structure in causal connectives: A cross-linguistic perspective. *Journal of Pragmatics* 44(2). 169–190.

Sweetser, Eve. 1990. *From etymology to pragmatics: The mind-body metaphor in semantic structure and semantic change*. Cambridge: Cambridge University Press.

Sweetser, Eve & Gilles Fauconnier. 1996. Cognitive links and domains: Basic aspects of mental space theory. In Gilles Fauconnier & Eve Sweetser (eds.), *Spaces, worlds, and grammar*, The University of Chicago Press, 1–28. Chicago and London: The University of Chicago Press Chicago and London.

Traxler, Matthew J., Michael D. Bybee & Martin J. Pickering. 1997. Influence of connectives on language comprehension: eye tracking evidence for incremental interpretation. *The Quarterly Journal of Experimental Psychology: Section A* 50(3). 481–497.

Traxler, Matthew J., Anthony J. Sanford, Joy P. Aked & Linda M. Moxey. 1997. Processing causal and diagnostic statements in discourse. *Journal of Experimental Psychology: Learning, Memory, and Cognition* 23(1). 88.

Van Belle, William. 1989. Want, omdat en aangezien: een argumentatieve analyse. *Leuvense Bijdragen/Leuven Contributions to Linguistics and Philology* 78. 435–456.

Véronis, Jean, Guimier De Neef, Emilie, 2006. Le traitement des nouvelles formes de communication écrite. In: Sabah, G. (Ed.), Compréhension des langues et interaction. Paris: Hermès-Lavoisier, pp. 227–248.

Zufferey, Sandrine. 2012. *Car, parce que, puisque* revisited: Three empirical studies on French causal connectives. *Journal of Pragmatics* 44(2). 138–153.

Zufferey, Sandrine, Willem Mak, Sara Verbrugge & Ted Sanders. 2018. Usage and processing of the French causal connectives *car* and *parce que*. *Journal of French Language Studies* 28(1). 85–112.

Zufferey, Sandrine, Ekaterina Tckhovrebova, Matias Wetzel & Pascal Gygax. this volume. Individual differences in the ability to master connectives: The importance of exposure to print.

Sandrine Zufferey, Ekaterina Tskhovrebova, Mathis Wetzel and Pascal Gygax

4 Individual differences in the ability to master connectives: The importance of exposure to print

Abstract: Important individual differences exist in the way language is acquired by children, and processed by adult native speakers. So far, studies demonstrating those individual differences have focused on lexical and syntactic aspects, yet not on discursive competences. However, we argue that discourse connectives are particularly well suited to investigate individual differences, as the ability to handle them lies at the interface of lexical, syntactic and discursive competence. In this chapter, we report a series of studies designed to investigate the ability of teenagers, learners and adults to use connectives typical of the written mode, and to assess its correlation with their degree of exposure to print. Taken together, these studies demonstrate that connectives that are less frequent in corpus data are also mastered less well even by adult native speakers, and that exposure to print explains the mastery of these connectives in all three groups.

Keywords: connectives, language production task, judgement task, exposure to print, author recognition test, French

1 Individual differences in linguistic competence are broad and persistent

Traditionally, experimental research in linguistics has tended to downplay the importance of individual differences, because the focus was placed on group comparisons, and variations in such designs are often ignored or treated as noise in the data (Kidd, Donnelly, and Christiansen 2007). Yet, a large number of studies have now convincingly demonstrated that these differences exist from the onset

---

Sandrine Zufferey, University of Bern, sandrine.zufferey@unibe.ch
Ekaterina Tskhovrebova, University of Bern, ekaterina.tckhovrebova@unibe.ch
Mathis Wetzel, University of Bern, mathis.wetzel@unibe.ch
Pascal Gygax, University of Fribourg, pascal.gygax@unifr.ch

https://doi.org/10.1515/9783110790351-004

of language development, and that they also influence linguistic attainment several years later (Brito et al. 2016; Cristia et al. 2013). These differences concern all aspects of language development, namely the lexicon (e.g., Weisleder and Fernald 2013), syntax (e.g., Kidd 2012), and even though studies are still scarce in this domain, recent research has shown that individual differences extend to pragmatic competences as well (e.g., Matthews et al. 2018).

Moreover, individual differences are not limited to the period of first language acquisition. In fact, there are still widespread differences in the way adult native speakers process language, as well as their ultimate level of linguistic competence. Differences among adults involve the breadth and depth of lexical knowledge, which in turn affects reading patterns and reading strategies (e.g., Andrews 2015). Differences are also found in linguistic contexts involving a high degree of structural complexity, such as the comprehension of complex syntactic structures like object relative clauses (Wells et al. 2003), and the ability to resolve syntactic ambiguities (Swets et al. 2007). Compared to spoken language competences, linguistic competence in the written mode is typically even more variable among adult speakers, as individual differences are wide-ranging in reading comprehension (Braze et al. 2007) and spelling skills (Kamhi and Hinton 2001).

To the best of our knowledge, individual differences have so far not been studied extensively at the discourse level, but a few studies do indicate that individual differences may play an important role in discourse comprehension. For example, Daneman and Carpenter (1980) found that the ability of adults to correctly identify pronoun references was quite variable, and that it was linked to readers' working memory capacities. Regarding connectives, McClure and Geva (1983) found that some adult native speakers struggle to infer subtle meaning distinctions between closely related connectives such as *but* and *although* (e.g., Many people like to ski although/but skiing is dangerous), and that their judgements depend on their syntactic placement within the sentence. More recently, Scholman, Demberg and Sanders (2020) found that some adult native speakers also use contextual signals within a discourse segment (expressions such as *a few* and *multiple*) as indications that a list relation is expected in the next segment. They report that this ability is correlated with people's degree of exposure to print (we explain this factor in detail in Section 2). Even though empirical evidence is still scarce, these studies provide a good indication that individual differences do exist and that they should be investigated more systematically. The research reported in this chapter is an attempt in that direction.

In addition to these empirical findings, there are also several reasons stemming from the theoretical descriptions of connectives that lead us to expect that their mastery is likely to be quite variable, even among adult native speakers. Most importantly, as connectives' usage lies at the interface between lexical, syntactic and discursive skills, they raise specific challenges within each of these domains. First, in the lexical domain, connectives encode procedural rather than conceptual meaning, contrary to most other lexical items (Sperber and Wilson 1993). One of the main characteristics of procedural meaning is that it is typically harder to bring to consciousness (Wilson 2011). Because of this, the meaning of connectives is difficult to learn explicitly, and must be inferred based on their usage. In this respect, learning the meaning of a connective is more akin to learning a grammatical rule than a lexical item. The implicit characteristic of such learning leaves more room for incorrect interpretations, at least compared to explicitly learning concepts related to lexical items. At the syntactic level, connectives often serve to link complex clauses. Sometimes, their use involves the embedding of a clause through subordination, placing a high cognitive load on syntactic processing. Even when such embedding is not required, connectives often link segments that are remote from each other within the text and cover large spans of texts, placing high demands on working memory. Finally, at the discourse level, the role of connectives is to explicitly indicate the type of discourse relation holding between discourse segments (e.g., Halliday and Hasan 1976). However, in most cases, no one-to-one mapping can be made between connectives and relations. In fact, many connectives can convey several discourse relations depending on context. Thus, mastering all these connectives involves the ability to form complex form-function mappings, which has been shown to be problematic, at least for non-native speakers (Zufferey and Gygax 2017).

In addition to all the previously mentioned difficulties, the category of connectives raises yet another challenge. In most Indo-European languages, the repertoire of connectives is vast, and regularly includes from one hundred to several hundred connectives. For example, the French lexicon of connectives Lexconn (Roze, Danlos, and Muller 2012) contains 328 entries. Yet, in the spoken mode, few of these connectives are frequently used (Crible and Cuenca 2017). A large proportion of these connectives is therefore mostly bound to the written mode. As we argued above, individual differences may be particularly acute in this mode. We can therefore expect that these connectives give rise to important individual variations in the way they are mastered. Yet, studies assessing the role of connectives for language processing and comprehension (e.g., Traxler et al. 1997; Canestrelli, Mak, and Sanders 2013) have mostly focused on connectives frequently used in speech. The role of connectives from the written mode remains therefore largely unexplored. In this chapter, we will focus precisely on these connectives, and the difficulties they create compared to connectives frequently used in speech.

In a nutshell, all the arguments presented above regarding the complexity of connectives and their link to the written mode lead us to expect a high degree of individual variation in the ability to use and understand them. In this chapter, we present several experiments from our laboratory that have actually assessed this variability in adult native speakers (Section 3), teenagers (Section 4) and learners (Section 5). But before turning to the presentation of these experiments, we introduce in the next section the notion of exposure to print, and discuss its role as a variable explaining individual differences in many aspects of linguistic competences.

2 Exposure to print: How important is it and how is it measured?

Studies of individual variations have strived to identify the factors at the foundation of linguistic abilities. In the domain of language processing, studies have focused on the relationship between language competences and other cognitive abilities such as working memory capacity (e.g., Caplan and Waters 1999) and executive control (e.g., Vuong and Martin 2014). In the domain of language acquisition, a frequently tested social factor is the socioeconomic status of families (e.g., Hoff 2003). For adults, one of the most common factors analyzed is the degree of familiarity that people have with the written mode, measured through their degree of exposure to print. This factor has turned out to be a strong predictor for a wide array of linguistic and even cognitive skills, as we now outline.

First, a high exposure to print is linked to better sentence processing ability and superior performance on verbal portions of the ACT test (Acheson, Wells, and MacDonald 2008). In addition, relations between the degree of exposure to print and reading skills are found for all age groups from kindergarten to university students, and the role of exposure to print as a predictor of oral language skills grows stronger as children get older: while exposure to print accounts for 12% of the variance in oral skills for kindergarteners, it goes up to 34% for university students (Mol and Bus 2011). Thus, the role of exposure to print tends to become more prevalent with age, as time spent reading also increases with age. Higher exposure to print is also linked with more efficient reading skills in older readers in their seventies (e.g., Payne et al. 2012).

Exposure to print has also been related to a better vocabulary and world knowledge for both university students and older adults (Stanovich, West, and Harrison 1995), as well as to orthographic competence (Stanovich and West 1989). Interestingly, exposure to print does not only improve spoken and written language skills in readers' mother tongue, but also influences competence in second language learning. More specifically, exposure to print in L1 is linked to L2 reading comprehension, L2 decoding, L2 writing, and L2 listening/speaking competence (Sparks et al. 2012).

Exposure to print is also linked to better performances in other cognitive skills such as theory of mind abilities. Comer Kidd and Castano (2013) studied the link between mental state attribution competence and exposure to print, as reading may attune readers' sensitivity to interpersonal issues, a capacity underlying theory of mind skills. Their results indicated that reading fictional texts (as opposed to texts pertaining to other discourse genres) was linked to better theory of mind abilities, as measured in a variety of standard tests such as the reading the mind in the eyes test.

In all the studies discussed above, the degree of exposure to print was measured using variants of the Author Recognition Test (ART), developed by Stanovich and West (1989) in order to provide a more objective measure compared to self-assessments that typically lead to socially-desirable biases. This test is very easy to administer, as it simply consists of a list of real and fake literary authors that people are asked to recognize. Half of the list usually comprises names of real authors, and half comprises fake author names. Participants' scores on the test are computed by subtracting incorrectly identified fake names to correctly identified real ones. We have used different versions of the Author Recognition Test in the experiments we now turn to, and we therefore discuss its effectiveness as a factor explaining individual differences in the ability to use connectives.

3 Invididual variations among adult native speakers

It is often the case in studies on first language acquisition and second language learning that a group of adults is included in the experimental design in order to provide a gold standard of connective competences, against which the performance of children and learners is compared. These studies thus make two implicit assumptions about adults, but none of which may turn out to be fully correct. First, adults are presumed to be fully competent, and second, they are presumed to represent a homogenous group. Traditionally, the adults included in psycholinguistic experiments were groups of university students in linguistics or psychology participating for course credits. These students indeed represented a linguistically highly proficient and rather homogenous group. However, things have radically changed recently with the arrival of online recruitment platforms such as Prolific (Palan and Schitter 2018), which have given researchers easier access to a larger pool of participants from more diverse backgrounds (even though a lot of university students are still present on these platforms). This new recruitment method has opened new avenues of enquiry for the study of individual variations among adults. And indeed, many recent studies reporting individual variations were conducted on participants from these platforms (e.g., Scholman et al. 2020; see also Blochowiak and Grisot this volume, chapter 3).

This is also the recruitment method that we used in an experiment designed to assess the existence of individual variations in adult native speakers' ability to master connectives typical of the written mode (Zufferey and Gygax 2020a). This experiment targeted the ability of adult native speakers to discriminate between correct and incorrect uses of four French connectives from the written mode. We tested a group of 60 participants, all recruited on Prolific. The four French connectives included in this experiment were chosen because they enabled us to assess the role of several factors that could potentially affect participants' ability to use them. These connectives were *aussi* to convey a consequence relation (similar to *therefore* in English), *en outre* to convey an additive relation (similar to *in addition* in English), *en effet* to convey a causal relation (the best equivalent in English is *for*, but bear in mind that these two connectives are also quite different in several respects), and *toutefois* to convey a concessive relation (similar to *however* in English).

The first factor that could affect participants' ability to use these connectives according to the literature is the degree of cognitive complexity of the relation they encode. This factor has indeed been found to play a role in the order of acquisition between relations (Evers-Vermeul and Sanders 2009), and the online processing of sentences containing connectives (Traxler et al. 1997; Canestrelli et al. 2013; Zufferey et al. 2018). According to Sanders, Spooren and Noordman (1992), connectives' meaning can be decomposed into four primitives (basic operation, order of the segments, polarity, and source of coherence), with each of them having two possible values. For each primitive, one of the values is deemed to be cognitively more complex than the other. For example, the values for the primitive of polarity are 'positive' and 'negative', and negative relations are considered to be more complex than positive ones (see, for example, Morera et al. 2017 for an empirical validation of this claim). Each of these dimensions are cumulated to account for the cognitive complexity of each of them. Thus, following this model, *en outre* conveys the easiest type of relation (additive), followed by *aussi* (forward causal connective), then *en effet* (backward causal connective), and finally *toutefois* (concessive connective). Based on this classification, if cognitive complexity is an important factor for adults' competence with connectives, we expected that participants in our experiment would have lower scores for *en effet* and *toutefois* compared to *aussi* and even more *en outre*, because the former encode relations with a higher degree of cognitive complexity.

Yet, cognitive complexity is not the only factor that could play a role for adults' competence with connectives. Another possibility that we tested is that the frequency with which connectives are used in the written mode might also play a role. The rationale is this: as people encounter less frequent connectives less often while reading, they have less opportunity to integrate their meaning. This factor was indeed found to play a role for the ability of teenagers to master connectives (Nippold, Schwartz, and Undlin 1992; see Section 3 for an experiment with teenagers), and this effect might well continue to influence the competences of adults. From our sample, the two connectives *en effet* and *toutefois* are used significantly more frequently in written corpora (around 200 occurrences per million words) compared to *en outre* and *aussi* (around 100 occurrences per million words). Thus, if frequency plays an important role for people's ability to master connectives from the written mode, then the scores for *aussi* and *en outre* should be lower than those for *en effet* and *toutefois*. Note that this is a reverse pattern compared to the one expected on the basis of cognitive complexity, which enables us to pitch the role of these two factors against each other.

Finally, a third factor that could be important for speakers' competence – and that we also tested – is the fact that while some connectives have only one meaning, others are polyfunctional and can encode several meanings depending on context. For example, in English, the connective *since* sometimes encodes a temporal relation and in other cases a causal relation. In our sample, two connectives are monofunctional (*en outre* and *toutefois*) and two polyfunctional (*en effet* and *aussi*). In addition to its causal meaning, *en effet* can also be used to convey a relation of confirmation (similar to the English *indeed*), and in addition to its meaning of consequence, the connective *aussi* can also take an additive meaning (similar to the English *also*). However, these alternative meanings are not found in sentence initial position (the syntactic placement tested in our experiment), and could therefore not create ambiguities in our experimental items. Coming back to the role of polyfunctionality, if this factor played an important role in the ability to master connectives from the written mode, then we expected that the scores of *en effet* and *aussi* would be lower than those of the other two connectives, which are monofunctional.[1]

In order to assess the impact of these three factors, we created 64 experimental sentences: 16 per connective. Each connective was correctly used in 8 sentences and incorrectly used in 8 other sentences. In other words, in the correct version, the meaning of the connective was compatible with the content of the linguistic segments, as in (1), in which aussi coherently expresses a consequence relation between breaking one's tooth and making an appointment at the dentist. In the incorrect version however, the connective provided an indication incompatible

---

[1] Note that other factors could still play a role, such as the existence of close competitors (e.g., *ainsi* and *aussi*). The role of these additional factors will need to be tested in future experiments.

with the information from the linguistic segment, as in (2). In this example, *en outre* indicates that there is no causal link but only an addition of two independent facts between breaking a tooth and going to the dentist, thus creating an incoherence.

(1) *Roger s'était cassé une dent en mangeant. Aussi, il prit rendez-vous rapidement chez son dentiste.*

(2) *Roger s'était cassé une dent en mangeant. En outre, il prit rendez-vous rapidement chez son dentiste.*
'Roger had broken his tooth while eating. CONNECTIVE he quickly made an appointment with his dentist'.

During the experiment, participants were asked to evaluate the coherence of sentences on a continuous scale ranging from "very incoherent" on the left to "very coherent" on the right, by moving a cursor along the scale. Results clearly indicated that participants had a higher ability to correctly judge sentences containing *en effet* and *toutefois* compared to *aussi* and *en outre*, thus indicating that frequency rather than cognitive complexity or polyfunctionality seems to be the most relevant factor to explain people's competence with connectives from the written mode, as these are the two less frequent connectives in corpus data.

To investigate whether there would be individual differences in these effects, and whether we could explain them in terms of exposure to print, participants completed a French version of the Author Recognition Test (ART-F), newly developed by us. Results showed that when participants were split into two groups depending on their score on the ART-F test, interesting differences emerged, confirming the idea that exposure to print is a relevant variable to explain variations among adults. While all participants had an equal ability to deal with the two more frequent connectives (*en effet* and *toutefois*), participants with a higher score on the ART-F test achieved significantly better results with the two less frequent ones (*aussi* and *en outre*). This study has therefore shown that the ability of adult native speakers to deal with connectives from the written mode is variable, and that this variability can be explained by the degree of exposure that people have with the written mode. In other words, even though all adult native speakers seem to master frequent connectives from the written mode, their degree of exposure to print makes the difference between people who know and do not know how to use the less frequent connectives.

The variability of adults' competences was further tested in another set of experiments (Tskhovrebova, Zufferey, and Gygax 2022) involving the same connectives in two sentence completion tasks, but this time comparing two samples that we argued would vary in their level of competence with connectives. A sample of university students actually studying French, and a sample of participants from Prolific not studying French. Participants were also administered the ART-F and showed notable differences in their exposure to print. In the first experiment, involving a context limited to two sentences that had to be linked by choosing the appropriate connective between *aussi, en effet, toutefois* and *en outre*, adults recruited on Prolific systematically reached a lower performance compared to a group of university students studying French. In the second task, involving blanks to be filled with connectives in short texts rather than two sentences only, adults recruited on Prolific again reached a lower performance compared to students, which was this time more pronounced for the two less frequent connectives than for more frequent ones. Thus, the greater context present in the second task decreased the general performance across all connectives and reduced the differences between the results of the two groups for more frequent connectives. However, the discrepancy between the two populations still remained for the two less frequent connectives, suggesting that adults recruited on Prolific mastered them less well, and that this was due to their lower exposure to print.

These experiments thus confirm that adults' limitations are not found only in judgement tasks, but are also evidenced in fill-in-the-blank tasks that simply involve choosing the appropriate word between a set of four connectives. For the portion of adults who do not fully master connectives from the written mode, the clues given by context are not enough to help them make the correct choices.

Finally, in another set of experiments (Wetzel, Zufferey, and Gygax 2020) comparing the ability of native and non-native speakers to use a broader range of connectives from the spoken and the written modes, we also found that native-speakers' score on the ART-F was a significant predictor of their ability to fill in blanks within sentences with the appropriate connective.

In a nutshell, in all three experiments, we found that native speaking adults' level of competence with connectives was quite variable, and that participants' degree of exposure to print was an important factor to explain variability among them. However, these studies did not document the onset of such a variability – especially in terms of exposure to print – a question we now turn to.

4 Individual variations among teenagers

In the literature, many studies have investigated the early productions of connectives during the first years of life in corpus data (e.g., Evers-Vermeul and Sanders 2009; Zufferey 2010). Another trend of research has focused on the ability of young readers aged 8 to 12 to integrate the meaning conveyed by connectives (e.g., Cain and Nash 2011; Pyykkönen and Järvikivi 2012). All these studies have focused on connectives frequently used in speech, and many of them have found that cognitive complexity is an important factor explaining both the order of acquisition between connectives, and also their degree of complexity for young readers.

Few studies have addressed the issue of the later acquisition of connectives typical of the written mode. For example, Nippold et al. (1992) found that between the ages of 12 to 23 years, familiarity with the connective matters more than the cognitive complexity of the relation. The notion of familiarity was measured based on the proportion of teenagers who knew each connective in every age group. Even though this experiment included both connectives frequently used in speech and limited to the written mode, these results seem to indicate that frequency might play an important role, as it is related to the notion of familiarity. However, these studies did not directly test this factor.

In order to investigate the roles of frequency and cognitive complexity for teenagers' ability to master connectives from the written mode, we compared the ability of 40 teenagers aged 16 years to use the same four French connectives described above: *en effet, toutefois, aussi* and *en outre* (Zufferey and Gygax 2020b). The teenagers were divided into two groups based on their academic level (i.e., applied vs. theory-driven), which we used as the operationalization of exposure to print, as teenagers coming from the more applied academic level only spent part of the week doing curricular activities involving reading, with the rest being spent in practical work. In this experiment, students simply had to insert the appropriate connective in blank spaces between two sentences. Even though neither group of teenagers reached a performance comparable to that of university students, interesting differences also emerged between them. While both groups received equally low scores for the two less frequent connectives (*en outre* and *aussi*), the group of teenagers with the more theory-driven academic background outperformed the other group with the two more frequent connectives (*en effet* and *toutefois*). It seems therefore that individual differences are already apparent between teenagers. Yet, even though the differences were likely caused by the different level of academic background between them, and the varying levels of exposure to print they entailed, teenagers' individual exposure to print was not measured directly in this experiment. In addition, as only 16-year-olds were tested, this experiment gave no indications as to how teenagers progressed in their ability to use connectives from the written mode.

In order to gather more data on these issues, we ran a new set of experiments, in which we considerably expanded the cohort of teenagers, to include 191 participants aged 12 to 22 years (Tskhovrebova, Zufferey, and Gygax 2022). These teenagers either frequented a secondary school in French-speaking Switzerland (aged 12 to 15 on average) or high-school in the same geographic region (aged 16 to 18 on average). At both levels, participants were divided into groups based on the academic level of their curricula. Indeed, in these age groups, the Swiss school system separates students into different levels based on their academic achievements. In a first experiment, these participants did the same experiment conducted with the 16-year-olds and described above. In other words, they inserted one of the four connectives in a completion task limited to two sentences. Results from this task indicated that students do indeed progress in their mastery of connectives from secondary to high-school, but these improvements were apparent only for the two frequent connectives *en effet* and *toutefois*. Scores for the less frequent connectives remained low even for high-school students (less than 30% of correct choices). In addition, within each education level (secondary school and high school), teenagers from a higher academic background reached a higher score than the other students for all connectives, independently of their age. These results thus confirm that individual variations are already quite strong during teenage years, and that academic level is an important predictor of competence. In these experiments, we also included the ART-F described above. The ART-F did correlate with the mastery of connectives, but this effect was never as clear as for our adult populations. One explanation for this difference could be that the ART-F test we have compiled is not adapted to capture differences in reading experiences between teenagers, as some of the authors on the list were not recognizable enough for such a young population.

A possible explanation for teenagers' rather low scores with less frequent connectives could be that the task they had to perform did not correctly mimic normal reading situations, in which more context is provided, which could potentially give more information about the intended coherence relation. In order to assess the role of context for teenagers' competence with connectives, we conducted a second experiment with 85 teenagers aged 13 to 19, involving the same four connectives, but this time they had to be inserted into short texts (around 250 words each) rather than isolated sentence pairs. Results from this new experiment confirmed once again that teenagers master the two frequent connectives (*en effet* and *toutefois*) better than the two infrequent ones (*en outre* and *aussi*). In this version of the task, teenagers from a higher academic background again reached a higher performance compared those from a lower background, yet only for the two more frequent connectives. Finally, it is noteworthy that the scores were globally significantly lower in this task compared to the first one. For example, the ability of teenagers from a higher academic background to choose *en effet* in causal sentences dropped from 81% to 62% of correct choices. It seems therefore that having to insert connectives within a richer context also increases rather than decreases the difficulty of the task for teenagers. This also means that the low scores evidenced in the sentence completion task were not due to the lack of relevant clues to complete the task.

To summarize, results from studies involving teenagers reported in this section provide evidence for the fact that individual differences already exist early on in the process of mastering connectives from the written mode. This ability additionally appears to be strongly dependent on academic level, which in turn is linked to the degree of exposure to print involved in the school curricula. However, current measures of exposure to print such as the ART-F test do not seem fit to capture individual differences within this population, and will need to be further adapted to the reading materials of teenagers. We will come back to this issue in Section 6. Before that, we will now turn to studies that have assessed the competence of second language learners.

5 Data on second language learners

The ability of learners to master connectives in a second language has been assessed in many studies analyzing natural productions in corpus data (e.g., Granger and Tyson 1996; Tapper 2005). Comparatively, this issue has seldom been tackled from an experimental perspective (but see Degand and Sanders 1999; Zufferey et al. 2015). In this body of literature, one of the main goals is to determine the causes of learners' difficulties with connectives, but this issue remains for the time being largely unsettled. While many studies emphasize the role of negative transfer effects (e.g., Leedham and Cai 2013; Hamed 2014; Shi 2017), others relate them to more general limitations in proficiency in the second language (e.g., Chen 2014; Tazegül 2015), and others still trace these difficulties to limitations that might also be present in learners' first language (Bolton, Nelson, and Hung 2012). This latter point of view is interesting from the perspective of individual variations, because it implies that learners' cognitive and linguistic competence might be related across languages, and therefore individual variations in the first language might be helpful to explain individual variations observed in the second language. Even though the topic of individual variations has been discussed in relation to the second language acquisition of pragmatic competences in general (Taguchi 2012), this question has not been tackled specifically in relation to the mastery of connectives.

In order to address this issue, we designed an experiment meant to assess the ability of German-speaking learners of French to use 12 French connectives (Wetzel, Zufferey, and Gygax 2020). These connectives conveyed six different coherence relations: *addition*, *consequence*, *contrast*, *concession*, *cause* and *condition*. For each relation, two connectives from the written mode were included: one of them with a high frequency in corpus data and another with a low frequency. For the high frequency group, these connectives were: *par ailleurs, ainsi, cependant, par contre, dans le cas où* and *car*. In the low frequency group, the connectives were: *en outre, c'est pourquoi, néanmoins, en revanche, pourvu que* and *puisque*. The task was a simple sentence completion task in which participants were asked to fill in blanks between two sentences presented in isolation with one of six connectives (the two groups of connectives were presented separately). In addition, learners' level of competence in French was assessed using two tests. In the first, participants evaluated the grammatical correctness of 40 given sentences, among which 20 contained typical grammatical errors of written language (Zufferey and Gygax 2020). The second language proficiency test used was the vocabulary test Lextale in French, targeting the ability to discriminate existing from invented words. This test was chosen because it has been shown to correlate strongly with other measures of language proficiency (Brysbaert 2013). Participants were finally also administered the Author Recognition Test in two versions: French authors (the ART-F mentioned above) and German authors (Grolig, Tin-Richards, and Schroeder 2020). The rationale for using two different versions of the test was that performance on the ART test in people's mother tongue was shown to correlate with various aspects of second language proficiency in previous studies, as discussed in Section 3.

Contrary to native speaking teenagers and adults, results from this experiment indicated that frequency is not always the most relevant factor to explain learners' difficulties with connectives from the written mode. While some high frequency connectives from the written mode were indeed better mastered than their less frequent counterpart (*car* was mastered better than *puisque* and *par contre* was mastered better than *en revanche*), there were no significant differences for other pairs (*en outre* and *par ailleurs, dans le cas où* and *pourvu que, cependant* and *néanmoins*). For one pair, the frequent connective even triggered a significantly lower score than its less frequent counterpart (*ainsi* and *c'est pourquoi*). These findings also indicate that learners' difficulties with connectives might not come from the cognitive complexity of the discourse relation they encode, as no significant differences were found between the relations.

Thus, it seems that in the case of learners, other explanations than those put forward for native-speaking teenagers and adults must be called for to get a full picture of their strengths and difficulties with connectives from the written mode. For example, as hinted by our results, learners may at times rely on what Hasselgren (1994) called "comfort words", that is, words that they know and feel comfortable using, independently of their frequency. In the case of connectives, Crewe (1990) already observed that learners tend to rely first on a small subset of connectives that they tend to overuse in corpus data compared to native speakers, before progressively expanding their repertoire. This factor could explain why in some cases, learners do not struggle with some less frequent connectives. These connectives may be part of their curricula and hence already integrated into the learners' lexicon. The results from the Grammar task and the Lextale proficiency measures indicate that the group of learners tested is not yet at an advanced proficiency level. They might therefore still be in a phase of overreliance to a reduced "comfort" vocabulary.

However, the pair made of *par contre* and *en revanche* provides some indications that frequency may still be at play, at least for some connective pairs. The strong preference for *par contre* may reflect the fact that learners prefer words that have a high frequency in spoken language. Indeed, *par contre* is very frequently used in colloquial speech, with a variety of functions extending from a contrastive connective to discourse marker uses (i.e., topic change), whereas the overall less frequent connective *en revanche* is associated with a higher language register and more frequently used in literary works. Leedham and Cai (2013) also observed that learners use more informal connectives than natives. Other studies have found that even native speakers are better at using connectives used in speech than in writing, even in the same sentences (Zufferey and Gygax 2020a).

In the case of the pair made of *c'est pourquoi* and *ainsi*, for which results seem to counterintuitively indicate that learners master the less frequent word better, the discrepancy might be due to the fact that *c'est pourquoi* is still partially transparent semantically (the meaning is literally "it is why", and this might have helped learners to guess its meaning, even though it was probably less familiar). The role of transparency will need to be further assessed in future experiments.

Coming now to the question of individual variations, scores on the French version of the ART test did not seem to predict the mastery of connectives. However, this lack of effect is hardly surprising given that learners reached very low scores, probably reflecting the fact that they did not read much in French. However, quite interestingly, their performance on the connective task was linked with their score on the German version of the ART test. Thus, results from this experiment confirmed that being exposed to print in one's native language has advantages extending beyond the mastery of that particular language (similar to what suggested Bolton et al. 2012), which is also the case for the mastery of connectives. The relationship between L1 and L2 competences will need to be further assessed in more detail in future work.

To summarize, the analysis of learners' competence with connectives from the written mode has provided a more nuanced picture compared to native speaking adults and teenagers. While frequency also seems to play a role, this factor is also mediated by other factors such as the overuse of a restricted number of "comfort words" already acquired and the reliance on semantic clues for partially transparent items, in order to guess the meaning of some connectives.

6 Taking stock and looking ahead

The goal of this chapter was to provide new evidence that individual differences exist in the mastery of discourse connectives, even in samples of adult native speakers, especially for the numerous ones that are bound to the written mode. Another aim was to illustrate the fact that individual differences also affect teenagers and second language learners. Finally, a third aim was to specifically link these differences to the degree of exposure to print that each person has. Overall, we found ample evidence in all three groups that exposure to print greatly matters for the ability to handle connectives from the written mode. As was found in other domains of language competence, the role of exposure to print starts early and becomes even greater for adults, as the gap between frequent and infrequent readers increases as years go by.

Coming back to the case of connectives from the written mode, the main lesson from the studies presented in this chapter is that their mastery is not perfect and not homogenous between readers. Their competences should therefore not be taken for granted. In addition to this, given that even the less frequent connectives included in our experiments still have a very high frequency compared to most other content words, the problems that may be caused by a lack of understanding of these connectives should not be underestimated. The experiments conducted so far focused on this ability to use these connectives appropriately. Future work will need to determine the consequence of these observed difficulties for reading and text comprehension.

One of the main challenges emerging from our experiments concerns the methods that can be used to measure exposure to print in populations that are not adult native speakers. In the case of learners, we have seen that using an ART test in learners' first language is a good way to track individual differences. The situation is more complex, however, in the case of teenagers, for whom the test also needs to be adapted. However, identifying the type of print exposure that may help to separate frequent from infrequent readers in this age group remains a challenge. In some studies (e.g., Cunningham and Stanovich 1990; Deportes et al. 1996), researchers opt for a Title Recognition Test (TRT) rather than the Author Recognition Test for children up to 13. Using the titles of the specific books may be cognitively easier for young children and, thus, allow their exposure to non-school print to be captured better. Yet, there is evidence that author names can also be well processed by children already from the age of 10. This means that ART can be an efficient predictor of the exposure to print for younger populations too if the latter are well targeted (Allen, Cipielewski, and Stanovich 1992; Stainthorp 1997; Spear-Swerling, Brucker, and Alfano 2010). There are several strategies that can be used to better target the recognition test for the tested population. One of them is to ask school instructors and other educational professionals for the lists of books or authors that they expect to be popular among the children of the tested age bracket in the tested cultural context. Another possibility is to base the test on the best-seller lists for children and teenagers from big web platforms selling books in the tested geographical area. Finally, it is also possible to ask a relatively large number of children from the region of interest to name book titles or authors with which they are familiar, and to build the task based on a sample from the generated list. Thus, to increase the chances of capturing individual variations in exposure to print among children and teenagers, future studies should probably combine the proposed strategies to select the items for a form of the Author Recognition Test.

Another avenue of enquiry that will need to be explored in future work concerns the granularity of frequency effects. In our experiments, we simply compared a group of frequent to a group of less frequent connectives. One of the questions arising from our results is to determine from which frequency rank a connective becomes too infrequent to be mastered by most speakers. In order to address this issue, future studies will need to take a scalar rather than a categorical measure of frequencies.

Finally, all the experiments presented in this chapter were conducted with a limited range of French connectives. In order to assess the generalizability of our findings, future work is still needed, with a broader range of connectives, across different languages. A particularly fruitful avenue of enquiry seems to be the comparison between languages with a bigger and smaller repertoire of connectives. It can be expected that languages with fewer connectives may trigger less challenges, as all of them are likely used with a greater frequency and might therefore be mastered better by a majority of speakers.

To conclude, the study of individual variations represents a stepping stone for the study of connectives. It will provide important insights into the mastery of connectives across various populations, with a potentially great impact for language teaching. It would also have a strong resonance for initiatives advocating plain language writing, which aims at the production of texts that are understandable for a wider audience. In this respect, controlling the type of connectives used might be an important step ahead.

References

Acheson, Daniel, Justine Wells & Maryellen MacDonald. 2008. New and updated tests of print exposure and reading abilities in college students. *Behavior Research Methods* 40(1). 278–289.

Allen, Linda, Jim Cipielewski & Keith Stanovich. 1992. Multiple indicators of children's reading habits and attitudes: Construct validity and cognitive correlates. *Journal of Educational Psychology* 84(4). 489–503.

Andrews, Sally. 2015. Individual differences among skilled readers: the role of lexical quality. In Alexander Pollastek & Rebecca Treiman (eds.) *The Oxford Handbook of Reading*, 1–37. Oxford: Oxford University Press.

Bolton, Kingsley, Gerald Nelson & Joseph Hung. 2011. A corpus-based study of connectors in student's writing. *International Journal of Corpus Linguistics* 7(2). 165–182.

Braze, David, Whitney Tabor, Donald Shankweiler & Einar Menkl. 2007. Speaking up for vocabulary: reading skill differences in young adults. *Journal of Learning Disabilities* 40(3). 226–243.

Brito, Natalie, William Fifer, Michael Myers, Amy Elliott & Kimberly Noble. 2016. Associations among family socioeconomic status, EEG power at birth, and cognitive skills during infancy. *Developmental Cognitive Neuroscience* 19. 144–151.

Brysbaert, Marc. 2013. Lextale_FR a fast, free, and efficient test to measure language proficiency in French. *Psychologica Belgica* 53. 23–37.

Cain, Kate & Hannah Nash. 2011. The Influence of Connectives on Young Readers' Processing and Comprehension of Text. *Journal of Educational Psychology* 103. 429–441.

Canestrelli, Anneloes, Willem Mak & Ted Sanders. 2013. Causal connectives in discourse processing: How differences in subjectivity are reflected in eye-movements. *Language and Cognitive Processes* 28(9). 1394–1413.

Caplan, David & Gloria Waters. 1999. Verbal working memory and sentence comprehension. *Behavioral and Brain Sciences* 22. 77–126.

Chen, Ping. 2014. The comparison of intermediate and advanced Chinese learners' use of English adverbial connectors in academic writing. *International Journal on Studies in English Language and Literature* 2. 85–92.

Comer Kidd, David & Emanuele Castano. 2013. Reading literary fiction improves theory of mind. *Science* 342 (6156). 377–380.

Crewe, W. 1990. The illogic of logical connectives. *ELT Journal* 44. 316–325.

Crible, Ludivine & Maria Josep Cuenca. 2017. Discourse markers in speech: characteristics and challenges for annotation. *Dialogue and Discourse* 8(2). 149–166.

Cristia, Alejandrina, Amanda Seidl, Caroline Junge, Melanie Soderstrom & Peter Hagoort. 2013. Predicting individual variation in language from infant speech perception measures. *Child Development* 85(4). 1130–1345.

Cunningham, Anne & Keith Stanovich. 1990. Assessing print exposure and orthographic processing skill in children: A quick measure of reading experience. *Journal of Educational Psychology* 82(4). 733–740.

Daneman, Meredyth & Patricia Carpenter. 1980. Individual differences in working memory and reading. *Journal of Verbal Learning and Verbal Behavior* 19. 450–466.

Degand, Liesbeth & Ted Sanders. 2002. The Impact of Relational Markers on Expository Text Comprehension in L1 and L2. *Reading and Writing* 15. 739–757.

Deportes, Laura, Richard West, Keith Stanovich & Kathleen Zehr. 1996. Using children's literacy activities to predict growth in verbal cognitive skills: A longitudinal investigation. *Journal of Educational Psychology* 88(2). 296–304.

Evers-Vermeul, Jacqueline & Ted Sanders. 2009. The emergence of Dutch connectives: How cumulative cognitive complexity explains the order of acquisition. *Journal of Child Language* 36. 829–54.

Granger, Sylviane & Stephanie Tyson. 1996. Connector usage in the English essay writing of native and non-native EFL speakers of English. *World Englishes* 15. 17–27.

Grolig, Lorenz, Simon Tin-Richards & Sascha Schroeder. 2020. Print exposure across the reading life span. *Reading and Writing* 33. 1423–1441.

Halliday, Michael & Ruqaiya Hasan. 1976. *Cohesion in English*. London: Longman.

Hamed, Muftah. 2014. Conjunctions in Argumentative Writing of Libyan Tertiary Students. *English Language Teaching* 7. 108–120.

Hasselgren, Angela. 1994. Lexical teddy bears and advanced learners: A study into the ways Norwegian students cope with English vocabulary. *International Journal of Applied Linguistics* 4. 237–258.

Hoff, Erika. 2003. The specificity of environmental influence: socioeconomic status affects early vocabulary development via maternal speech. *Child Development* 72. 1368–1378.

Kamhi, Alan & Linette Hinton. 2001. Explaining individual differences in spelling ability. *Topics in Language Disorders* 20(3). 37–49.

Kidd, Evan. 2012. Individual differences in syntactic priming in language acquisition. *Applied Psycholinguistics* 22. 393–418.

Kidd, Evan, Seamus Donnelly & Morten Christiansen. 2017. Individual differences in language acquisition and processing. *Trends in Cognitive Sciences* 22(2). 154–169.

Leedham, Maria & Guozhi Cai. 2013. Besides. . . on the other hand: Using a corpus approach to explore the influence of teaching materials on Chinese students' use of linking adverbials. *Journal of Second Language Writing* 22. 374–389.

Matthews, Danielle, Hannah Biney & Kirsten Abbot-Smith. 2018. Individual differences in children's pragmatic ability: a review of associations with formal language, social cognition, and executive functions. *Language Learning and Development* 14(3). 186–223.

McClure, Erica & Esther Geva. 1983. The development of the cohesive use of adversative conjunctions in discourse. *Discourse Processes* 6. 411–432.

Mol, Suzanne & Adriana Bus. 2011. To read or not to read: A meta-analysis of print exposure from infancy to early adulthood. *Psychological Bulletin* 137(2). 267–296.

Morera, Yurena, José León, Inmaculada Escudero & Manuel de Vega. 2017. Do causal and concessive connectives guide emotional expectancies in comprehension? A double-task paradigm using emotional icons. *Discourse Processes* 54(8). 583–598.

Nippold, Marilyn, Ilsa Schwartz & Robin Undlin. 1992. Use and understanding of adverbial conjunctions: A developmental study of adolescents and young adults. *Journal of Speech and Hearing Research* 35. 108–118.

Palan, Stefan & Christian Schitter. 2018. Prolific.ac – A subject pool for online experiments. *Journal of Behavioral and Experimental Finance* 17. 22–27.

Payne, Brennan, Xuefei Gao, Soo Rim Noh, Carolyn Anderson & Elizabeth Stine-Morrow. 2012. The effects of print exposure on sentence processing and memory in older adults: evidence for efficiency and reserve. *Aging Neuropsychology and Cognition* 19(1–2). 122–149.

Pyykkönen, Pirita & Juhani Järvikivi. 2012. Children and situation models of multiple events. *Developmental Psychology* 48(2). 521–529.

Roze, Charlotte, Laurence Danlos & Philippe Muller. 2012. LEXCONN: A French lexicon of discourse connectives. *Discours* 10. 1–15.

Sanders, Ted, Wilbert Spooren & Leo Noordman. 1992. Toward a taxonomy of coherence relations. *Discourse Processes* 15. 1–35.

Scholman, Merel, Vera Demberg & Ted Sanders. 2020. Individual differences in expecting coherence relations: Exploring the variability in sensitivity to contextual signals in discourse. *Discourse Processes* 57(10). 844–861.

Shi, Jiangang. 2017. A Corpus-Based Study of Contrastive/Concessive Linking Adverbials in Spoken English of Chinese EFL Learners. *Studies in Literature and Language* 14. 17–25.

Sparks, Richard, Jon Patton, Leonore Ganschow & Nancy Humbach. 2012. Do L1 Reading Achievement and L1 Print Exposure Contribute to the Prediction of L2 Proficiency? *Language Learning* 62(2). 473–505.

Spear-Swerling, Louise, Pamela Brucker & Michael Alfano. 2010. Relationships between sixth-graders' reading comprehension and two different measures of print exposure. *Reading and Writing: An Interdisciplinary Journal* 23(1). 73–96.

Sperber, Dan & Deirdre Wilson. 1993. Linguistic form and relevance. *Lingua* 90. 1–25.

Stainthorp, Rhona. 1997. A Children's Author Recognition Test: A useful tool in reading research. *Journal of Research in Reading* 20(2). 148–158.

Stanovich, Keith & Richard West. 1989. Exposure to print and orthographic processing. *Reading Research Quarterly* 24(4). 402–433.

Stanovich, Keith, Richard West & Michele Harrison. 1995. Knowledge growth and maintenance across the life span. The role of print exposure. *Developmental Psychology* 31(5). 811–826.

Swets, Benjamin, Timothy Desmest, David Hambrick & Fernanda Ferreira. 2007. The role of working memory in syntactic ambiguity resolution. A psychometric approach. *Journal of Experimental Psychology: General* 136. 64–81.

Taguchi, Naoko. 2012. *Context, Individual Differences and Pragmatic Competence*. Bristol: Multilingual Matters.

Tapper, Marie. 2005. Connectives in advanced Swedish EFL learners' written English – preliminary results. *The Department of English: Working Papers in English Linguistics* 5. 116–144.

Tazegül, Assiye. 2015. Use, misuse and overuse of 'on the other hand': A corpus study comparing English of native speakers and learners. *International Online Journal of Education and Teaching* (IOJET) 2. 53–66.

Tskhovrebova, Ekaterina, Sandrine Zufferey & Pascal Gygax. 2022. Individual variations in the mastery of discourse connectives from teenage years to adulthood. *Language Learning*, published online ahead of print.

Traxler, Matthew, Antony Sanford, Joy Aked & Linda Moxey. 1997. Processing causal and diagnostic statements in discourse. *Journal of Experimental Psychology: Learning Memory, and Cognition* 23(1). 88–101.

Vuong, Loan & Randi Martin. 2014. Domain-specific executive control and the revision of misinterpretations in sentence comprehension. *Language, Cognition and Neuroscience* 29(3). 313–325.

Weisleder, Adriana & Anne Fernald. 2013. Talking to children matters: early language experience strengthens processing and builds vocabulary. *Psychological Science* 24. 2143–2152.

Wells, Justine, Morten Christiansen, David Race, Daniel Acheson & Maryellen MacDonald. 2003. Experience and sentence processing: statistical learning and relative clause comprehension. *Cognitive Psychology* 58. 250–271.

Wetzel, Mathis, Sandrine Zufferey & Pascal Gygax. 2020. Second language acquisition and the mastery of discourse connectives: assessing the factors that hinder L2-learners from mastering French connectives. *Languages* 5. 1–26.

Wilson, Deirdre. 2011. Procedural meaning: past, present and future. In Victoria Escandell-Vidal, Manuel Leonetti & Aoife Ahern (eds.) *Procedural Meaning: Problems and perspectives*, 33–54. Emerald: Bingley.

Zufferey, Sandine. 2010. *Lexical Pragmatics and Theory of Mind: The Acquisition of Connectives*. Amsterdam: John Benjamins.

Zufferey, Sandrine & Pascal Gygax. 2017. Processing connectives with a complex form-function mapping in L2: the case of French 'en effet'. *Frontiers in Psychology: Language* 8. 1–11.

Zufferey, Sandrine & Pascal Gygax. 2020a. "Roger broke his tooth. However, he went to the dentist": why some readers struggle to evaluate wrong (and right) uses of connectives. *Discourse Processes* 57(2). 184–200.

Zufferey, Sandrine & Pascal Gygax. 2020b. Do teenagers know how to use connectives from the written mode? *Lingua* 234. 1–12.

Zufferey, Sandrine, Willem Mak, Liesbeth Degand & Ted Sanders. 2015. Advanced learners' comprehension of discourse connectives: The role of L1 transfer across on-line and off-line tasks. *Second Language Research* 31. 389–411.

Zufferey, Sandrine, Willem Mak, Sara Verbrugge & Ted Sanders. 2018. Usage and processing of the French causal connectives 'car' and 'parce que'. *Journal of French Language Studies* 28(1). 85–112.

Mathis Wetzel, Sandrine Zufferey and Pascal Gygax

5 Do non-native readers rely on connectives? The processing of coherence relations in L2

Abstract: In this chapter, we discuss the extent to which non-native readers rely on discourse connectives to build coherence relations, and whether their reading fluency is affected by missing or misleading connectives. Our hypothesis is that the information conveyed by connectives is less salient when reading in a second language, as L2 processing has been shown to be shallower than that of native readers. In order to substantiate this claim, we conducted two self-paced reading experiments with native and non-native readers of French. Results show that while non-native readers were generally able to efficiently retrieve the meaning of connectives, their reading fluency was somewhat less affected than the one of native readers when confronted to sentences that contained no connective or an inappropriate one. We conclude that non-native readers rely less on functional and more on lexical cues than native readers do. Our findings also indicate that the reading of native and non-native speakers was affected by the complexity of the coherence relation, suggesting that processing in L2 follows the same cognitive principle of continuity as in L1.

Keywords: discourse connectives, L2 acquisition, processing, coherence relations

1 Introduction

Discourse connectives are linguistic elements that are known to be helpful to establish coherence within a discourse, as they guide and instruct readers on how to interpret the underlying coherence relations (e.g., Halliday and Hasan, 1976). Still, research in second language acquisition has shown that connectives remain highly difficult, even for proficient L2 learners (e.g., Lei, 2012; Zufferey and Gygax, 2017). Many corpus studies have reported for instance that non-native writers struggle to use discourse connectives appropriately in their text productions, at times overusing (e.g., Granger & Tyson, 1996; Leedham and

Mathis Wetzel, University of Bern, mathis.wetzel@unibe.ch
Sandrine Zufferey, University of Bern, sandrine.zufferey@unibe.ch
Pascal Gygax, University of Fribourg, pascal.gygax@unifr.ch

https://doi.org/10.1515/9783110790351-005

Cai, 2013), at times underusing (e.g., Shi, 2017; Tazegül, 2015) and even misusing particular connectives (e.g., Myung-Jeong, 2017; Jameel et al., 2014).

Given that the mastery of connectives in L2 appears to be quite challenging, one might assume that non-native speakers cannot benefit from their presence to the same extent as native speakers even while reading. In the present chapter, we address this question by examining how non-native readers of French process discourse connectives and coherence relations. We do so on the basis of the following research questions:

1) To what extent do non-native readers of French benefit from the presence of discourse connectives while reading?

2) In the case of a wrongly used connective, do non-native readers still rely on the information conveyed by the connective?

Our hypothesis is that non-native readers rely less on connectives, as research has shown that they are more strongly guided by lexical cues than by functional ones (Papadopoulou and Clahsen, 2003). This lower sensitivity to connectives should also result in less pronounced processing disruptions compared to native speakers when encountering a wrongly used connective.

However, there might be also similarities between the processing of connectives in L1 and L2, especially when considering general cognitive processes whilst reading. For example, readers expect discourse to unfold in a continuous manner (Segal et al., 1991; Murray, 1995, 1997) and are able to infer causal relations even in the absence of a connective, whereas concessive relations need to be marked explicitly (Murray, 1995; Sanders, 2005). As one can assume that these principles apply to non-native readers as well, we additionally assess the following two research questions:

3) Do non-native readers of French process discontinuous relations more slowly than continuous ones?

4) Is the effect of the coherence relation equally visible when comparing incorrectly marked concession relations and correctly marked ones?

Our hypothesis is that non-native readers should show similar processing patterns as native readers regarding the complexity of the coherence relation. In other terms, they should read concessive relations more slowly than causal ones, regardless of whether they are indicated by an appropriate or an inappropriate connective.

We start by discussing more generally whether non-native readers understand and recall texts better when they contain connectives. Then, we focus more precisely on what happens during reading by discussing the processing of coherence relations in L2, and the potential benefit that connectives might bring to it. In order to test our assumptions that non-native readers rely less on connectives and are affected by more complex coherence relations, we present two self-paced reading experiments, in which native and non-native readers read sentences that are marked with or without a connective (Experiment 1) and with a correct or incorrect connective (Experiment 2). As expected, the results of both experiments confirm our hypotheses and replicate existing finding of L2-research. We conclude this chapter with potential avenues for research in this domain.

2 Do non-native readers benefit from connectives?

Several studies have demonstrated that L2 learners struggle to understand a text due to a poor mastery of connectives (e.g., Cohen and Fine, 1978; Clerehan, 1995). Cohen et al. (1979), for example, investigated the way non-native students read and understood different types of expository texts, and showed that the insufficient mastery of connectives led, amongst other factors, to a lower understanding of the texts. Cohen et al. (1979) anecdotally reported that one participant thought that the only function of the connective *thus* was to mark off sentences. Geva (1986) also found that an explicit marking of connectives did not bring much benefit to non-native readers for their understanding of a text. However, her study also indicated that advanced learners did show a better comprehension, unlike less proficient ones, when texts contained connectives that were typographically highlighted. This finding thus indicates that L2 learners can actually benefit from the presence of connectives provided specific conditions and a higher level of language proficiency. Similarly, when testing non-native speakers with a higher level of proficiency (i.e., learners that were actually able to understand the meaning of the connectives), Degand and Sanders (2002) demonstrated that L2 learners can benefit from the presence of connectives, and understand texts marked with causal connectives better than texts that did not contain them. In line with Degand and Sanders (2002), Crosson and Lesaux (2013) observed that a good knowledge of connectives had a positive effect on learners' text comprehension and concluded that highly proficient readers' understanding of text does benefit from connectives. The ability to benefit from connectives and to better understand a text written in L2 thus depends highly on readers' level of language proficiency. This is not surprising, given that it is well known that the meaning of connectives is better retrieved with a higher language proficiency (Goldman and Murray, 1992; Wetzel et al., 2020), especially for speakers with a high *spoken* language proficiency (Geva, 1992, 2007).

Still, observations from other studies attenuate these findings and point out the role of the connective under scrutiny, as more complex connectives have been shown to complicate the construction of the intended coherence relation, even for highly proficient non-native readers. Zufferey and Gygax (2017), for example, have shown that when a connective is polyfunctional and therefore ambiguous, even highly proficient non-native readers show a preference for sentences that do not contain it. Also, in a sentence evaluation task, non-native readers preferred implicit specifications such as: 'The neighbor, the old lady who lives above, is very nice.' over specifications that contained a correct connective such as: 'The neighbor, that is, the old lady who lives above, is very nice.'(Wetzel et al., in press). One possible explanation for this result could be that highly optional connectives might be somewhat unexpected for non-native readers and might lead to confusion.

Taken together, non-native readers do seem to struggle to use discourse connectives, which lowers their chances to understand a text. However, when a generally higher language proficiency is attained, their understanding can benefit from discourse connectives. In the next section, we discuss whether the benefit of connectives for text comprehension in L2 also produces beneficial effects not only for understanding but also for reading fluency. While the facilitative effect of connectives on reading fluency is well-documented for native readers (e.g., Millis and Just, 1994; Sanders and Noordmann, 2000), there are indications that non-native readers may not obtain a direct benefit from connectives, as they process on a shallower level than L1 readers (Clahsen and Felser, 2006a, 2006b).

3 Processing of coherence relations in L2

Generally, theories assume shallower, and therefore more limited, processing when reading in L2 compared to reading in L1. For example, Clahsen and Felser (2006a, 2006b) suggest that the processing of non-native readers is generally less automatic than the processing of native readers, which might be partly explained by a greater cognitive effort when reading in a L2 compared to reading in a L1. Also, it is known that non-native readers rely more on lexical-semantic cues, and less on syntactical and functional ones (see also Marinis et al., 2005; Papadopoulo and Clahsen, 2003). As a consequence, while native readers show high processing disruption for incorrect sentences, L2 learners are less (or at least differently) affected (e.g., Weber-Fox and Neville, 1996). Studies using ERP (i.e., event related potentials) have found support for this by showing that L2 learners – even bilinguals – process semantic and syntactic anomalies differently than monolingual readers (e.g., Hahne and Friederici, 2001; Weber-Fox and Neville, 1996, Ardal et al. 1990, Felser et al., 2003). Some studies have also shown that more proficient L2 readers tend to develop native-like reading processing (Hahne et al. 2006; Sabourin, 2003; McLaughlin et al, 2004).[1]

With respect to the processing and benefit of discourse connectives, shallower processing of non-native readers could lead to different assumptions. Firstly, one could assume that non-native readers should benefit from the presence of connectives, as the clear-cut and valuable instructions of connectives could strongly release cognitive resources otherwise used to infer coherence relations. However, as discussed above, connectives are also known to be complex linguistic elements that can carry multiple functions and have nuanced pragmatic overtones (e.g., Schumann et al., 2020), which makes them, potentially, more complicated for L2 learners. Thus, their potential benefit for online processing – while being well-documented in L1 research (Millis and Just, 1994; Sanders and Noordman, 2000) – appears rather open in L2.

In Zufferey and Gygax (2017), non-native readers showed no processing disruption for sentences that were incorrectly marked with the French connective *en effet* ('indeed'), hinting that even highly proficient language learners do not master the different uses of this polyfunctional connective. Moreover, Wetzel et al. (in press) demonstrated that non-native readers, contrarily to native readers, showed no processing disruptions for sentences containing misuses of connectives. Interestingly, however, in the same study, errors were still detected by non-native readers, but only after reading (i.e., in an offline task). The lack of fluency effects during online reading might be due to processing capacity limitations induced by the temporal pressure of online reading.

Taken together, the evidence presented in this section indicates that non-native readers might not experience immediate benefits of connectives during reading. The general reliance on lexical rather than on syntactical cues (Clahsen and Felser, 2006a, 2006; Marinis et al., 2005; Papadopoulo and Clahsen, 2003), together with the complexity of connectives and their uses (Zufferey and Gygax, 2017; Wetzel et al., in press) might lead to shallower processing of the procedural

---

1 It is still debated whether non-native readers can actually achieve a full native-like processing (see for instance Clahsen and Felser, 2006a; Yuan, 2017; Bond et al., 2011, Sabourin and Stowe, 2008).

instructions provided by a connective. Yet, there might also be cognitive processes that apply to all readers, independently of whether they read in L1 or L2, as we now outline.

4 Cognitive theories for native speakers potentially applying to L2 processing

In the preceding sections, we have discussed the idea that non-native readers' understanding of text could benefit from connectives, provided that these readers are highly proficient and that the connectives are easily accessible to them. We also discussed the fact that non-native readers might rely less on connectives during reading, as L2 processing is known to be shallower than that of native readers. We now discuss the processing of connectives in the light of the cognitive theories that have been established for native readers, and try to extend them, despite important differences between L1 and L2 processing, to non-native readers.

The *causality-by-default* hypothesis, put forward by Sanders (2005), states that readers expect, unless indicated otherwise, causal links between sentences. In line with this hypothesis, causal sentences should be easy to understand without explicit connective marking, as in example (1).

(1) Paul was hungry. He ordered food.

Causal sentences are also known to be cognitively less complex than concessive ones (Sanders et al., 1992), resulting in a faster processing for causal relations than for concessive ones (e.g., Köhne and Demberg, 2013). These findings can also be explained by the *continuity*-hypothesis (e.g., Murray, 1995, 1997; Segal et al., 1991), which states that readers tend to interpret sentences in narratives as if they were following one another in a continuous manner (Murray, 1997:228). Continuity (such as the fulfillment of an expectation) thus facilitates the processing of a text whereas discontinuity, such as sudden topic changes or general violations of an expectation, render a text more difficult to process. In the context of coherence relations, this means that continuous connectives, such as causal and additive ones, should facilitate processing whereas concessive and contrastive connectives – marking a disruption of continuity – are processed at a greater effort. In line with this hypothesis, Murray (1997) showed by conducting reading experiments that non-appropriate concessive connectives produced a higher processing disruption in reading fluency than non-appropriate causal and additive connectives.

In the case of non-native reading, some evidence suggests that these cognitive principles also apply to non-native readers. Recio Fernández (2020), for example, investigated the link between language proficiency and the ability to process coherence relations in L2. In four experiments using eye-tracking, she compared reading fluency of sentences containing the Spanish connective *por lo tanto* ('therefore') and *sin embargo* ('however') by native speakers of Spanish and Spanish learners of different proficiency levels (B1 – C1). More precisely, Recio Fernández (2020) tested (i) whether whether specific relations (cause vs concession) would affect the online-processing of non-native readers of Spanish, (ii) whether an implicit causal relation would affect processing to the same extent as an explicit causal one, (iii) whether incorrect connectives would affect processing of causal relations, as well as of concessive relations (iv). The results obtained in these experiments not only suggested a clear link between language proficiency and the processing of coherence relations, but also indicated that L2 learners of Spanish were generally affected by the complexity of coherence relations. However, the compelling results obtained by Recio Fernández (2020) also raise intriguing questions that remain open.

For example, there is still a lack of documentation on the interaction between the type of relation and the processing of implicitly or explicitly marked sentences. In other words, it is still unknown whether a concessive relation (implicit or explicit) is processed differently by non-native readers in comparison to a causal one (implicit or explicit). As a reminder, according to the *causality-hypothesis* by Sanders (2005), implicit causal relations should not create the same processing disruption as implicit concessive ones. Also, we do not know whether the effect of the complexity of coherence relations is also apparent when sentences are incorrectly marked.

Furthermore, although the use of eye tracking measures allows for fine-grained examinations, it is highly beneficial to complement these with other processing methodologies to assess online reading, as recently shown by Müller and Mari (2021). By using self-paced reading measures, they demonstrated that *definite descriptions* (e.g., Roberts, 2003) led to longer reading times when produced in implausible contexts, and were thus able to replicate findings of Singh et al. (2016) in French. However, when using eye-tracking measures (first fixation duration, first-pass reading times and regression path times), Müller and Mari (2021) failed to observe similar reading time differences in the measurements corresponding to the online processing. The findings of the study thus show that complementing online measurements is highly beneficial to obtain a wider and more reliable picture of the effects under scrutiny.

Finally, there is also uncertainty whether the findings of Recio Fernández (2020) can be applied to other languages than Spanish. Given that coherence relations are expressed differently across languages (e.g., Kanno, 1986) and since cross-linguistic studies demonstrate that readers from differing L1 process discourse and connectives differently (Blumenthal-Dramé, 2020), reading experiments in other languages (and L1 – L2 pairs) are necessary to reach appropriate generalizability.

5 Our study and hypotheses

In order to obtain a comprehensive picture of the processing of coherence relations in L2, and to assess the potential benefit that connectives can bring to L2 reading, we present two experiments, based on the work of Recio Fernández (2020) and Wetzel et al. (2022), which will enable us to answer the following research questions:
a) To what extent do non-native readers of French benefit from the presence of discourse connectives while reading?
b) In the case of a wrongly used connective, do non-native readers still rely on the connective?
c) Do non-native readers of French process discontinuous relations more slowly than continuous ones (cf. Recio Fernández, 2020)?
d) Is the effect of the coherence relation equally visible when comparing incorrectly marked concession relations and correctly marked ones?

In order to assess these research questions, we measured self-paced reading times of native and non-native readers of French for causal and concessive sentences that are presented either *with* or *without* a correct connective (experiment 1) and either with a *correct* or with an *incorrect* connective (experiment 2).

Testing these two types of relations enables us to assess whether reading in L2 follows the cognitive principles established for native readers by Sanders (2005) and Murray (1997; see also Segal et al., 1991). These principles suggest that readers expect discourse to proceed in a continuous and causal manner and show disruptions when these expectations are not fulfilled. Continuous and discontinuous relations are, in consequence, read at a different pace and readers need more time to integrate the meaning of more complex relations (Köhne and Demberg, 2013). In the context of L2 reading, there is supporting evidence to this hypothesis by Recio Fernández (2020) for Spanish.

Also, causal and concessive relations differ in their degree of implicitness, as causes can be easily identified even without an explicit marking (Sanders, 2005), whereas concessions need to be marked explicitly (Murray, 1995). Given that these principles are grounded in general cognitive ones, we expect a similar effect for non-native readers of French, however with generally slower reading times compared to native readers, since reading in L2 is generally more demanding than reading in L1.

We also expect differences regarding the reliance on connectives, as non-native readers might not have a native-like sensibility to connectives and rely more on the propositional content of a sentence. Hence, they should not be able to detect losses of coherence, especially for concessive relations in which the connective is missing. Thus, while native readers should be affected by implicitly marked concessions, non-native readers should show less pronounced disruptions of reading fluency in this condition.

6 Experiment 1: Implicit marking of coherence relations

In this experiment, we test how missing connectives affect the online processing of native and non-native readers of French. We measure reading times for two types of relations, a causal relation and a concessive one, that are either marked with a connective or conveyed implicitly. We have the following hypotheses:

Hypothesis 1: When comparing explicitly marked concessions and causes, segments introduced by concessions should trigger slower reading times, given their higher cognitive complexity (Sanders et al., 1992). As this assumption is based on general cognitive principles, we expect the same effect for both speakers' groups, native or non-native.

Hypothesis 2: Segments introduced by implicit causes should not trigger slower reading times compared to segments introduced by explicit causes, as causality can be understood when left implicit (Sanders, 2005). Once more, this effect should be the same for both native and non-native readers.

Hypothesis 3: In the case of segments introduced by implicit concessions, the absence of the connective creates incoherence (Murray, 1995), which should negatively affect reading times in native readers. Yet, for non-native readers implicit concessions should not trigger reading disruption of following segments in comparison to explicitly marked ones, as non-native readers tend to rely more on lexical propositional cues than on functional procedural ones (Papadopoulou and Clahsen, 2003).

6.1 Participants

We recruited participants via the online platform *Prolific* (Oxford, UK, www.prolific.co). For the non-native speakers' group, we recruited 53 non-native participants that had English as their L1 and that indicated to be able to speak French (participants who declared to be bilingual were excluded). As we had to exclude four participants due to failed attention checks (see below), the data from 49 non-native participants was analyzed (44f, in mean 36.6 yo, SD = 12.8). Language proficiency scores (as reported below) indicated a rather high level of language proficiency. For the control group, we recruited 65 French native participants (33f, in mean 27.5 yo, SD = 8.2).

All participants were compensated with 3.15 GBP and gave informed content for inclusion. We only recruited participants that showed a satisfying participation in previous studies on the *prolific* platform (minimum of 95% approved participations).

6.2 Design

We conducted a web-based self-paced reading task with two variables: the *type of coherence relation* (cause vs. concession) and the *type of marking* (explicit vs. implicit), using 4 lists of items that were presented in a 2x2 Latin square design. We additionally measured French proficiency by using the French version of the vocabulary task *Lextale* (Brysbaert, 2013). Lextale scores have been shown to be a valid and robust measurement of second language proficiency, and they have been shown to correlate with connectives' mastery in offline tasks (e.g., Wetzel et al. 2020). The task will be presented in more detail in Section 5.4.

6.3 Materials

We created 40 experimental and 45 filler items, based on the items used by Wetzel, Zufferey and Gygax (2022). More precisely, we took the correct versions of concessions and causes of Wetzel et al.'s first experiment in order to obtain explicitly marked causes and concessions (example 2 and 3). In order to obtain implicit versions, we simply removed the connectives, as in examples (4) and (5).

(2) *Nadia adore tous les animaux à fourrure, donc elle a toujours eu un chat.*
    'Nadia loves all furry animals, so she always had a cat.'

(3) *Nadia a peur de tous les animaux à fourrure, mais elle a toujours eu un chat.*
'Nadia is afraid of all furry animals, but she has always had a cat.'

(4) *Nadia adore tous les animaux à fourrure, elle a toujours eu un chat.*
'Nadia loves all furry animals, she always had a cat.'

(5) *Nadia a peur de tous les animaux à fourrure, elle a toujours eu un chat.*
'Nadia is afraid of all furry animals, she has always had a cat.'

Filler items also consisted of two clauses that were linked by different French pronouns (such as *à laquelle* 'to which' or *duquel* 'from which'). As shown in example (6), we segmented each item into seven segments for which we measured reading times (the segments' numbers are given in parentheses).

(6) *Nadia adore (1) // tous les animaux (2) // à fourrure, (3) // donc (4) // elle a (5) // toujours eu (6) // un chat. (7) //*
'Nadia loves (1) // all animals (2) // with fur, (3) // so (4) // she has (5) // always had (6) // a cat. (7) //'

In order to preserve reading as natural as possible, we did not instruct readers to read these segments as quickly as possible. After every item (including the filler items) a verification question, as in (7) was presented to which participants responded either affirmatively (by pressing *v* for *vrai* 'true') or negatively (by pressing *f* for *faux* 'false').

(7) *Nadia a toujours eu un chien. Vrai ou faux ?*
'Nadia has always had a dog. True or false?'

While verification questions that followed experimental items referred to the second part of the sentence, the verification questions for the filler items referred to the first part of the sentence. Thus, participants were obliged to read attentively all parts of the sentences, as they could not guess which part of the sentence the question would address. As these questions functioned as wrap-up segments of the preceding sentence, recording response times enabled us to observe potential spill-over effects of the reading fluency (as in Wetzel et al., 2022; Crible et al., 2021). In addition, based on the response given to the question, we excluded participants who did not truly read the sentences (at a threshold of 75% of correct answers).

6.4 Procedure

Before the experiment, a consent form was displayed using *Qualtrics* (Qualtrics LLC, Provo, UT, USA). After participants agreed to it, they were guided off *Qualtrics* to the actual experiment which was designed using the *Psychopy* software (Peirce et al., 2019; version 2020.20) and hosted on *Pavlovia* servers.

Participants were instructed to read each sentence, segment by segment, and to respond to the corresponding verification question. Two training items were presented before the actual experiment in order to familiarize the participants with the task. Before every sentence, participants had to press the space bar in order to start reading the first segment, and to confirm that they were ready. After doing so, a red cross lasted for 1 second at the place where the first segment of the sentence would appear. Each segment of the sentence was presented isolated in mid-screen in an easy-to-read black font. The participants had to press the space bar in order to move on to the next segment, allowing us to measure reading times for each segment. After completing the main task, the participants performed the French version of the vocabulary task *Lextale* (Brysbaert, 2013). In this task, we presented 56 real existing French and 28 non-existing but morphologically plausible words, for each of which participants had to decide whether they identified it as a real existing French word or not. For every correctly identified word we awarded one point, for every incorrectly identified word we deducted one point. Hence, the maximum score was 56 points. The whole experiment lasted approximatively 30 minutes.

6.5 Analysis

6.5.1 Lextale scores

Lextale scores are reported in Table 1.[2] As expected, native and non-native readers significantly differed in their language proficiency, as measured by the Lextale task ($t[55]= 14.44, p < .00001$).

Table 1: First experiment: Lextale scores for all participants.

	Mean	SD	%
Native readers	45.2	6.9	81
Non-native readers	23.2	9.4	42

---

[2] In comparison, in Wetzel et al. (2020), non-native French learning students at a B1 – B2 level were tested. Their mean score in the Lextale task was of 14.69 (SD = 8.37, 26%).

6.5.2 Main analyses

We conducted linear mixed models using the *R* software (R Core Team, 2020) on the reading times of the last three segments as well as the response times to the verification questions (i.e., all regions that did not differ across all conditions). All models were built following the procedure of Baayen (Baayen, 2008), meaning that for each added fixed effect, the resulting model was compared to the model that did not contain it. We assessed the improvement of the models by conducting log-likelihood-tests using the *anova()* function of the *stats* package (version 3.6.2, R Core Team, 2020). We obtained significance levels using the *summary()* function of the *base* package (version 3.6.2, R Core Team, 2020); for interactions we conducted post-hoc comparisons using the *glht()* function of the *multcomp* package (Hothorn et al., 2008). All our models, including the null models, contained *Participants* and *Items* as random effects. As the reading times were positively skewed (as measured by the *skewness()* function of the *moments* package, Komsta and Novomestky, 2015), we set cut-off values at 0.5 and 4 sec for the sentence's segments and 0.5 and 8 seconds for the comprehension question and conducted log-transformations (as in Crible et al., 2021). Visual representations of our data then indicated a normal distribution. When analyzing response times, we did not dissociate between correct and incorrect answers, as we were merely interested in potential spill-over effects of reading at this wrap-up region. As we anticipated a high difference in reading times between native and non-native readers, we conducted separate analyses for both language groups (as in Crible et al., 2021). The outputs of all our models are reported in Table 2.

Table 2: Outputs from our models.

Native readers						
Segment 5		β	SE	df	t	Pr(>|t|)
	(Intercept)	−1.12	.06	70.61	−20.44	< 2^{e-16} ***
	Marking implicit	.11	.02	2453.16	6.42	1.67^{e-10} ***
Segment 6						
	(Intercept)	−1.09	.06	71.28	−18.29	< 2^{e-16} ***
	Marking implicit	−0.05	.02	2442.28	−2.91	.0036 **
Segment 7						
	(Intercept)	-1.00^{e+00}	5.40^{e-02}	7.96^{e+01}	−18.58	< 2^{e-16} ***
	Relation consequence	-1.08^{e-03}	2.15^{e-02}	2.45^{e+03}	−0.05	.96
	Marking implicit	6.20^{e-02}	2.16^{e-02}	2.44^{e+03}	2.87	< .01 **
	Relation consequence: Marking implicit	-7.56^{e-02}	3.05^{e-02}	2.44^{e+03}	−2.48	< .05 *

Table 2 (continued)

Verification question						
	(Intercept)	1.07	.02	111.50	43.95	< 2^{e-16} ***
	Relation consequence	−0.04	.01	2461.88	−3.48	< .001 ***
	Marking implicit	0.04	.01	2463.13	3.36	< .001 ***
	Relation consequence: Marking implicit	−0.03	.02	2461.96	−1.95	.05
Non–native readers						
Segment 5						
	(Intercept)	−0.66	.06	75.93	−11.67	< 2^{e-16} ***
	Marking implicit	.04	.02	1860.28	2.29	.022 *
Segment 6						
	(Intercept)	−0.56	.06	70.77	−9.19	1.07^{e-13} ***
	Marking implicit	−0.07	.92	1865.31	−3.96	7.81^{e-05} ***
Segment 7						
	(Intercept)	−0.52	.06	68.65	−9.31	8.68^{e-14} ***
	Relation consequence	−0.06	.02	1866.51	−4.00	6.53^{e-05} ***
Verification question						
	(Intercept)	2.24	.03	87.45	43.36	< 2^{e-16} ***
	Relation consequence	−0.04	.01	1843.84	−3.16	< .005 **
	Marking implicit	.03	.01	1842.59	2.18	< .05 *
	Relation consequence: Marking implicit	−0.04	.02	1843.82	−1.94	.05

Significant codes: > 0: '***', > 0.001: '**', > 0.01: '*'

In Segment 5, for both native and non-native models, the fit of the model improved by adding *Marking* (i.e., implicit or explicit marking; improvement for the model for the L1 group: χ^2 = 40.82, df = 1, p = 1.67^{e-10}; L2 group: χ^2 = 5.24, df = 1, p < .05). As apparent in Table 2, reading times of Segment 5 were faster when explicitly marked, both for native and non-native readers. In the following segment (i.e., Segment 6), *Marking* also improved the models (L1 group: χ^2 = 8.48, df = 1, p < .005, L2 group: χ^2 = 15.61, df = 1, p = 7.79^{e-05}), but for both groups reading times were this time faster for implicitly marked segments (see Table 2).

For Segment 7, models differed when considering native and non-native readers (see Figure 1). For native readers, adding *Marking* did not improve the random model's fit (χ^2 = 2.44, df = 1, p = .12), yet *Relation* did (χ^2 = 6.37. df = 1, p <.05). Adding *Marking* (main and interaction effects) further improved the model (χ^2 = 8.63, df = 2, p <.05). Post-hoc comparisons revealed that Segment 7 was read more slowly when introduced by implicit concessions (compared to *explicit concessions*: β = .06, SE = .02, z = 2.87, p < .05; to *implicit causes*: β = .01, SE = 0.02, z =-0.6, p < .01; and to *explicit causes*: β = .06, SE =.02; z = -2.91, p < .05).

For non-native readers, adding *Marking* did not improve the random model's fit (χ^2 = .12, df = 1, p = .73). Adding *Relation* did (χ^2 = 15.95, df = 1, p = 6.52^{e-05}). This time, adding *Marking* (main and interaction effects) did not further improve the model (χ^2 = .64, df = 2, p = .73). For non-native readers, differences in reading times were only apparent when comparing relations, independent of marking (see also Figure 1).

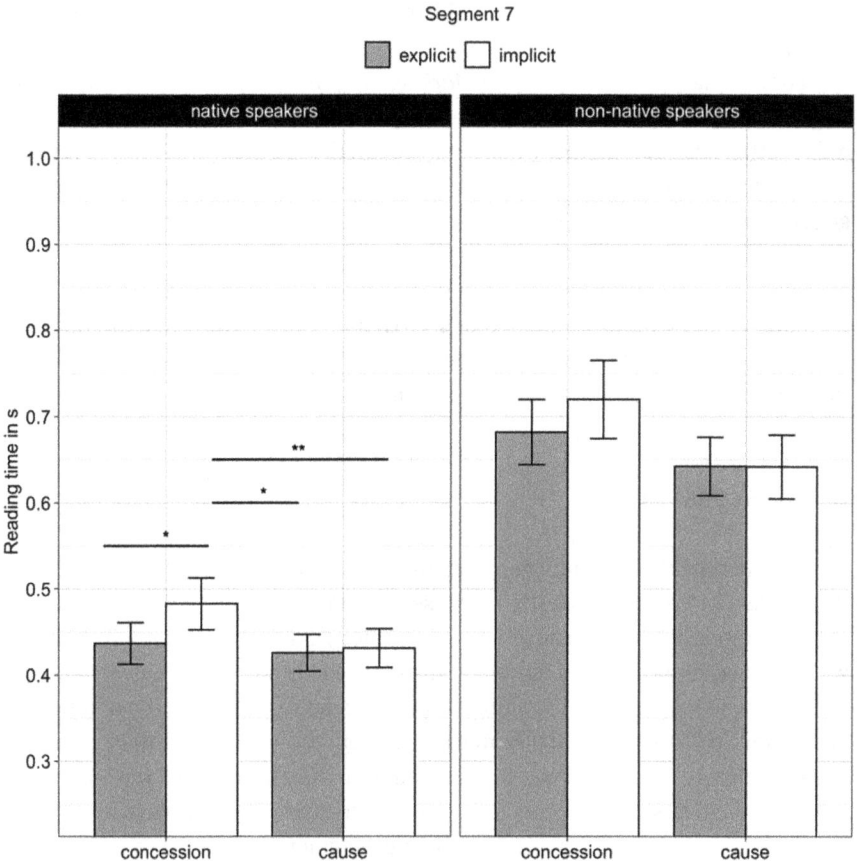

Figure 1: First experiment: reading times for segment 7. Main effect of *Relation* for non-native readers. Post-hoc comparisons indicated for native readers (CI of 95% as error bars).

For native readers, in the wrap up region of the sentence (i.e., the response times to the verification question), adding *Marking* improved the random model's fit

(χ^2 = 7.55, df = 1, p < .01). Further adding *Relation* (main and interaction effects) also did (χ^2 = 50.27, df = 2, p = 1.22$^{e\text{-}11}$). Although the interaction of Marking by Relation was at the limit of significance[3] (p =.05, see Table 2 and Figure 2), simultaneous tests for general linear hypotheses using the *glht()* function of the *multcomp* package (Hothorn et al., 2008) showed that response times in the *implicit concession* condition differed from all other conditions (compared to *explicit concessions*: β =.04, SE = .01, z = 3.36, p < .01; to *implicit causes*: β = .08, SE = .01, z = −6.2, p < .001; and to *explicit causes*: β = .08, SE = .01, z = −6.82, p < .001). Also, we observed that native readers also responded faster to questions that were primed by explicit causes than those primed by explicit concessions (β = −0.04, SE =.01, z = −3.48, p < .01).

For non-native readers, adding *Marking* did not improve the random model's fit (χ^2 = 1.21, df = 1, p = .27). However, adding *Relation* (χ^2 = 40.27, df = 1, p = 2.21$^{e\text{-}10}$) did. Further adding *Marking* (main and interaction effects) did only marginally improve the model's fit (χ^2 = 5.06 df = 2, p = .08). Additional simultaneous tests for general linear hypotheses showed no significant differences between response times for implicit and explicit concessions (β = .03, SE = .01, t = 2.18, p = .13), as well as no difference between implicit and explicit causes, (β = .01, SE = .01, t = −0.57, p = .94). Non-native readers were not really affected by the different markings (i.e., implicit or explicit); yet, were always slower to respond to questions related to sentences introduced by concessions than by causes.

6.6 Discussion

In this experiment, we conducted a self-paced reading task for native and non-native readers of French, in which we presented sentences containing two types of coherence relations (i.e., cause and concession) that were presented with and without an appropriate connective (see also Loureda et al., this volume, chapter 2).

Firstly, we observed in segment 5 that all readers, independently of language group, tended to read implicitly marked sentences more slowly than explicitly marked ones. As segment 5 was the segment that directly followed the connective in the explicit versions, we conclude that connectives speeded up reading, even for non-native readers. Then, in the following segment, we observed that readers needed time to integrate the meaning of the connectives in the explicit version.

---

[3] When adopting a 50% threshold for correct responses to the verification questions (i.e., instead of 75%), the interaction seemed to become clearer (p<.05). We would suggest that shallower readers (i.e., less accurate ones) may struggle even more with implicitly marked concessions (i.e., the source of the interaction).

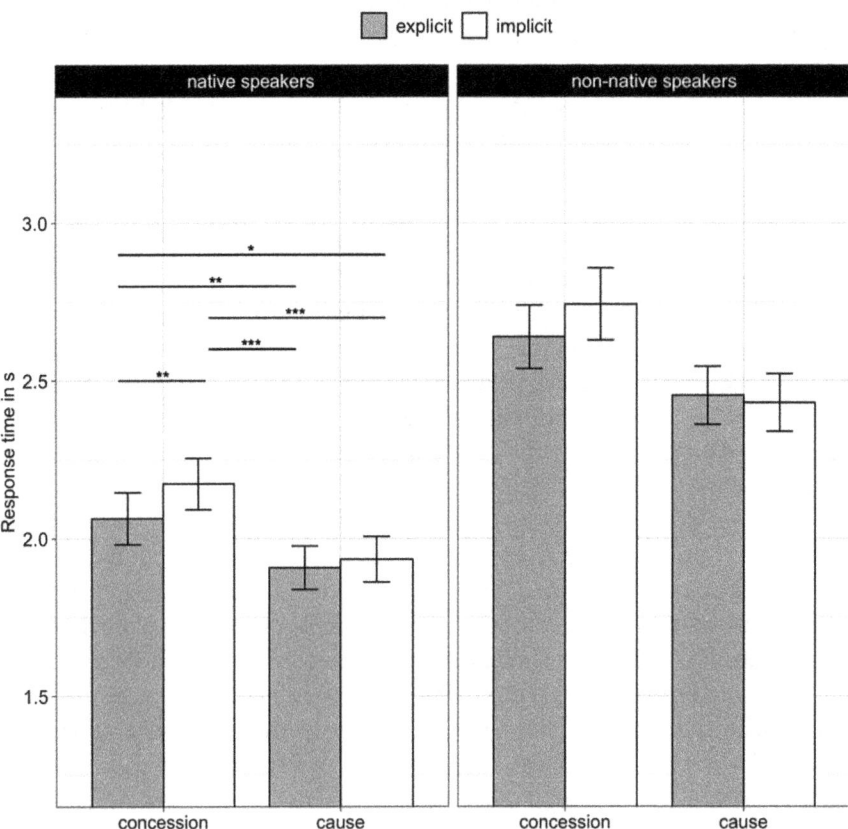

Figure 2: First experiment: response times to the verification question. General effect of *Relation* for non-native readers. Post-hoc comparison indicated for native readers (CI of 95% as error bars).

While this effect was once more expected for native readers (e.g., Zufferey and Gygax, 2017), the fact that non-native readers also showed an immediate benefit from the connective confirms that they actively processed the sentences.

In the following segments, both native and non-native readers consistently processed causal sentences faster than concessions (confirming Hypothesis 1), which is indicative of the higher complexity of concessive over causal relations (Sanders, 2005). This finding is remarkable, especially in the context of second language reading, as it indicates that reading in a L2, although cognitively more demanding than reading in a L1, follows the same cognitive principles. Also, the finding that implicit causes did not trigger longer reading times than explicit causes for non-native readers shows that they were able to construct a causal meaning despite a 'missing' connective (confirming Hypothesis 2). Yet, we also observed important differences between native and non-native readers in the last segment and the verification questions: contrary to native readers, it appeared that non-native readers were not affected by implicit concessions (confirming Hypothesis 3). It appears, therefore, that the non-native readers relied less on the presence of connectives and were focusing on the linguistic content of the segments.

Taken together, the results of this first experiment indicate that L2 processing follows similar cognitive principles as L1 processing regarding the complexity of coherence relations, but that non-native readers focus less on connectives. It appears that non-native readers rely more on the content of the segments than on the signal provided by the connective. This became visible especially for the implicit concessions, as non-native readers did not process versions with a missing connective differently than explicit ones, although the implicit concession created incoherence, as evidenced by the observed processing disruption for native readers.

Still, one could argue that the incoherence of implicit concessions can be resolved, as it is caused by missing, not contradictory, information. This finding raises an intriguing question: are non-native readers also unaffected by incoherence that cannot so easily be resolved? For example, in the case of a wrong use of a connective, non-native readers might not be able to easily draw alternative coherent interpretations. To address this question, we assessed in the following experiment whether incoherence due to incorrectly used connectives affects the reading fluency of non-native readers of French, and compared it to the data collected in Wetzel et al. (2022) for the same experiment on L1 readers.

7 Experiment 2: Incorrect marking of coherence relations

In our second experiment, we assess whether native and non-native readers are affected by non-resolvable (or at least, hardly resolvable) incoherence due to an incorrect use of connectives. We have the following hypotheses:

Hypothesis 1: Native readers should show slower reading times of segments that are introduced by incorrect connectives, regardless of the coherence relation.

Hypothesis 2: As non-native readers may rely more on lexical cues, reading disruption of segments introduced by incorrect uses of frequent connectives should only be – if present – temporary or limited (i.e., they should become apparent in some segments but not all).

Hypothesis 3: When comparing reading times for segments introduced by incorrectly used connectives, an incorrect concessive connective should trigger (even) slower reading times than an incorrect causal one – for both native and non-native readers –, as concession involves more complex processing (as evidenced in Experiment 1).

7.1 Participants

We recruited participants via the internet platform *prolific*[4] and analyzed the reading times of 61 French native participants (27 female; in mean 31.4 yo, SD = 11.3y) and, after excluding 10 participants due to failed attention checks, of 47 non-native participants (35 female; in mean 42 yo, SD = 15.8y). As in Experiment 1, we measured, for both groups, language proficiency in French using the *Lextale* task. Also, all participants were compensated with 3.15 GBP. All participants gave informed consent for inclusion and none of the participants had participated in Experiment 1.

7.2 Design

The design of this experiment was the same as for the first experiment, but this time we tested – instead of *implicit* and *explicit* marking – *correct* and *incorrect* markings of the causal and concessive sentences.

7.3 Materials

For the correct versions of the items, we used the explicit items of Experiment 1. In order to obtain incorrect versions, we simply exchanged the connectives, in other words we used the concessive connective in causal sentences (8) and the causal connective in concessive sentences (9).

---

[4] As mentioned earlier, we used Wetzel et al.'s (2022) data for the exact same experiment on native readers to compare to the present non-native readers' results.

(8) *Nadia adore tous les animaux à fourrure, mais elle a toujours eu un chat.*
    'Nadia loves all furry animals, but she always had a cat.'

(9) *Nadia a peur de tous les animaux à fourrure, donc elle a toujours eu un chat.*
    'Nadia is afraid of all furry animals, so she has always had a cat.'

As these examples illustrate, the incorrect uses of connectives create incoherence that cannot be easily resolved.

7.4 Procedure

The procedure was the same as in Experiment 1, as described in Section 6.5.

7.5 Analysis

7.5.1 Lextale scores

Lextale scores are reported in Table 3. The language proficiency scores in this experiment were highly comparable to the one of the first experiment, and showed significant differences between language groups ($t[55]= 13.02, p < .00001$).

Table 3: Second experiment: Lextale scores for all participants.

	Mean	SD	%
Native readers	45.4	6.6	81
Non-native readers	26.0	10.1	47

7.5.2 Main analysis

We conducted our analyses following the same strategy as in Experiment 1, described in Section 5.5. The outputs of all our models are reported in Table 5.

For the two groups of readers, we did not observe any effect of *Marking* (correct or incorrect) nor of the type of *Relation* in Segment 5 (see Table 4 for the lack of improvement of the models when fixed effects were added to the model).

Table 4: Experiment 2, Segment 5: improvement of models when fixed effects were added.

Native readers

added fixed effect	improvement of the model		
	CHI	df	Pr(>Chisq)
Marking	.16	1	.68
Relation	2.39	1	.12

Non-native readers

Marking	1.15	1	.28
Relation	2.86	1	.10

For reading times of Segment 6, adding *Marking* to the model improved the random model's fit, for both native (χ^2= 4.83, df =1, p <.05) and non-native readers (χ^2=17.59, df = 1, p = 2.74^{e-05}). When Segment 6 was introduced by an incorrect connective, it was read more slowly than when introduced by a correct one, and this for all readers (see Table 5).

Table 5: Outputs for all our models.

Native readers						
Segment 6		B	SE	df	t	Pr(>|t|)
	(Intercept)	−1.11	.06	67.22	−17.61	< 2^{e-16}***
	Marking incorrect	.04	.02	2293.21	2.20	.03*
Segment 7						
	(Intercept)	−0.90	.05	75.85	−16.73	< 2^{e-16}***
	Marking incorrect	−0.70	.02	2310.89	−3.25	<.005**
	Relation consequence	−0.06	.02	2317.26	−2.76	<.01**
	Marking incorrect: Relation consequence	.05	.03	2316.56	1.55	.12
Verification question						
	(Intercept)	.66	.04	109.36	17.77	< 2^{e-16}***
	Marking incorrect	−0.06	.02	2324.06	−3.52	<.001***
	Relation consequence	−0.08	.02	2326.00	−4.32	1.63^{e-05}***
	Marking incorrect: Relation consequence	.02	.03	2326.25	.65	.52
Non –native readers						
Segment 6						
	(Intercept)	−0.50	.06	65.08	−8.09	2.00^{e-11}***
	Marking incorrect	.08	.02	1756.48	4.20	2.75^{e-05}***

Table 5 (continued)

Segment 7					
(Intercept)	−0.48	.06	62.65	−8.60	**3.29^{e-12}***
Marking incorrect	.10	.02	1761.95	5.50	**4.27^{e-08}***
Verification question					
(Intercept)	−0.22	.06	65.79	−3.46	**<.001***
Marking incorrect	0.12	.02	1680.55	5.20	**2.22^{e-07}***
Relation consequence	−0.48	.02	1680.66	−2.00	**<.05***
Marking incorrect: Relation consequence	−0.07	.03	1680.59	−1.99	**<.05***

Significant codes: > 0: '***', > 0.001: '**', > 0.01: '*'

For Segment 7, models differed when considering native and non-native readers (see Figure 3). For native readers, adding *Marking* improved the random model's fit (χ^2 = 9.30, df = 1, p <.005). Adding *Relation* (main and interaction effects) further improved the model (χ^2 = 7.91, df = 2, p <.05). Although the interaction of Marking by Relation was marginal (p = .12; see Table 5), simultaneous tests for general linear hypotheses using the *glht()* function of the *multcomp* package (Hothorn et al., 2008) showed that reading times for incorrectly marked concessions differed from all other conditions (in comparison to correctly marked concessions: β = .07, SE = .02, z = 3.25, p < .01; to correctly marked causes: β = .08, SE = .02, z = 3.82, p < .001; and to incorrectly marked causes: β = .06, SE = .02, z = −2.76, p < .05).

For non-native readers, adding *Marking* improved the random model's fit (χ^2 = 25.24, df = 1, p = 5.06^{e-07}). Further adding the *Relation* (main and interaction effects) did not (χ^2 = 2.71, df = 2, p = .26). For non-native readers, slower reading times were only apparent when Segment 7 was introduced by an incorrect connective, but independent of the relation conveyed.

For the native readers, in the wrap up region of the sentence (i.e., the response times to the verification question, see Figure 4), adding *Marking* improved the random model's fit (χ^2 =18.36, df = 1, p = 1.83^{e-05}). Further adding *Relation* (main and interaction effects) also did (30.14, df = 2, p = 2.85^{e-07}). As the interaction of *Marking* by *Relation* was not even close to the limit of significance (see Table 5 and Figure 4), we did not perform post-hoc comparisons.

For the non-native readers, adding *Marking* did improve the random models' fit (χ^2 = 28.43, df = 1, p = 9.73^{e-08}). Further adding *Relation* (main and interaction effects) also did (χ^2 =26.67, df = 2, p = 1.62^{e-06}). Post-hoc comparisons showed that only the condition of incorrectly marked concessions differed significantly from correctly marked concessions (β = .10, SE = .02, z = 5.19, p < .001), from correctly

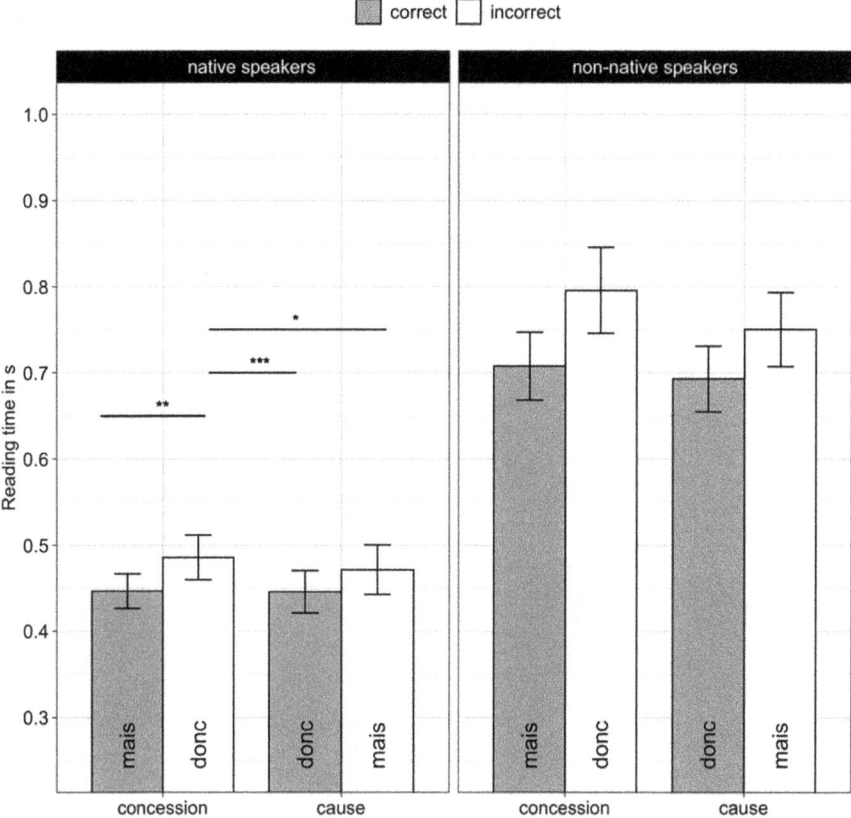

Figure 3: Second experiment: reading times for segment 7 for both native and non-native readers. Effect of marking for non-native readers, post-hoc comparisons indicated for native readers (CI of 95% as error bars.)

marked causes (β = .15, SE = .02, z = 7.5, p < .001), and from incorrectly marked causes (β = .12. SE = .02, z =−5.42, p < .001). Conversely, response times did not significantly differ whether the preceding causal sentences were correctly marked or not (β = .04, SE = .02, z = 2.02, p = .18).

7.6 Discussion

In this second experiment, we assessed the extent to which reading in L2 was affected when connectives provide a misleading instruction to interpret target sentences (i.e., creating incoherence). We expected, given that non-native readers

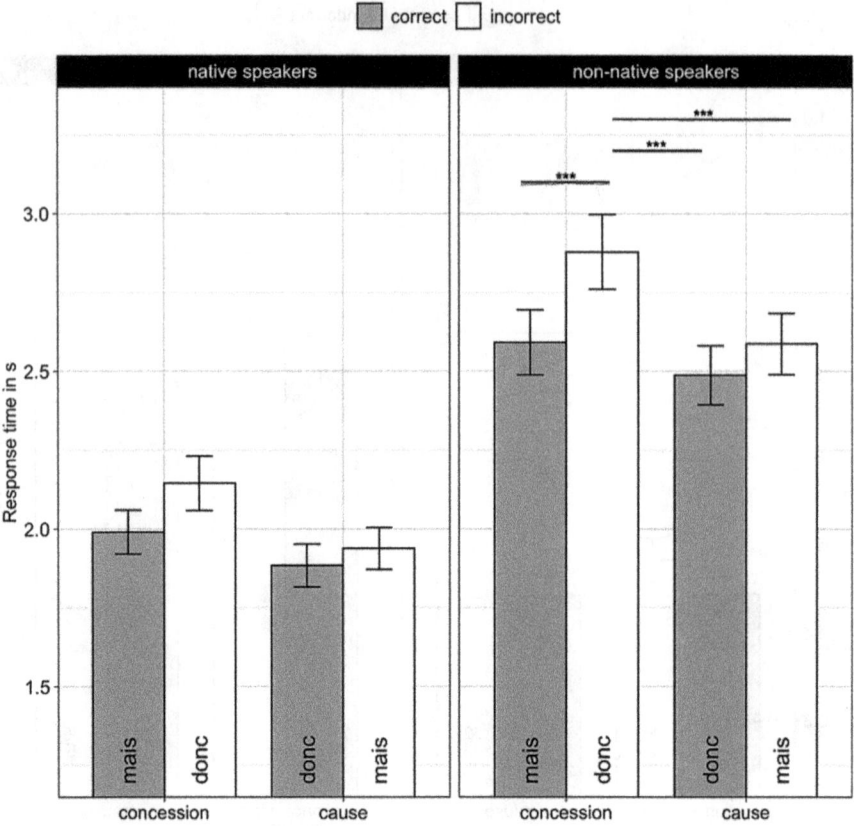

Figure 4: Second experiment: response times to the verification question for native and non-native readers. Post-hoc comparisons indicated (CI of 95% as error bars).

appeared to rely less on connectives in the first experiment, that we would observe less pronounced effects for an incorrect marking as well. As in Experiment 1, we measured once more the reading times of native and non-native readers of French for causal and concessive relations, that were however this time *correctly* and *incorrectly* marked by connectives.

In segment 5, we did not observe an effect of marking, which is not surprising, given that all sentences in this experiment were explicit and that different outcomes of the sentence were still possible at this time. In contrast, we observed in the pre-final segment (i.e., segment 6), that incorrectly marked sentences were read more slowly than correctly marked ones, showing that both native and non-native readers were affected by incoherence quite early during processing.

Our results indicate that, generally, native readers were affected by incorrectly marked relations (confirming Prediction 1). However, segments introduced by incorrectly marked concessive relations appeared to be slower to read, the highest disruptive effects being present for the final segment (confirming Prediction 3). It appears thus that processing disruptions due to incorrect marking emerges especially for more complex relations.

Non-native readers were affected by incorrectly marked sentences throughout the experiment. Interestingly, non-native readers were also affected by incorrectly marked concessions (confirming Prediction 3), yet showed only a somewhat delayed effect, that is, only response times to the verification questions were affected (confirming Prediction 2). Also, the incoherence due to incorrect marking for causal relations did only temporarily affect reading, as we did not observe any difference between incorrectly and correctly marked causes in the response times to the verification questions (confirming Prediction 2). These findings cannot be explained by a low level of language proficiency: Lextale scores indicated that all non-native readers were quite proficient. In addition, non-native readers were affected by incoherence quite early, showing that they read the sentences attentively.

In line with our first experiment, our results hint therefore to the conclusion that non-native readers rely less on connectives and focus more on the lexical content. Yet, these results should be taken with a pinch of salt, and that for two reasons. First, there was no true interaction effect of *Marking* by *Relation* when native readers responded to the verification questions, making it difficult to run the same post-hoc comparisons for both speaker groups. Secondly, as can be seen in the data visualizations, the (potential) effects look rather subtle (if they are true). Future research should assess if (and if so, how) incoherent sentences are generally resolved or rejected differently depending on the coherence relation.

Still, non-native readers were affected by incoherence introduced by incorrect connectives, thus indicating that they do process the connective, even if some effects were only apparent in later measures (i.e., response times to verification questions for sentences introduced by a concessive connective, and the final segment for sentences introduced by a causal connective).

8 General discussion

In this chapter, we tested the hypothesis that, in comparison to native readers, non-native readers would rely less on connectives while reading, as reading in L2 is a cognitively demanding task (Clahsen and Felser, 2006a; 2006b). Also, we argued that cognitive principles evidenced for native readers, such as a higher cognitive cost for concessive relations (Sanders et al. 1992) would also apply to reading in a L2. In order to substantiate these assumptions, we conducted two reading experiments with native and non-native readers in French.

The findings of both experiments consistently indicate that reading in L2 follows L1 cognitive principles, as non-native readers generally read concessive sentences more slowly than causal ones. This is in line with theoretical claims (e.g., Sanders, 2005) as well as experimental evidence (e.g., Köhne and Demberg, 2013) for native readers. Causal relations are read faster, due to their simpler structure (e.g., Sanders et al., 1992) and to the expectation that discourse unfolds in a causal manner (Sanders, 2005). As we observed similar reading patterns for non-native readers, we conclude that they were also able to infer the intended coherence relation. As such, our results replicate those obtained by Recio Fernández (2020) for Spanish, suggesting that complex coherence relations affect reading fluency in general, not only in specific languages.

Furthermore, our results suggest that non-native readers rely somewhat less on connectives than native readers. In our first experiment, non-native readers did not read implicit concessions differently than explicit concessions, although this condition strongly affected the reading fluency of native readers. In addition, in our second experiment, non-native readers showed only delayed or temporal disruptions for incorrectly used connectives. Given that we tested extremely frequent connectives, we still believe that non-native readers were able to retrieve the meaning of connectives, presumably even in an effortless manner (considering that they reacted to an incorrect marking already in Segment 6 in Experiment 2). Yet, the processing disruptions due to misleading connectives only occurred temporarily. A possible interpretation is that non-native readers construct coherence relations mainly based on lexical propositional content and rely in comparison to native readers less on functional cues (such as connectives). As a consequence, when the signal of the connective clashes with the overall meaning of a sentence, non-native readers tend to rely more on lexical and semantic content. In this regard, the stronger reliance on lexical cues might be the reason why non-native readers showed only little processing disruptions for implicitly marked concessions (Experiment 1).

This finding is in line with Papadopoulo and Clahsen (2003; see also Felser et al., 2003), who found that non-native and native readers differed in their parsing strategies of sentences containing complex relative clauses (such as "A man called the student of the teacher who seemed disappointed by the new educational system"). According to the authors, non-native readers might struggle to integrate different sources of information and are more strongly guided by lexical cues than by functional ones (Papadopoulou and Clahsen, 2003). Native speakers in contrast show greater ease integrating the meaning of functional cues and to align them with the lexical or thematic content. Our results support this interpretation with regards to connectives.

Importantly, higher reliance on lexical cues does not imply that L2 learners cannot benefit from connectives, nor that they fail to retrieve their meaning. Indeed, non-native readers were still affected by incoherence due to misleading connectives in Experiment 2, meaning that they were generally able to infer the meaning of the connectives. However, given that these processing disruptions did not persist, or emerged only at a later stage when reading target sentences, we believe that non-native readers were also able to easily ignore the misleading signal of connectives as they relied more on the linguistic content of the sentence.

A potential limitation of our experiments might be that our connectives could be considered polyfunctional (e.g., *mais* can also indicate a contrastive relation). Although we tested the very frequent and primary functions of the connectives (i.e., reducing the possibility that readers struggle to disambiguate their meaning), the polyfunctionality of the connectives tested might have had potential disruptive effects on reading fluency, as participants may have needed time to disambiguate the connective (i.e., choosing its correct meaning). While reading appears to be rather robust for native readers even for less frequent and polyfunctional connectives (Wetzel et al., 2022), especially non-native readers might be affected by their uses and would probably not detect when these connectives are used incorrectly. In this respect, the findings of Zufferey and Gygax (2017) already provide some indication for this claim, as they observed that German speaking non-native readers were unaffected by the loss of incoherence due to an insufficient mastery of the polyfunctional French connective *en effet* ('indeed'). Yet, it remains open whether the observed insufficient mastery of *en effet* is really due to its polyfunctionality or to other characteristics of this connective – such as orthographic similarity to other French connectives (*en fait* 'actually') –, or even to crosslinguistic inferences of a possible L3, such as English (*in fact* or *in effect*). In order to make solid assertions about the potential bias of polyfunctionality in our study, further research is needed.

Another potential limitation and, thus, a question worth investigating, is the impact of readers' profiles (for a discussion of individual differences, see Zufferey et al., this volume, chapter 4). In our experiments, the scope was to address how non-native readers react to incoherence due to missing or misleading connectives and whether this depended on the type of coherence relation. We did so, however, only under the condition that they understood the sentences and regardless of their language proficiency in French. Indeed, in order to address the correlation between the level of language proficiency of non-native readers and their reaction to incoherence, we should have assessed the linguistic profile of our participants in more detail.

Since there might be an additional interaction with the language proficiency in L2, we conclude that more research is needed to assess which dimensions of language proficiency can generally predict a better processing and understanding of discourse connectives and coherence relations.

Finally, research about the way non-native readers process discourse connectives could also take into account pragmatic functions, as for example the function of indicating subjective point of views in causality (e.g., Degand and Pander Maat, 2003). Hence, the findings presented in this chapter are a promising starting point to encourage future research on L2 acquisition and mastery, and more generally on the way non-native readers process discourse.

References

Ardal, Sten, Merlin Donald, Renata Meuter, Shannon Muldrew & Moira Luce. 1990. Brain responses to semantic incongruity in bilinguals. *Brain and Language* 39(2). 187–205. https://doi.org/10.1016/0093-934X(90)90011-5

Baayen, Harald. 2008. *Analyzing Linguistic Data: A Practical Introduction to Statistics Using R*. Cambridge: Cambridge University Press.

Bond, Kristi, Alison Gabriele, Robert Fiorentino & José A. Bañón. 2011. Individual differences and the role of the L1 in L2 processing: An ERP investigation. In Julia Herschensohn & Darren Tanner (eds.), *11th Generative Approaches to Second Language Acquisition (GASLA 2011)*, 17–29. Somerville: Cascadilla Proceedings Project.

Blumenthal-Dramé, Alice. 2021. The Online Processing of Causal and Concessive Relations: Comparing Native Speakers of English and German. *Discourse Processes* 58(7). 642–661. https://doi.org/10.1080/0163853X.2020.1855693

Brysbaert, Marc. 2013. Lextale_FR a fast, free, and efficient test to measure language proficiency in French. *Psychologica Belgica* 53(1). 23–37.

Clahsen, Harald & Claudia Felser. 2006a. Continuity and shallow structures in language processing. *Applied Psycholinguistics* 27(1). 107–126. https://doi.org/10.1017/S0142716406060206

Clahsen, Harald & Claudia Felser. 2006b. How native-like is non-native language processing? *Trends in Cognitive Sciences* 10(12). 564–570. https://doi.org/10.1016/j.tics.2006.10.002

Clerehan, Rosemary. 1995. Taking it down: Notetaking practices of L1 and L2 students. *English for specific purposes* 14(2). 137–155.

Cohen, Andrew & Jonathan Fine. 1978. Reading history in English: Discourse analysis and the experience of native and non-native readers. *Working Papers on Bilingualism* 16. 55–74.

Cohen, Andrew, Hilary Glasman, Phyllis Rosenbaum-Cohen, Jonathan Ferrara & Jonathan Fine. 1979. Reading English for Specialized Purposes: Discourse Analysis and the Use of Student Informants. *TESOL Quarterly* 13(4). 551–564. https://doi.org/10.2307/3586449

Crible, Ludivine, Mathis Wetzel & Sandrine Zufferey. 2021. Lexical and Structural Cues to Discourse Processing in First and Second Language. *Frontiers in Psychology* 12. 1–16. https://doi.org/10.3389/fpsyg.2021.685491

Crosson, Amy & Nonie Lesaux. 2013. Does knowledge of connectives play a unique role in the reading comprehension of English learners and English-only students? *Journal of Research in Reading* 36(3). 241–260. https://doi.org/10.1111/j.1467-9817.2011.01501.x

Degand, Liesbeth & Ted Sanders. 2002. The impact of relational markers on expository text comprehension in L1 and L2. *Reading and writing* 15(7). 739–757.

Degand, Liesbeth & Henk Pander Maat. 2003. A contrastive study of Dutch and French causal connectives on the Speaker Involvement Scale. In Arie Verhagen & Jeroen van den Weijer (eds), *Usage-Based Approaches to Dutch*, 105–199. Utrecht: LOT Netherlands. Graduate School of Linguistics. https://dspace.library.uu.nl/handle/1874/295389

Geva, Esther. 1986. Reading Comprehension in a Second Language: The Role of Conjunctions. *TESL Canada Journal* 3. 85–96. https://doi.org/10.18806/tesl.v3i0.996

Geva, Esther. 1992. The Role of Conjunctions in L2 Text Comprehension. *TESOL Quarterly* 26(4). 731–747. https://doi.org/10.2307/3586871

Geva, Esther. 2007. Second-Language Oral Proficiency and Second- Language Literacy. In Diane August & Timothy Shanahan (eds.), *Developing literacy in second-language learners: Report of the National Literacy Panel on Language-Minority Children and Youth*, 123–139. Oxfordshire: Routledge.

Goldman, Susan & John Murray. 1992. Knowledge of Connectors as Cohesion Devices in Text: A Comparative Study of Native-English and English-as-a-Second-Language Speakers. *Journal of Educational Psychology* 84(4). 504–519.

Granger, Sylviane & Stephanie Tyson. 1996. Connector usage in the English essay writing of native and non-native EFL speakers of English. *World Englishes* 15(1). 17–27. https://doi.org/10.1111/j.1467-971X.1996.tb00089.x

Felser, Claudia, Leah Roberts, Theodore Marinis & Rebecca Gross. 2003. The processing of ambiguous sentences by first and second language learners of English. *Applied Psycholinguistics* 24(3). 453–489. https://doi.org/10.1017/S0142716403000237

Hahne, Anja & Angela Friederici. 2001. Processing a second language: Late learners' comprehension mechanisms as revealed by event-related brain potentials. *Bilingualism: Language and Cognition* 4(2). 123–141. https://doi.org/10.1017/S1366728901000232

Hahne, Anja, Jutta Mueller & Harald Clahsen. 2006. Morphological Processing in a Second Language: Behavioral and Event-related Brain Potential Evidence for Storage and Decomposition. *Journal of Cognitive Neuroscience* 18(1). 121–134. https://doi.org/10.1162/089892906775250067

Halliday, Michael & Ruqaiya Hasan. 1976. *Cohesion in English*. London: Longman.

Hothorn, Torsten, Frank Bretz & Peter Westfall. 2008. Simultaneous Inference in General Parametric Models. *Biometrical Journal* 50(3). 346--363.

Jameel, Irum, Muhammad A. Mahmood, Zahida Hussain & Aleem Shakir. 2014. A corpus-based analysis of linking adverbials in Pakistani English. *International Journal of Linguistics* 6(3). 133–140.

Kanno, Yasuko. 1989. The Use of Connectives in English Academic Papers Written by Japanese Students. In Yukio Otsu (ed), *MITA Working Papers in Psycholinguistics* 2, 41–54. Tokyo: Keio University Tokyo. https://eric.ed.gov/?id=ED358721

Köhne, Judith & Vera Demberg. 2013. The time-course of processing discourse connectives. *Proceedings of the Annual Meeting of the Cognitive Science Society* 35(35). 2760–2765.

Komsta, Lukasz & Frederick Novomestky. 2015. *moments: Moments, cumulants, skewness, kurtosis and related tests*. R package version 0.14. https://CRAN.R-project.org/package=moments

Leedham, Maria & Guozhi Cai. 2013. Besides . . . on the other hand: Using a corpus approach to explore the influence of teaching materials on Chinese students' use of linking adverbials. *Journal of Second Language Writing* 22(4). 374–389. https://doi.org/10.1016/j.jslw.2013.07.002

Lei, Lei. 2012. Linking adverbials in academic writing on applied linguistics by Chinese doctoral students. *Journal of English for Academic Purposes* 11(3). 267–275. https://doi.org/10.1016/j.jeap.2012.05.003

Loureda, Óscar, Inès Recio Fernández, Adriana Cruz & Martha Rudka. this volume. Principles of discourse marking: An experimental approach of general and contrastive perspectives.

Marinis, Theodore, Leah Roberts, Claudia Felser & Harald Clahsen. 2005. Gaps in second language sentence processing. *Studies in Second Language Acquisition* 27(1). 53–78.

McLaughlin, Judith, Lee Osterhout & Albert Kim. 2004. Neural correlates of second-language word learning: Minimal instruction produces rapid change. *Nature Neuroscience* 7(7). 703–704. https://doi.org/10.1038/nn1264

Millis, Keith & Marcel Just. 1994. The influence of connectives on sentence comprehension. *Journal of memory and language* 33(1). 128–147.

Müller, Misha-Laura & Magali Mari. 2021. Definite Descriptions in the Light of the Comprehension vs. Acceptance Distinction: Comparing Self-Paced Reading with Eye-Tracking Measures. *Frontiers in Communication* 6. 1–17. https://doi.org/10.3389/fcomm.2021.634362

Murray, John. 1995. Logical connectives and local coherence. In Robert Lorch & Edward O'Brien (eds.), *Sources of cohesion in text comprehension*, 107–127. Hillsdale, NJ: Erlbaum.

Murray, John. 1997. Connectives and narrative text: The role of continuity. *Memory & Cognition* 25(2). 227–236. https://doi.org/10.3758/BF03201114

Myung-Jeong, Ha. 2016. Linking adverbials in first-year Korean university EFL learners' writing: A corpus-informed analysis. *Computer Assisted Language Learning* 29(6). 1090–1101. https://doi.org/10.1080/09588221.2015.1068814

Papadopoulou, Despina & Harald Clahsen. 2003. Parsing strategies in L1 and L2 sentence processing: A Study of Relative Clause Attachment in Greek. *Studies in Second Language Acquisition* 25(4). 501–528.

Peirce, Jonathan, Jeremy Gray, Sol Simpson, Michael MacAskill, Richard Höchenberger, Hiroyuki Sogo, Erik Kastman & Jonas Lindeløv. 2019. PsychoPy2: Experiments in behavior made easy. *Behavior Research Methods* 51(1). 195–203. https://doi.org/10.3758/s13428-018-01193-y

R Core Team. 2020. *R: A language and environment for statistical computing*. Vienna, Austria: R Foundation for Statistical Computing. https://www.R-project.org/

Recio Fernández, Inés. 2020. *The Impact of Procedural Meaning on Second Language Processing: A Study on Connectives*. PhD dissertation, Universität Heidelberg. https://doi.org/10.11588/heidok.00028641

Roberts, Craige. 2003. Uniqueness in Definite Noun Phrases. *Linguistics and Philosophy* 26(3). 287–350. https://doi.org/10.1023/A:1024157132393

Sabourin, Laura. 2003. *Grammatical gender and second language processing: An ERP study*. PhD dissertation, Rijksuniversiteit Groningen.

Sabourin, Laura & Laurie Stowe. 2008. Second language processing: When are first and second languages processed similarly? *Second Language Research* 24(3). 397–430. https://doi.org/10.1177/0267658308090186

Sanders, Ted, Wilbert Spooren & Leo Noordman. 1992. Toward a taxonomy of coherence relations. *Discourse Processes* 15(1). 1–35. https://doi.org/10.1080/01638539209544800

Sanders, Ted & Leo Noordman. 2000. The Role of Coherence Relations and Their Linguistic Markers in Text Processing. *Discourse Processes* 29(1). 37–60. https://doi.org/10.1207/S15326950dp2901_3

Sanders, Ted. 2005. Coherence, causality and cognitive complexity in discourse. In Michel Arnauage, Myriam Bras, Anne Le Draoulec & Laure Vieu (eds), *Proceedings/Actes SEM-05, First International Symposium on the exploration and modelling of meaning*, 105–114. Toulouse: University of Toulouse-le-Mirail.

Schumann, Jennifer, Sandrine Zufferey & Steve Oswald. 2020. The Linguistic Formulation of Fallacies Matters: The Case of Causal Connectives. *Argumentation* 35. 361–388. https://doi.org/10.1007/s10503-020-09540-0

Segal, Erwin, Judith Duchan & Paula Scott. 1991. The role of interclausal connectives in narrative structuring: Evidence from adults' interpretations of simple stories. *Discourse Processes* 14(1). 27–54. https://doi.org/10.1080/01638539109544773

Shi, Jiangang. 2017. A Corpus-Based Study of Contrastive/Concessive Linking Adverbials in Spoken English of Chinese EFL Learners. *Studies in Literature and Language* 14(2). 17–25. https://doi.org/10.3968/9273

Singh, Raj, Evelina Fedorenko, Kyle Mahowald & Edward Gibson. 2016. Accommodating Presuppositions Is Inappropriate in Implausible Contexts. *Cognitive Science* 40(3). 607–634. https://doi.org/10.1111/cogs.12260

Tazegül, Assiye Burgucu. 2015. Use, misuse and overuse of 'on the other hand': A corpus study comparing English of native speakers and learners. *International Online Journal of Education and Teaching (IOJET)* 2(2). 53–66.

Yuan, Boping. 2017. Can L2 sentence processing strategies be native-like? Evidence from English speakers' L2 processing of Chinese base-generated-topic sentences. *Lingua* 191–192. 42–64. https://doi.org/10.1016/j.lingua.2017.04.001

Weber-Fox, Christine & Helen Neville. 1996. Maturational Constraints on Functional Specializations for Language Processing: ERP and Behavioral Evidence in Bilingual Speakers. *Journal of Cognitive Neuroscience* 8(3). 231–256. https://doi.org/10.1162/jocn.1996.8.3.231

Wetzel, Mathis, Sandrine Zufferey & Pascal Gygax. 2020. Second Language Acquisition and the Mastery of Discourse Connectives: Assessing the Factors That Hinder L2-Learners from Mastering French Connectives. *Languages* 5. 1–26. https://doi.org/10.3390/languages5030035

Wetzel, Mathis, Ludivine Crible & Sandrine Zufferey. in press. Processing Clause-Internal Discourse Relations in a Second Language. A Case Study of Specifications in German and French. *Journal of Second Language Studies*.

Wetzel, Mathis, Sandrine Zufferey & Pascal Gygax. 2022. How Robust Is Discourse Processing for Native Readers? The Role of Connectives and the Coherence Relations They Convey. *Frontiers in Psychology* 13. 1–13. https://doi.org/10.3389/fpsyg.2022.822151

Zufferey, Sandrine & Pascal Gygax. 2017. Processing Connectives with a Complex Form-Function Mapping in L2: The Case of French "En Effet." *Frontiers in Psychology* 8. 1–11. https://doi.org/10.3389/fpsyg.2017.01198

Zufferey, Sandrine, Ekaterina Tckhovrebova, Mathis Wetzel & Pascal Gygax. this volume. Individual differences in the ability to master connectives: the importance of exposure to print.

Zoé Broisson and Liesbeth Degand

6 How egocentric is discourse marker use? Investigating the impact of speaker orientation and cognitive load on discourse marker production

Abstract: Language has often been described as produced 'for the hearer'. A case in point is the study of discourse markers (DMs), often presented as linguistic expressions that 'provide instructions to the hearer' (Hansen, 2006: 25). But what about their role for the speaker? Psycholinguistic research showing that speakers demonstrate egocentric behavior when their cognitive load increases (e.g. Keysar et al. 1998, Roßnagel 2000, Vogels et al. 2015) suggests that the lack of consideration for the role played by constraints on the speaker leaves us with an incomplete account of language production. To assess whether speakers use DMs with a communicative intention, i.e. purposefully and intentionally, this contribution reports on two experiments investigating the impact of speaker orientation (allocentric vs. egocentric) and cognitive load on the use of DMs. Results show that speakers use DMs both in the allocentric and egocentric conditions, but with systematic differences in terms of frequency, diversity and DM types. Cognitive load, however, does not seem to have any of the hypothesized effects on DM use.

Keywords: Discourse markers, cognitive load, speaker orientation, speech elicitation, spoken interaction, French

1 Introduction

Language is an inherent part of human communication. Despite its ubiquity in our everyday lives, using language for comprehension or production remains a demanding task from a cognitive and motor perspective (Levelt 1989: 1). As Tanenhaus (2013: 1) explains, understanding is difficult because it involves making inferences about a speaker's intentions on the basis of (sometimes vague) acoustic cues, and this under a limited time constraint. But equally taxing is the act of speaking, as it represents the engagement of our motor commands to allow the

Zoé Broisson, Université catholique de Louvain
Liesbeth Degand, Université catholique de Louvain, liesbeth.degand@uclouvain.be

https://doi.org/10.1515/9783110790351-006

translation of a complex conceptual piece of information into a series of sounds or hand gestures (MacDonald 2013: 2). From either perspective, it seems that attending to the competing demands of both the speaker and the hearer is crucial to achieve successful communication in any interaction.

While dividing the efforts involved in language use evenly between speaker and hearer would be optimal, it has been suggested that one of the two may well have the upper hand in the cognitive processing-driven organization of grammar. But whose processing considerations shape the way that we use language to express ourselves (see e.g. Pijpops et al. 2018)? Those of our interlocutors, or our own? Many theorists and researchers have attempted to answer this question, which continues to resonate in recent research (e.g. Debska and Raczaszek-Leonardi 2018, Galati et al. 2018, Hawkins 2004, Horton and Gerrig 2016, Jaeger and Tily 2011, Yoon and Brown-Schmidt 2018). Nevertheless, the scientific community shows little convergence on this issue. Classical theories of language assume that spoken conversation is only successful when it is collaborative (Grice 1975). For this reason, most scholars believe that it makes more sense to think that language is produced directly for the hearer: if speakers put effort into producing language that is tailored to their addressee, their own intentions will be understood better and more quickly, which in turn will reduce the overall effort required in communication (e.g. Achim, Achim and Fossard 2017, Yoon and Brown-Schmidt 2017, Brennan and Hanna 2009, Clark 1996). Next to the cooperation principle (Grice 1975), several theories and models of language production embrace this hearer-oriented or allocentric view, among them the audience design model (Blokpoel et al. 2012); common ground theory (Clark and Carlson 1981, 1982) or the perspective-taking model (Galinsky et al. 2008). Following Levelt's (1989) model for the speaker, these theories place audience design processes during the early stages of language production. However, certain researchers have challenged this assumption that audience design would be a systematic step in the planning process. In Barr and Keysar's (2006: 902) words, "the question is no longer whether speakers design their speech for their listeners, but how and when they do so." More precisely, the hearer-oriented speech planning would require far too many cognitive resources to be used efficiently in every day speech (e.g. Bard et al. 2000, Brown and Dell 1987, Horton and Keysar 1996). Instead, it has been suggested that speakers may well produce language as if it was intended for themselves, at first, and then, only if they have enough time or memory resources or strong enough cues (Vogels et al. 2020), adapt it to their addressee. Models and theories defending this speaker-oriented view comprise the generic- vs. partner-listener adaptation model (Dell and Brown 1991), the perspective monitoring and adjustment model (Horton and Keysar 1996, Keysar et al. 1998, 2000), and the dual-process model (Bard et al. 2000, Roßnagel 2000). These theories of language assume that the incorporation of common ground during language processing (be it production or comprehension) is controlled, optional and subject to restrictions on memory capacity, and that it takes place during the later stages of processing such as monitoring, rather than in the initial utterance plan. Concretely, when speech production is difficult (e.g. low working memory, high cognitive load), hearer-oriented (utterance) planning is impaired and might be supplanted by egocentric strategies (MacDonald 2013). These two divergent lines of thought have governed the field of language processing research from its development in the late 1980s until today.

In this contribution, we propose to focus on discourse markers as a linguistic category having the potential to offer an innovative vantage point on the issues tied to language production in terms of speaker vs. hearer orientation.

2 Discourse markers as a lens

Discourse markers (henceforth, DMs) are words or expressions such as well, you know, I mean, anyway that are highly frequent and widespread in language in use, and therefore have the potential to inform us about inherent aspects of human communication. While the related literature shows little agreement on the limits of the DM category as a linguistic class (see Introduction to the volume), authors do agree on the fact that one specific DM can fulfil more than one function, either simultaneously (multifunctionality) or in different discourse contexts (polyfunctionality) given their high degree of polysemy (Bolden 2015, Crible 2017b: 107, Fischer 2006). A great deal of research supports the view of DMs as a multi-faceted phenomenon, with a general consensus that DMs operate as a pragmatic category in the metalinguistic domain, beyond the syntactic and semantic aspects of discourse (Martín Zorraquino and Portolés Lázaro 1999: 4057). Regarding their role and function in language processing, it seems that DM studies are marked by a strong hearer-oriented bias, both in Coherence Theory and in Relevance Theory, the two main theoretical perspectives regarding the function of DMs.

The Coherence Theory approach to DMs defines their role as one that signals and explicitly embodies the coherence relations that bind the elements of discourse together, therefore facilitating its overall comprehension (Schiffrin 1987: 49, Taboada 2006: 567–568). However, this model has been criticized for relying too heavily on the textual aspect of discourse focusing on connectivity and therefore failing to account for other aspects of meaning that might be signalled differently than through relationality, such as ones expressing the speaker's attitude towards their discourse or issues of speaker-hearer management, mostly present in speech (see e.g. Maschler 2009, Crible and Cuenca 2017). The second leading theoretical approach to the functional definition of DMs is based on Sperber and Wilson's (1986) Relevance Theory. In terms of discourse analysis, this framework defines the role of DMs as one that facilitates the cognitive aspects of discourse processing. According to Blakemore (1987), DMs fulfil this function by signalling the relevance of an utterance within the discourse context, therefore making the processing efforts involved in the interpretative process of the speaker's intended meaning by the hearer less cognitively costly. In other words, this theoretical framework mostly focuses on the procedural meaning conveyed by DMs, which consists in providing metadiscursive instructions to ease the interpretation of information (Brinton 2008: 1, Hansen 2006: 25).

Thus, both of the "mainstream" theoretical frameworks describe DMs in terms of hearer benefit, their purpose being mostly understood as facilitating comprehension one way or another. Yet, a few scholars have suggested that DM use may also benefit speakers in some ways, such as by facilitating their own integration of common ground (Fuller 2003, Jucker and Smith 1998), or by 'adding some spatiality to the temporality of speech' (Crible 2018: 48) and allowing both speaker and hearer to project or backtrack their attention along the flux of speech. As far as processing is concerned, the study of DMs has shown that their use reflects the underlying processes of language planning, as they constitute major indicators of (dis)fluency besides other linguistic signals of fluency and disfluency ('fluencemes' in Götz' (2013) words), such as filled or unfilled pauses and repetitions (Crible, Degand and Gilquin 2017). However, these accounts remain scarce and the dominant paradigm in DM research continues to follow a bias towards the hearer, made evident by the majority of psycholinguistic studies investigating a restricted set of DMs (mainly connectives) and their impact on comprehension, and this mainly in non-interactive contexts (e.g. Brehm-Jurish 2005, Canestrelli, Mak and Sanders 2013, Sanders and Noordman 2000, Traxler, Bybee and Pickering 1997).

One might argue that this approach fails to account for one of the key aspects of language by not considering the role of DMs vis-à-vis production. Indeed, a closer look at results from corpus analyses reveals evidence suggestive of an 'easy-on-the-speaker' use (MacDonald 2013). For instance, DM polyfunctionality could be interpreted as benefitting the speaker by allowing him or her to (re) use the same forms in different contexts to express different functions, keeping them easily retrievable. In a similar logic, DM multifunctionality could allow the speaker to mitigate planning demands by using one form to perform several functions at once. Finally, a phenomenon known as underspecification (Spooren 1997), that is 'the mismatch between a discourse marker's semantics and its enriched interpretation in context (e.g *and* in a contrastive relation)' (Crible et al.

2019: 142), could well be used as a mechanism to reduce processing costs if we consider that speakers allocate underspecified meanings to ambiguous DMs to avoid making further disambiguation steps, in that they do not develop a detailed mental representation of the relation expressed by the DM but rather stop at one that is 'good enough' to save resources (Crible et al. 2019, Ferreira, Bailey and Ferraro 2002, Frisson 2009, Irmer 2011). This type of corpus evidence, however indirect, highlights the potential for more related work in the area of language processing to investigate if and how the functional-pragmatic DM category could be used in ways that are not always communicative in nature but rather represent speaker strategies. This, in turn, would further inform us about how humans may mitigate the demands of utterance planning, and about the extent to which these impact speech production and speakers' capacity to adapt to their addressee.

In this study, we will try to find out whether DMs are (primarily) used as a signal to facilitate the addressee's comprehension and/or as a trace of the speaker's production difficulties. This research question is addressed through one primary research question: What is the impact of allocentric v. egocentric speaker orientation on DM production? And a secondary research question: What is the impact of cognitive load on DM production, especially in the allocentric condition? More concretely, do (allocentric) speakers behave more egocentrically when put under augmented cognitive load?

3 Rationale of the study and hypotheses

To assess whether speakers use DMs with a deliberate communicative intention, this chapter proposes to investigate the use of discourse markers in a set of two experiments manipulating speaker orientation (egocentric vs. allocentric), in one of two cognitive load conditions (high vs. low). The expected outcome of this experiment is to identify potential speaker-oriented DMs and potential listener-oriented DMs. The cognitive load manipulation will aim at furthering the results obtained by assessing whether, in the allocentric experiment, high cognitive load elicits the use of more speaker-oriented DMs, while low or normal cognitive load elicits the use of more listener-oriented DMs. Thus, we expect an interaction between the two variables, such that under high cognitive load speakers become more egocentric, using less listener-oriented DMs in the allocentric condition. The strong assumption underlying this design is that advancing knowledge about how DMs work and why speakers use them will in turn shed more light on who between the speaker or hearer ultimately has the upper hand in the processing-driven shaping of grammar.

In this respect, the following two research questions will be addressed:

- RQ1. Is there a difference between the allocentric and the egocentric output, in terms of DM density, diversity and functional use?

Obviously, we expect to find more listener-oriented DMs in the allocentric task, and more speaker-oriented DMs in the egocentric task. Yet, what characterizes these two types of DMs is not clearly established. Based on the literature review, we expect to find higher density and lower diversity of DMs in the output of the allocentric task than in that of the egocentric task, due to the naturally demanding nature of the linguistic processing inherent to interactive communication (Levelt 1989) and the strong link between DMs and disfluency due to processing pressure (Crible 2018, Crible, Degand and Gilquin 2017, Götz, 2013), which is characterized by the increased use of DMs and the repetition of the same forms (Crible 2018: 87). In this (high-pressure) interactive context, speakers can be hearer-oriented, dedicating sufficient resources to the needs of the listeners, or may turn to more egocentric behaviour, if the cognitive demands of the communicative task are too high. Our assumption is that speakers will be able to dedicate sufficient resources to their hearers under "normal cognitive load" in the allocentric task. Therefore, we expect that speakers will use fewer polysemous (different meanings) DMs, because polysemy is known to be harder to process (Frisson 2009, Rice et al. 2019), and is therefore more taxing on the hearer. Also, given the obvious influence of the communicative situation on DM use, we expect to find more interpersonal (speaker-hearer management) DMs in the allocentric condition. In terms of meaning relations, it is also expected to find more markers of reformulation, specification and contrast of information in the allocentric task since these have been identified as representative of discourse functions geared towards the hearer's needs (Ciabarri 2013, Cuenca 2003, Cuenca and Bach 2007). Spelling out the hypotheses for RQ1, these are:

- H1: There is a higher density of DMs in the allocentric task than in the egocentric task
- H2: There is a lower diversity of DMs in the allocentric task than in the egocentric task
- H3: Speakers use fewer polysemous DMs in the allocentric condition than in the egocentric task (under "normal cognitive load")
- H4: There are more interpersonal DMs in the allocentric task than in the egocentric task.
- H5: Speakers use more DMs with a hearer-benefitting meaning (reformulation, specification, contrast) in the allocentric task than in the egocentric task

In addition to these specific hypotheses, we will sketch a distributional picture of DM use in the two speaking conditions in order to find out which DMs, if any, can be considered as indices of speaker v. listener orientation.

- RQ2. Is there a difference between the high and low cognitive load conditions, in terms of DM density, diversity and functional use?

The general hypothesis for the second research question is that increased cognitive load should make speakers in the allocentric condition more egocentric. Yet, given the relation between DMs and (dis)fluency (cf. supra), it is expected that a higher density and a lower diversity of DMs will be found in the high cognitive load condition, both in the egocentric and in the allocentric condition. In addition, for a similar reason, DMs performing 'symptom' rather than 'signal' uses (i.e. those with a monitoring or repairing function), in the words of Crible (2018: 53), are expected to be found in larger proportions in the high cognitive load condition. Finally, DMs that display a high degree of polysemy are expected to be found in larger proportions in the high cognitive load condition, in line with their previously hypothesized 'easy-on-the-speaker' use. The hypotheses for RQ2 are spelled out as follows:

- H6: There is a higher density of DMs in the high cognitive load cognition than in the low cognitive load condition
- H7: There is a lower diversity of DMs in the high cognitive load cognition than in the low cognitive load condition
- H8: Speakers use more polysemous DMs in the high cognitive load cognition than in the low cognitive load condition.

To answer the two research questions presented above and test their related hypotheses, a usage-based, empirical approach to DMs in elicited speech will be employed, therefore requiring a set of experimental data as working material. These data along with the methods employed in their collection and analysis are detailed in the following section.

4 Experimental design

In this study, speech was elicited from participants performing two speaking tasks carried out consecutively as part of an experiment in which we manipulated two variables, the cognitive load of both participants as well as speaker orientation. In this design, the dependent variable is the DM output produced by participants.

In the first task, two participants had to jointly assemble a tangram puzzle. The dialogic and collaborative nature of this task determined its orientation as allocentric, that is centred on the addressee. One participant, the director, had to give blind verbal instructions to another participant, the matcher. The perspectives of the director and the matcher were dissociated by giving access to the puzzle silhouette to the director only. This was done in an attempt to trigger the use of potential hearer-oriented DMs as part of perspective-adaptation mechanisms. In this task, cognitive load was manipulated by having both participants conduct a (secondary) verbal memory task while assembling the puzzle. The use of dual tasks is an established method for eliciting cognitive load which researchers have been employing for a few decades. In this study, a verbal rather than visual dual task (e.g. Rosa and Arnold 2017) was selected to ensure that it would interfere with memorizing processes or attending to discourse information (tied to the phonological loop of working memory, cf. Baddeley et al. 2020) rather than with visually attending to the geometrical shapes and the silhouette of the tangram puzzle (tied to the visuo-spatial sketchpad of working memory). This design choice was inspired by Vogels et al. (2015), who followed recommendations from a study testing the effectiveness of various dual tasks on verbal, visual and spatial working memory conducted by Kellog, Olive and Piolat (2007).

In the second task, all participants had to retell themselves the instructions to the puzzle they had solved (or had attempted to solve) in the first task, using verbal cues only. The monologic nature of this task determined its orientation as egocentric, that is centred on the self. In this task, no perspective difference was therefore induced. However, cognitive load was manipulated by asking participants who were in the high cognitive load condition to recall these instructions from memory, a method previously employed in Roßnagel (2000). Participants in the low cognitive load condition were presented with the assembled puzzle while giving their instructions. Since the cognitive load manipulation for the egocentric task was very different from that for the allocentric task, the comparison between the effects of cognitive load in the allocentric and egocentric tasks may be hard to interpret.[1] Therefore, comparisons will be made only within each speaker orientation task. Our focus will be mainly on the allocentric task where we expect a clear impact of the cognitive load manipulation, with the cognitive load manipulation in the egocentric task serving mainly as a control.

---

[1] We would like to sincerely thank one of the reviewers for pointing out this potential methodological flaw in our data.

4.1 Participants

Data was collected from twenty-four participants (12 male, 12 female) recruited as acquaintances of the first author. As a result of this sampling method, all participants knew each other to some degree. This is a limitation to the present study, due to the established negative effect of the 'closeness-communication bias' on humans' ability to take their addressee's perspective into account (cf. Savitsky et al. 2011). However, since the degree of closeness was relatively stable across participants, all being either friends, partners or family members, we believe the bias was similar across all pairs. This method of participant selection was chosen due to its convenience. All participants reported being native speakers of Belgian French, and all were residents of the Hainaut province. Their age ranged from 19 to 55 years old (μ=28.9, s.d.=12.8, Md=24), although younger speakers between the ages of 19 and 26 were preferred due to the known effect of age on the mitigation of demands created by dual tasks (cf. Kemper et al. 2009), and therefore formed the majority of the sample (n=17, 70.83%). Half of the participants acted as directors in the first speaking task, and the other half acted as matchers. Half of the speakers (n=12, 8 males, 4 females) performed the elicitation tasks under high cognitive load conditions, while the other half (n=12, 4 males, 8 females) performed the tasks under low/normal cognitive load conditions.

4.2 Materials

The experimental items consisted of a set of seven printed color-coded geometrical shapes commonly used to solve tangram puzzles, and two puzzle silhouettes alternatively given to participants, one representing a cat, as shown in Figure 1, and the other one representing a butterfly. Participants were also provided with a written copy of instructions to keep with them at all times, a bell which they could ring to call the experimenter into the room if a (substantial) problem arose, as well as a timer.

4.3 Procedure

The recordings took place in a quiet but non-acoustically treated room premised at a private home. Before taking part in the experiment, participants were asked to provide information about their age and first language, and to sign a consent.

At the beginning of the first speaking task, participants were randomly assigned to the role of director or matcher. They were told that the experiment was investi-

Figure 1: Cat tangram puzzle (silhouette on the left, coloured solution on the right).

gating the way pairs of friends, partners or family members gave each other verbal instructions in problem-solving settings. For this purpose, they would have to keep communicating as much as possible during the task and avoid blanks. The experimenter gave detailed instructions about how the two phases of the experiment would proceed, and gave each participant an individual written copy of those instructions in case it was needed for future reference. Then, the experimenter explained how tangram puzzles could be assembled. After participants had time to ask questions, they were seated at a table opposite each other. A blind attached to the table prevented participants from establishing visual contact and had participants communicate purely verbally. Finally, the experiment could begin and participants were given ten minutes to solve the tangram puzzle together. The experimenter exited the room and gave a signal to the participants to start solving the puzzle.

In the high cognitive load group, participants were each given a laptop at the same time as they were being seated at the table. Then, the experimenter gave them additional instructions and demonstrated how the secondary verbal memory task was to be performed. A questionnaire created on the www.typeform.com platform was loaded onto each laptop. As participants completed the questionnaire, words such as MOT and LOT (French for 'word' and 'prize', respectively), chosen for their close graphic and phonetic representations, were continually prompted onto the screen throughout the experiment. Every time a new word appeared, participants were asked whether it was the same as the first word presented to them at the start of the experiment and had to press a 'Yes' or 'No' button. Participants did not receive feedback on their answers. These dual-task stimuli were an adaptation of Vogels et al. (2015). It was designed in such a way to have participants keep a verbal item in their working memory at all times, thereby burdening it.

After having completed the first part of the experiment, participants were given a five minutes break. Then, they orally received detailed instructions about the second speaking task from the experimenter, and once again were given a hardcopy. In this phase of the experiment, participants were told they would be recorded while verbally retelling themselves how to solve the puzzle they had just assembled with their partner, as if they would need to use these instructions (and these instructions exclusively) to assemble it again in three months' time. Participants were given a time limit of ten minutes to complete this task, and had access to the tangram puzzle and its assembled solution the whole time. After having left time for both participants to ask questions, the experimenter and one of the participants left the room, and gave the other participant a signal that he or she could start recording themselves and started the timer. Once the first person was finished, he or she rang the bell to call back the experimenter into the room (as previously instructed). Then, the other participant repeated the protocol by themselves.

In the high cognitive load condition, participants were given an additional five minutes to remember how to assemble the puzzle after being given the instructions about the task, and before beginning to record themselves. Again, they were given a time limit of ten minutes to complete the task, although this time they did not have access to the puzzle nor its solution while recording themselves, but rather had to recall the instructions entirely from memory.

4.4 Data set

The speech data collected through the elicitation tasks was compiled as a corpus, which we will onwards refer to using the acronym TACO, which stands for 'TAngram COrpus', in reference to the main topic represented in its contents. TACO can be defined as a synchronic, monolingual Belgian French corpus of elicited speech displaying a low degree of formality collected in the year 2018 in Belgium. It contains 36 oral texts, has a total duration of almost 3 hours (2:53:17s), and comprises 25,473 word tokens. TACO is (approximately) balanced between both conditions: the high cognitive load (HCL) component makes up 53% of the corpus with 13,406 word tokens, and the low cognitive load (LCL) component makes up 47% of the corpus with 12,067 word tokens.

Each text composing TACO was transcribed orthographically in standard French (retaining standard contracted forms only) and aligned to its corresponding audio file using the annotation software Praat (v. 6.1) (Boersma and Weenink 2019). The following technical guidelines were used for the transcription: individual tiers were created for each speaker and assigned an ID created using the following structure: [Speaker's initials (2 letters) + Sex (M, F) + Age], e.g. VEF55 [VE + F + 55]. Any instance of a person's name was anonymized and transcribed either as 'NAME' or using the appropriate participant ID. Silent pauses were marked by an underscore ('_'), filled pauses were transcribed as *euh, euhm, hum, m/, mm/, h/, pf/, hm, tch/, ts/*, or FP if their articulation was ambiguous, and both types of pauses were transcribed within their own boundaries (i.e. separate from spoken language). Truncations were marked by a forward slash ('/'), and any unclear text was marked as 'UNCLEAR'. The textual output of each transcript was extracted from Praat's .textgrid format into a .txt file using a Praat script ('save_conversation_tiers_as_text_file.praat') written by Lennes (2019).

Table 1 provides an overview of the data set of the transcribed contents in TACO. All 24 participants performed both the allocentric and the egocentric tasks, either in the high or the low cognitive load condition, and either as director or matcher in the allocentric task.

Table 1: Overview of contents in TACO.

TASK	COGNITIVE LOAD	TEXTS	WORD TOKENS	DURATION
Dialogic (allocentric)	High	6	9511	59:26s
	Low	6	8169	53:43s
Monologic (egocentric)	High	12	3898	30:41s
	Low	12	3895	29:27s
Total		36	25473	2:53:17s

Examples (1) and (2) illustrate the kind of speech available in the data set, with identified DMs marked in bold.

Allocentric High Cognitive Load condition

(1) SAF24: **bon alors** euh le carré mauve tu le places sur sa pointe en face de toi
'well then uhm the purple square you put it on its tip in front of you'

ASF24: **okay** ouais
'okay yeah'

SAF24: **okay**
okay

ASF24: ouais
'yeah'

SAF24: **ensuite** attends je teste non merde c'est pas ça euh
'then wait I test it out no shit that's not it uhm'

ASF24: **ben limite** essaye de me décrire la forme
'well maybe try to describe the form to me'

SAF24: ouais c'est un chat
yeah it's a cat

Egocentric High Cognitive Load condition

(2) COM19: **donc** euh je commence par le parallélogramme qui se met euh en bas à droite **ensuite** je fais la tête du chat **donc** la tête du chat c'est euh le carré **mais** qui se met euh en biais **donc** de manière à former quasi un losange **puis** j'assemble les deux petits triangles sur le carré de manière à faire les deux euhm les deux oreilles **puis** je reviens au parallélogramme

'so uhm I start with the parallelogram that is put uhm at the bottom on the right then I make the head of the cat so the head of the cat that is uhm the square but that is put uhm across so in such a way to form nearly a diamond then I join the two small triangles on the square in order to make the two uhm the two ears then I come back to the parallelogram'

4.5 DM identification and annotation

The full annotation of the TACO data was carried out in two consecutive steps by a single annotator for the whole corpus. To ensure the validity of the annotation, Kappa statistics (Cohen, 1960) were computed as intra-annotator reliability measures for each level of disambiguation. In this section, their results and the procedure involved in each of the annotation steps are described in more detail.

The first step of the annotation process consisted in the chronological and manual identification of DM candidates in the TACO corpus. This was done by carefully reading and listening to the sound-aligned transcripts using the EXMARaLDA software (Schmidt and Wörner 2012). The identification of DMs was carried out using the following open-class definition of DMs taken from Crible (2018) and a set of additional restrictive criteria added by the same author in Crible and Zufferey (2015):

DMs are a grammatically heterogeneous, syntactically optional, polyfunctional type of pragmatic marker. Their specificity is to function on a metadiscursive level as procedural cues to constrain the interpretation of the host unit in a co-built representation of on-going discourse. They do so by either signaling a discourse relation between the host unit and its context, making the structural sequencing of discourse segments explicit, expressing the speaker's meta-comment on their phrasing, or contributing to the speaker-hearer relationship.

The restrictive criteria further applied to this definition in view of improving its replicability are the following, quoted directly from Crible and Zufferey (2015: 4):
- [strict] syntactic optionality: their removal does not alter the grammaticality of the utterance;

- scope over syntactically and semantically independent units: there must be a finite or implicit predicate, which excludes relative and non-finite clauses, and nominal phrases except when these are acting as a-verbal predicates;
- high degree of grammaticalization: fixed multi-word units, frequently used (not idiosyncratic) and semantically non-compositional;
- incompatibility with membership in the categories of fillers, interjections, response signals, epistemic parentheticals, general extenders, tag questions and editing terms.

The combined use of the definition and the criteria was tested on a recording (HCL_SAAS_ALLO) representing approximately 7% of the whole TACO corpus, at three weeks' interval. It allowed for the identification of 242 DMs with a Kappa value of 0.935, which is indicative of almost perfect agreement according to Landis and Koch (1977).

The second and final step of the annotation process consisted in the chronological and manual classification of the previously identified DMs using Crible and Degand's (2019) functional annotation model. Of particular interest in this model are the two independent dimensions of analysis that aim at accounting for the full functional spectrum of DMs. On the one hand, DMs are coded according to the discourse domain in which they work, corresponding more or less to the communicative intention of the speaker, what he or she aims at achieving through their contribution. Four domains are distinguished, depending on whether a given DM is used to link events in the world (ideational domain), to link mental states or attitudes (rhetorical domain), to structure the discourse (sequential domain) or to manage the speaker-hearer interaction (interpersonal domain). Independently from the domain annotation, DMs also receive a discourse function corresponding to the specific meaning of the marker in the given context (one of fifteen functions among which [consequence], [addition], [temporal], [specification], [contrast], etc.). Theoretically, any function can combine with any of the four domains giving rise to sixty (4x15) possible domain-function combinations visualized in Table 2. Cross-linguistic corpus studies have indeed demonstrated that many functions can combine with the four domains, but that languages differ in the ways DMs may actually express specific combinations (Degand, Broisson, Crible, and Grzech 2022).

Given the theoretical weight of the combinations made possible between domains and functions to encompass DM poly- and multifunctionality, the annotation was carried out on a DM-by-DM basis following the operationalisations for domains and functions in Crible and Degand (2019). No double tags were used as part of the disambiguation method. Once again, the reliability of the annotation was tested, this time by coding a sample of 250 DMs (10% of the whole DM

Table 2: Crible and Degand's (2019) functional annotation scheme.

DOMAINS	[Ideational] [Rhetorical] [Sequential] [Interpersonal]
FUNCTIONS	[Addition] [Alternative] [Cause] [Concession] [Condition] [Consequence] [Contrast] [Hedging] [Monitoring] [Temporal] [Specification] [Agreeing] [Disagreeing] [Topic] [Quoting]

sample). Kappa scores of 0.84 and 0.70 were obtained for domains and functions respectively, indicating almost perfect and substantial levels of agreement.

Following the completion of the annotation procedure, the data were processed using MS Excel and R Studio (RStudio Team, 2015) for subsequent analyses. The R packages 'vcd' and 'dplyr', were used to carry out chi-squared tests. Visual representations of the data were produced with the packages 'ggplot2'. Measures of intra-rater agreement were computed using Geertzen's (2012) online kappa calculator.

5 Analysis and discussion

5.1 Discourse markers frequency (density)

Table 3 presents an overview of the DMs frequency in the TACO data. A total number of 2700 DMs were identified.

Table 3: Raw and relative frequencies (ptw) of DMs by speaking task and cognitive load condition

	ALLOCENTRIC TASK			EGOCENTRIC TASK			TOTAL
	High	Low	High+Low	High	Low	High+Low	
Corpus size (words)	9,511	8,169	17,680	3,895	3,898	7,793	25,473
DMs	1,158	981	2,139	284	277	561	**2,700**
ptw	121.75	120.08	120.98	72.91	71.06	71.99	**105.99**

Zooming in on the figures reported in Table 3 for each subcorpus of TACO, two general observations can be made. The first concerns the much higher overall relative frequency of DMs in the allocentric task (120.98 ptw) than in the egocentric task (71.99 ptw). This difference was found to be statistically significant by using a log-likelihood test (LL=131.76, p<0.01) (Brezina 2018: 84–85). On the basis of the reported frequencies and the significant log-likelihood test, we may thus confirm H1 (RQ1): speakers use more DMs in the allocentric task than in the egocentric task, both in raw and in relative frequencies.

The second observation to be made concerns the apparent stability of relative frequencies found for DMs across cognitive load conditions, in both the allocentric (high cognitive load: 121.75 ptw, low cognitive load: 120.08 ptw) and the egocentric (high cognitive load: 72.91 ptw, low cognitive load: 71.06 ptw) task. Indeed, the differences between the frequencies reported in each condition were not found to be statistically significant, whether it be in the allocentric task (LL=0.1, p>0.05) or its egocentric counterpart (LL=0.09, p>0.05). These results contradict H6 (RQ2), according to which a higher density of DMs would be found in the high cognitive load condition of each task, due to their established link to planning pressure as markers of disfluency.

5.2 Discourse markers diversity

Moving onto diversity, comparing the type-token ratios (TTR) in the different speaking tasks is a way to uncover to what extent the speaking situation influences the number of different DM types speakers use. It is known, however, that TTR is a simple measure of lexical density which is sensitive to text length, in that it decreases when a text becomes longer and the same words are used again (Brezina, 2018: 58). As a consequence, its reliability can be questioned when texts of different lengths are compared against each other, as it is the case here with the allocentric and the egocentric speaking tasks. As Figure 2 shows, texts produced in the allocentric task and those produced in the egocentric task possess different typical lengths, as characterized by the key values of their distributions. This may be due to a number of factors, including how fast pairs of participants solved the puzzle in the collaborative task (3 out of 12 pairs of speakers [25%] finished under their allocated time limit of ten minutes), the role held by speakers in the collaborative task (texts produced by directors have a mean length of 1,003.92 words, whereas that of matcher texts is 469.42 words), and potentially the fact that giving instructions to oneself simply requires a lot less time and effort than it does to give instructions to someone else, as the chance of misunderstanding is lifted (although given the same time limit to perform both tasks, most speakers completed the egocentric task in under three minutes, M=2.5'). In addition, since the egocentric speaking task systematically took place after the allocentric task, we cannot exclude that the repetition of two similar tasks impacted on the number of words produced as previous studies have shown that repetition of (conversational) tasks leads to lesser word use (e.g. Clark and Wilkes-Gibbs 1986).

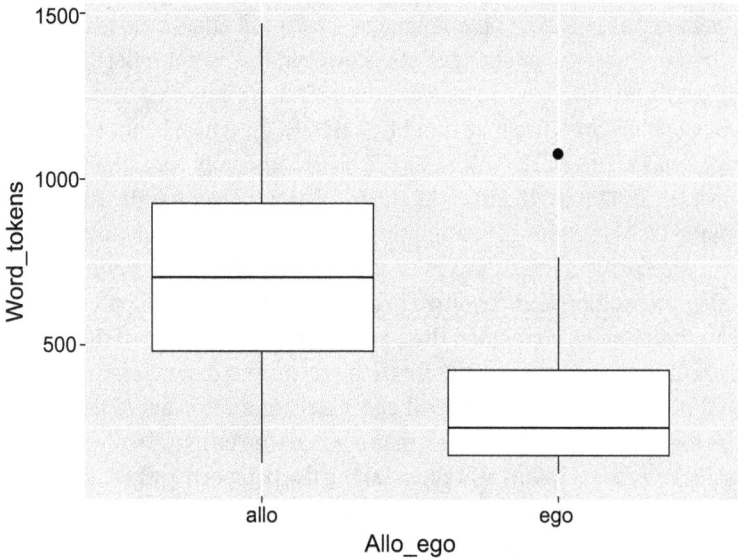

Figure 2: Dispersion of text length (in words), per speaker per speaking task.

Since texts produced by matchers in the allocentric task and texts produced in the egocentric task have relatively more comparable lengths (M=469.42 for the matcher group, M=324.71 for the egocentric task), we resampled the data set according to this criterion of individual text length. Table 4 displays the type-to-ken ratios for the different speaking tasks on the basis of the restriction applied to the allocentric dataset.

Table 4: Type-token ratio of DMs per speaking task (resampled data set) and cognitive load condition.

	ALLOCENTRIC TASK			EGOCENTRIC TASK			TOTAL
	High	Low	High+Low	High	Low	High+Low	
Types	46	41	54	32	34	47	56
TTR	11.5	11.11	7.02	11.27	12.27	8.38	8.19

The figures in Table 4 show that as expected (H2, RQ1), DMs are used less diversely by speakers in the allocentric task (TTR=7.02) than in the egocentric task (TTR=8.38), although the difference between the two is very slight. This is interesting, as in previous work Crible (2018: 87) noted a sharp TTR gap between the more monologic and prepared speech and those involving a higher degree of interaction and a lower degree of preparation. The latter are assumed to entail a greater pressure on working memory as speakers plan language – as is the allocentric task here – and thereby trigger the reuse of similar DMs. However, this is not reflected by the present findings. As for the cognitive load manipulation, we expected a lower diversity of DMs in the high cognitive load condition (H7, RQ2), which is not confirmed in the allocentric task (HCL: TTR=11.5; LCL: TTR=11.11), and only very slightly in the egocentric task (HCL: TTR=11.27, LCL: TTR=12.27). Given the similarities shared by the two speaking tasks in terms of content (instructions on a tangram puzzle), any differences (or similarities) in DM diversity are likely to be due to the manipulations of speaker orientation and cognitive load applied during the data collection process. It can therefore be concluded that, as shown by the results of the experiment so far, speakers appear to use DMs for their addressees more than they do for themselves, although both allocentric and egocentric motives seem to drive their use, given the high density of DMs overall in the egocentric output. While speakers use DMs significantly more frequently when taking the perspective of an addressee is required for communication, the increased burden this entails on the speakers does not seem to prevent them from varying their use of these discourse-structuring devices. Whether they use the same or different DM types, and for what functions, will be investigated throughout the following sections.

5.3 Discourse markers distribution: Descriptive account

Before turning to the hypotheses concerning the use of polysemous DMs in the different conditions (H3, H8), we want to give an overview of the types of DMs used, focussing on their frequency as a potential characteristic of speaker-oriented v. listener-oriented DMs.

As mentioned above, the design of the experiment carried out for the present purposes resulted in an imbalance of data between the allocentric and egocentric subcorpora of TACO, due to their corresponding speaking tasks producing different amounts of output (17,689 words vs. 7,793 words, respectively). As the present study focuses on a highly frequent and pervasive phenomenon, viz. DMs, this shortcoming arguably has limited impact on the normalized frequencies and diversity information presented thus far. However, in order to prevent this bias from influencing type and function distributions, and for comparability purposes, the further analyses will be carried out on a resampled dataset comprising a (near-)equal number of DMs in all conditions. This balanced dataset was obtained by matching the number of DMs in the lowest category (n=561), the egocentric task, with that of the highest category, the allocentric task. To do this, an equal number of DMs (n=24) were randomly selected from the allocentric output of each of the 24 speakers represented in the dataset (n=576), and compiled with the existing egocentric output. The new dataset presented in Table 5 comprises 1137 DMs of 66 unique types.

Table 5: Distribution of DMs in the balanced sample, per speaking task and cognitive load condition.

	ALLOCENTRIC TASK	EGOCENTRIC TASK	Total
High cognitive load	288	284	572
Low cognitive load	288	277	561
Total	**576**	**561**	**1,137**

The following sections describe the peculiarities of this frequency distribution and its variations across experimental conditions.

5.3.1 Discourse markers types and frequency bands

To investigate a potential interaction between frequent vs. infrequent DMs and speaker orientation and/or cognitive load, all 66 DM types found in the dataset were sorted into four groups or 'bands' of frequency, identified as apparent gaps between clusters of DMs displaying similar frequency ranges in the data. The four groups classify DM frequency as 'very high' (>169 tokens, n=2 types, *donc* 'so', *et* 'and'), 'high' (49–81 tokens, n=5 types, *mais* 'but', *ensuite* 'then', *okay*, *alors* 'well, then', *voilà* 'that's it'), 'moderate' (6–35 tokens, n=22 types, e.g. *ben* 'well', *en fait* 'in fact', *hein* 'right', *maintenant* 'now', *tu vois* 'you see'), . . .), and 'low' (<6 tokens, n=35 types, e.g. *puisque* 'since', *par consequent* 'as a consequence', *écoute* 'listen', *par contre* 'in contrast', . . .). The full list of DM types is provided in Table A1 in the appendix. This skewed DM frequency distribution with few DMs being used very frequently, and many DMs being used with a moderate or low frequency has been found to be typical of the class of DMs (e.g. Crible 2018, Martín Zorraquino and Portolés Lázaro 1999). The distribution of frequency bands across speaker orientation (allocentric vs. egocentric) is shown in Table 6 below.

Overall, DM tokens are distributed rather evenly across the top three categories, namely 'very high', 'high', and 'moderate', only the bottom category, 'low', counts approximately five times fewer tokens than the others despite counting the highest number of distinct types (n=35). A closer look at the distribution of more vs. less frequent DMs per speaking task (or 'orientation') reveals that more 'very high' frequency DMs seem to occur in the egocentric task than in the allocentric task, while more 'high', 'moderate' and even 'low' frequency DMs appear more

Table 6: Distribution of frequency bands across speaker orientation.

	VERY HIGH	HIGH	MODERATE	LOW	Total
Allocentric	95	201	234	46	576
Egocentric	271	149	120	21	561
Total	**366**	**350**	**354**	**67**	**1137**

often in the allocentric task. A chi-squared test of independence was performed to examine the relationship between speaker orientation and DM frequency bands. A significant association was found: $X^2(3)=138,23$, $p<0.0001$. The overall effect is moderate: Cramér's V=0.3549. All cells but the 'high' frequency were found to contribute significantly to the chi-squared value at the level of $p<0.05$. 'Moderate' and 'low' frequency band DMs were found to be overrepresented in the allocentric task and underrepresented in the egocentric task, whereas 'very high' frequency band DMs were found to be strongly overrepresented in the egocentric task and underrepresented in the allocentric task. A possible explanation is that those 'very high' frequency DMs (*et, donc*) are frequent because they are underspecified and multifunctional (Crible et al. 2019), and as a consequence easier for speakers to retrieve from memory. Thus, their use is potentially triggered not by the intention to accommodate speech to a particular addressee's perspective one way or another, but rather by production economy habits on the part of the speaker. Therefore, they are more likely to be found in the egocentric task where they are not in competition with other, more hearer-oriented DMs.

If highly frequent DMs are 'easy-on-the-speaker', then their use should increase together with the amount of cognitive load imposed on speakers. As Table 7 reveals, this holds true in the two speaking tasks, although the difference between the high and low cognitive load conditions appears rather slight.

Table 7: Distribution of frequency bands per cognitive load condition, per speaker orientation.

		VERY HIGH	HIGH	MODERATE	LOW	Total
Allocentric	High	50	101	114	23	288
	Low	45	100	120	23	288
Egocentric	High	144	71	58	11	284
	Low	127	78	62	10	277
Total		**366**	**350**	**354**	**67**	**1137**

Once again, chi-squared tests of independence were performed, this time to examine the relation between cognitive load and DM frequency bands within each speaking task. Significant associations were found neither in the allocentric task nor the egocentric task ($X^2(3)=1.49$, $p>0.05$), meaning that cognitive load had no effect on DM frequency bands, similarly to what we found for their frequency and diversity.

5.3.2 Discourse markers frequency and polysemy

To assess whether the high frequency of some DMs could indeed be linked to their polysemy, the degree of polysemy of the DM types found in the dataset was measured in each condition. It was operationalized as follows: DMs characterized by 'monosemy' were defined as those performing a single function (cf. Section 4.5, the functions level in the annotation); those characterized by 'low polysemy' as performing two to three functions; and those characterized by 'high polysemy' as performing five or more functions. DMs with a frequency of three or less were discarded as hapax legomena of which the polysemy could not be established. This leaves us with 1097 DM tokens and 36 DM types. The resulting annotations per DM frequency band are presented in Table 8.

Table 8: Distribution of polysemy levels per DM frequency band.

	HIGH POLYSEMY	LOW POLYSEMY	MONOSEMY	Total
Very high freq.	366	0	0	366
High freq.	181	169	0	350
Moderate freq.	76	181	97	354
Low freq.	0	0	27	27
Total	623	350	124	1097

These figures clearly suggest a relationship between the two variables: all of the DMs identified as 'very high' frequency also display a high degree of polysemy (100%), while all DMs identified as 'low' frequency (yet with a frequency of more than three tokens in the dataset) are monosemous (100%). The other two frequency bands, 'high' and 'moderate', span more polysemy categories, where 'high' frequency shows a slight tendency to attract 'high' polysemy DMs (in 51.71% of cases), and 'moderate' an affinity for low polysemy DMs (in 51,13% of cases), without excluding highly polysemous and monosemous DMs. By means of a chi-squared test, a significant association was found between frequency band and polysemy ($X^2(6)=760.85$, $p<0.0001$). The overall effect is large, Cramér's $V=0.589$. The analysis of the standardized residuals indicates that all but one cell (high frequency * high polysemy) contributed significantly to the chi-squared value at the level of p<0.01 with residual values above or below +2.58 and −2.58 respectively (Levshina 2015: 221).

Together with the previously established egocentric preference for 'very high' frequency DMs, and allocentric preference for 'high', 'moderate' and 'low' frequency DMs, these results suggest that speaker-oriented DMs uses are characterized by a higher degree of polysemy, and listener-oriented DMs are characterized by a lower degree of polysemy. In other words, speaker orientation would not as much impact the selection of high or low frequency DMs per se, but rather their degree of polysemy.

Indeed, as Table 9 shows, greater counts of highly polysemous DMs are found in the egocentric output than in its allocentric counterpart, while monosemous, although less frequent overall, seem to be typical of the allocentric orientation.

Table 9: Distribution of polysemy levels per speaker orientation.

	HIGH POLYSEMY	LOW POLYSEMY	MONOSEMY	Total
Allocentric	262 (47.46%)	201 (36.41%)	89 (16.12%)	552
Egocentric	361 (66.24%)	149 (27.34%)	35 (6.42%)	545
Total	623	354	122	1097

To assess the significance of this relationship, a chi-squared test of independence was performed. A significant association was found between speaker orientation and degree of DM polysemy ($X^2(2)=46.93$, $p<0.0001$), with an overall small effect (Cramér's V=0.207). There is a significant positive association at the level of p<0.01 between monosemous DMs and allocentric speech, and another between highly polysemous DMs and egocentric speech. On the other hand, allocentric speech significantly disprefers highly polysemous DMs, while monosemous DMs are dispreferred in egocentric speech. These results support H3 (RQ1), that speakers use fewer polysemous DMs in the allocentric condition. On this basis, we may tentatively conclude that certain DMs and uses may well be indices of speaker orientation: listener-oriented DMs leaning towards monosemy, which is easier to process for the hearer, and speaker-oriented DMs being those of the highly polysemous kind.

The fact that highly polysemous DMs occurring in the 'high' and 'very high' frequency bands, make up approximately half (49,86%, see Table 8) of the total number of DMs found in the output of the (resampled) allocentric task point to a use of DMs that is less heavily centred on the hearer's needs than previously thought (e.g. Hansen, 2006), but rather balanced between those of both speakers and hearers.

To find out whether a higher cognitive load triggers the use of more 'speaker-oriented' highly polysemous DMs within each task (H8, RQ2), similar tests were run contrasting the data in the high vs. low condition (Table 10).

Table 10: Distribution of polysemy levels per cognitive load condition, per speaker orientation.

		HIGH POLYSEMY	LOW POLYSEMY	MONOSEMY	Total
Allocentric	High	133	96	46	275
	Low	129	105	43	277
Egocentric	High	183	71	22	276
	Low	178	78	13	269
Total		623	350	124	1097

Unsurprisingly in light of the inconclusive results previously obtained regarding the distribution of frequency bands across cognitive load conditions, no significant associations were found between cognitive load and degree of DM polysemy, be it in the allocentric data ($X^2(2)= 0.56$, $p>0.05$), or in the egocentric data ($X^2(2)= 2.62$, $p>0.05$). At this point, we cannot state that polysemous DMs are "easy-on-the-speaker" (nor "hard-on-the-speaker", for that matter), but rather that they are listener-unfriendly. In the following Section we will further deepen the impact of speaker orientation on DM use, matters of cognitive load will not be further analysed given the inconclusive results so far.

5.4 Discourse markers distribution: Domains and functions

The analysis so far has focused on providing a more descriptive account of the DM category and its formal behaviour in the experimental conditions under study. In this Section, we turn to the more functional potential of DMs to provide insight into the debated allocentricity of language. To this end, we will make use of the two-dimensional annotation in Domains and Functions, following Crible and Degand's (2019) protocol (cf. Section 4.5).

5.4.1 Domains across conditions

Table 11 displays the number of DM tokens used in the different domains across the two speaker orientation tasks.

Table 11: Distribution of domain tokens per speaker orientation (balanced sample).

	IDEATIONAL	RHETORICAL	SEQUENTIAL	INTERPERSONAL	Total
Allocentric	29	105	174	268	576
Egocentric	86	91	368	16	561
Total	115	196	542	284	1,137

Overall, the sequential domain displays the highest frequency in the balanced TACO sample. This higher sequential use is in line with previous results across different languages (Crible 2018, Crible and Degand 2019, Degand et al. in press). Here, the results are skewed by the egocentric output, however, where the sequential domain dominates by far in comparison with its three alternatives. In the allocentric output, it is the interpersonal domain which seems to have the upper-hand, although DM tokens are distributed relatively more evenly in this condition, that is with a large number of DMs also found in the sequential and rhetorical domains. Interestingly, a small yet noticeable amount of interpersonal domain tokens can be found in the egocentric task. Upon closer analysis of those instances, it seems that their use stems from one of two possible explanations, or a combination of both. The first is related to the fact that participants were asked to give instructions to themselves 'as if they had to use these instructions again in three months' time to reassemble the puzzle'. A number of them did indeed just that, and addressed an impersonated version of their future self in the recording, such as by using the second person singular (*tu*). Their speech was thus punctuated with 'interpersonal' monitoring DMs including *hein*, *attends* and *quoi*, whenever they stalled due to having to recall information (3) and/or had to apply a repair (4,5), for instance, even though no addressee was there to whom they had to indicate their willingness to keep their speaking turn.

(3) *et tu vas le placer m [filled pause]* **attends hein** *je ne sais plus le triangle vert*
  'and then you put it uh [filled pause] wait hang on I don't know anymore the green triangle' HCL_CHF52_EGO

(4) *à côté du des deux côtés euh m non* **attends** *du côté des deux côtés*
  'next to the the two sides uhm no wait on the same side as the two sides' HCL_MAM19_EGO

(5) *un centimètre au-dessus euh collé euh un elle doit elle doit dépasser d'un centimètre sur le triangle jaune* **quoi**
  'one centimetre above um stuck on uh a it needs it needs to cover one centimetre of the yellow triangle actually' LCL_VEF55_EGO

The alternative explanation is that due to the observer's paradox (Labov, 1972), participants behaved in the egocentric task as they would have if the experimenter had been present, due to knowing they were being recorded. The feeling of being observed would have therefore triggered the use of such DMs. This suggests one of two things, either that the experimental condition was overall not constraining enough to prevent speakers from using these particular interpersonal DMs, or that they are not truly 'interpersonal' (i.e. produced 'for the hearer'). The latter option would imply that the use of such DMs is more automatic than controlled, as it does not appear to be affected by reduced working memory capacity, and more 'universal' at that, as suggested by Fuller (2003).

Returning to the distribution of domains in the two speaking tasks, their relative proportions are presented in Figure 3.

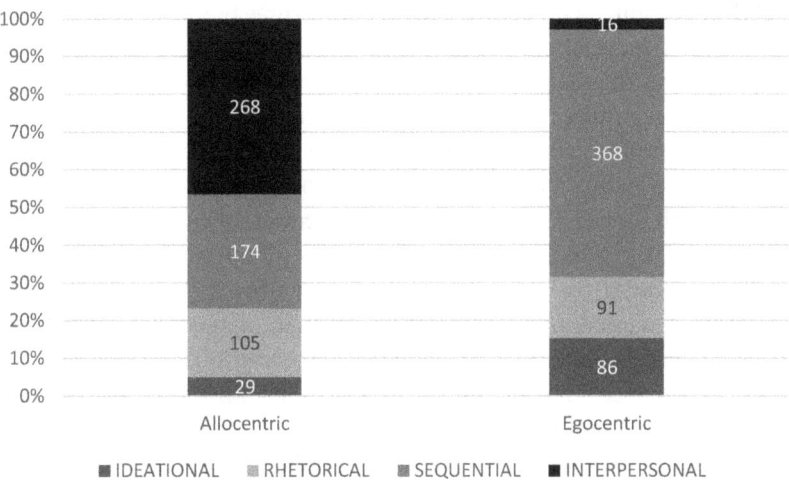

Figure 3: Proportions of DM domains per speaker orientation.

This visualization of the relative density of domains in the dataset clarifies the gaps distinguishing the speaking tasks. Overall, DMs produced in the allocentric task appear more functionally diverse than those produced in the egocentric task at this level of analysis. A chi-squared test revealed a significant association between domain distribution and speaker orientation: $X^2(3)=322.16$, $p<0.001$, with an overall large effect (Cramér's V=0.532). The results of the analysis revealed three significant positive associations, two between the ideational and the sequential domains and the egocentric speaker orientation, and one between the interpersonal domain and the allocentric orientation. Negative significant associations were found between the ideational and the sequential domain and the allocentric orientation, and between the interpersonal domain and the egocentric orientation.

While the association between the interpersonal domain and the allocentric speaker orientation seems obvious, confirming H4 (RQ1), it is less straightforward to interpret the results indicating that DMs used to structure discourse (sequential) and to express (relations between) facts (ideational) are not likely to be used for communicative purposes, but are rather associated with the egocentric perspective of speakers. Apparently, the structuring function of DMs is more about organizing discourse from one's own perspective, than it is to facilitate the listener's comprehension. A closer look at the specific DM meanings (discourse functions) expressed in the sequential domain nuances this observation. A qualitative analysis of the functional DM distribution in the two speaker orientations focusing on the sequential domain only suggests a number of tendencies (see Table 12). The egocentric condition seems to attract three types of discourse relations. In order of decreasing frequency these are: monitoring, marked by DMs such as *alors* ('well, then'), *donc* ('so'), *okay*, *voilà* ('that's it'), temporal relations, marked mainly by *ensuite* ('then, after that'), *maintenant* ('now'), *puis* ('then') to express chronological ordering, and additive relations marked mainly by *et* ('and'). In the allocentric condition, there is only one type of discourse relation that stands out in terms of frequency, namely monitoring, with a larger variety of DMs to mark the relation. In addition to the DMs used in the egocentric task, *ben* ('well') and *ouais* ('yeah') seem to be more specific of the allocentric condition. Strikingly, a number of discourse relations occur (almost) only in the allocentric task, namely causal (marked by *parce que* 'because'), concessive (*mais*, 'but') and consequence (marked by *donc*, 'so') relations, when used sequentially. Such uses are not present in the egocentric dataset. While they fulfil primarily a sequential role in organizing the flow of speech they also directly address the listener, as in (6).

(6) Receiver : ***et donc*** *tu veux que je fasse l'inverse que je mette les pointes contre les pointes*
'and so you want me to do the opposite to put the tips against the tips'
Director: ouais mais moi je sais pas le truc que tu dessines **hein** NAME
'yeah but I don't know the thing that you are drawing right'

This preliminary description of which type of DMs are put to use to express different types of discourse relations in the sequential domain suggests that when speakers make the structure and organization of their discourse flow explicit, they do this in different ways depending on the speaker orientation they take.

Table 12: Distribution of DM meanings in the sequential domain across speaker orientation.

	ADD	ALT	CAU	CCS	CSQ	HDG	MNT	SPE	TMP	TOP	Total
ALLOCENTRIC	12	9	2	5	12	2	102	1	20	9	174
EGOCENTRIC	71	18	0	0	5	2	153	8	105	6	368
Total	83	27	2	5	17	4	255	9	125	15	542

ADD: additive, ALT: alternative, CAU: causal, CCS: Concession, HDG: hedging, MNT: monitoring, SPE: specification, TMP: temporal, TOP: topic

Coming now to the higher proportion of ideational DM uses in the egocentric domain, the (relational) meaning distribution across the two speaker orientations displayed in Table 13 shows that ideational uses in the egocentric task are on the account of mainly two discourse relations, i.e. addition (marked exclusively by *et*) and consequence (marked by *donc* ('so'), *et donc* ('and so') *du coup* ('consequently')), accounting together for nearly 77% of the cases. It does seem that when speakers are giving instructions to themselves, they mainly describe the events in a list like way, or, more rarely, as following from one another.

Table 13: Distribution of DM meanings in the ideational domain across speaker orientation.

	ADD	ALT	CAU	CCS	CSQ	CDN	CTR	SPE	TMP	Total
ALLO	6	6	3	3	2	1	2	1	5	29
EGO	55	0	4	4	11	0	2	4	6	86
Total	61	6	7	7	13	1	4	5	11	115

ADD: additive, ALT: alternative, CAU: causal, CCS: concession, CSQ: consequence, CDN: condition, CTR: contrast, SPE: specification, TMP: temporal

5.4.2 Speaker- and hearer-oriented functions of discourse markers

At this level of analysis, it was hypothesized (H5, RQ1) that DMs functioning as markers of reformulation, specification and contrast of information were expected to be found in larger proportions in the allocentric output than in the egocentric output, as previous literature had identified them as representative of discourse functions geared towards the hearer's needs (Ciabarri 2013, Cuenca 2003, Cuenca and Bach 2007). In Crible and Degand's (2019) taxonomy, specification (SPE) and contrast (CTR) do have their own label, but reformulation (paraphrastic or non-paraphrastic) is expressed via the combination of the rhetorical domain and the 'alternative' function (ALT) for the reformulation of two full units, while repairs due to a change in phrasing, or the reformulation of incomplete units is marked by the combination of the sequential domain and the alternative function. An additional function in the taxonomy that may be relevant for the present discussion on hearer-orientation is concession (CCS), when "the marker signals that the segment it connects denies one or several expectations related to the other segment" (Crible and Degand, 2019). Table 14 zooms in on the distribution of these alleged hearer-oriented discourse relations across the two speaker orientations in the balanced sample. For ease of presentation, reformulation here groups sequential and rhetorical alternative.

Table 14: Distribution of "hearer-oriented" functions per speaker orientation (balanced sample).

	ADD	ALT	CAU	CCS	CSQ	CDN	CTR	SPE	TMP	Total
ALLO	6	6	3	3	2	1	2	1	5	29
EGO	55	0	4	4	11	0	2	4	6	86
Total	61	6	7	7	13	1	4	5	11	115

At first glance, the data in Table 14 show that there is no association between speaker orientation and alleged hearer-oriented DM functions. With the exception of concession, none of the other functions of contrast, specification and reformulation associate with the expected speaker orientation. Yet, when we look at the type of DMs used, we see a different distribution pattern across the conditions. Strikingly, the polysemous DM *donc* is used overwhelmingly in the egocentric task (24 out of the 41 egocentric reformulation markers) to express reformulation, while speakers resort to more variation to reformulate in the allocentric condition (*enfin* ('I mean'), *donc* ('so'), *ou alors* ('or else'), *alors* ('then')). The same pattern arises for the specification relation, where *donc* again takes the majority of the egocentric uses on its account (15 out of the 25 DMs used in the egocentric task), thus confirming the selection of highly frequent, polysemous DMs when speakers take an egocentric perspective, regardless of the type of discourse domain or discourse relation. In contrast, the allocentric speaker orientation associates with concessive relations, overwhelmingly expressed by *mais* ('but'). So, while speakers may reformulate, specify and even contrast for themselves or for others, establishing an explicit concessive relation is most often directed towards the hearer.

Figure 4 displays the full range of DM functions per speaker orientation in the balanced sample. The most frequent function across the two is monitoring, corresponding to speakers' need to manage the discourse flow. In the allocentric task, top DM uses also include expressing agreement with an interlocutor and contradicting or nuancing (conceding) information. In the egocentric task, speakers mostly use DMs to add information and define the temporality of the events they talk about.

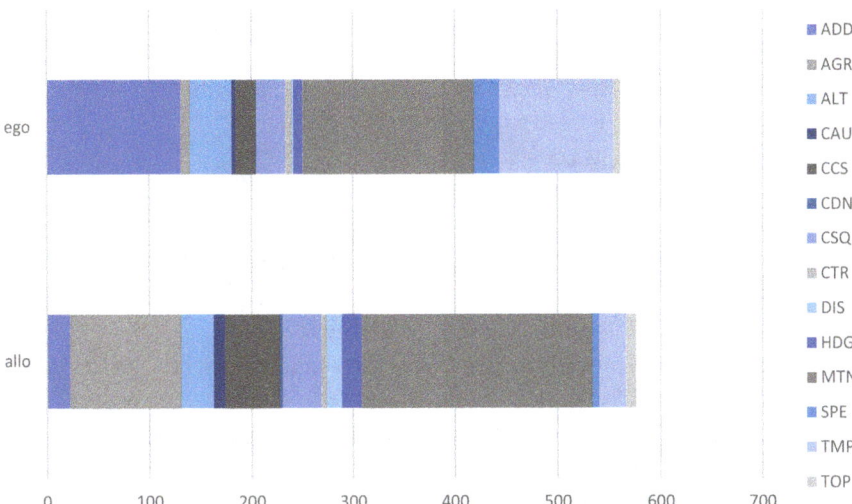

Figure 4: Raw frequency of DM functions per speaker orientation (balanced sample). Legend: ADD: additive, AGR: agreement, ALT: alternative, CAU: causal, CCS: concession, CDN: condition, CSQ: consequential; CTR: contrastive, DIS: disagreement, HDG: hedging, MTN: monitoring, SPE: specification, TMP: temporal, TOP: topic.

To assess whether the trends of attraction detailed above were statistically valid, a chi-squared test of independence was computed. To do so, three functions had to be regrouped as 'other' due to their low number of occurrences: cause, condition and disagreement. A significant association was found between speaker orientation and DM function ($X^2(11)= 267.89$, $p<0.001$). An overall moderate effect was found (Cramér's V=0.485). A significant positive association was found between the allocentric orientation and agreement, concession, hedging, monitoring and other, and between the egocentric orientation and the addition, specification and temporal functions.

From these results, it seems that more hearer-oriented uses of DMs include mostly showing agreement (AGR) to confirm (7) or check (MTN) (8) the correspondence of information between speaker and hearer information states. Indicating a shift in perspective orientation on the part of the hearer may be necessary through approximation (HDG) (9) or concession (CCS) (10). Arguably, most are uses that would indeed be more in line with an addressee-oriented definition of discourse markers such as Hansen's (2006), and could be defined as more 'conscious', controlled uses linked to the integration and/or negotiation of common ground between interlocutors. Exceptions could perhaps include some 'interpersonal' monitoring DMs linked to floorholding which apparently also occur in egocentric situations and could potentially perform more universal functions, as discussed in the previous section.

(7) ***d'accord*** *et euh est-ce que ça doit longer euh le triangle euh*
'alright and does it need to go along uh the triangle um' HCL_ASF24_ALLO

(8) *comme ça tu as les deux oreilles **tu vois** (pause) **bon***
'that way you have both ears, see (pause) alright' LCL_ANM55_ALLO

(9) *tu le fais rentrer de **genre** deux trois millimètres*
'you make it go inwards by like two or three millimetres' LCL_PAF25_ALLO

(10) *il faut qu'on prenne le bleu et le vert **mais** je sais pas comment les mettre*
'we need to use the blue one and the green one but I don't know how to place them' LCL_CAF39_ALLO

DMs identified as associated to the egocentric orientation, on the other hand, tend to be used by speakers to signal the introduction of discourse-new information or express the continuity linking two consecutive ideas or segments (ADD) (11); elaborate on a previous segment by providing a detail which can be 'subjectively appreciated by the speaker' (Crible and Degand, 2019) (SPE) (12), and structure the temporality (or order) of the events or arguments presented (TMP) (13). These are uses that could be seen as 'framing' and enhancing the way information is presented (Jucker and Smith, 1998).

(11) *le parallélogramme qui euh va venir faire la la deuxième pointe **et** qui va toucher à la fois le carré*
'the parallelogram which uh is going to complete the the second peak and at the same time come into contact with the square' LCL_VIM19_EGO

(12) *l'un de ses petits côtés **à savoir** celui qui est le plus haut dans ta forme*
'one of its smaller sides that is the one placed higher inside your shape' HCL_SAF24_EGO

(13) *l'hypoténuse étant ainsi diagonale **ensuite** on vient prendre le grand triangle*
'the hypothenuse therefore being diagonal then we shall take the big triangle'
LCL_CLF21_EGO

6 Conclusions

The aim of this contribution was to pursue the following two research objectives: (1) uncover potential speaker-oriented and hearer-oriented uses of DMs based on their frequency distribution, linguistic features and functional behaviour in an experiment manipulating speaker orientation and cognitive load; and (2) to situate evidence from DMs within the wider discussion concerning the egocentric or allocentric basis of language production.

Our main findings are that DMs occur with a higher overall relative frequency in the allocentric task than in the egocentric task. This frequency effect does however not extend to the cognitive load manipulations. Beyond mere frequency, DMs were found to be used more diversely in the egocentric experiment than in its allocentric counterpart, although the overall difference was not great. Similarly to frequency, no major differences were found between DMs identified in either cognitive load condition, be it in one task or the other. This pattern of findings is repeated throughout the analysis, as the results tend to show a greater impact of speaker orientation over cognitive load on the production of DMs. Overall, these results confirm the hypotheses formulated for RQ1 in terms of DM frequency and diversity, but not those of RQ2 which predicted that DMs would be produced more frequently but less diversely under a higher mental load.

A more fine-grained approach to DM frequency distribution and their linguistic behavior revealed that speakers in the egocentric context used a more restricted set of highly frequent DM types characterized by their high degree of polysemy (more than five different senses). On the other hand, speakers in the interactive context preferred a wider variety of less polysemous types distributed more evenly across frequency bands, including a number of monosemous DMs. These results were taken as evidence that speakers, when they behave egocentrically, show an affinity for forms that are more economical in terms of processing, such as underspecified DMs that can perform several functions. On the other hand, the use of fewer polysemous and more monosemous DMs in the allocentric condition leads us to conclude that speakers do indeed take their hearers' processing cost into account using more specific DMs that are easier to interpret in context.

Turning to the functional analysis of DMs, the objective was to try identifying potential speaker- or hearer-oriented uses within the limitations of the present off-line experimental design to elicit such information, and the reliability of its accompanying approach to DM annotation. Regarding domain distribution corresponding more or less to the speaker's communicative intention, the data revealed that hearer-oriented DM use performs mostly in the interpersonal domain, as well as in the rhetorical domain to a lesser extent. More speaker-oriented DMs, on the other hand, operate in the sequential and ideational domains of discourse and function as 'frames' that structure the temporality of discourse, fillers, or serve as markers of self-monitored adaptations or repair of speech content.

From a theoretical point of view, the starting point of the present study lies in the widespread claim that discourse phenomena, and language more generally, take place 'for the hearer'. A case in point are the numerous contributions focusing on a restricted number or types of DMs and the role they play in guiding comprehension processes. Such studies have led authors to extrapolate that DMs are indeed hearer-oriented, despite a wealth of psycholinguistic research claiming that speakers' processing considerations may be more central to language production and grammar shaping than previously thought. This claim is based mostly on evidence that speakers display egocentric behavior when their working memory is impaired, although this is hotly debated.

The present research showed that the way speakers used DMs varied depending on whether they gave instructions to themselves or to an addressee, suggesting that specific DM types or uses may be geared towards the hearer, and others to the self. The fact that DMs identified as speaker-oriented were found in large proportions in both the egocentric and allocentric tasks goes to show that, while DMs appear to be hearer-oriented to a certain extent, their speaker-oriented and hearer-oriented functions seem to co-exist and competitively weigh in the decisions that determine use in context to ultimately benefit both interlocutors when it comes to processing cost.

Importantly, the results stemming from the cognitive load manipulation applied in the experiments were mostly inconclusive, indicating minor to no differences across conditions. The first explanation coming to mind is that the cognitive load manipulation imposed on speakers during the experiment simply was not efficient. Arguably, however, this is unlikely for two reasons: first, high cognitive load was elicited differently across the two speaking tasks (verbal memory task in the allocentric task and recalling instructions from memory in the egocentric task), thus not relying on a single cognitive task. Second, the ways in which high cognitive load was elicited here were chosen for their established effectiveness in previous linguistic studies (Vogels et al. 2015, Roßnagel 2000). Therefore, the fact that stability was found across the treatment conditions in both tasks is interesting, and suggests that higher memory demands do not substantially affect the production of DMs. One could argue that this claim is conditional to the assumption that speech produced in the low cognitive load condition was in fact produced under low cognitive load. This being said, the notion of 'low' cognitive load here (and in similar studies) needs to be taken with a grain of salt, as it is widely acknowledged that language production in itself is demanding processing-wise (Levelt 1989, Tanenhaus 2013), and therefore prone to requiring a certain level of mental effort from speakers regardless of any additional (artificial) burdens. In sum, no matter how high or low the cognitive load of the participants in this study was to begin with, the methodology employed in the treatment conditions should in any case increase it. Our general conclusion therefore goes against the hypothesis of an egocentric bias in language production put forward by Keysar and colleagues (Keysar et al. 1998, Keysar et al. 2000) bringing new perspectives to the table that carry potential weight as they concern a phenomenon highly pervasive in language-in-use, namely DMs.

Appendix

Table A1: Overview of DM types per frequency band (N= 1137).

Very high frequency >169 tokens	High frequency 49–81 tokens	Moderate frequency 6–35 tokens	Low frequency <6 tokens
donc (so), et (and)	mais (but), ensuite (then), okay, alors (so/well/then), voilà (that's it)	allez (come on), après (after), attends (wait), ben (well), bon (well), c'est ça (that's it), d'abord (first), du coup (consequently), en fait (actually), en gros (approximately), enfin (finally/well), et alors (and then), et donc (and so), hein (you know) , là (there), maintenant (now), non (no), oui (yes), parce que (because), puis (then), quoi (hé), tu vois (you see)	à savoir (that is), bah, bien (good), ça va (right), d'accord (okay), de toute façon (in any case), déjà (already), écoute (listen), eh, eh ben (well), en tout cas (in any case), en vrai (for real), enfin bon (well then), et après (and after), et ensuite (and then), et puis (and then), finalement (finally), genre (like), je vois (I see), limite (limit), mec (dude), ou (or), ou alors (or else), par conséquent (as a consequence), par contre (in contrast), premièrement (first), puisque (since), quand même (anyway), si (if), si tu veux (if you want), t'inquiète (no worries), une fois (once), vas-y (go), viens (come)

Note: Translations of DMs are very approximate

References

Achim, Amélie M., André Achim & Marion Fossard. 2017. Knowledge likely held by others affects speakers' choices of referential expressions at different stages of discourse. *Language, Cognition and Neuroscience* 32(1). 21–36. doi:10.1080/23273798.2016.1234059.

Baddeley, Alan, Michael W. Eysenck & Michael C. Anderson. 2020. *Memory*. 3rd edn. London: Psychology Press.

Bard, Ellen Gurman, Anne H. Anderson, Catherine Sotillo, Matthew Aylett, Gwyneth Doherty-Sneddon & Alison Newlands. 2000. Controlling the Intelligibility of Referring Expressions in Dialogue. *Journal of Memory and Language* 42(1). 1–22. doi:10.1006/jmla.1999.2667.

Barr, D. J. & Boaz Keysar. (2006). Perspective Taking and the Coordination of Meaning in Language Use. In M. J. Traxler & M. A. Gernsbacher (eds.), *Handbook of Psycholinguistics*. 2nd edn, 901–938. London: Academic Press.

Blakemore, Diane Lesley. 1987. *Semantic constraints on relevance*. Oxford: Basil Blackwell.

Blakemore, Diane. 1993. The relevance of reformulations. *Language and Literature* 2(2). 101–120. doi:10.1177/096394709300200202.

Blokpoel, Mark, Marlieke van Kesteren, Arjen Stolk, Pim Haselager, Ivan Toni & Iris van Rooij. 2012. Recipient design in human communication: Simple heuristics or perspective taking? *Frontiers in Human Neuroscience* 6. Article 253. doi:10.3389/fnhum.2012.00253.

Boersma, Paul & Daniel Weenink. 2019. *Praat: doing phonetics by computer* (Version 6.1). from http://www.praat.org/.

Bolden, Galina B. 2015. Discourse Markers. *The International Encyclopedia of Language and Social Interaction*. Hoboken, NJ: John Wiley and Sons, Inc. doi:10.1002/9781118611463. wbielsi031.

Brehm-Jurish, Eva Ute. 2005. *Connective ties in discourse : three ERP-studies on causal, temporal and concessive connective ties and their influence on language processing*. Potsdam: University of Potsdam Doctoral Dissertation.

Brennan, Susan E. & Joy E. Hanna. 2009. Partner-Specific Adaptation in Dialog. *Topics in Cognitive Science* 1(2). 274–291. doi:10.1111/j.1756-8765.2009.01019.x.

Brezina, Vaclav. 2018. *Statistics in Corpus Linguistics: A Practical Guide*. Cambridge: Cambridge University Press. doi:10.1017/9781316410899.

Brinton, Laurel J. 2008. *The Comment Clause in English: Syntactic Origins and Pragmatic Development*. Cambridge: Cambridge University Press.

Broisson, Zoé. 2019. *How egocentric is language production? Evidence from discourse marker use under cognitive load*. Louvain-la-Neuve: Université Catholique de Louvain. Master thesis.

Brown, Paula M. & Gary S. Dell. 1987. Adapting production to comprehension: The explicit mention of instruments. *Cognitive Psychology* 19(4). 441–472. doi:10.1016/0010-0285(87)90015-6.

Canestrelli, Anneloes R., Willem M. Mak & Ted J. M. Sanders. 2013. Causal connectives in discourse processing: How differences in subjectivity are reflected in eye movements. *Language and Cognitive Processes* 28(9). 1394–1413. doi:10.1080/01690965.2012.685885.

Ciabarri, Federica. (2013). Italian reformulation markers: a study on spoken and written language. In Catherine Bolly & Liesbeth Degand (eds.), *Across the Line of Speech and Writing Variation*, 113–128. Louvain-la-Neuve: Presses universitaires de Louvain.

Clark, Herbert H. 1996. *Using language*. Cambridge: Cambridge University Press.
Clark, Herbert H. & Thomas B. Carlson. 1981. Context for comprehension. In John Long & Alan Baddeley (eds.), *Attention and performance* IX, 313–330. Hillsdale, NJ: Lawrence Erlbaum Associates.
Clark, Herbert H. & Thomas B. Carlson. 1982. Hearers and Speech Acts. *Language* 58(2). 332–373. doi:10.2307/414102.
Clark, Herbert H. & Deanna Wilkes-Gibbs. 1986. Referring as a collaborative process. *Cognition* 22 (1). 1–39.
Crible, Ludivine. 2017. Towards an operational category of discourse markers: A definition and its model. In Chiara Fedriani & Andrea Sanso (eds.), *Discourse markers, Pragmatics Markers and Modal Particles: New Perspectives,* 101–126. Amsterdam and Philadelphia: John Benjamins.
Crible, Ludivine. 2018. *Discourse Markers and (Dis)fluency. Forms and functions across languages and registers*. Amsterdam and Philadelphia: John Benjamins. doi:10.1075/pbns.286.
Crible, Ludivine, Ágnes Abuczki, Nijolė Burkšaitienė, Péter Furkó, Anna Nedoluzhko, Sigita Rackevičienė, Giedrė Valūnaitė Oleškevičienė & Šárka Zikánová. 2019. Functions and translations of discourse markers in TED Talks: A parallel corpus study of underspecification in five languages. *Journal of Pragmatics* 142. 139–155. doi:10.1016/j.pragma.2019.01.012.
Crible, Ludivine & Maria-Josep Cuenca. 2017. Discourse Markers in Speech: Distinctive Features and Corpus Annotation. *Dialogue and Discourse* 8(2). 149–166.
Crible, Ludivine & Liesbeth Degand. 2019. Domains and Functions: A Two-Dimensional Account of Discourse Markers. *Discours. Revue de linguistique, psycholinguistique et informatique. A journal of linguistics, psycholinguistics and computational linguistics* (24). doi:10.4000/discours.9997. http://journals.openedition.org/discours/9997 (8 November, 2019).
Crible, Ludivine, Liesbeth Degand & Gaëtanelle Gilquin. 2017. The clustering of discourse markers and filled pauses: a corpus-based French-English study of (dis)fluency. *Languages in Contrast* 17(1). 69–95.
Crible, Ludivine & Sandrine Zufferey. 2015. Using a unified taxonomy to annotate discourse markers in speech and writing. In Harry Bunt (ed.), *Proceedings of the 11th Joint ACL – ISO Workshop on Interoperable Semantic Annotation* (isa-11). 14–22. London, UK: ACL.
Cuenca, Maria-Josep. 2003. Two ways to reformulate: a contrastive analysis of reformulation markers. *Journal of Pragmatics* 35(7). 1069–1093. doi:10.1016/S0378-2166(03)00004-3.
Cuenca, Maria Josep & Carme Bach. 2007. Contrasting the form and use of reformulation markers: *Discourse Studies* 9(2). 149–175.
Dębska, Agnieszka & Joanna Rączaszek-Leonardi. 2018. What Makes Us More Egocentric in Communication? The Role of Referent Features and Individual Differences. *Discourse Processes* 55(1). 1–11. doi:10.1080/0163853X.2016.1198137.
Degand, Liesbeth, Zoé Broisson, Ludivine Crible & Karolina Grzech. 2022. Cross-linguistic variation in spoken discourse markers: Distribution, functions, and domains. In Elizabeth Peterson, Turo Hiltunen & Joseph Kern (eds.), *Discourse-Pragmatic Variation and Change: Theory, Innovations, Contact,* 83–103. Cambridge: Cambridge University Press.
Dell, Garry S. & Paula M. Brown. 1991. Mechanisms for listener-adaptation in language production Limiting the role of the "model of the listener.". In Donna Jo Napoli & Judy Anne Kegl (eds.), *Bridges between psychology and linguistics*. 105–129. New York: Academic Press.

Ferreira, Fernanda, Karl G. D. Bailey & Vittoria Ferraro. 2002. Good-Enough Representations in Language Comprehension. *Current Directions in Psychological Science* 11(1). 1–15. doi:10.1111/1467-8721.00158.

Frisson, Steven. 2009. Semantic Underspecification in Language Processing. *Language and Linguistics Compass* 3(1). 111–127. doi:10.1111/j.1749-818X.2008.00104.x.

Fischer, Kerstin (ed.). 2006. *Approaches to discourse particles.* (Studies in Pragmatics 1). Bingley, UK: Emerald Group Publishing.

Fuller, J.M. 2003. Discourse marker use across speech contexts: A comparison of native and non-native speaker performance. *Multilingua* 22(2). 185–208.

Galati, Alexia, Anthi Diavastou & Marios N. Avraamides. 2018. Signatures of cognitive difficulty in perspective-taking: is the egocentric perspective always the easiest to adopt? *Language, Cognition and Neuroscience* 33(4). 467–493. doi:10.1080/23273798.2017.1384029.

Galinsky, Adam D., William W. Maddux, Debra Gilin & Judith B. White. 2008. Why it pays to get inside the head of your opponent: The differential effects of perspective taking and empathy in negotiations. *Psychological Science* 19(4). 378–384. doi:10.1111/j.1467-9280.2008.02096.x.

Geertzen, Jan 2012. *Inter-Rater Agreement with multiple raters and variables.* Retrieved March 23, 2019, from https://nlp-ml.io/jg/software/ira/

Götz, Sandra. 2013. *Fluency in native and nonnative English speech.* Amsterdam and Philadelphia: John Benjamins. doi:10.1075/scl.53.

Grice, Herbert Paul. 1975. *Logic and conversation. Speech Acts.* 41–58. New York: Academic Press.

Hansen, Maj-Britt Mosegaard. 2006. A dynamic polysemy approach to the lexical semantics of discourse markers (with an exemplary analysis of French 'toujours'). In Kerstin Fischer (ed.), *Approaches to discourse particles,* 21–41. Oxford: Elsevier.

Hawkins, John A. 2004. Efficiency and Complexity in Grammars. Oxford: Oxford University Press.

Horton, William S. & Richard J. Gerrig. 2016. Revisiting the memory-based processing approach to common ground. *Topics in Cognitive Science* 8(4). 780–795. doi:https://doi.org/10.1111/tops.12216.

Horton, William S. & Boaz Keysar. 1996. When do speakers take into account common ground? *Cognition* 59(1). 91–117. doi:10.1016/0010-0277(96)81418-1.

Irmer, Matthias. 2011. Bridging inferences. Constraining and resolving underspecification in discourse interpretation. Berlin and Boston: De Gruyter Mouton.

Jaeger, T. Florian & Harry Tily. 2011. On language 'utility': Processing complexity and communicative efficiency. Cognitive Science 2(3). 323–335. doi:10.1002/wcs.126.

Jucker, Andreas H. & Sara Smith. 1998. And people just you know like 'wow'. Discourse markers as negotiating strategies. In Andreas H. Jucker & Yael Ziv (eds.), *Discourse Markers. Descriptions and theory,* 171–201. (Pragmatics and Beyond New Series 57). Amsterdam and Philadelphia: John Benjamins.

Kellogg, Ronald T., Thierry Olive & Annie Piolat. 2007. Verbal, visual, and spatial working memory in written language production. *Acta Psychologica* 124(3). 382–397. doi:10.1016/j.actpsy.2006.02.005.

Keysar, Boaz, Dale J. Barr & William S. Horton. 1998. The egocentric basis of language use: Insights from a processing approach. *Current Directions in Psychological Science* 7(2). 46–49. doi:10.1111/1467-8721.ep13175613.

Keysar, Boaz, Dale J. Barr, Jennifer A. Balin & Jason S. Brauner. 2000. Taking perspective in conversation: The role of mutual knowledge in comprehension. *Psychological Science* 11(1). 32–38. doi:10.1111/1467-9280.00211.

Landis, J. Richard & Gary G. Koch. 1977. The measurement of observer agreement for categorical data. *Biometrics* 33(1). 159–174. doi:10.2307/2529310.

Lennes, Mietta 2019. SpeCT – *The speech corpus toolkit for Praat*. Retrieved May 13, 2019, from https://lennes.github.io/spect/

Levelt, William J. M. 1989. *Speaking: From intention to articulation*. Cambridge, Mass.: The MIT Press.

Levshina, Natalia. 2015. *How to do Linguistics with R: Data exploration and statistical analysis*. Amsterdam and Philadelphia: John Benjamins. doi:10.1075/z.195.

MacDonald, Maryellen C. 2013. How language production shapes language form and comprehension. *Frontiers in Psychology* 4. 226. doi:10.3389/fpsyg.2013.00226.

Maschler, Yael. 2009. *Metalanguage in Interaction: Hebrew Discourse Markers*. Amsterdam and Philadelphia: John Benjamins.

Martin Zorraquino, Maria Antonia & José Portoles Lazaro. 1999. Los marcadores del discurso. In Ignacio Bosque & Violeta Demonte (eds.), *Gramatica descriptiva de la lengua espanola*, 4051–4213. Madrid: Espasa-Calpe.

Pijpops, Dirk, Dirk Speelman, Stefan Grondelaers & Freek Van De Velde. 2018. Comparing explanations for the Complexity Principle: Evidence from argument realization. *Language and Cognition* 10(3). 514–543. doi:10.1017/langcog.2018.13.

Rice, Caitlin A., Natasha Tokowicz, Scott H. Fraundorf & Teljer L. Liburd. 2019. The complex interactions of context availability, polysemy, word frequency, and orthographic variables during lexical processing. *Memory and Cognition* 47(7). 1297–1313. doi:10.3758/s13421-019-00934-4.

Rosa, Elise C. & Jennifer E. Arnold. 2017. Predictability affects production: Thematic roles can affect reference form selection. *Journal of Memory and Language* 94. 43–60. doi:10.1016/j.jml.2016.07.007.

Roßnagel, Christian. 2000. Cognitive load and perspective-taking: applying the automatic-controlled distinction to verbal communication. *European Journal of Social Psychology* 30(3). 429–445. doi:10.1002/(SICI)1099-0992(200005/06)30:3<429::AID-EJSP3>3.0.CO;2-V.

Sanders, Ted J. M. & Leo G. M. Noordman. 2000. The role of coherence relations and their linguistic markers in text processing. *Discourse Processes* 29(1). 37–60.

Savitsky, Kenneth, Boaz Keysar, Nicholas Epley, Travis Carter & Ashley Swanson. 2011. The closeness-communication bias: Increased egocentrism among friends versus strangers. *Journal of Experimental Social Psychology* 47(1). 269–273. doi:10.1016/j.jesp.2010.09.005.

Schiffrin, Deborah. 1987. *Discourse markers*. Cambridge: Cambridge University Press.

Schmidt, T. & K. Worner. (2012). EXMARaLDA. In Jacques Durand, Ulrike Gut & Gjert Kristoffersen (eds.), *The Oxford handbook on corpus phonology*, 402–410. Oxford: Oxford University Press.

Sperber, Dan & Deirdre Wilson. 1986. *Relevance: Communication and cognition*. Cambridge MA: Harvard University Press.

Spooren, Wilbert. 1997. The Processing of Underspecified Coherence Relations. *Discourse Processes* 24(1). 149–168.

Taboada, Maite. 2006. Discourse markers as signals (or not) of rhetorical relations. *Journal of Pragmatics* 38(4). 567–592. doi:10.1016/j.pragma.2005.09.010.

Tanenhaus, Michael K. 2013. All P's or mixed vegetables? *Frontiers in Psychology* 4. doi:10.3389/fpsyg.2013.00234.

Traxler, Mathew J., Michael D. Bybee & Martin J. Pickering. 1997. Influence of connectives on language comprehension: eye tracking evidence for incremental interpretation. *Quarterly Journal of Experimental Psychology: Human Experimental Psychology* 50(3). 481–497.

Vogels, Jorrig, Emiel Krahmer & Alfons Maes. 2015. How cognitive load influences speakers' choice of referring expressions. *Cognitive Science* 39(6). 1396–1418. doi:10.1111/cogs.12205.

Vogels, Jorrig, David M. Howcroft, Elli Tourtouri & Vera Demberg. 2020. How speakers adapt object descriptions to listeners under load. *Language, Cognition and Neuroscience* 35(1). 78–92. doi:10.1080/23273798.2019.1648839.

Yoon, Si On & Sarah Brown-Schmidt. 2018. *Aim low: Mechanisms of audience design in multiparty conversation*. Discourse Processes 55(7). 566–592. doi:10.1080/0163853X.2017.1286225

Ruiqi Li, Liesbeth Allein, Damien Sileo
and Marie-Francine Moens

7 When do discourse markers affect computational sentence understanding?

Abstract: The capabilities and use cases of automatic natural language processing (NLP) have grown significantly over the last few years. While much work has been devoted to understanding how humans deal with discourse connectives, this phenomenon is understudied in computational systems. Therefore, it is important to put NLP models under the microscope and examine whether they can adequately comprehend, process, and reason within the complexity of natural language. In this chapter, we introduce the main mechanisms behind automatic sentence processing systems step by step and then focus on evaluating discourse connective processing. We assess nine popular systems in their ability to understand English discourse connectives and analyze how context and language understanding tasks affect their connective comprehension. The results show that NLP systems do not process all discourse connectives equally well and that the computational processing complexity of different connective kinds is *not always* consistently in line with the presumed complexity order found in human processing. In addition, while humans are more inclined to be influenced *during* the reading procedure but *not* necessarily in the final comprehension per-

---

Acknowledgement: This work was realized with the collaboration of the European Commission Joint Research Centre under the Collaborative Doctoral Partnership Agreement No 35332. The research was designed and the experiments were conducted and analyzed when Liesbeth Allein was at KU Leuven; further analyses were performed and the chapter was written when she was at the European Commission. The scientific output expressed does not imply a policy position of the European Commission. Neither the European Commission nor any person acting on behalf of the Commission is responsible for the use which might be made of this publication. This work is also part of the CALCULUS[1] project: Damien Sileo and Marie-Francine Moens are funded by the ERC Advanced Grant H2020-ERC-2017 ADG 788506. Ruiqi Li is funded by the State Scholarship Fund of China Scholarship Council (CSC).

---

1 https://calculus-project.eu/

Ruiqi Li, KU Leuven & National University of Defense Technology, ruiqi.li@kuleuven.be
Liesbeth Allein, KU Leuven & European Commission, Joint Research Centre (JRC), liesbeth.allein@kuleuven.be
Damien Sileo, KU Leuven, damien.sileo@kuleuven.be
Marie-Francine Moens, KU Leuven, sien.moens@kuleuven.be

https://doi.org/10.1515/9783110790351-007

formance, discourse connectives have a significant impact on the final accuracy of NLP systems. The *richer* knowledge of connectives a system learns, the *more negative* effect inappropriate connectives have on it. This suggests that the correct explicitation of discourse connectives is important for computational natural language processing.

Keywords: discourse markers, sentential semantics, computational language understanding, sentence embeddings, English

1 Introduction

Human language learning is a complex process involving many capabilities. Humans acquire vocabulary, order words in accepted sequences to form meaningful messages and consider the physical and social context to convey intentions and understand those of others. Computational systems – or models – working with natural language now aim to acquire such knowledge and proficiency with a single *pretraining* stage, during which they learn to perform a task requiring linguistic capabilities such as masked word prediction. Natural language processing (NLP) practitioners provide a randomly initialized model with a large number of texts in natural language and let it predict output for a predefined training task. For example, when the model is pretrained on the *masked word prediction task*, it tries to predict which word is hidden behind the mask in a given sentence: *The lioness hunts the [MASK]* → *zebra*. The correct answers are used to optimize the model and consequently improve its capabilities. By doing so, the model looks for patterns and important information in the input to adequately perform the pretraining task. These pretrained models can then be reused for other tasks. For example, NLP models can be used to tag the parts of speech in a sentence (Manning 2011; Plank, Søgaard, and Goldberg 2016), correct language-specific grammar errors (Heyman et al. 2018; Allein, Leeuwenberg, and Moens 2020), locate the correct answer to questions (Choi et al. 2018; Cartuyvels, Spinks, and Moens 2020) or even detect offensive or incorrect information (Ghadery and Moens 2020; Allein, Augenstein, and Moens 2021). To achieve high performance on these tasks, pretrained computational models need to acquire in-depth knowledge and understanding of syntax, semantics, pragmatics, and discourse. Given the scope of this volume, we focus on a special type of discourse markers, discourse connectives, and evaluate how they are leveraged by state-of-the-art NLP models to comprehend the discourse contained within a sentence. More specifically, we assess whether the presence or absence of discourse connectives affect a model's discourse understanding and compare the ease of comprehension between different connective types. Drawing parallels with the literature on human processing, this chapter also sheds light on the differences between humans and computers in terms of discourse comprehension. Last, we bridge the gap between computational and general linguistics by explaining and illustrating the core components in computational NLP models in a step-by-step manner.

The remainder of this chapter is structured as follows: Section 2 situates this chapter in the body of work that evaluated the discourse processing capabilities of humans and language processing abilities of computational NLP models; Section 3 illustrates step by step how these models turn language into a task output; Section 4 introduces the research questions and motivates them using findings from the linguistic literature on discourse connectives; Section 5 presents the nine sentence processing models and the three tasks we use in our evaluation; Section 6 elaborates on the methodology and contains the analyses and discussion; lastly, Section 7 concludes the chapter.

2 Related work

Our work contributes to the analysis of discourse markers in use. Discourse marker usage has been analyzed from the standpoint of corpus analysis (e.g., Schiffrin 2006; Prasad et al. 2008; Taboada 2006; Crible 2018). Many psycholinguistics studies focus on different methods by which discourse markers influence understanding. For example, Millis and Just (1994) and Haberlandt (1982) studied the influence of discourse markers on short-term word retention and reading speed, respectively. Degand, Lefèvre, and Bestgen (1999) and Degand and Sanders (2002) explored the influence of discourse relation marking understanding with question answering tests. Yung et al. (2017) developed a psycholinguistic model for discourse relation marking with an evaluation on the Penn Discourse Treebank dataset (Prasad et al. 2008). Studies on natural language processing models are valuable additions to psycholinguistics (Brysbaert, Keuleers, and Mandera 2014), as parallels can be established between NLP models and human processing (Mei et al. 2019; Ettinger 2020). Although many other evaluations have been proposed to assess their capabilities, our work is the first to assess the effect of discourse connectives on various computational models.

Sentence embedding models have been evaluated with many language understanding tasks, including natural language inference (NLI), sentence similarity, paraphrase detection, sentiment analysis, and question answering (e.g., Conneau and Kiela 2018; Wang et al. 2018, 2019). However, such results have been criticized for their lack of interpretability (Ribeiro et al. 2020). Conneau et al. (2018) proposed ten linguistic probing tasks: sentence length, word content, bigram shift, tree depth, top constituent, tense, subject number, object number, semantic odd man out, and coordination inversion. Wang et al. (2018) introduced a diagnostics-topic dataset that evaluates NLI accuracy when dealing with a more focused set of linguistic phenomena (lexical semantics, logic, knowledge, and propositional structure). Perone, Silveira, and Paula (2018) combined language understanding tasks and probing tasks and evaluated six sentence embedding models (ELMo, BoW, p-mean, Skip-Thoughts, InferSent and USE). They compared the embeddings on classification tasks (sentiment analysis, subjectivity/objectivity classification, question answering, and opinion polarity), semantic relatedness and textual similarity (image-caption retrieval, paraphrase detection, similarity and entailment), and the abovementioned ten linguistic probing tasks. Krasnowska-Kieras´ and Wróblewska (2019) evaluated six sentence embedding models (FastText, BERT, BiLSTM concatenated word and character embeddings, Sent2Vec, USE, and LASER) on some of the aforementioned linguistic probing tasks, other probing tasks (such as passive-active and sentence type classification), and two language understanding tasks (relatedness and entailment), and extended their evaluation to a multilingual setup. They compared sentence embedding performance for English and Polish. In contrast to the abovementioned research, we perform a more fine-grained evaluation of sentence embeddings by assessing their ability to grasp the meaning of connectives. Discourse connectives, including conjunctions and connective adverbials, have been leveraged for the training and evaluation of sentence embedding models (Jernite, Bowman, and Sontag 2017; Nie, Bennett, and Goodman 2019; Sileo et al. 2019, 2020) and there has been interest in measuring discourse coherence as a linguistic probing task when evaluating sentence embeddings (Chen, Chu, and Gimpel 2019).

However, these works focus on predicting a discourse connective or discourse relation between two sentences. Even though they show the value of discourse connective prediction as training/evaluation tasks, none of them measure the models' abilities to correctly make use of a connective within a sentence.

3 Computational models: Step-by-step

We first provide an overview of the three main processing steps involved in computational models performing sentence understanding tasks. Consider the two following sentences:

(1) *The lioness hunts the zebra.*

(2) *I go to the doctor because I am sick.*

3.1 From input to word representations

In order to process text, a computational model maps each word to a numerical word representation. Over the years, word representations have moved from categorical (Scott and Matwin 1999) to continuous representations (Naseem et al. 2020), illustrated in Figure 1. Categorical word representations are sparse,[2] multidimensional vectors in which each dimension corresponds to a unique word in the vocabulary.[3] If we consider the two example sentences (1) and (2) as corpus, the vocabulary contains eleven words[4] and the categorical word vector for lioness is a vector with ten zero values and one non-zero value. The non-zero value can be either '1' (one-hot encoding), the word's absolute count in a sentence (Bag of Words), or its weighted importance compared with the occurrence frequency of other words in the entire corpus (term frequency-inverse document frequency, or TF-IDF). When adopting the TF-IDF approach, the non-zero value in the *lioness* word representation will be higher than the non-zero value in the word representation of *the* as the latter word is more frequent and therefore less unique. These categorical representations, however, do not encode a word's meaning a priori. For example, the categorical representations for *lioness* and *zebra* in Figure 1 do not reflect the relatedness we could expect between two mammals: the word *lioness* is equidistant[5] from both *zebra* and *sick*. Continuous word representations, or **word embeddings**, can encode such information. Instead of a specific word, the vector dimensions here represent word *aspects*. Continuous representations have a fixed dimensionality that is independent of the vocabulary size of a language. The word embeddings and their values are obtained by applying statistical learning techniques over a large collection of textual data. In a continuous multidimensional space, related words can be grouped, and unrelated words can be far apart. For example, when using the continuous representation, *lioness* is closer to *zebra*

---

2 Most dimensions of a vector are zeros, except for one dimension.
3 NLP models usually have a fixed-size vocabulary that is extracted from a tokenized corpus and a minimum frequency criterion.
4 the, lioness, hunts, zebra, I, go, to, doctor, because, am, sick.
5 Using metrics that measures the distance between two representations such as the Euclidean Distance.

than to *sick* (Figure 1). The sentence representation models in this chapter represent words using continuous word embeddings.

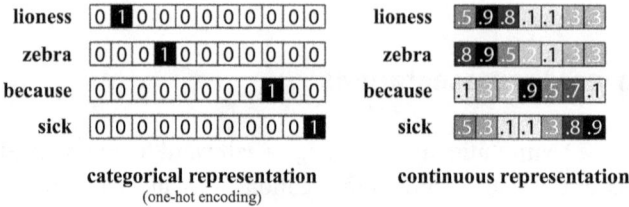

Figure 1: Examples of categorical and continuous word representations.

3.2 From word representations to sentence representation

Once words are turned into numerical representations, a composition model now has to relate them to one another in a sentence in order to derive meaning. Given a sequence of word embeddings, a composition model computes a sentence representation, also called **sentence embedding**. Some sentence embedding models simply use the presence of words, and not their order or interaction to construct sentence representations. They often do this by taking the average of all the word embeddings in a sentence. Other models take into account the word order and relate the words to each other to derive the meaning of a sentence. For this, the models need to apply more complex statistical learning techniques. Sentence (2), illustrates the importance of processing word order. The causal connective (*because*) combines an action (*I go to the doctor*) and a situation (*I am sick*). The connective signals the motivation for the action. Both the action and situation refer to common real-world events, and the causal relationship between the two is plausible. Switching the position of the action and situation (i.e., *I am sick because I go to the doctor*) alters the original sentence's meaning.

State-of-the-art NLP systems use sentence embedding models to construct representations of natural language sentences. These models are trained using statistical learning techniques that incentivize the encoders to capture sentential semantics. In this chapter, we evaluate nine widely used sentence embedding models. More specifically, we look at how they behave on sentences with connective words.

3.3 From sentence representation to task prediction

After a sentence embedding model has constructed a sentence embedding, another computational model reasons over the sentence embedding to predict the desired outcome for a given task such as sentiment classification illustrated in Figure 2. This is generally done with a classifier using sentence embeddings as features. The classifier is an algorithm that implements a mathematical function to transform the multidimensional sentence embedding to the expected task output. When the model is learning a classification task, the classifier learns to relate features to the desired output labels based on annotated examples.

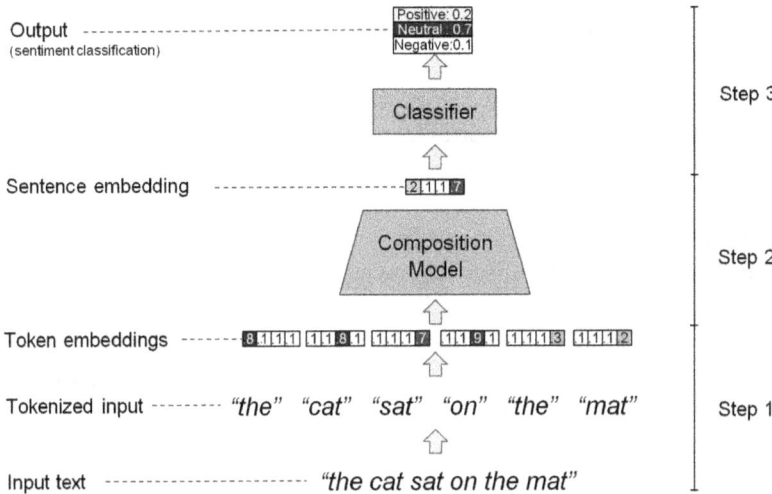

Figure 2: Overall architecture of a computational classification model.

4 Research questions

We assess nine state-of-the-art sentence embedding models in their ability to represent sentences containing a discourse connective. We follow Fraser (1988) and regard discourse connectives as a category of discourse markers.[6] Discourse connectives signal a predicate between two discursive objects (Asher 1993), which are clauses in our work. We focus on discourse connectives because of their pre-

---

6 We do note that different acceptations of this term cohabit in the literature (Chen 2019).

dominance in the datasets containing mainly written texts and the availability of semantic annotations (Prasad et al. 2008) of discourse connective roles. We address the following research questions:
1. Do sentence embedding models adequately capture the meaning of sentences containing a discourse connective?
2. How well do sentence embedding models deal with different connective types?
3. What is the effect of discourse connective removal on a sentence embedding?
4. If a connective is replaced with another connective, how much does this affect the sentence embedding?

RQ 1 *Do sentence embedding models adequately capture the meaning of sentences containing a discourse connective?*

The ability to recognize and create connections between words and sentence parts to infer relations and meaning is crucial for text comprehension (Best et al. 2005; Crosson and Lesaux 2013). A person's mastery of discourse markers and reading comprehension accuracy is shown to be positively correlated (Khatib and Safari 2011). The presence of discourse connectives facilitates text comprehension, as they explicitly mark the relation between two sentence parts (Sanders and Noordman 2000; Degand and Sanders 2002). Nonetheless, humans still heavily rely on world and individual knowledge when inferring discourse meaning and relations (Singer and Gaskell 2007; Noordman and Vonk 2015), even when connectives are present (Noordman et al. 2015). Like humans, computational sentence embedding models need to have encountered various connectives denoting various relations when learning a language to recognize, understand and leverage connectives for meaning construction. The models also need to gain in-depth knowledge of the real world to verify whether the discourse relations are valid or to infer relations when discourse connectives are absent. The pretrained sentence embedding models discussed in this chapter learn that world from the millions of sentences they were exposed to in the pretraining phase.

We first compare the nine sentence embedding models' performances on three language understanding classification tasks for sentences containing a connective word. As we aim to directly evaluate the sentence representations, we always use the same simple classifier, namely, a logistic regression classifier. This ensures a controlled comparison of the sentence embedding models. We assume that the model's ability to adequately capture all the needed information contained within the sentences will translate into adequate performance on language understanding tasks. Therefore, low language understanding task performance indicates an inadequate encoding of connectives in the sentence embeddings. Conversely, high model performance indicates a sufficient integration of a connective's semantics.

RQ 2 *How well do sentence embedding models deal with different connective types?*

Not all discourse relations are equally easy and fast to comprehend. The discourse connectives' relative cognitive complexities are often defined in terms of the order in which they are acquired in childhood. In this regard, Sanders (2005) hypothesized that causal relations are more complex than additive relations as additive connectives are first acquired when learning a language before causal connectives. That causal complexity hypothesis is supported by Bloom et al. (1980), who investigated the order in which English connectives appeared in the complex sentences of four children between two and three years old. They found that additive connectives are used earlier than those signaling temporal, causal, and adversative relations. Crosson, Lesaux, and Martiniello (2008) and Cain, Patson, and Andrews (2005) also confirmed that additive relations are cognitively the least complex of the four. Murray (1997) showed that the duration of human processing differs according to discourse connective types and that adversative connectives lead to the highest processing disruption. In contrast, Cain and Nash (2011) found that people process complex and specific connectives more quickly than the simpler, more general additive connective 'and', suggesting that higher complexity does not necessarily indicate longer processing or reading time.

We investigate deeper into the different types of connectives and compare sentence embedding behavior models in the presence of various connective types. We use the following connective types: additive, adversative, causal, and sequential[7] (Bernhardt 1980). Other categorizations of connectives or, more broadly, discourse markers have been adopted in the literature. For example, Fraser (1996) focused on the pragmatics behind discourse markers and categorized them as a type of pragmatic marker that only bears a procedural meaning and connects a message to a previous discourse. His proposed subcategories are topic change, contrastive, elaborative, and inferential markers. We refer to Alami (2015) for a more elaborate discussion on discourse marker categorizations. We hypothesize that sentence embedding models – like humans – will display differences in connective comprehension across the connective types.

---

[7] Instead of *sequential* connectives, the literature also uses temporal connectives; they can be considered synonymous as they both signal a sequence of events in time (Cain and Nash 2011).

RQ 3 *What is the effect of discourse connective removal on a sentence embedding?*

Humans process explicit information more easily than implicit information (Florit, Roch, and Levorato 2011). When discourse connectives are absent and discourse relations are implicit, they need to rely on higher-order skills to fill in the gaps (Rapp et al. 2007). Research on the effect of discourse connectives on human processing polarizes. Some studies (Al-Surmi 2011; Cevasco, Muller, and Bermejo 2020) conclude that the presence of a discourse connective does not affect the accuracy of following reading comprehension tasks, but some other studies (Loman et al. 1983; Meyer, Brandt, and Bluth 1980) confirm that discourse connectives facilitate human text representation. Some researchers (Millis, Graesser, and Haberlandt 2010) even report a negative impact.

We remove connectives from the language understanding task input text and measure the influence of this removal on prediction accuracy. Drawing parallels with the negative effects of connective removal on human discourse understanding, we hypothesize that connective removal will negatively affect the sentence embedding models' discourse comprehension and task performance. If the accuracy drops, the sentence embedding models have learned to incorporate the meaning of the connectives when representing sentences. If it does not, this suggests that the sentence encoders ignore the connectives for sentence representation.

RQ 4 *If a connective is replaced with another connective, how much does this affect the sentence embedding?*

Replacing a connective with another connective that signals a different discourse relation can lead to incoherence, thus making a sentence inexplicable or incomprehensible (Van Dijk 1977). Humans also need more time to process two-clause sentences when the connective signals an incorrect discourse relation that opposes the meaning of the two clauses (Cain and Nash 2011). As discussed in RQ1, both humans and computational systems need to rely on in-depth knowledge of the real world to verify whether a signaled discourse relation presents a state or event that can occur in the real world as perceived and acquired by the human or model.

We assess whether sentence embedding models can distinguish the discourse relations signaled by the connectives. We first replace each connective with a connective signaling a similar discourse relation. We expect that this substitution should not strongly affect model performance as the discourse relation remains fairly intact. We then substitute each connective with a connective signaling another discourse relation. We expect this switch to negatively affect model performance, as the sentence's meaning might be drastically altered and/or the sentence now presents an improbable reality.

5 Sentence embedding models and tasks

5.1 Sentence embedding models

Table 1: Sentence embedding models evaluated in the experiments.

Class	Model
Word order invariant	BOW
	SIF
	p-Mean
Word order aware: RNN-based	SkipThought
	QuickThoughts
	DiscSE
	InferSent
Word order aware: Transformer-based	BERT
	USE

Table 1 summarizes the nine sentence embedding models used in our study. We selected these particular models based on their popularity and their potential ability to capture the meaning of connectives. We group the sentence embedding models based on their encoding scheme: word order invariant (WO-invariant) and word order aware (WO-aware).

5.1.1 WO-invariant

WO-invariant embedding models represent a sentence by averaging all word embeddings (Figure 3). These models do not take into account the order of the input words.

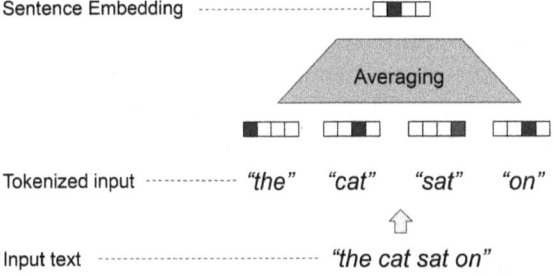

Figure 3: WO-invariant sentence embedding models: BOW, SIF, *p*-Mean.

Continuous Bag Of Word (BOW) is a widely-used baseline (Perone, Silveira and Paula 2018; Arora, Liang and Ma 2017; Tai, Socher and Manning 2015) which represents a sentence as the average of the embeddings of its words. In our experiments, we use two types of word embeddings: GloVe[8] and fastText,[9] denoted as **BOW-GloVe** and **BOW-fastText**, respectively.

Smooth Inverse Frequency (SIF) model (Arora, Liang, and Ma 2017) is an extension of BOW where the word embeddings are weighted during averaging. The weight of a word is inversely proportional to the frequency of that word in the training corpus. Following Arora, Liang, and Ma (2017), we use GloVe as word embeddings (denoted as **SIF-GloVe**) and set a, the parameter that adjusts the influence of word frequency on word vector weight, to $a=0.0003$ as suggested by the authors.

***p*-power Mean Concatenation (p-mean)** technique (Rücklé et al. 2018) computes a sentence embedding with a geometric average of the word embeddings instead of the previously used arithmetic average. In our experiments, we use the four word embedding models provided by the authors and set of powers $p \in \{1, 2, 3\}$, denoted as ***p*-mean-1**, ***p*-mean-2**, and ***p*-mean-3**, respectively.

5.1.2 WO-aware

WO-aware sentence embedding models take into account the order in which word embeddings are presented (Figure 4).

SkipThoughts (Kiros et al. 2015) trains an encoder-decoder neural network to predict the previous and next sentences based on the current sentence. Both the encoder and decoder are Recurrent Neural Networks, namely Gated Recurrent Units (GRU). This model is trained on the BookCorpus (Zhu et al. 2015) dataset.

QuickThoughts (Logeswaran and Lee 2018) is similar to SkipThought, but here, the network has to predict the next sentence among a group of candidates from the further neighborhood. We use two QuickThoughts versions, one trained on the Book Corpus and the other on the UMBC webBase corpus (Han et al. 2013). We refer to them as **QuickThoughts-BC** and **QuickThoughts-UMBC**, respectively.

---

[8] The GloVe vectors have 300 dimensions and were trained on the 840 billion words Common Crawl corpus, available at https://nlp.stanford.edu/projects/glove/
[9] The fastText vectors have 300 dimensions and were trained on the 600 billion words Common Crawl corpus, available at https://fasttext.cc/docs/en/english-vectors.html

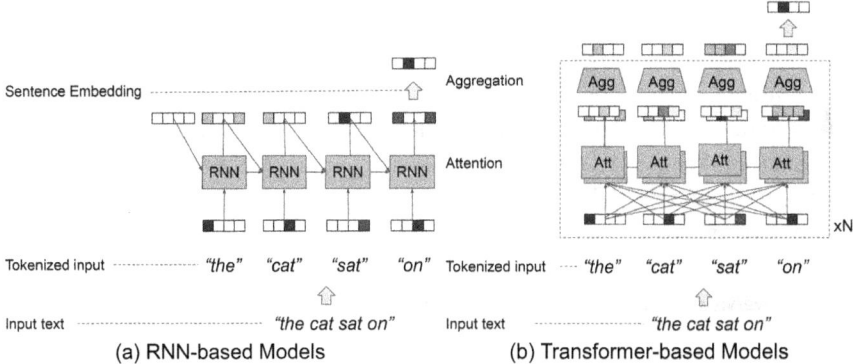

Figure 4: WO-aware sentence embedding models. Their architecture can either be based on a recurrent neural network (RNN) or a Transformer.

DiscSE (Sileo et al. 2019) is obtained with a RNN network that is trained to predict the discourse marker between two input sentences. The model is trained on a dataset derived from the Depcc corpus (Panchenko et al. 2018).

InferSent model (Conneau et al. 2017) builds sentence embeddings with a RNN network trained on a natural language inference task on the Stanford Natural Language Inference (SNLI) corpus (Bowman et al. 2015) and the Multi-Genre Natural Language Inference (MultiNLI) corpus (Williams, Nangia, and Bowman 2018). We use InferSent initialized with GloVe and fastText word embeddings as done in (Conneau et al. 2017). The resulting models are referred to as **InferSent-GloVe** and **InferSent-fastText**, respectively.

BERT (Devlin et al. 2019) is a bidirectional Transformer network trained with language modeling and next sentence prediction objectives, using data from the BookCorpus and the English Wikipedia. In our experiment, we use the BERT-Base and BERT-Large pretrained models containing 12 layers and 24 layers, respectively, and denoted as **BERT-12** and **BERT-24**.

Universal Sentence Encoder (USE) (Cer et al. 2018) is a Transformer encoder trained on multiple tasks including unsupervised tasks[10] (next sentence prediction and a conversational input-response task) and one supervised task (natural language inference). We refer to this model as **USE**.

---

[10] The data is crawled from a variety of web sources including Wikipedia, Web news, Web question-answer pages and discussion forums.

5.2 Tasks

The sentence embedding models are evaluated using the three following language understanding tasks: sentiment classification, paraphrase detection, and coordination inversion detection. Each task evaluates a different aspect of sentence understanding. Table 2 presents an overview of the tasks and datasets used in our experiments.

Table 2: Overview of the tasks and datasets used in the extrinsic evaluation of sentence embeddings.

Task	Dataset	#Test examples	#Examples with connective words	#Labels
Sentiment classification	MR	10662	7635	positive (5331) negative (5331)
	SST2	1821	1245	positive (909) negative (912)
	CR	3775	2603	positive (2407) negative (1368)
	OSCAR	2689	1970	positive (923) negative (1320) mix (174) neutral (272)
Paraphrase detection	MRPC	1725	1244	paraphrase (1147) non-paraphrase (578)
	PAWS	8000	5675	paraphrase (3536) non-paraphrase (4464)
Coordination inversion detection	CoordInv	10002	10002	invalid (5001) valid (5001)

Sentiment classification For a given sentence, the goal is to predict whether the sentence conveys a neutral, positive, or negative sentiment. The sentiment of a sentence depends on the words and the connections between them. Consider the following sentences:

(3) *The lioness hunts the zebra.* (neutral)

(4) *The magnificent and fearless lioness hunts the zebra.* (positive)

(5) *I like this movie because it contains violent scenes.* (positive-positive)

(6) *I like this movie although it contains violent scenes.* (positive-negative)

Sentence (3) is neutral because it simply describes an action without presenting an opinion or a sentiment. By adding words that convey a positive sentiment (magnificent, fearless), the sentiment of the entire sentence becomes positive (sentence (4)). Similarly, discourse connectives can influence the sentiment of a sentence or clause. In sentence (5), violent scenes are considered a positive aspect of the movie – or even movies in general – and reinforce the overall positive sentiment of the entire sentence. On the contrary, this aspect is presented as negative by using an adversative instead of causal connective in sentence (6). As a consequence, the overall positive sentiment towards the movie is weakened.

Coordination inversion detection The goal is to predict the natural ordering of two clauses. Given sentences composed of two coordinate clauses and a binding connective, 50% of the sentences are modified by inverting the position of the two clauses. The task is to predict whether the sentence was modified and thus *invalid*, or not (*valid*). Consider the following two sentences:

(7)   *I go to the doctor because I am sick.* (valid)

(8)   *I am sick because I go to the doctor.* (invalid)

Sentence (7) could naturally occur in a corpus, and sentence (8) is the coordination inversion of it. Due to the inversion, sentence (8) does not follow a plausible reasoning. Sentence embedding models should correctly encode semantic relations between coordinate clauses in order to fully solve this task. Discourse markers have a clear influence on this task, since replacing *because* by *therefore* in sentence (8) would make it much harder to detect a coordination inversion.

Paraphrase detection The goal is to predict whether two sentences convey the same meaning.

(9)   *The lioness hunts the zebra.* vs. *The zebra hunts the lioness.* (non-paraphrase)

(10)   *I go to the doctor because I am sick.* vs. *I go to the doctor even though I am sick.* (non-paraphrase)

(11)   *I go to the doctor because I am sick.* vs. *I am not feeling well so I am going to see my doctor.* (paraphrase)

Once again, this task is sensitive to word order, as illustrated in sentence (9). This task is by definition sensitive to semantic changes: sentences (10) and (11) show that changing a discourse marker is enough to change the expected outcome of a paraphrase detection.

6 Evaluation and discussion

6.1 Methodology

Many studies have explored the characteristics of human discourse processing, with a focus on discourse markers. For example, the presence and absence of markers elicit different reading behaviors in humans (Canestrelli, Mak, and Sanders 2013; Cain and Nash 2011), and different types of discourse markers also provoke varying reading responses (Murray 1997; Cain and Nash 2011). In order to investigate the mechanisms associated with the processing of discourse connectives by sentence embedding models, we set up four experiments corresponding to the four research questions described in Section 4. Unlike human language learners who have standardized language proficiency assessment systems such as TOEFL and IELTS, sentence embedding models do not have a standardized assessment system. It is therefore necessary to test the overall language processing ability of such models for sentences containing discourse connectives through designed experiments. We first set up a general evaluation to measure the models' ability to process and comprehend discourse connectives (General evaluation; RQ1). In controlled setups, we further study the influence of the presence of various connectives on model performance (Connective type evaluation; RQ2) and evaluate the language understanding tasks under specific connective perturbations (Connective omission/switch; RQ3/RQ4).

We select one-word connectives from the lexicons of Halliday and Hasan (1976). A manual annotation by two annotators was conducted to ensure that our evaluation focuses on the intended function. For each sentence, the connective words are selected and labeled with one category. The reliability of the annotations is ensured by a high inter-annotator agreement score of 98.82% (estimated from 150 randomly selected sentences with 254 candidate connective words). To base our findings on sufficient data, for each dataset, we only consider connective words that belong to the 5% most frequent words. We adopt the standard train/validation/test splits for each dataset, where a sentence that contains two or more connectives will appear in all relevant subtest sets. For the CoordInv dataset, we evaluate the split of the test set in valid and invalid sentences. We report the average of 5 runs per task and perform one-tailed t-test comparisons when applicable.

6.2 General evaluation

RQ1: *Do sentence embedding models adequately capture the meaning of sentences that contain a connective?*

This general evaluation answers RQ1 by measuring the model's overall ability to deal with discourse connectives. We select sentences containing one or more connectives in each dataset and evaluate the error rates (complementary to one of the accuracies) of the nine different sentence embedding models for these sentences.

Category	Model	MR	CR	SST2	OSCAR	MRPC	PAWS	CoordInv
Word Order Invariant	BOW-GloVe	0.23	0.21	0.20	0.37	0.27	0.43	0.47
	BOW-fastTex	0.22	0.20	0.18	0.35	0.27	0.44	0.48
	SIF-GloVe	0.44	0.31	0.40	0.42	0.32	0.43	0.50
	p-mean-1	0.22	0.20	0.17	0.36	0.27	0.43	0.46
	p-mean-2	0.36	0.32	0.21	0.48	0.29	0.43	0.50
	p-mean-3	0.27	0.26	0.21	0.43	0.27	0.43	0.48
Word Order Aware	SkipThought	0.24	0.20	0.18	0.35	0.27	0.36	0.32
	QuickThoughts-BC	0.20	0.17	0.15	0.51	0.24	0.32	0.30
	QuickThoughts-UMBC	0.18	0.15	0.13	0.51	0.24	0.30	0.31
	BERT-12	0.19	0.14	0.14	0.32	0.28	0.42	0.31
	BERT-24	0.16	0.12	0.11	0.30	0.31	0.42	0.29
	DiscSE	0.22	0.16	0.17	0.39	0.25	0.27	0.31
	InferSent-GloVe	0.20	0.15	0.17	0.36	0.25	0.26	0.33
	InferSent-faslText	0.26	0.25	0.18	0.42	0.26	0.26	0.37
	USE	0.20	0.14	0.14	0.30	0.28	0.41	0.41

Figure 5: Average absolute error rate for each sentence embedding model per task (General evaluation). For each dataset, color darkness is proportional to error rate.

Figure 5 confirms that WO-aware sentence embedding models (e.g., Quick-Thoughts, BERT, InferSent) outperform WO-invariant models (e.g., SIF, p-mean). On average, the former has a 24% lower error rate than the latter. The advantage of WO-aware models is particularly noticeable for the coordination inversion task (CoordInv). On this task, the error rates of the WO-invariant models approximate the accuracy of a random guess (i.e., 50% accuracy), which is substantially higher than those for the WO-aware sentence embedding models.

This can be explained by the fact that WO-invariant methods and WO-aware models dramatically differ in structure: WO-invariant methods simply take the (weighted) average of word embeddings. Each word is independently processed, and swapping the word order does not result in a change in the final sentence embedding. Therefore, they suffer from a very limited ability to capture semantic relationships. However, WO-aware models are designed with more complex neural network structures with multiple layers that can handle complex patterns.

Through layer-by-layer interaction, words convey information to each other. As a result, WO-aware models capture more subtle semantics between words and are better at processing words like discourse connectives that specialize in expressing the interplay of words/discourses.

Conclusion WO-aware sentence embedding models outperform WO-invariant models ($p < 10^{-3}$) in presence of discourse connectives.

6.3 Connective type evaluation

RQ2: *How well do sentence embedding models deal with different connective types?*

We now focus on individual connectives and evaluate the performance of the sentence embedding models for each connective type. The connectives are divided into four types based on the denoted discourse relation: additive, adversative, causal, and sequential (Bernhardt 1980). Although these types can be further divided into more specific subtypes, we opted for these four generalized types because each type should have a statistically sufficient number of samples and because they are often used in other studies of discourse markers' impact on readability.

We start by evaluating the general trend of error rate change caused by the presence of a specific connective. For sentence embedding model M and dataset D, we compute the connective-specific error rate $\epsilon_c^{M,D}$ when classifying sentences containing the connective c (Eq 1) and the overall error rate $\epsilon_{all}^{M,D}$ for all sentences in all the benchmark test set of dataset D (Eq 2). Subsequently, we calculate the error rate difference $\Delta\epsilon_c^{M,D}$ between $\epsilon_c^{M,D}$ and $\epsilon_{all}^{M,D}$ (Eq 3). For brevity, we compute all the average error rate change $\overline{\Delta\epsilon}_c^{D}$ (Eq 4) of all three ($N = 3$) WO-invariant and all six ($N = 6$) WO-aware sentence embedding models for each dataset D.

$$\epsilon_c^{M,D} = \frac{\#\text{misclassified c-type samples}}{\#\text{c-type samples}} \quad (1)$$

$$\epsilon_{all}^{M,D} = \frac{\#\text{misclassified test samples}}{\#\text{test samples}} \quad (2)$$

$$\Delta\epsilon_c^{M,D} = \epsilon_c^{M,D} - \epsilon_{all}^{M,D} \quad (3)$$

$$\overline{\Delta\epsilon}_c^{D} = \frac{1}{N}\sum_{i=1}^{N}\Delta\epsilon_c^{M_i,D} \quad (4)$$

The results (Figure 6) for each individual connective show great differences in error rates across the different connective types, suggesting that not every discourse relation is equally easy to process. Sequential connectives decrease the error rate in five out of six datasets that contain its kind (Figure 6(a)–(f)). In the sentiment analysis task (Figure 6(a)–(d)), the error rate of adversative connectives is the highest ($p < 0.003$ for all datasets). Adversative connectives such as *however, although,* and *but* are a source of confusion, showing that sentence embeddings overall have difficulties capturing the meaning of adversative connectives. The causal connective *so* is consistently associated with high error rates. Regarding additional connectives, *or* is more difficult to handle than *also* and *and*. Overall, the adversative and causal connectives lead to significantly higher error rates than the additive and sequential connectives ($p < 10^{-4}$).

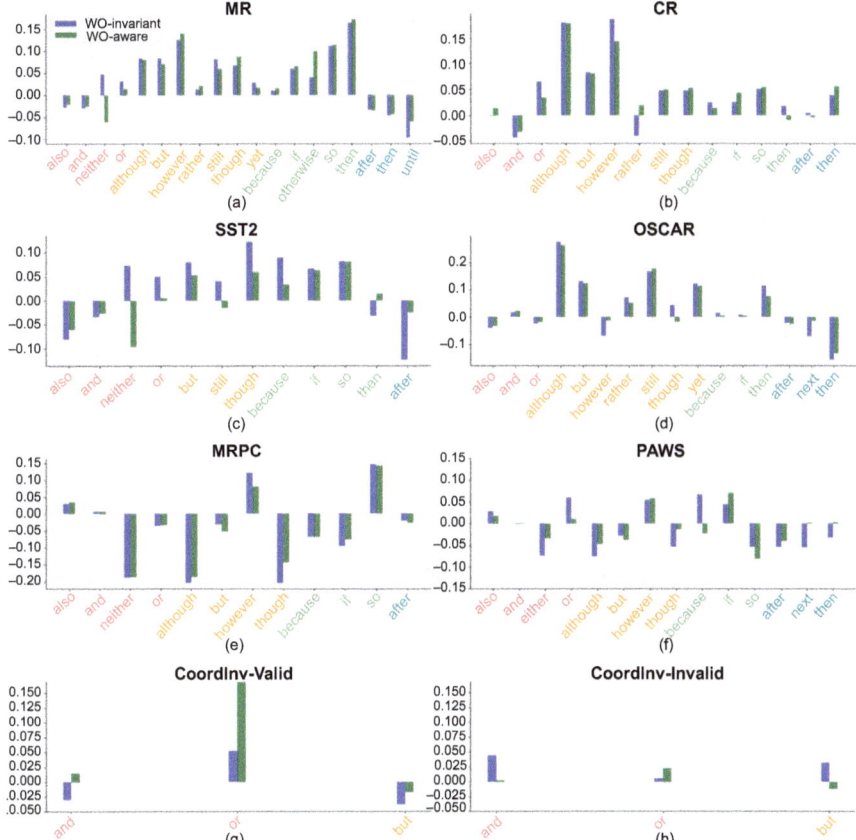

Figure 6: Error rate increase/decrease of WO-invariant (blue) and WO-aware (green) sentence embeddings for individual connectives (Connective type evaluation).

We observe different results for the paraphrasing task (Figure 6(e)–(f)). Additive connectives *also* and *and* slightly increase the error rate while adversative connectives largely lower the error rate. In the coordination inversion detection task (Figure 6(g)–(h)), connective *or* again correlates with a higher error rate than *and* and *but* ($p < 10^{-4}$). Overall, the impact of connectives depends on task type. The sentiment analysis task yields performance differences between connective types that are similar to their presumed complexity in the linguistic literature: higher performance with additive and sequential connectives and lower performance with causal and adversative connectives. This is in line with the complexity order of connectives established by Bloom et al. (1980): additive – sequential – causal – adversative (low to high complexity). However, in paraphrase detection and coordination inversion, the additional ones become the most difficult to process. This suggests that the effect of different types of connectives on computational language processing varies with tasks: paraphrase detection and coordination inversion are very sensitive to word order. Next, a person's mastery of discourse markers and reading comprehension accuracy is said to present a positive correlation (Khatib and Safari 2011). However, our study notes that the same phenomenon does not hold with sentence embedding models. Although WO-aware models have a richer knowledge of discourse connectives than WO-invariant models – as established in the general evaluation – both of them are similarly influenced by the different connective types. This suggests that sentence embeddings can use discourse connectives as superficial cues instead of using them to articulate discourse units. Concerning discourse processing speed, we cannot explore the difference between humans and computational models, as in most NLP models, sentences are all transformed into vectors of the same dimension and with the same computational cost.

Conclusion The sequential connectives are the easiest to handle across computation language understanding tasks. Adversative connectives are difficult to process in sentiment analysis tasks and additive ones are hard to deal with in paraphrase detection and coordination inversion.

6.4 Connective omission

RQ3: *What is the effect of discourse connective removal on sentence embeddings?*

We now modify connectives to directly evaluate their influence on sentence embeddings. For this, we leave out one connective in each input sentence by masking it with a special [MASK] token. This way, the sentence embedding models construct sentence embeddings that are not influenced by a discourse connective. We compare the error rate for all sentences in which the connectives are masked/omitted to the general error rate. The error rate change incurred by the omission is a measure of discourse connective importance. As connectives can strongly contribute to sentence meaning, we expect the error rate to increase in the case of connective omission.

Figure 7 displays the relative error rate variations when connectives are removed. Connective omission leads to an overall increase in error rates ($p < 10^{-6}$), suggesting that most sentence embedding models productively use the connective when computing embeddings. However, we observe that the effect of connective omission differs across the connective types. For example, omitting adversative connectives (e.g., *however*, *although*) affects error rates more strongly than omitting additive connectives (e.g., *and*, *also*) – with the highest error rate increase for *though* and *instead* ($p < 10^{-4}$). This suggests that sentence embedding models either heavily rely on adversative connectives or infer additive discourse relations better than adversative relations when a connective is missing. Intriguingly, we detect little difference in error rate change across connective types between WO-invariant sentence embedding models, which do not allow for non-additive interactions between words, and the more expressive WO-aware models. This could be attributed to a spurious correlation, which is confirmed upon dataset inspection. For instance, 58% of SST-2 reviews containing *instead* have a negative sentiment while only 20% are positive.

This highlights further differences between computational processing and human processing. Degand and Sanders (2002) suggested that discourse-insensitive tasks cannot present the significant effect of discourse connectives on human text processing. However, removing connectives in all datasets in our study results in consistent changes in error rates of computational models, suggesting that discourse connectives are a major factor in computational text processing, even for discourse-insensitive tasks. This conclusion is consistent with the observations in Section 6.2 that the explicitation of discourse connectives is essential for current sentence embedding models to infer pragmatic relations. By contrast, humans use discourse markers in a flexible way. For example, Cuenca (this volume, chapter 9) argues that even in academic text translation, where literal translations are predominant, omission of discourse markers is significant.

Conclusion The sentence embedding models appear to encode intra-sentential discourse relations relying on both the connective and the other words in the sentence. The processing of an adversative relation is the most dependent on the connective presence. Without correct connectives, the performance of sentence embedding models decreases across language understanding tasks. The depend-

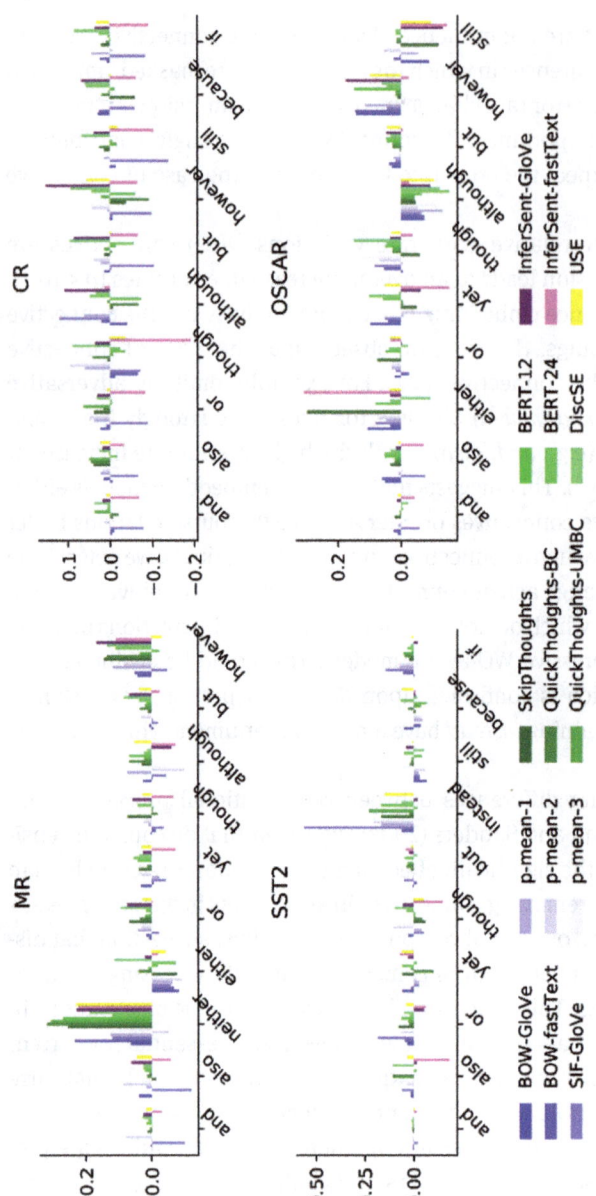

Figure 7: Error rate increase/decrease for each type of sentence embedding when corresponding connective words are removed (Connective omission).

ence on correct discourse connectives for computational language understanding systems is larger than that for humans.

6.5 Connective switch

RQ4: *When a connective is replaced with another connective, how much does this affect the sentence embedding?*

We observed in the previous section that the presence of a connective word can have a strong influence on the error rate. In order to assess whether the models fully exploit connectives and not the mere presence of a connective word, we measure how a switch in connective type influences model performance. For this, we switch a connective with a connective that conveys a different discourse relation (e.g., *because* → *but*). We specifically focus on changing causal connective *because* with additive connective *also*, sequential connective *then* and adversative connective *but* in the sentiment classification and paraphrase detection datasets (Figure 8).

Although connective omission has led to similar performance variations for WO-invariant and WO-aware sentence embedding models (Section 3.4), connective switches cause higher error rate increases in WO-aware models. This suggests that WO-aware sentence embedding models make more non-trivial use of the inappropriate connectives than WO-invariant models. Overall, switching connectives cause an increase in error rate for all switches – with the highest error rate increase for *because* → *but*. As observed in Section 6.4, we see that sentence embedding models are again most sensitive to adversative connective *but*. This sensitivity indicates that the models not only strongly rely on *but* when computing embeddings, but also correctly embed the discourse relation it conveys.

The connective switching results suggest similarities between computational models and humans when faced with unsuitable discourse connectives. However, inappropriate discourse relations caused by a switch in connective type affect humans and computational models differently: humans are more inclined to produce changes in reading behavior (Canestrelli, Mak, and Sanders 2013) and reading time (Cain and Nash 2011; Murray 1997; Loureda et al, this volume, chapter 2), but not always in eventual reading comprehension accuracy (Al-Surmi 2011; Cevasco, Muller, and Bermejo 2020). Computational models have the opposite behavior: inappropriate discourse connectives greatly increase the error rate in reading tasks. Further, humans with a deeper knowledge of discourse connectives are more likely to reject the inappropriate connectives (Cain and Nash 2011), but computa-

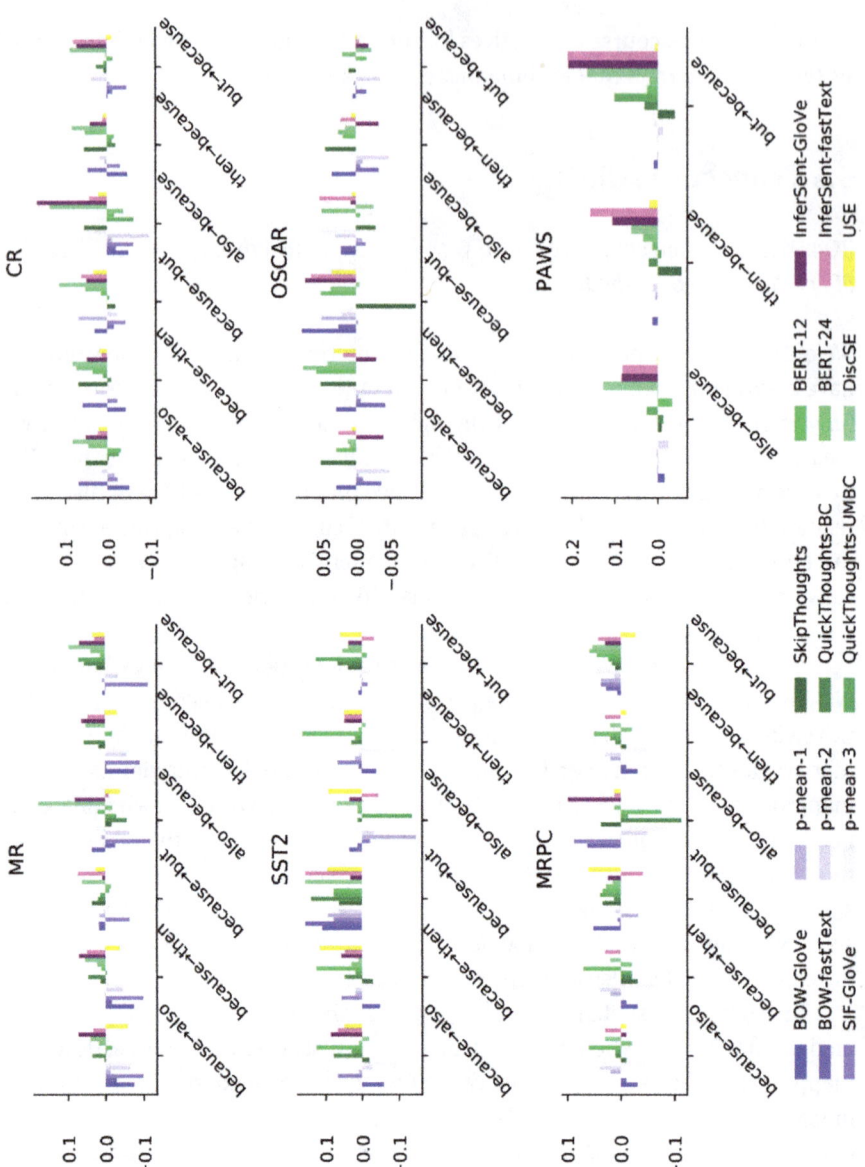

Figure 8: Error rate increase/decrease for each type of sentence embedding when corresponding connective words are switched (Connective switch).

tion systems with a richer knowledge of discourse connectives are more likely to be negatively affected.

Conclusion Substituting a connective with another connective that establishes a different discourse relation harms model performance, especially when it involves adversative connectives. The WO-aware sentence embedding models are more sensitive to connective switches than WO-invariant models. Contrary to humans, richer knowledge of discourse connectives makes a computational language understanding system more susceptible to the negative effects of incorrect connectives.

7 Conclusions

This chapter focused on assessing how connectives are leveraged in sentence embedding models and how the process differs from human processing.

As for the first general questions, our conclusions are: (a) The sequential connectives are the easiest to handle. Adversative connectives are difficult for computational sentiment analysis and additive ones for order-sensitive tasks. (b) Omitting connectives actually influences computational language processing. Models with rich (WO-aware) and poor (WO-invariant) discourse connective knowledge are influenced to a similar extent, showing the connectives alone have a substantial predictive power. (c) The connective switch generally has a negative influence on computational language understanding. Systems with rich discourse knowledge suffer the most from inappropriate discourse connectives.

Concerning the difference between the processing mechanism for discourse connectives of computational models and humans: discourse connectives promote reading continuity and reduce the time that humans need to process utterances but they do not necessarily have an effect on reading comprehension accuracy, while the opposite is true for sentence embedding models. Current sentence embedding models cannot infer intersentential relations without discourse connectives as accurately as humans. Consequently, the presence and appropriate position of discourse connectives significantly reduces the error rate of sentence embedding models in subsequent classification tasks. In summary, our evaluation sheds light on the extent to which sentence embedding models make use of connectives and can be used to pinpoint the strengths and weaknesses of current models.

References

Alami, Manizheh. 2015. Pragmatic functions of discourse markers: A review of related literature. *International Journal on Studies in English Language and Literature* 3(3). 1–10.

Allein, Liesbeth, Isabelle Augenstein & Marie-Francine Moens. 2021. Time-aware evidence ranking for fact-checking. *Journal of Web Semantics*. 100663.

Allein, Liesbeth, Artuur Leeuwenberg & Marie-Francine Moens. 2020. Automatically correcting Dutch pronouns "die" and "dat". *Computational Linguistics in the Netherlands Journal* 10. 19–36.

Arora, Sanjeev, Yingyu Liang & Tengyu Ma. 2017. A simple but tough-to-beat baseline for sentence embeddings. In *Proceedings of 5th International Conference on Learning Representations (ICLR)*.

Asher, Nicholas. 1993. *Reference to abstract objects in discourse*. (Studies in Linguistics and Philosophy 50). Dordrecht: Kluwer Academic Publishers.

Bengio, Yoshua, R'ejean Ducharme, Pascal Vincent & Christian Janvin. 2003. A neural probabilistic language model. *The Journal of Machine Learning Research* 3. 1137–1155.

Bernhardt, Stephen A. 1980. Review of cohesion in English M.A.K. Halliday and R. Hasan. *Style* 14(1). 47–50.

Best, Rachel M, Michael Rowe, Yasuhiro Ozuru & Danielle S McNamara. 2005. Deep-level comprehension of science texts: The role of the reader and the text. *Topics in Language Disorders* 25(1). 65–83.

Bloom, Lois, Margaret Lahey, Lois Hood, Karin Lifter & Kathleen Fiess. 1980. Complex sentences: Acquisition of syntactic connectives and the semantic relations they encode. *Journal of Child Language* 7(2). 235–261.

Bowman, Samuel R., Gabor Angeli, Christopher Potts & Christopher D. Manning. 2015. A large annotated corpus for learning natural language inference. In *Proceedings of the 2015 Conference on Empirical Methods in Natural Language Processing (EMNLP)*. 632–642.

Brysbaert, M., Emmanuel Keuleers & Pawel Mandera. 2014. A plea for more interactions between psycholinguistics and natural language processing research. *Computational Linguistics in the Netherlands Journal* 4. 209–222.

Cain, Kate & Hannah Nash. 2011. The influence of connectives on young readers' processing and comprehension of text. *Journal of Educational Psychology* 103(2). 429–441.

Cain, Kate, Nikole Patson & Leanne Andrews. 2005. Age- and ability-related differences in young readers' use of conjunctions. *Journal of Child Language* 32(4). 877–892.

Canestrelli, Anneloes R., Willem M. Mak & Ted J. M. Sanders. 2013. Causal connectives in discourse processing: How differences in subjectivity are reflected in eye movements. *Language and Cognitive Processes* 28(9). 1394–1413.

Cartuyvels, Ruben, Graham Spinks & Marie Francine Moens. 2020. Autoregressive reasoning over chains of facts with transformers. *Proceedings of the 28th International Conference on Computational Linguistics (COLING)*. 6916–6930.

Cer, Daniel, Yinfei Yang, Sheng-yi Kong, Nan Hua, Nicole Limtiaco, Rhomni St John, Noah Constant, Mario Guajardo-Cespedes, Steve Yuan, Chris Tar, Brian Strope & Ray Kurzweil. 2018. Universal sentence encoder for English. *Proceedings of the 2018 Conference on Empirical Methods in Natural Language Processing: System Demonstrations*. 169–174.

Cevasco, Jazmin. 2009. The role of connectives in the comprehension of spontaneous spoken discourse. *The Spanish journal of psychology* 12(1). 56–65.

Cevasco, Jazmin, Felipe Muller & Frederico Bermejo. 2020. Comprehension of topic shifts by Argentinean college students: Role of discourse marker presence, causal connectivity and prior knowledge. *Current Psychology* 39(3). 1072–1085.

Chen, Jiahuang. 2019. What are discourse markers? In *2nd Symposium on Health and Education 2019 (SOHE 2019)*, 1–9. (Advances in Social Science, Education and Humanities Research, Vol. 268). Atlantis Press.

Choi, Eunsol, He He, Mohit Iyyer, Mark Yatskar, Wen-tau Yih, Yejin Choi, Percy Liang & Luke Zettlemoyer. 2018. QuAC: Question answering in context. *Proceedings of the 2018 Conference on Empirical Methods in Natural Language Processing (EMNLP)*. 2174–2184.

Conneau, Alexis & Douwe Kiela. 2018. SentEval: An evaluation toolkit for universal sentence representations. *Proceedings of the Eleventh International Conference on Language Resources and Evaluation (LREC)*. 1699–1704.

Conneau, Alexis, Douwe Kiela, Holger Schwenk, Loic Barrault & Antoine Bordes. 2017. Supervised learning of universal sentence representations from natural language inference data. *Proceedings of the 2017 Conference on Empirical Methods in Natural Language Processing (EMNLP)*. 670–680.

Conneau, Alexis, German Kruszewski, Guillaume Lample, Loic Barrault & Marco Baroni. 2018. What you can cram into a single &!#* vector: Probing sentence embeddings for linguistic properties. *Proceedings of the 56th Annual Meeting of the Association for Computational Linguistics (ACL)*. 2126–2136.

Crible, Ludivine. 2018. *Discourse markers and (dis)fluency: forms and functions across languages and registers*. (Pragmatics and Beyond New Series 286). Amsterdam: John Benjamins Publishing Company.

Crosson, Amy C & Nonie K Lesaux. 2013. Does knowledge of connectives play a unique role in the reading comprehension of English learners and English-only students? *Journal of Research in Reading* 36(3). 241–260.

Crosson, Amy C, Nonie K Lesaux & Maria Martiniello. 2008. Factors that influence comprehension of connectives among language minority children from Spanish-speaking backgrounds. *Applied Psycholinguistics* 29(4). 603–625.

Degand, Liesbeth, Nathalie Lefevre & Yves Bestgen. 1999. The impact of connectives and anaphoric expressions on expository discourse comprehension. *Document Design* 1. 39–51.

Degand, Liesbeth & Ted Sanders. 2002. The impact of relational markers on expository text comprehension in L1 and L2. *Reading and Writing* 15(7). 739–757.

Devlin, Jacob, Ming-Wei Chang, Kenton Lee & Kristina Toutanova. 2019. BERT: Pre-training of deep bidirectional transformers for language understanding. *Proceedings of the 2019 Conference of the North American Chapter of the Association for Computational Linguistics: Human Language Technologies (NAACL-HLT)*. 4171–4186.

Dolan, Bill, Chris Quirk & Chris Brockett. 2004. Unsupervised construction of large paraphrase corpora: exploiting massively parallel news sources. *Proceedings of the 20th International Conference on Computational Linguistics*. 350–356.

Ettinger, Allyson. 2020. What BERT is not: Lessons from a new suite of psycholinguistic diagnostics for language models. *Transactions of the Association for Computational Linguistics* 8. 34–48.

Florit, Elena, Maja Roch & M Chiara Levorato. 2011. Listening text comprehension of explicit and implicit information in preschoolers: the role of verbal and inferential skills. *Discourse Processes* 48(2). 119–138.

Fraser, Bruce. 1988. Types of English discourse markers. *Acta Linguistica Hungarica* 38(1/4). 19–33.
Fraser, Bruce. 1996. Pragmatic markers. *Pragmatics* 6(2). 167–190.
Ghadery, Erfan & Marie Francine Moens. 2020. LIIR at *SemEval* – 2020 task 12: A cross-lingual augmentation approach for multilingual offensive language identification. *Proceedings of the Fourteenth Workshop on Semantic Evaluation (semEval)*. 2073–2079.
Haberlandt, Karl. 1982. Reader expectations in text comprehension. *Advances in Psychology* 9. 239–249.
Halliday, Michael Alexander Kirkwood & Ruqaiya Hasan. 2014. *Cohesion in English*. Routledge.
Han, Lushan, Abhay L Kashyap, Tim Finin, James Mayfield & Jonathan Weese. 2013. UMBC EBIQUITY-CORE: Semantic textual similarity systems. In *Second Joint Conference on Lexical and Computational Semantics (*SEM). Volume 1: Proceedings of the main conference and the shared task: semantic textual similarity*. 44–52.
Heyman, Geert, Ivan Vulic, Yannick Laevaert & Marie-Francine Moens. 2018. Automatic detection and correction of context-dependent dt-mistakes using neural networks. *Computational Linguistics in the Netherlands Journal* 8. 49–65.
Hu, Minqing & Bing Liu. 2004. Mining and summarizing customer reviews. *Proceedings of the 10th ACM SIGKDD International Conference on Knowledge Discovery and Data Mining*. 168–177.
Jernite, Yacine, Samuel R. Bowman & David Sontag. 2017. Discourse-based objectives for fast unsupervised sentence representation learning. *arXiv preprint arXiv:1705.00557*. https://arxiv.org/abs/1705.00557.
Khatib, Mohamad. 2011. Comprehension of discourse markers and reading comprehension. *English Language Teaching* 4. 243–250.
Kiros, Ryan, Yukun Zhu, Ruslan Salakhutdinov, Richard S. Zemel, Raquel Urtasun, Antonio Torralba & Sanja Fidler. 2015. Skip-thought vectors. *Advances in Neural Information Processing Systems (NeurIPS)*. 3294–3302.
Krasnowska-Kieras, Katarzyna & Alina Woblewska. 2019. Empirical linguistic study of sentence embeddings. *Proceedings of the 57th Annual Meeting of the Association for Computational Linguistics (ACL)*. 5729–5739.
Lai, Alice & Julia Hockenmaier. 2014. Illinois-LH: A denotational and distributional approach to semantics. *International Workshop on Semantic Evaluation*. Proceedings of the 8th International Workshop on Semantic Evaluation (SemEval 2014). 329-334. Dublin, Ireland.
Logeswaran, Lajanugen & Honglak Lee. 2018. An efficient framework for learning sentence representations. *Proceedings of the 6th International Conference on Learning Representations (ICLR)*.
Loman, Nancy, L. Mayer, Richard & E. 1983. Signaling techniques that increase the understandability of expository prose. *Journal of Educational Psychology* 75(3). 402–412.
Manning, Christopher D. 2011. Part-of-speech tagging from 97% to 100%: is it time for some linguistics? In A F Gelbukh (ed.), *Computational Linguistics and Intelligent Text Processing. (CICLing) 2011*, 171–189. (Lecture Notes in Computer Science, vol 6608). Berlin, Heidelberg: Springer.
Mei, Ning, Usman Sheikh, Roberto Santana & David Soto. 2019. How the brain encodes meaning: Comparing word embedding and computer vision models to predict fMRI data during visual word recognition. *2019 Conference on Cognitive Computational Neuroscience*. 1088.

Meyer, Bonnie J. F., David M. Brandt & George J. Bluth. 1980. Use of top-level structure in text: key for reading comprehension of ninth-grade students. *Reading Research Quarterly* 16(1). 72–103.

Millis, Keith K., Arthur C. Graesser & Karl Haberlandt. 2010. The impact of connectives on the memory for expository texts. *Applied Cognitive Psychology* 7(4). 317– 339.

Millis, Keith K. & Marcel Adam Just. 1994. The influence of connectives on sentence comprehension. *Journal of Memory and Language* 33(1). 128–147.

Murray, John D. 1997. Connectives and narrative text: The role of continuity. *Memory & Cognition* 25(2). 227–236.

Naseem, Usman, Imran Razzak, Shah Khalid Khan & Mukesh Prasad. 2021. A comprehensive survey on word representation models: From classical to state-of-the-art word representation language models. *Transactions on Asian and Low-Resource Language Information Processing* 20(5). 1–35.

Nie, Allen, Erin Bennett & Noah Goodman. 2019. DisSent: Learning sentence representations from explicit discourse relations. *Proceedings of the 57th Annual Meeting of the Association for Computational Linguistics (ACL)*. 4497– 4510.

Noordman, Leo G. M. & Wietske Vonk. 2015. Inferences in discourse, psychology of. In J. D. Wright (ed.), *International Encyclopedia of the Social & Behavioral Sciences*. Vol. 12, 37–44. 2nd edn. Amsterdam: Elsevier.

Noordman, Leo, Wietske Vonk, Reinier Cozijn & Stefan Frank. 2015. Causal inferences and world knowledge. In *Inferences During Reading*, 260–289. Cambridge: Cambridge University Press.

Panchenko, Alexander, Eugen Ruppert, Stefano Faralli, Simone Paolo Ponzetto & Chris Biemann. 2018. Building a web-scale dependency-parsed corpus from CommonCrawl. *Proceedings of the Eleventh International Conference on Language Resources and Evaluation (LREC)*, 1816–1823.

Pang, Bo & Lillian Lee. 2005. Seeing stars: Exploiting class relationships for sentiment categorization with respect to rating scales. *Proceedings of the 43rd Annual Meeting of the Association for Computational Linguistics*. 115– 124.

Perone, Christian S., Roberto Silveira & Thomas S. Paula. 2018. Evaluation of sentence embeddings in downstream and linguistic probing tasks. *arXiv preprint arXiv:1806.06259*. https://arxiv.org/abs/1806.06259.

Plank, Barbara, Anders Søgaard & Yoav Goldberg. 2016. Multilingual part-of-speech tagging with bidirectional long short-term memory models and auxiliary loss. *Proceedings of the 54th Annual Meeting of the Association for Computational Linguistics (ACL)*. 412–418.

Prasad, Rashmi, Nikhil Dinesh, Alan Lee, Eleni Miltsakaki, Livio Robaldo, Aravind Joshi & Bonnie Webber. 2008. The Penn Discourse TreeBank 2.0. *Proceedings of the Sixth International Conference on Language Resources and Evaluation (LREC)*. 2961–2968.

Rapp, David N, Paul van den Broek, Kristen L. McMaster, Panayiota Kendeou & Christine A. Espin. 2007. Higher-order comprehension processes in struggling readers: A perspective for research and intervention. *Scientific Studies of Reading* 11(4). 289–312.

Ruckle, Andreas, Steffen Eger, Maxime Peyrard & Iryna Gurevych. 2018. Concatenated p-mean word embeddings as universal cross-lingual sentence. *CoRR* abs/arXiv preprint arXiv:1803.01400. URL: https://arxiv.org/abs/1803.01400.

Sanders, Ted. 2005. Coherence, causality and cognitive complexity in discourse. *Proceedings of the First International Symposium on the Exploration and Modelling of Meaning*. 105–114.

Sanders, Ted J.M. & Leo G.M. Noordman. 2000. The role of coherence relations and their linguistic markers in text processing. *Discourse Processes* 29(1). 37–60.

Schiffrin, Deborah. 2006. Discourse marker research and theory: revisiting 'and'. In Kerstin Fischer (ed.), *Approaches to Discourse Particles*, 315–338. Oxford, UK: Elsevier.

Sileo, Damien, Tim Van de Cruys, Camille Pradel & Philippe Muller. 2019. Mining discourse markers for unsupervised sentence representation learning. *Proceedings of the 2019 Conference of the North American Chapter of the Association for Computational Linguistics: Human Language Technologies (NAACL-HLT)*. 3477–3486.

Sileo, Damien, Tim Van de Cruys, Camille Pradel & Philippe Muller. 2020. DiscSense: Automated semantic analysis of discourse markers. English. *Proceedings of the 12th Language Resources and Evaluation Conference (LREC)*. 991–999.

Singer, Murray & M. Gareth Gaskell. 2007. Inference processing in discourse comprehension. In M. Gareth Gaskell (ed.), *The Oxford Handbook of Psycholinguistics*, 343–359. Oxford, UK: Oxford University Press.

Socher, Richard, Alex Perelygin, Jean Wu, Jason Chuang, Christopher D. Manning, Andrew Y. Ng & Christopher Potts. 2013. Recursive deep models for semantic compositionality over a sentiment treebank. *Proceedings of the 2013 Conference on Empirical Methods in Natural Language Processing (EMNLP)*. 1631–1642.

Al-Surmi, Mansoor. 2011. Discourse markers and reading comprehension: Is there an effect? *Theory and Practice in Language Studies* 1(12). 1673–1678.

Taboada, Maite. 2006. Discourse markers as signals (or not) of rhetorical relations. *Journal of Pragmatics* 38(4). 567–592.

Tackstrom, Oscar & Ryan T. McDonald. 2011. Discovering fine-grained sentiment with latent variable structured prediction models. *Proceedings of Advances in Information Retrieval – 33rd European Conference on IR Research*. 368–374.

Tai, Kai Sheng, Richard Socher & Christopher D. Manning. 2015. Improved semantic representations from tree-structured long short-term memory networks. *Proceedings of the 53rd Annual Meeting of the Association for Computational Linguistics and the 7th International Joint Conference on Natural Language Processing of the Asian Federation of Natural Language Processing (ACL-IJCNLP)*. 1556–1566.

Van Dijk, Teun A. 1977. Semantic macro-structures and knowledge frames in discourse comprehension. *Cognitive Processes in Comprehension* 332. 3–31.

Wang, Alex, Yada Pruksachatkun, Nikita Nangia, Amanpreet Singh, Julian Michael, Felix Hill, Omer Levy & Samuel R. Bowman. 2019. SuperGLUE: a stickier benchmark for general-purpose language understanding systems. *Proceedings of the 33rd International Conference on Neural Information Processing Systems (NeurIPS)*. 3266–3280.

Wang, Alex, Amanpreet Singh, Julian Michael, Felix Hill, Omer Levy & Samuel Bowman. 2018. GLUE: a multi-task benchmark and analysis platform for natural language understanding. In *Proceedings of the 2018 EMNLP Workshop BlackboxNLP: Analyzing and Interpreting Neural Networks for NLP*. 353–355.

Williams, Adina, Nikita Nangia & Samuel Bowman. 2018. A broad-coverage challenge corpus for sentence understanding through inference. *Proceedings of the 2018 Conference of the North American Chapter of the Association for Computational Linguistics: Human Language Technologies (NAACL-HLT)*. 1112–1122.

Yung, Frances, Kevin Duh, Taku Komura & Yuji Matsumoto. 2017. A psycholinguistic model for the marking of discourse relations. *Dialogue & Discourse* 8(1). 106–131.

Zhang, Yuan, Jason Baldridge & Luheng He. 2019. PAWS: Paraphrase adversaries from word scrambling. *Proceedings of the 2019 Conference of the North American Chapter of the Association for Computational Linguistics: Human Language Technologies, NAACL-HLT 2019, Minneapolis, USA, June 2–7, 2019, Volume 1: long and short papers.* 1298–1308.

Zhu, Yukun, Ryan Kiros, Rich Zemel, Ruslan Salakhutdinov, Raquel Urtasun, Antonio Torralba & Sanja Fidler. 2015. Aligning books and movies: towards story-like visual explanations by watching movies and reading books. *Proceedings of the IEEE International Conference on Computer Vision (ICCV).* 19–27.

Darinka Verdonik

8 Discourse markers and dialogue act annotation for computational dialogue systems

Abstract: The aim of this study is to uncover the interaction between DM functions and dialogue segmentation. More precisely, we investigate to what extent DMs are used as autonomous dialogue acts or as part of a larger dialogue act. Dialogue acts are defined as speech acts following Austin's definition of illocutionary force. We hypothesize that the dialogual behaviour of DMs is informative of the function they will fulfil in discourse. The aim of the present study is thus to answer the following research question: Which DMs in what types of contexts can perform as dialogue acts on their own? Authentic conversation data in Slovene is used to conduct the analysis. As a result of the analysis, six criteria are defined that help distinguish DMs that are dialogue acts on their own. The importance of contextual bondedness and non-verbal, especially prosodic, features of speech in the interpretation of dialogue acts and DMs is outlined. The findings show that the majority of DM usages are not dialogue acts on their own, and at least some of those that are represent borderline DM usages.

Keywords: conversation, dialogue, speech act, basic unit of annotation, Slovene

1 Introduction

Dialogue acts are minimal units of interaction that express the speaker's intention (AMI 2005), or minimal stretches of communicative behaviour that have a communicative function (ISO 24617-2 2012). In addition to traditional speech acts such as asking for information (e.g., *What would you call it?*), providing information (*One of the things that you were doing was running a marathon.*) or giving

---

Acknowledgment: This work was funded by the Slovenian Research Agency, project HUMANIPA (research core funding No. J2-1737). Furthermore, I would like to thank the anonymous reviewers and the editors for their valuable comments and suggestions that helped improve this contribution to the volume.

Darinka Verdonik, University of Maribor, darinka.verdonik@um.si

https://doi.org/10.1515/9783110790351-008

instructions (*Come here!*), dialogue acts include discourse management acts such as making a pause and holding the floor (*Just a minute.*).

The concept of dialogue acts is tightly connected to computational work in building dialogue systems, i.e., systems where a computer communicates with humans by speaking. Early examples include the TRAINS project (Allen et al. 1994), map task studies – HCRC (Carletta et al. 1996), appointment scheduling and travel planning – Verbmobil (Alexandersson 1997), and in-car spoken dialogues – CIAIR (Irie et al. 2006). Today, such systems are termed conversational agents/personal assistants (e.g., Google Assistant) and are launched on the market by international IT corporations.

The origin of the notion of the dialogue act can be traced back to speech act theory (Austin 1975; Searle 1979), in which an illocutionary act is considered as the "performance of an act in saying something" (Austin 1975: 99); for example, apologising, offering help, stating information, etc. In computational linguistics, researchers worked with actual (albeit studio imitated and/or domain-specific) dialogues with the aim of developing a computer program that can communicate with humans by speaking. It was soon clear that the theoretically driven speech act theory was not prepared for field data, as some basic questions remained unresolved, such as: "How many types are there, and are they universal or culturally specific? How are they expressed in language? And how are they recognized or attributed in actual language use?" (Levinson 2017: 200). Speech act annotation schemes were therefore developed anew, with a strong empirical orientation. Types of acts such as signal-understanding, correct-misspeaking and tentative agreement were added to more traditional acts such as statement, offer, commitment, etc. Moreover, the core notion of speech acts was changed and the term *dialogue act* was introduced instead.

Today, dialogue act annotation of corpus data is a well-established field of research. Although tightly connected to the development of technology in the beginning, dialogue act annotation is also an active field of research in linguistics, especially in corpus pragmatics (Weisser 2016). A number of annotation schemes have been developed so far. Some are designed for domain-specific types of data, while others are generic, such as DAMSL (Allen and Core 1997), SWBD-DAMSL (Jurafsky, Shriberg, and Biasca 1997) or ISO 24617-2 (2012). Jurafsky, nonetheless, warns that "[t]he phrase 'dialogue act' is unfortunately ambiguous. As Bunt and Black (2000) point out, it has been variously used to loosely mean 'speech act, in the context of a dialogue' (Bunt 1994), a combination of the speech act and the semantic force of an utterance (Bunt 1995), or an act with internal structure related specifically to its dialogue function (Allen and Core 1997)" (Jurafsky 2004: 588). The present study follows Bunt's (1994) definition, whereby a dialogue act means a speech act in the context of dialogue.

Discourse markers (DMs) are "small words", typical of spoken language, fulfilling a series of non-propositional functions in discourse. They come in a variety of grammatical forms, including adverbs, conjunctions, multi-word phrases, etc. Among the numerous approaches to or definitions of DMs (overviews can be found, for example, in Fischer 2006; Crible and Zufferey 2015; Maschler and Schiffrin 2015), Maschler's approach to DMs was selected for the present research. Maschler (1994, 2009) defines DMs with regard to metalanguaging, whereby we use language to "look at the process of using language itself" (Maschler 1994: 327), in contrast to the general usage of language, whereby we "look at the world through the process of using language" (Maschler 1994: 327). With respect to the relation between discourse segmentation and DM use, Maschler (1994: 357) defines DMs as "the category of utterances used to metalanguage discourse boundaries", i.e., they signal switches between verbal-activity boundaries.

The approach adopted here is based on a similar type of data as Maschler's work, i.e., informal spoken conversation. It covers all of the expressions that have been previously identified as DMs in Slovene spoken dialogues. The first efforts to provide guidelines for DMs annotation in Slovene spoken interaction were presented by Verdonik, Rojc, and Stabej (2007). Later, the use of DMs in different spoken genres was examined (Verdonik, Žgank, and Pisanski Peterlin 2008; Verdonik 2010) and the procedure of automatic extraction of multi-word DMs from corpora was investigated (Dobrovoljc 2017). In these previous approaches to DMs in Slovene spoken interaction, DMs were commonly identified based on the distinction between propositional content and metadiscourse.

In the present study, the Slovene metadiscoursive expressions previously identified are included along with several additional expressions that appear in the data set, such as *ej* (e.g., *res sta izvirna **ej*** 'you really are original **though**') and *ma* (e.g., ***ma** taka ta prava* '**well** such a true one').

The problem dealt with in this chapter is the relationship between dialogue acts and DMs. Following Maschler's (1994) definition of DMs, some DM usages can represent a dialogue act on their own.[1] Below is an example from the Slovene data in the present study:

---

[1] All of the examples in this paper have been interpreted based on audio and video recording, not only on the transcription. For the general public, audio for each utterance is available at http://www.korpus-gos.net/, medium 'Television', event type 'Moderated show'.

(1) A is one of two evening talk show hosts and B is their guest on the show. A and B discuss the time of the year in which farmers cut grass.

A: *Eee v katerem letnem [času] pa je to? | Poleti, ne?*
'Uhm in what [time] of the year is this? | In summer, right?'
B: *[Ja.]*
'[Yes.]'
B: *Ja pa tudi še delno v jeseni.*
'Yes and partially also in the autumn.'
A: **Glej**, *| jaz kosim travo, ko je toliko* [hand gesture showing hight] *visoka.*
'**Look**, | I cut the grass when it is this [hand gesture showing hight] high.'[2,3,4,5]

A starts his turn with the DM *glej* 'look'. In this context, considering the non-verbal features along with the verbal expression, the functions of *glej* 'look' are primarily interpersonal and can be described as: grabbing the turn, grabbing the hearer's attention, stressing the content that is about to follow, connecting the utterance that is to follow with previous discourse, etc. Some of these functions have often been defined as dialogue act units, e.g., turnGrab (ISO 24617-2 2012), or as initiating a new phase of dialogue (Weisser 2019). From a pragmatic perspective, such functions of the DM *glej* 'look' are distinct from the functions of the following utterance ('I cut the grass when it is this high'). In this context, *glej* 'look' tries to influence B's discourse behaviour (to pay attention), while the continuation of the turn provides information and expresses A's attitude.

The present study focuses on DM usages of this kind in order to examine the boundaries between DM usages that could be treated as separate dialogue acts and usages in which the DM should be considered as part of a dialogue act, such as in (2).

---

[2] All of the English translations of Slovene DMs in this chapter are merely intended to approximately illustrate the original DM functions. DMs are language- and culture-specific and cannot be directly translated from Slovene to English.
[3] All of the examples in this chapter are from our data and are taken from the Slovene reference speech corpus GOS. We strongly recommend that readers listen to the examples in order to gain an acoustic impression. This can be done by copying the text into http://www.korpus-gos.net/, search option 'Search by standardized spelling'.
[4] In all of the examples in this chapter, the vertical line is used to mark borders between dialogue acts. Capitalisation and punctuation are added in order to facilitate understanding.
[5] Square brackets indicate overlapping speech.

(2) A TV host is teasing his guest that she and her friends have often (more than once) played a particular game with boys, trying to charm them:

A: *Slišim da je to kar nedovršni glagol, da kar se to dogaja.*
'I hear that this is a continuous verb form, that this is going on.'
B: *Ah ja no.* [laughter]
'Oh well.' [laughter]
A: ***Torej** greš | daj a si ti upaš iti do onega?*
'**So** you say: | go, do you dare to talk to him?'

In (2), the DM *torej* 'so' signals that the speaker will continue the discussion on a previously started topic that was interrupted by the interlocutor's comment. *Torej greš* 'so you say' could be considered as a single dialogue act, introducing the reported speech and/or describing the circumstances.

However, some cases are ambiguous, as in (3).

(3) The evening show starts with a set-up scene in which the TV hosts meet their guest on the staircase behind the stage and invite her to come with them, using a false excuse. While they accompany her to the stage, one of the show hosts explains to her:

C: *Ja leča je, **veš eee**, Ladotu padla na tla, | če bi lahko... | Ti imaš pa tanke roke | pa če bi lahko...*
'Well Lado's contact lens, **you know uhm**, has fallen on the floor, | if you could... | And you have thin fingers | so if you could...'

In (3), the speaker starts a dialogue act of explanation. After the initial words, he hesitates, taking time to formulate the second part of the utterance. Hesitation is marked with the DM *veš* 'y'know' and the filled pause *eee* 'uhm'. Hesitation is defined as a special dialogue act, i.e., "stalling", in ISO 24617-2 (2012: 80). According to this dialogue act annotation scheme, the DMs *veš eee* 'y'know uhm' could be treated as a separate dialogue act, but we cannot assign any particular illocutionary force to it.

In summary, the problem encountered during dialogue act annotation is the lack of specifications as to whether some DM uses should be treated as separate dialogue acts, and if so, which ones. The present study attempts to fill this gap and find answers to the following research question: Which DMs in what types of contexts can perform as dialogue acts on their own?

In order to answer this question, data in Slovene were collected and qualitative analyses performed. The study follows Austin's (1975) initial definition of illocutionary acts to interpret the dialogue act sequences. The analyses of DMs include all of the previously defined DMs in Slovene (see Verdonik, Rojc, and Stabej 2007; Verdonik, Žgank, and Pisanski Peterlin 2008; Dobrovoljc 2017) as well as some additional DMs that may be specific to this new type of data and that correspond to Maschler's (1994) definition of DMs. In interpreting the functions and meanings of DMs, the conversation analysis qualitative approach (Toerien 2014) is followed.

The following sections provide a brief overview of dialogue act annotation for computational systems (Section 2) and describe the methodology (Section 3) and results (Section 4). Section 5 includes the conclusions.

2 Dialogue act annotation

In dialogue act annotation, an utterance is commonly considered as the basic unit of annotation. But identifying when a DM performs as an utterance on its own is anything but a clearly distinguishable unit. Dialogue act annotation was initially inspired by speech act theory as formulated by Austin (1975) and Searle (1979). Some authors still annotate dialogue acts according to Austin's (Kang, Kim, and Seo 2010) or Searle's classifications (Qadir and Riloff 2011). Yet, a number of schemes differ significantly from the original theory. The following paragraphs provide a detailed overview of how several dialogue act annotation schemes define the basic unit of annotation with regard to DMs.

One of the most widely known and applied dialogue act annotation schemes is DAMSL (Allen and Core 1997). The DAMSL scheme "assumes an utterance is a set of words by one speaker that is homogeneous with respect to Information Level and Forward and Backward Communicative Functions" (Core and Allen 1997). This definition refers to the tagset defined in this scheme. The drawback of such a definition is that if we are faced with dialogue functions that the tagset does not include, we have no reliable theoretical guidelines as to how to treat such units. The DAMSL tagset does not define many communicative functions that directly correspond to DM functions. One exception is the Acknowledge (Backward-looking) function, which corresponds to backchannel signals. Specifically regarding DMs, Core and Allen (1997) mention 'okay': "Usually the only utterances shorter than a clause are sentence initial words such as 'okay'." Furthermore, they point to DMs that are used as part of self-repairs: "Words such as 'um' and 'er' and phrases such as 'I mean' have communicative functions separate from the clauses in which they appear." However, they do not treat such DMs as separate dialogue acts, as "DAMSL is not designed for annotating speech repairs, reference, or other intra-clause relations so [they] decided to use a simple definition of utterance that leaves out such phenomena" (Core and Allen 1997).

The SWBD-DAMSL tagset (Jurafsky, Shriberg, and Biasca 1997) represents a simplification of the multidimensional DAMSL[6] into a single-dimensional scheme. SWBD-DAMSL uses slash units as the basic unit of annotation: "A slash-unit is maximally a sentence but can be a smaller unit" (Meteer 1995: 16). Meteer (1995) points out that in speech it is common for units of speech to be shorter than complete sentences, but nevertheless to be felt as complete utterances. Furthermore, "[a]ny turn consisting of only continuers or assessments (expressions such as *uh-huh, right, yeah, oh really*) is also coded as a slash-unit. In a series of continuers/assessments, each one constitutes its own slash-unit" (Meteer 1995: 16). According to this interpretation, so-called backchannels are again considered as special dialogue acts.

An independent dialogue act annotation scheme was developed within the AMI project (AMI 2005). Dialogue act annotation in the AMI project "is about the type of intention the speaker has. Intuitively, each time a new intention is expressed, you should mark a new segment" (AMI 2005: 6). According to the AMI scheme, it is also possible to annotate a new segment if "the speech that might be a second segment adds any new information" (AMI 2005: 6). According to the AMI scheme, DMs are generally integral parts of the dialogue act that they introduce: "[C]onjunctions that introduce whole new clauses such as 'so', 'because', and some uses of 'and', 'but', and 'or' can be hints that a new segment is starting" (AMI 2005: 6). However, "not everything in the transcription really conveys a speaker intention" (AMI 2005: 8). Three dialogue act classes are therefore introduced that "aren't really dialogue acts but let us mark up everything" (AMI 2005: 9). Two of these three classes will typically capture some DMs: backchannels (AMI 2005: 9) and stalls: "Sometimes people start speaking before they are really ready, or keep speaking when they haven't figured out what to say, just to try to get or keep the attention of the group. When they do this, they often use special sounds called 'filled pauses', which are transcribed as 'uh', 'um', or 'mm' depending on how they sound, but they might also use words that don't commit them too much, like 'OK', 'yeah', 'like', or 'but'" (AMI 2005: 10).

The ISO 24617-2 (2012) guidelines for dialogue act annotation offer one of the most recent and state-of-the-art dialogue act definitions and annotation standards. The basic unit of annotation is defined as "a minimal stretch of communicative behaviour that has a communicative function" (ISO 24617-2 2012: 13).

---

[6] Further transformations of the DAMSL scheme can be found in the MRDA scheme (Dhillon et al. 2004), the MALTUS scheme (Clark and Popescu-Belis 2004) and others.

The basic units of annotation are very flexible: one basic unit can be embedded into another, or it may spread over multiple turns. Moreover, they are not limited to verbal behaviour, but can apply to non-verbal behaviour, as well. There are explicit guidelines so that annotators can choose either maximal or minimal approaches depending on their needs (Bunt 2019: 6). ISO 24617-2 (2012) includes a number of dialogue dimensions and belonging dialogue functions that could be considered as metadiscursive, such as turn-management functions, time-management functions, feedback functions and discourse structuring functions. DMs perform such functions. The examples already listed in ISO 24617-2 (2012) are: 'uh-huh', 'yes' or 'okay' as the "autoPositive" function of the feedback dimension, 'okay' as the opening function of discourse-structuring dimension, etc. The ISO scheme opens up the possibility of treating DMs as specific dialogue acts, especially if we choose to follow the minimal approach. DMs have communicative functions on their own. In the most extreme interpretation following these guidelines, each particular DM usage could be treated as a separate dialogue act.

The DART scheme (Weisser 2016; see Weisser 2019 for its latest release, DART 3.0) is a successor of the EAGLES recommendations (Leech et al. 1998), which also devote significant attention to dialogue act annotation and produced a generic taxonomy for dialogue act annotation (Leech and Weisser 2003). The DART scheme uses the C-unit as the basic unit of dialogue act annotation defined in Biber et al. (1999) as "[. . .] clausal and non-clausal units [. . .] that [. . .] cannot be syntactically integrated with the elements that precede or follow them" (Biber et al. 1999: 1070). C-units are maximal (or independent) units of conversational syntax consisting of clausal units, i.e., an independent clause together with any dependent clause embedded within it, and of non-clausal units, which are neither clausal units nor part of clausal units, e.g., response words, interjections, greetings, apologies, thanks, or expressions like 'oh', 'well', 'oh yeah', 'no', 'uh huh', etc. According to this definition of C-units, at least some DMs (e.g., 'oh', 'well') can be treated as separate dialogue acts. We can observe a shift from more traditional annotation guidelines in which only DMs that are somehow isolated, "on their own", in speech are treated as separate utterances or basic units of dialogue act annotation, to the recent approach of the ISO 24617-2 (2012) guidelines in which, at least theoretically, a number of DM usages could be treated as such. There are no clear borders regarding the extent to which this approach can be applied, as it has not been observed empirically thus far. In addition, dialogue acts are commonly annotated in imitated or studio-recorded dialogues; authentic data are rarely used. The language of the data is almost always English.

Based on the previous generic schemes, which are well documented and used to annotate a larger amount of data, the present research offers an analysis of authentic dialogue in Slovene.

3 Methodology

The data used in the present study are from a 44-minute video recording from the EVA Corpus (Mlakar et al. 2019). The recording contains a casual multiparty conversation from the Slovene evening entertainment TV show *As ti tud not padu* ('Did you fell in as well?'), broadcasted in 2008. A total of four different participants are engaged in the discourse, all of whom are public figures used to cameras and audiences. Since they also know each other privately, their social relationships are very informal, containing vivid emotional expressions. This results in discourse with a lot of overlapping speech, non-propositional material, unfinished utterances and self-repairs, hints, implied meanings, irony and humour. While this makes analysis more challenging, it reveals the processes of non-propositional meaning creation and expression to a higher degree than scripted data. The transcription and audio of this same recording is also part of the Slovene reference speech corpus GOS (Verdonik et al. 2013).

In order to answer the research questions, a theoretical perspective of dialogue acts is first established (see Section 2). Following Austin's (1975) original theory, dialogue acts are identified focusing on illocutionary force. It can be problematic to assign illocutionary force to DMs if we reduce the notion of illocutionary force to speaker's intent. However, Austin's original definition of illocutionary force was not defined as speaker's intent (such an interpretation was adopted later), but rather as a function or the type of use, and this can be assigned to DMs:

> For there are very numerous functions of or ways in which we use speech, and it makes a great difference to our act in some sense – sense (B) – in which way and in which sense we were on this occasion 'using' it. It makes a great difference whether we are advising, or merely suggesting, or actually ordering [. . .]. (Austin 1975: 99)

The most important emphasis of Austin's definition is on the notion of 'force', as he distinguishes between "force and meaning in the sense in which meaning is equivalent to sense and reference" (Austin 1975: 100).

Additionally, based on data observation, three guidelines were established in this study to define the segments of speech with illocutionary force on their own. First, illocutionary force is always defined based on the context of use, since "the occasion of an utterance matters seriously, and [. . .] the words used are to some extent to be 'explained' by the 'context' in which they are designed to be" (Austin 1975: 100). Second, illocutionary force needs to be directed towards the hearer/audience, i.e., it needs to be a social act. Self-repair segments or production problem signals may have their own distinctive sense or discourse function, but they carry no energy to influence the hearer/audience. Third, illocutionary force is expressed through the voice and other non-verbal modalities that accompany speech, not merely through the text. Prosodic or other non-verbal cues have a very important impact on which speech segment we define as a separate dialogue act that carries illocutionary force.

The example in (4) provides an instance of a metadiscourse segment that can have a specific illocutionary force:

(4)   A: *No ampak Špela zaenkrat eee še ni eee . . . | A si voditeljica tudi te eee celebrity te Kmetije slavnih?*
'Well however Špela for now isn't uhm . . . | Are you the host of this uhm celebrity the Celebrities' Farm?'
B: *Ne.*
'No.'
A: *Nisi ti voditeljica?*
'You are not the host?'
B: *Ne.*
'No.'
A: ***Aha**. | No, kajti tukaj je nov del in nove peripetije iz Kmetije slavnih.*
'**Aha**. | Well, because here is the new part and new adventures from Celebrities' Farm.'

The TV show host, A, asks his guest B (also a known TV host) if she is hosting the reality show Celebrities' Farm (this is not a real reality show, but a sketch in the present show). B denies this. A asks the same question one more time ('You are not the host?'), and B denies it again ('No.'). Using the DM *aha* 'aha', A then confirms that he has perceived and understood B's answer. He continues his turn with the announcement that the audience will now see the Celebrities' Farm sketch.

The data were examined carefully in order to answer the research question. Following Austin's theoretical perspective and the established guidelines for defining the segments of speech with illocutionary force on their own, manual qualitative analysis of each particular DM usage in the data was undertaken in an attempt to define whether or not it carries a specific illocutionary force, distinct from the illocutionary force of the previous or following speech segment. In doing so, it was also necessary to interpret the functions and meanings of each particular DM usage. No particular predefined DM annotation scheme was followed, as it would have limited the interpretations to pre-existing DM categories, which did not always correspond completely to the data or would need additional adjustment to Slovene. Instead, the conversation analysis qualitative approach was adopted (Toerien 2014).

All of the DM usages that were found to be dialogue acts on their own were observed separately, searching for repeating patterns, whether in the linguistic structure of the DMs or in the context of each particular DM usage. Thus, six criteria for annotation of dialogue acts that are commonly constituted from a single DM or a cluster of DMs were defined. Common patterns of all DM usages that were not dialogue acts on their own were also observed, in order to provide additional descriptions regarding which usages of DMs are not considered as individual dialogue acts.

4 Discourse markers used as separate dialogue acts

This section presents the results of the analysis by identifying two distinctive contexts. On the one hand, the types of DMs and usages in which they can perform as dialogue acts on their own. On the other hand, the DM types and usages in which they are not dialogue acts on their own.

4.1 Discourse markers as separate dialogue acts

Six different contexts may be identified where DMs function as separate dialogue acts.

First, DMs that are separated from the rest of the speech with longer or shorter pauses with an intonation fall can often be considered as dialogue acts on their own.

(5) A and C are TV talk show hosts. They start the show pretending that they do not have a guest for the show. They go behind the stage and decide to stop the first person who passes by to be their guest.

C: *Moment, | to je hec. | Šala, | mar ne. | Pojdiva, ja, | pojdiva, | pojdiva.*
'Just a moment, | this was a joke. | Just kidding, | you see. | Let's go, yes, | let's go, | let's go.'
A: *Tako. | Hitro, no.*
'That's right. | Hurry.'
A: *No. . .*
'Well. . .'

C: *Zdaj ta prvega, ki gre mimo . . .*
'Now the first one passing by . . .'
A: ***Okej.*** | *Okej jaz grem gor.*
'**Okay.** | Okay I will go upstairs.'

In (5), the first *okej* 'okay' is pronounced with an intonation fall and a short pause after it, and can therefore be interpreted as a separate utterance.

Backchannels like *mhm* or *aha* 'uhm' and *ja* 'yes' are another type of DM that is separated from the rest of the speech of the same speaker, acting as separate dialogue act units, as in (6).

(6) A, the TV show host, is describing his guest's (B) achievements in the Ljubljana Marathon. He prepares the ground to make a joke out of it, comparing his guest's results with the results of the winner. His guest uses backchannels *mhm* 'uhm' and *ja* 'yes' while A is talking:

A: *No eee . . . in evo le() Dan() Daneja Grandovec, [ne], letnik štiriinosemdeset, pa je zmagovalka.* | *Sicer iz Maribora.*
'Well uhm . . . and look le() Dan() Daneja Grandovec, [right], born in eighty-four, was the winner. | [From] Maribor.'
B: *[**Mhm.**]* | *[**Ja.**]*
'[**Uhm.**] | [**Yes.**]'
B: *Pa enkrat manj, ne?*
'Half less, right?'

When several backchannels are pronounced one after another with no pause between them, we will treat them as one dialogue act unit. In (7), B explains why it looks like the mayor of Ljubljana hugged her at the end of the marathon. The explanation is a joke. The TV show host C adds another joke. B uses two backchannels, *mhm mhm* 'uhm uhm' one after another to confirm her comprehension:

(7) B: *Sva drug drugega podpirala ne.*
'We supported one another y'know.'
C: *Midva se dostikrat podpirava, samo iz drugih [razlogov].*
'We often support one another but for different [reasons].'
B: *[**Aha aha.**]*
'[**Uhm uhm.**]'

8 Discourse markers and dialogue act annotation for computational dialogue systems — 203

Second, DMs that are prosodically emphasised function as a separate dialogue act. In (8), TV show host A is describing bizarre pornographic TV content at the TV station where his guest B started her career:

(8) A: *In on je to komentiral. | Na koncu oddaje je ponavadi pokazal eee tudi sam svojega pač, ne, [orodje].*
'And he commented on that. | At the end of the show he usually also showed uhm his own, y'know, [tool].'
B: *[Mhm].*
'[Uhm.]'
A: *Res res, to je teve Šiška. | Neverjetno.*
'Truly, truly. This is TV Šiška. | Incredible.'
A: ***In*** *| in potem se je stvar razvnela.*
'**And** | and then the thing got hot.'

A is describing the content of the TV show, then he makes a short pause to comment on what was described thus far ('Truly, truly. This is TV Šiška. Incredible.'), after which he continues his description, starting with the prosodically emphasised DM *in* 'and', the function of which is to convince the hearer and the audience to pay additional attention to what will follow.

Another instance of an emphasised DM is (9).

(9) A: *Eee začeli smo debato o tem, da . . . o tem, kaj si počela kaj, ono, tretje. . . | Ampak ena izmed zadnjih stvari, ki si ki si jih odmevno počela, je bilo to, da si šla maraton laufat oziroma polmaraton, |endvejs() enaindvajset kilometrov maratona.*
'Uhm we started a debate that . . . about what you have been doing, this, that. . . | However one of the last notable things you were doing was running the marathon or half-marathon actually, | twenty-o() twenty-one kilometres of marathon.'
A: *[**Ne?**] | In . . .*
'[**Right?**] | And . . .'
B: *[Tako], | to je zdaj štirinajst dni glih je od tega.*
'[Correct], | this is now fourteen days ago.'

Ne 'right' in (9) is pronounced after a short pause. It emphasises the given information and provokes B to confirm the information, which she does almost simultaneously. We should distinguish such usages from the usages of the DMs *ne*, *a ne* and *veš, a veš* (all of which are approximately translated with the English 'right' or 'y'know') as a segment ending and emphasis signal, which in Slovene is commonly prosodically integrated into the previous utterance and used quite automatically (see examples 19 and 20). This latter usage would not be considered as a separate dialogue act.

Third, DMs that are verbal imperatives in their grammatical structure may often express an attempt to affect the hearer's discourse behaviour. Such DMs are the Slovene verbs *glej* 'look', *veš kaj* 'y'know what', *čakaj* 'wait', etc. Two such usages can be found in (10).

(10) TV show host A explains how his guest B started her career at TV Šiška. She corrects him that it was not TV Šiška, after which A continues explaining what this TV was like:

B: *Tukaj je stacioniran, a veš. | **Čakaj**, | moraš biti eksakten, ne.*
'It was stationed there, you know. | **Wait**, |you have to be exact, y'know.'
A: *Tam . . .| **Glej**. | To j() to je televizija . . . | Ker jaz se je z() spomnim. | In sicer ko je bilo gor . . .*
'There . . .| **Look**. | This i() this is a television. . . | I re() remember it. | Because when they broadcasted. . .'

The DM *čakaj* 'wait' in (10) tries to influence the hearer to reconsider his own previous words, while the continuation of the turn introduces an argument why. *Glej* 'look' in (10) affects the hearer to pay additional attention, while the continuation of the turn provides information/argumentation.

Fourth, expressions that can either be used as DMs or not, and that have clear semantic meaning when not used as DMs, can be treated as separate dialogue acts especially in utterance-initial positions. Such expressions in the present data are *ne* 'no', *dobro* 'alright', *okej* 'okay', *mislim* 'I mean'. Many of their usages are often borderline and it is hard to decide whether they could be treated as DMs or not.

(11) C: *[Nekaj te rabiva no. | Saj ni nič takega zdaj, no.]*
'[We need you for something. | It's nothing special, y'know.]'
A: *[Da bi. . . eno . . . nekaj . . . | Če bi prijeti pomagala nekaj, če] . . .*
'That you would . . . one . . . something . . . | If you could help holding something, if. . .'
A: *Ne vem, če bi, no.*
'I don't know if I would.'
B: ***Ne**, | glej, saj pa bi lahko, a veš.*
'**No**, | look, you could, you know.'

In (11), *ne* 'no' expresses disagreement, while the following utterance introduces a contra-suggestion that is not explicit but implied through the DM *a veš* 'you know'. This usage of *ne* 'no' is borderline: it has some metalanguaging functions (grabbing a turn, introducing contra-argument), but its literal meaning (denial) is also outlined.

Furthermore, usages of DMs such as *dobro* 'alright' or *okej* 'okay' are frequently independent dialogue acts, as in (12).

(12) A: *In takoj na začetku je seveda ta pravi cajt, da jo posadiva in dava v luknjo slavnih.*
'And right at the beginning it is the right time to put her into the hole of celebrities.'
A: *Špela, može, lahko? | **Prav**.*
'Špela, agree, may we? | **Alright**.'
C: ***Dobro**, | si za, | to mi je všeč.*
'**Good**, | you agree, | I like this.'
B: *Nič nisem rekla, | ampak dobro.*
'I didn't say anything, | but okay.'

In (12), TV show host A asks his guest B if she is willing to put her head in a hole where only her face is visible, while around the face an unknown picture (in this case in the form of a chicken) is drawn. A does not wait for his guest to respond, but pretends that she has responded and that he has understood her response (using the DM *prav* 'alright'). Similarly, the second TV show host C uses the DM *dobro* 'good' to express that he understands that she agrees and that he is pleased with that, after which he explicitly outlines his interpretation that she agrees ('you agree') and at the end again explicitly expresses his satisfaction with this ('I like this'). As in (11), the usage of *dobro* 'good' as a DM in (12) may be ambiguous.

Fifth, if multiple DMs appear in a cluster, such as *ja ne* 'well no', *ja no* 'oh well', *ma ja* 'oh well', *okej nič* 'okay well', they are more likely to express their own specific illocutionary force, as in (13).

(13) A: *No, in daj mi povej, | a je eee kako a ka() kako je bilo delati. . . kako je delati na majhni, nikak(), torej eee zelo majhni televiziji, no.*
'So please tell me, | is it uhm how a h() how was it working . . . how is it working on a small, unimp(), so uhm very small television, right.'
B: ***Ja no**. | Saj veš sam, kako je z začetki, ne. | Začneš z majhnim, ne.*
'**Oh well.** | You know how it is with beginnings, y'know. |You start with small things, y'know.'

In (13), *ja no* 'oh well' expresses the attitude of the interviewee regarding what she was asked. The utterance following this DM cluster is an answer to a question.

Another instance from our data is (14).

(14) A: *Ne vem no.*
'I don't know.'
B: *No, kar, no.*
'Well, quite, well.'
C: *Redko.*
'Rarely.'
B: ***Ja no.***
[expresses hesitation, we find no English equivalents]

Example (14) represents the discourse segment in which the interlocutors express their opinion regarding how well TV show hosts A and C treat their guests (B in this example). There are sequences of DMs used to express personal opinions regarding the degree to which they think the guests are treated nicely or not.

Sixth, some DMs are used with the intention of starting an utterance or a turn, but the speaker is interrupted by another interlocutor, such as the DMs *eee* 'uhm' and *no* 'well' in (15).

(15) C: *Ne, ne [razumeš], | glej eee s(), midva nisva nikoli grda do svojih gostov... | [Eee]...*
'No, you don't [understand], | look uhm s(), we never treat our guests badly... | **[Uhm]**...'
A: *[No]...*
'**[Well]**...'
B: *[Mhm]. | Se samo malo pohecata, ne?*
'[Mhm]. |You just joke a little, right?'

In (15), TV show host A tries to grab a turn with the DM *no* 'well' (which overlaps with C's 'understand'), but then leaves the turn to his co-host C. At the end of his turn, C indicates with *eee* 'uhm' (which overlaps with B's 'mhm') that he will continue talking but stops and leaves the turn to B.

4.2 Discourse markers integrated in dialogue acts

The previous examples (5–15) show DM usages that are defined as separate dialogue acts. In order to provide a clearer presentation of when a DM usage can be considered as a separate dialogue act, we will now illustrate cases in which DMs cannot be considered as an individual dialogue act. We identified four different contexts.

First, turn-initial DMs that have a similar illocutionary force as the following utterance, such as *ja* 'yes', *ne* 'no', *aha* 'uhm', are usually integrated in the same dialogue act.

(16) C: *Samo moment, | dajte se majčkeno pogovarjat. | Kako ne veš, kdo je gost?*
'Just a minute, | please talk for a while. | How comes you don't know who the guest is?'
A: *Ja ne vem, | a ti nisi?*
'Well I don't know, | didn't you?'
C: *Ja ne, | jaz nimam . . . jaz nisem za to zadolžen,| jaz ne vem, kdo je gost.*
'Well no, | I don't have . . . I'm not in charge of that, | I don't know who the guest is.'
A: *Ja Bine bi moral reči, Bine.*
'Well Bine would have to say, Bine.'
C: *Kdo pa. . . | **Aha** ni ni() nimamo go() .. ni(). | Čakaj, | ne, kako ni?*
'Who then. . . | **Oh** he isn't is() we don't have gu() don(). | Wait, | no, how there is no?'

In (16), *aha* 'uhm' is a confirmation that the speaker has understood what was previously said, and so is the continuation of the turn: 'he isn't is() we don't have gu() don()'.

Second, DMs with an outlined connective function, such as ideational DMs (*in* 'and', *pa* 'and', *torej* 'so', *saj* 'because', *ampak* 'but', etc.), usually connect and maintain logical bonds between parts of the discourse. This cannot be considered as a specific illocutionary force. This is shown in (17) and (18).

(17) A: *[Jure, imamo?] | Hop, | Špela, stopiš na štengico tamle odzadaj.*
'[Jure, is it ready?] | Hop, | Špela, step on the stair back there.'
B: *[A kar takoj ali kaj?]*
'Right away or what?'
B: *Ja.*
'Yes.'
A: *Eee vključnjo s temle. | Daš obrašček skozi luknjo oziroma v luknjo.*
'Uhm including this. | You put your face into this hole.'
C: ***In** se nasmejiš.*
'**And** smile.'

Example (18) is the same segment as the example in (5), but a different DM is discussed here.

(18)   C: *Moment, | to je hec. | Šala, | mar ne. | Pojdiva, ja, | pojdiva, | pojdiva.*
'Just a moment, | this was a joke. | Just kidding, | you know. | Let's go, yes, | let's go, | let's go.'
A: *Tako. | Hitro, no.*
'That's right. | Hurry.'
A: *No. . .*
'Well. . .'
C: ***Zdaj** ta prvega, ki gre mimo . . .*
'**Now** the first one passing by . . .'

While (17) is very straightforward, (18) is less obvious. *Zdaj* 'now' is a connective element. It introduces the utterance, but also emphasises what is to follow. Emphasising the previous or following utterance is a rhetorical move, not an illocutionary force.

Third, turn-final DMs (*ne* 'right', *a ne* 'right', *veš* 'y'know', *no* 'though' – please note that the English translations are not real DM equivalents; to our knowledge, there are no such DM usages in English) are frequently used in Slovene. They are often used somewhat automatically and prosodically finish the speech segment, as in examples (19) and (20).

(19)   A: *A boš ti jo tam počakala | pa pridemo pol mi skupaj, no.*
'Will you wait for her there | and we come later together, y'know.'
C: *Glej, minutko nam daš **no**.*
'Look, give us a minute **y'know**.'
A: *Minutko.*
'A minute.'
C: *Špelci žiher **no**.*
'To Špela you could **y'know**.'
D: *Pa ne vem **no**.*
'Well I don't know **y'know**.'

(20)   A: *Ja ne na lokalni televiziji. | Na televiziji Šiška.*
'Well no, not on a local TV. | On TV Šiška.'
B: *Pa to ni Šiška **ne**.*
'But this is not Šiška **y'know**.'
A: *[Kaj ni Šiška?]*
'What is not Šiška?'

B: *[Tu je bil signal.]*
'[There was the signal.]'
B: *[Tukaj je stacioniran **a veš**... | Čakaj, /moraš bit eksakten **ne**.]*
'[It is stationed there **y'know**... | Wait, | you have to be precise **y'know**.]'
C: *[Ma Šiška, pusti... | Nima veze, Šiška.]*
['*Ma* Šiška, leave it... | Doesn't matter, Šiška.]

The utterance-final DMs in (19) and (20) would be treated as part of the previous utterance, not as dialogue acts on their own. However, if such utterance-final DMs are prosodically emphasised and provoke feedback from the hearer, like in Example (9) above, they can be considered as a separate dialogue act.

Fourth, fillers like *eee*, *eem* or *mmm* 'uhm' have no particular illocutionary force in most of the usages, as in (21).

(21) B: *Saj če sta resna, pol bi bilo najbrž dolgočasno, tako da...*
'Well if you were serious it would be boring, so...'
A: *Stari, to zveni kot tortura pri kakšnem **eee eee** zo() zobarju ali kaj.*
'Man this sounds like a torture at some sort of **uhm uhm** de() dentist or something.'
C: *Jaz se počutim, da sem jaz gost pri njej. | [Veš zdaj ona tukaj...]*
'I feel like I was her guest. | [You know, she now here...]'
A: *[Gledalci, poglejte si] **eee** poklic, | **eee** ki je, bi rekel, manj **eem**, kaj bi rekel temu, manj manj te je strah **eee** pri zobozdravniku kot očitno pri Špeli.*
'[Ladies and Gentlemen, take a look at] **uhm** a profession, | **uhm** which is, I would say, less **uhm**, how would you call it, less you are less scared **uhm** at the dentist than you are at Špela.'

The most general interpretation of fillers such as *eee* 'uhm' is that they signal that the speaker is searching for an appropriate expression; they do not express any specific force towards the hearer.

5 Conclusions

The present study has explored whether some DM usages should be treated as separate dialogue acts, and if so, what such usages are. The analysis of Slovene informal dialogue has led us to identify six criteria that can help us distinguish DM usages that can be treated as separate dialogue acts in some contexts:

- DMs that are separated from the rest of the speech with longer or shorter pauses with an intonation fall.
- DMs that are extremely emphasised in pronunciation.
- DMs that are verbal imperatives in their grammatical structure and used to affect the hearer's discourse behaviour (e.g., *glej* 'look', *veš kaj* 'y'know what', *čakaj* 'wait').
- Expressions that can either be used as DMs or not and have a clear semantic meaning when not used as DMs, especially in utterance-initial positions (e.g., *ne* 'no', *dobro* 'alright', *okej* 'okay', *mislim* 'I mean').
- DM clusters are more likely to express their own specific illocutionary force (e.g., *ja ne* 'well no', *ja no* 'oh well', *ma ja* 'oh well', *okej nič* 'okay well').
- DMs that are used with the intention of starting an utterance or a turn, but the speaker is interrupted by another interlocutor.

These findings are necessarily limited to casual conversation and additional research on other types of data is needed before drawing broader conclusions. The findings may be regarded as language independent, but some caution and additional validation is needed before applying them to other languages.

The criteria listed above depend on contextual bondedness and non-verbal, especially prosodic, features of speech. While defining the communicative functions of dialogue acts or DMs with regard to each particular context of use is already a wide practice (e.g., ISO 24617-2 2012; Crible and Degand 2019), the non-verbal features of speech do not always get the necessary attention in the annotation process (but see, e.g., Dhillon et al. 2004; Bartkova, Bastien, and Dargnat 2016). Yet, prosodic features have been shown to be key in determining their function in discourse or their status as DM (Aijmer 2002; Dehé and Wichmann 2010a, 2010b; Gonen, Livnat, and Amir 2015; Hansson 1999; Maschler 2009; Matzen 2004; Schiffrin 1987). Our study confirms that non-verbal features, especially prosodic cues, are among the central features of speech that need to be considered when interpreting the meaning of speech units. It makes a great difference whether a DM is pronounced in an emphasised, outlined manner, or almost automatically and prosodically merged with the previous or following speech.

We can conclude that DMs performing dialogue acts on their own (i.e., expressing illocutionary force on their own, considering the approach to dialogue acts in this study) function differently from DMs that are part of a broader dialogue act. The difference, however, is sometimes hard to draw, since the majority of the DM usages in the data used in the present study were not identified as dialogue acts on their own, as it was not possible to identify any specific illocutionary force they would express.

References

Aijmer, Karin. 2002. *English Discourse Particles*. Amsterdam: John Benjamins Publishing.
Alexandersson, Jan, Bianka Buschbeck-Wolf, Tsotumu Fujinami, Elisabeth Maier, Norbert Reithinger, Birte Schmitz & Melanie Siegel. 1997. *Dialogue Acts in VERBMOBIL-2*. Report 204. DFKI GmbH, Saarbrücken, Germany. http://www.jaist.ac.jp/~fuji/docs/papers/Verbmobil/report204/vmrep204.pdf.
Allen, James & Mark Core. 1997. *Draft of DAMSL: Dialog Act Markup in Several Layers*. https://www.cs.rochester.edu/research/cisd/resources/damsl/RevisedManual/.
Allen, James F., Lenhart K. Schubet, George Ferguson, Peter Heeman, Chung Hee Hwang, Tsuneaki Kato, Marc Light, Nathaniel G. Martin, Bradford W. Miller, Massimo Poesio & David R. Traum. 1994. *The TRAINS project: A case study in building conversational planning agent*. TRAINS technical note 94-3. Rochester, New York. http://people.ict.usc.edu/~traum/Papers/TRAINS93.pdf.
AMI. 2005. *Guidelines for Dialogue Act and Addressee Annotation*. Version 1.0. http://groups.inf.ed.ac.uk/ami/corpus/Guidelines/dialogue_acts_manual_1.0.pdf.
Austin, John L. 1975. *How to do things with words*. Oxford, New York: Oxford University Press.
Bartkova, Katarina, Alice Bastien & Mathilde Dargnat. 2016. How to be a Discourse Particle? Paper presented at the Speech Prosody 2016, Boston, United States, 31 May–3 June, 2016. https://hal.archives-ouvertes.fr/hal-01309251.
Biber, Douglas, Stig Johansson, Geoffrey Leech, Susan Conrad & Edward Finegan. 1999. *Longman Grammar of Spoken and Written English*. Harlow: Pearson Education.
Bunt, Harry. 1994. Context and Dialogue Control. *Think Quarterly* 3. 19–34.
Bunt, Harry. 1995. Dynamic interpretation and dialogue theory. In M. Martin Taylor, Françoise Néel & Don Bouwhuis (eds.), *The structure of multi-modal dialogue*, 139–166. Amsterdam: John Benjamins.
Bunt, Harry. 2019. *Guidelines for using ISO standard 24617-2*. [s.n]. https://research.tilburguniversity.edu/en/publications/guidelines-for-using-iso-standard-24617-2.
Bunt, Harry & Bill Black. 2000. The ABC of computational pragmatics. In Harry Bunt & William Black (eds.), *Abduction, belief and context: Studies in computational pragmatics*, 1–46. Amsterdam: John Benjamins.
Carletta, Jean, Amy Isard, Stephen Isard, Jacqueline Kowtko, Gwnyeth Doherty-Sneddon & Anne Anderson. 1996. *HCRC dialogue structure coding manual*. Technical Report HCRC, Research paper 82. Human Communication Research Centre, University of Edinburgh. http://www.justinecassell.com/discourse07/Week5Reading/Carletta_HCRCDialogStructure.pdf.
Clark, Alexander & Andrei Popescu-Belis. 2004. Multi-level Dialogue Act Tags. In *Proceedings of the 5th SIGdial Workshop on Discourse and Dialogue at HLT-NAACL 2004*, 163–170. Cambridge. https://aclanthology.org/volumes/W04-23/.
Core, Mark G. & James F. Allen. 1997. Coding dialogues with the DAMSL annotation scheme. In David R. Traum (ed.), *Working Notes: AAAI Fall Symposium on Communicative Action in Humans and Machines*, 28–35. Cambridge, MA: Publisher. http://www.justinecassell.com/discourse07/Week5Reading/Core_DAMSLannotation.pdf.
Crible, Ludivine & Liesbeth Degand. 2019. Domains and functions: A two-dimensional account of discourse markers. *Discourse: A journal of linguistics, psycholinguistics and computational linguistics* 24. Varia. http://journals.openedition.org/discours/9997.

Crible, Ludivine & Sandrine Zufferey. 2015. Using a unified taxonomy to annotate discourse markers in speech and writing. In Harry Bunt (ed.), *Proceedings of the 11th Joint ACL-ISO Workshop on Interoperable Semantic Annotation*. London, UK: Queen Mary University of London. https://aclanthology.org/W15-0202/.

Dehé, Nicole & Anne Wichmann. 2010a. Sentence-initial *I think (that)* and *I believe (that)*: Prosodic evidence for uses as main clause, comment clause and discourse marker. *Studies in Language* 34(1). 36–74.

Dehé, Nicole & Anne Wichmann. 2010b. The multifunctionality of epistemic parentheticals in discourse: Prosodic cues to the semantic-pragmatic boundary. *Functions of Language* 17(1). 1–28.

Dhillon, Rajdip, Sonali Bhagat, Hannah Carvey & Elizabeth Shriberg. 2004. *Meeting Recorder Project: Dialog Act Labeling Guide*. ICSI Technical Report TR-04-002. https://www1.icsi.berkeley.edu/ftp/global/pub/speech/papers/MRDA-manual.pdf.

Dobrovoljc, Kaja. 2017. Multi-word discourse markers and their corpus-driven identification: the case of MWDM extraction from the reference corpus of spoken Slovene. *International Journal of Corpus Linguistics* 22(4). 551–582.

Fischer, Kerstin (ed.). 2006. *Approaches to discourse particles*. Amsterdam, Boston, London: Elsevier.

Gonen, Einat, Zohar Livnat & Noam Amir. 2015. The discourse marker *axshav* ('now') in spontaneous spoken Hebrew: Discursive and prosodic features. *Journal of Pragmatics* 89. 69–84.

Hansson, Petra. 1999. Prosodic correlates of discourse markers in dialogue. *ETRW on Dialogue and Prosody*. Veldhoven, The Netherlands. http://www.isca-speech.org/archive_open/archive_papers/dia_pros/diap_099.pdf.

Irie, Yuki, Shigeki Matsubara, Nobuo Kawaguchi, Yukiko Yamaguchi & Yasuyoshi Inagaki. 2006. Layered speech-act annotation for spoken dialogue corpus. In Nicoletta Calzolari, Khalid Choukri, Aldo Gangemi, Bente Maegaard, Joseph Mariani, Jan Odijk, Daniel Tapias (eds.), *Proceedings of the International Conference on Language Resources and Evaluation 2006*, 1584–1589. Genoa, Italy: European Language Resources Association. http://www.lrec-conf.org/proceedings/lrec2006/.

ISO 24617-2. 2012. *ISO DIS 24617-2 Language resource management – Semantic annotation framework* (SemAF), Part 2: Dialogue acts. Geneva: ISO.

Jurafsky, Dan. 2004. Pragmatics and computational linguistics. In Laurence R. Horn & Gregory Ward (eds.), *The Handbook of Pragmatics*, 578–604. Malden, Oxford, Carlton: Blackwell Publishing Ltd.

Jurafsky, Dan, Elizabeth Shriberg & Debra Biasca. 1997. *Switchboard SWBD-DAMSL shallow-discourse-function annotation*. Coders manual, draft 13. University of Colorado at Boulder & +SRI International. https://web.stanford.edu/~jurafsky/ws97/manual.august1.html.

Kang, Sangwoo, Harksoo Kim & Jungyun Seo. 2010. A reliable multidomain model for speech act classification. *Pattern Recognition Letters* 31. 71–74.

Leech, Geoffrey & Martin Weisser. 2003. Generic speech act annotation for task-oriented dialogues. In Dawn Archer, Paul Rayson, Andrew Wilson & Tony McEnery (eds.), *Proceedings of the Corpus Linguistics 2003 Conference*. Lancaster University, UCREL Technical Papers, vol. 16, 441–446.

Leech, Geoffrey, Martin Weisser, Andrew Wilson & Martine Grice. 1998. *LE-EAGLES-WP4-4: Integrated Resources Working Group Survey and guidelines for the representation and annotation of dialogue*. Language Engineering Standards, LE-EAGLES-WP4-4 Integrated Resources Working Group. https://www.lancaster.ac.uk/fass/projects/eagles/delivera/wp4final.htm.

Levinson, Stephen C. 2017. Speech acts. In Yan Huang (ed.), *The Oxford Handbook of Pragmatics*, 199–216. Oxford: Oxford University Press.

Maschler, Yael. 1994. Metalanguaging and discourse markers in bilingual conversation. *Language in Society* 23. 325–366.

Maschler, Yael. 2009. Metalanguage in interaction: Hebrew discourse markers. In Turo Hiltunen & Irma Taavitsainen (eds.), *Pragmatics and beyond*. (New series 181). Amsterdam/Philadelphia: John Benjamins.

Maschler, Yael & Deborah Schiffrin. 2015: Discourse markers: Language, meaning and context. In Deborah Tannen, Heide E. Hamilton & Deborah Schiffrin (eds.), *The Handbook of Discourse Analysis*, 189–221. Malden, Oxford, Chichester: John Wiley & Sons, Inc.

Matzen, Laura. 2004. Discourse markers and prosody: A case study of so. *LACUS Forum XXX: Language, Thought and Reality* 30. 75–94.

Meteer, Marie. 1995. *Dysfluency Annotation Stylebook for the Switchboard Corpus*. Philadelphia: University of Pennsylvania. https://www.cs.brandeis.edu/~cs140b/CS140b_docs/DysfluencyGuide.pdf.

Mlakar, Izidor, Darinka Verdonik, Simona Majhenič & Matej Rojc. 2019. Towards pragmatic understanding of conversational intent: a multimodal annotation approach to multiparty informal interaction – the EVA corpus. In Carlos Martín-Vide, Matthew Purver & Senja Pollak (eds.), *Statistical language and speech processing: 7th international conference, SLSP 2019 Ljubljana, Slovenia, 14.–16. October, 2019*, 19–30. Springer, Lecture Notes in Computer Science.

Qadir, Ashequl & Ellen Riloff. 2011. Classifying sentences as speech acts in message board posts. In Regina Barzilay, Mark Johnson (eds.), *Proceedings of the 2011 Conference on Empirical Methods in Natural Language Processing*, 748–758. Edinburgh, United Kingdom.

Schiffrin, Deborah. 1987. *Discourse markers*. Cambridge: Cambridge University Press.

Searle, John R. 1979. *Expression and Meaning: Studies in the Theory of Speech Acts*. Cambridge University Press.

Toerien, Merran. 2014: Conversations and Conversation Analysis. In Uwe Flick (ed.), *The SAGE Handbook of Qualitative Data Analysis*, 327–340. London, Thousand Oaks, New Delhi, Singapore: SAGE Publications Ltd.

Verdonik, Darinka. 2010. Vpliv komunikacijskih žanrov na rabo diskurznih označevalcev. In Špela Vintar (ed.), *Slovenske korpusne raziskave*, 88–108. Ljubljana: Znanstvena založba Filozofske fakultete.

Verdonik, Darinka, Iztok Kosem, Ana Zwitter Vitez, Simon Krek & Marko Stabej. 2013. Compilation, transcription and usage of a reference speech corpus: the case of the Slovene corpus GOS. *Language Resources and Evaluation* 47(4). 1031–1048.

Verdonik, Darinka, Matej Rojc & Marko Stabej. 2007. Annotating discourse markers in spontaneous speech corpora on an example for the Slovenian. *Language Resources and Evaluation* 41(2). 147–180.

Verdonik, Darinka, Andrej Žgank & Agnes Pisanski Peterlin. 2008. The impact of context on discourse marker use in two conversational genres. *Discourse Studies* 10(6). 759–775.

Weisser, Martin. 2016. DART – The dialogue annotation and research tool. *Corpus Linguistics and Linguistic Theory* 12(2). 355–388.

Weisser, Martin. 2019. *The DART Taxonomy v. 3*. http://martinweisser.org/DART_scheme.html.

Maria-Josep Cuenca
9 Translating discourse markers: Implicitation and explicitation strategies

Abstract: In this paper, the strategies for translating connective DMs will be identified and illustrated by analyzing a parallel one directional corpus including papers from an academic journal publishing Catalan papers and their English translation. The DMs acting at the inter-sentential level have been identified and classified considering the source marker, the translated marker, the meaning of the coherence relation and the translation strategy. The analysis focusses on the factors favoring implicitation strategies (i.e. the omission of a DM or its substitution by a more general one) and explicitation strategies (i.e. the addition or specification of a DM) as clues to both the production and the interpretation process involved in the use of a DM. The results show that, although inter-sentential DMs in academic texts tend to be literally translated, implicitation and explicitation strategies are significant. The crucial factors to implicitate and explicitate are not only syntactic (scope, combination and collocation) and semantic (meaning of the marker and domain) but also more general aspects bound to the differences between the two languages involved and the translation process itself.

Keywords: implicitation, explicitation, connective DMs, Catalan, English

1 Introduction

Translating a DM is a two-fold task: first, the translator interprets the marker and then proposes a unit that transfers its relational meaning. The process implies the comprehension of the meaning and intended effects of the DM when produced and also a second-level production process by which the translator proposes a unit that transfers both the denotation and the connotation of its relational meaning. This comprehension-production task – based on an initial production in L1 by a different speaker – is affected by factors such as functional equivalence, frequency and conditions of use, including syntactic parameters (scope, position, co-occurrence and collocation). Both interpreting a DM and proposing a translation equivalent are also affected by the polyfunctionality and underspecification that a number of DMs typically show (see, e.g., Degand 2009; Crible et al. 2019).

Maria-Josep Cuenca, Universitat de València, maria.j.cuenca@uv.es

https://doi.org/10.1515/9783110790351-009

In this chapter, the general strategies and specific techniques used to translate DMs linking sentences or groups of sentences (inter-sentential or textual level) will be illustrated by analyzing a parallel one directional corpus including papers from a bilingual academic journal (*Catalan Historical Review*) that publishes the same paper in Catalan (source text) and in English (translated text). Special attention is paid to the factors favoring the omission of a DM or its substitution by a more general one (implicitation) and the addition or specification of a DM (explicitation).

Implicitation and explicitation are clues to both the production and the interpretation process involved in the use of a DM. Implicitation, mainly DM omission, has been observed in several contrastive analyses (e.g., Bazzanella and Morra 2000, Becher 2011a, Crible et al. 2019, Cuenca 2008, Dupont and Zufferey 2017, Hoek et al. 2017, Zufferey 2016). As for explicitation, several scholars have dealt with the addition of DMs in relation to the Explicitation Hypothesis, according to which translators tend to add linguistic material and thus translations are more explicit than non-translated texts (Blum-Kulka 1986). The Asymmetry Hypothesis (see Klaudy and Károly 2005, Klaudy 2008), a revised version of the Blum-Kulka's proposal, assumes that considering two languages explicitations in one translation direction tend to outnumber the corresponding implicitations in the other direction, an effect that has been observed as for the translation of DMs (see, e.g., Becher 2011a, 2011b; Marco 2018; Zufferey and Cartoni 2014).

The research questions that are addressed here are three:
a) Which are the strategies for translating DMs linking at the inter-sentential level?
b) Which factors (either syntactic or semantic/pragmatic) account for the implicitation or explicitation of a DM?
c) How can translation help uncover cross-linguistic differences in DMs use and processing?

The working hypotheses are the following:
(i) Underspecified DMs (such as *and*, *well* or *now* and their Catalan counterparts) are more frequently omitted or added in translation than DMs with a more specific meaning (such as *however*).
(ii) DMs are more frequently omitted or added when they act at the sequential domain (as opposed to the ideational domain, see Crible and Degand 2019).[1]

---

[1] Connectives can be used at different domains. In this paper, I assume three main domains: ideational or propositional, sequential or structural and interpersonal or modal. Crible and Degand

(iii)   Similar DMs show different frequencies and contexts of use cross-linguistically.

The analysis of the corpus of academic papers shows that inter-sentential DMs tend to be translated literally (or almost literally), but implicitation and explicitation strategies are also significant, especially when compared with other types of dynamic translation.

When translating a DM the translator takes into account the whole context of use, which can expand much further than in the case of other linguistic units. The crucial factors to implicitate and explicitate are syntactic – DM scope (either inter- or intra-sentential), combination and collocation –, semantic – meaning of the marker and domain – and more general aspects bound to the differences between the two languages involved and the translation process itself.

2 Methodology of analysis

The research described in this paper is a qualitative analysis of a corpus consisting of 10 papers in Catalan translated into English (*Catalan Historical Review*, volumes 11 and 12; total words: 99,958). The Catalan corpus includes 2997 sentences (i.e. units bracketed by full stop or equivalent), of which 532 (17.75%) are introduced by a connective DM. The relatively reduced sized of the corpus allows for a detailed analysis based on manual annotation. This process, although it is time-consuming, avoids the risk of misidentification of DMs either in the translated or in the source text, which would have an impact on the results.

The DMs in the source texts have been manually identified as a previous step to establish their English counterparts in the translated texts. The DMs in the translated text have also been manually identified in order to single out added DMs, that is, those lacking correspondence in the original.

The procedure followed to ensure that all DMs are identified entails several steps:
- Decomposition of the source text in sentences and identification of all the inter-sentential DMs, which generally occur in the second sentence left periphery but can also occur internally in the case of some connectives (e.g., parenthetical *però* 'though/however' and *doncs* 'then').

(2019) add a fourth domain, the rhetorical, which, in my opinion, overlaps with the sequential or the interpersonal domain. The DMs identified in the corpus act either at the ideational domain, linking propositional content, or at the sequential domain, indicating discourse organization.

- Search for the correspondence of each Catalan DM in the English translated version, either DM or other elements. This allows to identify correspondences as well as omissions.
- Decomposition of the English translation in sentences and identification of the inter-sentential DMs.
- Checking of the DMs in both versions in order to identify the DMs added in the translated version.

The examples have been included in a data-base and analyzed considering several features: The source marker, the translated marker, the meaning of the coherence relation and the translation strategies and specific techniques. Additionally, other features, such as the category of the marker, combinations or significant collocations have been taken into account.

The analysis of the data aims at uncovering the factors favoring implicitation and explicitation in the translation of inter-sentential DM in the Catalan-English direction.

3 Strategies and techniques for translating a DM: Literal and non-literal translation

The definition and classification of translation techniques is varied. Departing from Vinay and Darbelnet's (1958) seminal proposal of seven basic techniques classified as types of either direct or oblique translation, different authors have proposed an array of techniques, mainly applied to lexical units with a 'dictionary-like' meaning (see Molina and Hurtado 2002 for a critical review and a functional proposal). Oblique or dynamic translation includes a variety of procedures among which there is omission (as a type of reduction) and addition (as a type of amplification) of linguistic material.

In this research, six techniques to translate a DM will be distinguished:
a) Literal (or almost literal) translation, when the translated DM has a 'dictionary-like' correspondence in the source DM.
b) Omission of a DM.
c) Generalization of meaning.
d) Addition of a DM.
e) Specification of meaning.
f) Non-literal translation of an explicit DM by another DM or another linguistic unit, with a different semantic meaning.

For the purposes of this paper, the techniques have been grouped into three general strategies, namely, maintenance of the DM (including either literal translation or non-literal translation by a semantically unrelated lexical unit), implicitation of the DM or its meaning (i.e, omission and generalization of meaning) and explicitation of the DM or its meaning (i.e, addition and specification of meaning). Other non-literal or dynamic correspondences have been included under the general label of substitution. Table 1 shows the number of cases and percentage for each technique in the Catalan-English translation corpus.

Table 1: Techniques and strategies to translate inter-sentential DMs.

Technique	N/%	Strategy
Literal/almost literal translation	400 (75.2%)	Maintenance: 400 (75.2%)
DM omission	37 (7%)	Implicitation: 67 (12.6%)
Generalization of meaning	30 (5.6%)	
DM addition	34 (6.4%)	Explicitation: 53 (9.9%)
Specification of meaning	19 (3.5%)	
Non-literal translation	12 (2.2%)	Substitution: 12 (2.2%)
Total	532 (100%)	

a) A DM is literally translated (400 cases in the corpus, 75.2%) when the target DM keeps its semantic and pragmatic meaning. The translated marker can be a direct (or almost direct) counterpart of the source DM or a very close correspondence not affecting the meaning or conditions of use of the DM in the two languages considered.

(1) *Gaudí va optar des del primer moment per continuar l'obra sense fer un nou projecte global del temple. I mai no el faria.* (CHR12, González, 175)
'From the outset, Gaudí chose to carry on with the original project without making a new set of blueprints of the temple. **And** he never did'

(2) *Hi tingué força a veure el model d'estat liberal que es bastí, força similar al francès, uniforme i centralitzat, que havia d'exercir una tutela sobre la societat en tant que únic representant legítim dels interessos col·lectius, **però** també pel pes de la moral catòlica, molt present en les pràctiques polítiques.* (CHR12, Rubí, 178)
'This had a great deal to do with the model of liberal state which was being forged, which was quite similar to the uniform, centralised model in France that was supposed to oversee society as the sole legitimate representative of collective interests. **However**, it was also because of the importance of Catholicism in political practices'

In (1) the conjunction *i* is literally translated by its verbatim equivalent *and*. In (2) an intra-sentential DM corresponding to the conjunction *però* ('but') turns into an inter-sentential parenthetical connective (*however*), but the contrastive meaning of general opposition is kept.

b) DMs are omitted in 37 examples (7%). Omission (marked in the examples as ∅) can be either total or partial.

(3) *I,* **en la mateixa línia**, *cal prestar atenció a les discussions sobre el rol de la natura en la construcció de les identitats. S'ha treballat,* **per exemple***, el concepte de natura en el context de la formació dels estats moderns, la creació social dels paisatges a partir de la geografia catalana en el període entre 1870 i 1939, les consideracions dels estudis científics sobre la natura dins el marc de la Renaixença [. . .]* (CHR12, Martí, 15)
'∅ **In the same vein**, attention must be paid to the discussions on the role of nature in the construction of identities. Studies have examined ∅ the concept of nature within the context of education in modern states; the social creation of landscapes based on Catalan geography in the period from 1870 to 1939; the consideration of scientific studies on nature within the framework of the Renaixença [. . .]'

In (3) two DMs, namely *i* 'and' and *per exemple* 'for example', have been deleted. The first case is considered as partial omission, because only one of two co-occurring DMs has been deleted, whereas in the second case no DM is kept (total omission).

c) In 30 examples (5.6%) the DM in the translated text keeps the basic instruction of the source DM, but exhibits a more general meaning.

(4) *L'arquitecte va acollir la idea amb escepticisme, possiblement relacionat amb una certa por del fracàs o el desinterès, ja que creia que els francesos no comprenien la seva obra.* **Ben al contrari***, diu Martinell, Eusebi Güell es va manifestar entusiasmat amb la idea i es va oferir a patrocinar-la.* (CHR12, González, 173)
'The architect listened to his idea skeptically, perhaps because he was afraid of failing or not inspiring interest, since he thought that the French did not grasp his works. **However**, unlike Gaudí, says Martinell, Eusebi Güell expressed his enthusiasm for the idea and offered to sponsor the exhibition'.

In (4) the refutation meaning of *ben al contrari* 'on the contrary' turns into general contrast (*however*).

d) DMs are added in the translated text in 34 examples (6.4%).

(5) *Aquesta va ser una terra en la qual les famílies acabalades romanes i itàliques van invertir en terres per a fer vi, fet que també les va convertir en destinació d'immigrants. Ø L'exponent més clar de la introducció del sistema de la villa serà el cultiu de la vinya.* (CHR12, Prevosti, 128)
'This was a region where the wealthy Roman and Italic families invested in lands to produce wine, which also made it the destination of immigrants. **Indeed**, the clearest sign of the introduction of the villa system was the cultivation of grapes'.

In (5), the additive continuative marker *indeed* introduces a sentence that had no corresponding DM in the original.

e) In 19 examples (3.5%), the DM in the translated text has a more specific meaning than the original Catalan DM, as in (6), where the Catalan conjunction *i* 'and' is translated as *furthermore*.

(6) *Treien profit de l'espai sobre el qual tenien jurisdicció, que era fonamentalment agrícola i ramader, per bé que també explotaven els boscos, els rius i la costa i eventualment els metalls i les pedres. I val a dir que foren ciutats petites en el conjunt de l'Imperi, per bé que profundament aculturades.* (CHR12, Prevosti, 121)
'They exploited the space over which they held jurisdiction, essentially through crop and livestock farming, although they also harvested resources from forests, rivers and the coast, and eventually metals and stones as well. **Furthermore**, it is worth noting that they were small cities within the empire as a whole, albeit profoundly acculturated ones'.

f) The translated DMs seldom imply remarkable meaning change (12 cases, 2.2%). A non-literal translation can derive from an error either in the original or in the translation.

(7) *Tampoc no es documenta la producció d'àmfores oliàries al Conventus Tarraconensis, tot i que sí al sud de València, al taller d'Oliva, per exemple. En canvi, la importació d'àmfores oliàries de la Bètica és certament escadussera a l'àrea que tractem.* (CHR12, Prevosti, 125)
'Nor is there proof of the production of amphorae for oil in the Conventus Tarraconensis, even though there is in southern Valencia, such as in the Oliva workshop. **Likewise**, imports of oil amphorae from the Baetica are very scarce in the area we are examining'.

In (7) a contrastive marker, *en canvi* ('in contrast'), translates into a comparative marker, *likewise*. Interestingly, the translator seems to have corrected a weird use in the original, since there is no contrast between the two sentences linked by *en canvi*. In other cases, there is no error involved, as in (8).

(8) *Durant aquest llarg període temporal, societat civil, sociabilitat, associacionisme i ateneisme han anat molt sovint de la mà i s'han barrejat en una comunió gairebé perfecta.*
Però, *d'on ve el nom* d'ateneu? (CHR11, Izquierdo, 152)
'During this long period, civil society, sociability, associationism and membership in athenaeums have often gone hand-in-hand and have merged in an almost perfect communion.
So where does the name athenaeum come from?'

In (8) the DM introduces a topic change, which can be interpreted contrastively or as a continuation of discourse. The meaning of both ambiguous markers – at the sequential domain they do not indicate contrast or consequence but continuity – allows for a non-literal translation.

In summary, in the corpus analyzed, including academic papers in the field of History, most inter-sentential DMs are translated literally or almost literally (400 cases out of 532, 75.2%), with occasional changes in category or position. Implicitation strategies are relatively frequent (37 omissions and 30 generalizations of meaning, 12.6%). Explicitation is slightly less frequent in the corpus (34 additions and 19 cases of meaning specification, 9.9%). Dynamic translation of a DM by a DM or another lexical unit with a clearly different meaning is residual (12 cases, 2.2%). Let us take a closer look to implicitation and explicitation strategies.

4 Implicitation in DM translation

Implicitation in translation accounts for those cases in which the target text "is less explicit (more implicit) than the corresponding source text" (Becher 2011b: 19). According to Klaudy and Károly (2005), implicitation can derive from omission, contraction or generalization.

Omission has received some attention in the previous literature on DMs in translation. There are several papers that indicate that omission is a relatively frequent strategy in the translation of DMs, especially in oral interactive texts.[2] Omission has been reported as a frequent strategy in the case of underspecified markers. For instance, Bazzanella and Morra (2000) identify 39% of the occurrences of *well* that were deleted in an English novel translated into Italian. Similarly, in Cuenca's (2008) analysis of the translation of *well* in a dubbed English film, this DM was deleted in 25% of the cases in the Spanish and the percentage goes up to 46.4% in the Catalan version.

Bazzanella et al. (2007) compare the Italian DM *allora* and its French counterpart *allors* in two Italian novels translated into French, and find 18.3% of omission (20 cases out of 109), especially when *allora* shows a meta-textual function (not a temporal one equivalent to *then/at that moment*).

More recently, Crible et al. (2019) analyze 261 tokens of the general polyfunctional DMs *and, but, so, because* and *now* in three texts from TED Talks (subtitles of broadcast presentations) and identify 79 cases of omission in Lithuanian (30.3%), 101 in Czech (38.7%), 115 in French (44.1%) and 133 (50.1%) in Hungarian. Crible et al. (2019) conclude that omission "could be partly influenced by the presence or absence of a formal-functional equivalent in the target language, however it seems to be mainly motivated by the semantics and pragmatic function of the discourse markers in the original text" (2019: 153), specifically because of a "low information value either due to high polyfunctionality (as in the case of *and* and *so*) or to a highly bleached meaning (as in the case of *now*)" (2019: 145). Crible et al. also observe that "omission is not as frequent for discourse markers with more specific semantics (i.e. less polyfunctional items)" (2019: 145).

Beyond pointing out the importance of omission when translating DMs, some authors have tried to test the factors accounting for this strategy. Zufferey (2016) discusses the cognitive factors explaining why continuous coherence relations, such as time or cause, are easier to convey implicitly than discontinuous ones, such as concession, and how this semantic-pragmatic difference affects the omission of a marker. The case study deals with 200 occurrences of three polysemous French connectives, namely, *dans la mesure où* (indicating either *cause* or *condition*), *or* (indicating either *background* or *concession*) and *en effet* (indicating either *cause* or *confirmation*). The corpus includes original French texts from Europarl and their translations into English, German and Spanish. Just focusing on the French-English pair: *dans la mesure où* is omitted 13 times out of 200 examples, always with a causal meaning; *or* is omitted 70 times, most of them

---

[2] On the effects of implicitation (i.e. connective removal) in computational sentence understanding, see Li et al. (this volume, chapter 7). According to their data, the relation has an impact on machine processing. They also conclude that the dependence on the presence of a connective for a correct discourse understanding is larger in computation systems than in humans.

(59 examples) expressing background (i.e., temporal or argumentative continuation); *en effet* is omitted in 88 cases, 81 of which correspond to cause and only 7 to confirmation. Although in all the cases the continuous meaning (the first one) is more frequent than the discontinuous meaning (the second one), the data confirm that "[f]or all connectives and relations, the discontinuous discourse relations of condition, concession and confirmation lead to a higher number of explicit translations compared to continuous causal and temporal relations" (2016: 275). Zufferey (2016: 276) concludes:

> Similarities in the number of implicitations across languages were also found when comparing the translation equivalents on the three connectives. In all target languages, *en effet* produced the highest number of implicitations, followed by *or* and lastly *dans la mesure où*. This difference suggests that some intrinsic properties of connectives make them more or less likely to be translated implicitly.

In a more comprehensive approach, not restricted to a group of markers, Becher (2010, 2011a, 2011b) analyzes the explicitation and implicitation of connectives in a bi-directional English-German corpus of translated business texts (ca. 20,000 words in each language). Although his work is more focused on explicitation, his data are also informative for implicitation. According to Becher (2011a: 31), omitting a connective is less frequent than adding one, especially in German (32 omissions vs 114 added connectives in German translations).

Becher (2010, 2011a, 2011b) proposes 5 the factors to account for implicitation:
- if a particular lexical item in the source text has no straightforward equivalent in the target language.
- if the target language lacks a syntactic slot offered by the source language.
- in order to comply with typical communicative preferences of target language readers.
- to avoid stylistic awkwardness.
- to achieve a neat information structure, i.e. a distribution of given and new information that secures optimal processing in the target language. (Becher 2011b: 217)

However, it is often the case that translators do not implicitate although this would be licensed by one or more of the reasons listed above. This behavior can be accounted for because: (i) they are "risk-averse", (ii) "there is often no good reason to do so" or (iii) "taking things away tends to be more difficult in language than adding things" (Becher 2011b: 218).

In summary, the contributions to the analysis of implicitation show that the omission of a marker is related to several factors: the marker, and specifically its meaning and domain, the type of relation (e.g. continuous relations favor deletion), cross-linguistic differences (e.g. lack of equivalent, avoiding stylistic awkwardness), and extralinguistic factors such as the translation process *per se* (not taking the risk of omitting a word if there is no good reason to do so) or even the genre, e.g. subtitling is known to increase the deletion of linguistic material, especially when lexical content is low.

4.1 Omission in the corpus

In the corpus analyzed here, there are 37 cases of omission, which can be considered a modest amount, but it is significant considering that: (i) translators avoid omitting words, as a risk practice (Becher 2011a) and (ii) omission is much more frequent than (other types of) dynamic translation (12 cases).

Omission can be total and it can also be partial, when two DMs combine and only one is translated.[3] Total omission of a DM (29 cases) leads to the implicitation of a relationship, which means that only easily interpretable meanings allow for the omission of the marker.

Total omission is related to four main factors in the corpus: the meaning of the marker, the interaction with related markers or words in the near context, changes in the syntactic structure leading to meaning contraction and change from inter-sentential to intra-sentential connection.

a) Markers with a sequential meaning are more frequently deleted than DMs expressing ideational meanings. This is specially the case with continuity meanings.

(9) *Poc després, a petició del poeta Joan Maragall, Gaudí s'esforçaria a concretar una mica més el temple que estava fent sense plànols.* ***I*** *a la «vaguetat mantinguda fins al present», diu Casanelles, «va respondre amb una vaguetat de futur.* (CHR12, González, 175)
'Shortly thereafter, on the request of the poet Joan Maragall, Gaudí strove to come up with a more specific design for the temple which he was building sans blueprints. Ø According to Casanelles, 'he responded to the vagueness upheld until then with future vagueness".

---

[3] Omission of one marker in a DM cluster could be considered a case of contraction, following Klaudy and Károly (2005) proposal.

(10) *A Palau de Cerdanya, poble cedit a França, el bisbe d'Urgell va nomenar com a rector de la parròquia Rafel Prada, cerdà, però oriünd de Llívia, ara sota domini espanyol.* **Així**, *en 1666, les autoritats franceses es queixaren d'aquest nomenament, ja que consideraren Prada un estranger que no podia exercir el seu sacerdoci.* (CHR11, Pojada, 145)

'In Palau-de-Cerdagne, a town conceded to France, the bishop of Urgell appointed Rafel Prada, a Cerdagne resident originally from Llívia, which was now under Spanish control, as the parish rector. Ø In 1666, the French authorities complained of this appointment, as they regarded Prada as a foreigner who could not exercise his priesthood there'.

In (9) and (10) the underspecified DMs *i* 'and' and *així* 'thus' indicating continuity are omitted in the translated text.

b) The presence of more than one DM in the same sentence or in a subsequent sentence increases the possibility of deleting one of them.

(11) *O bé es poden fer càlculs de proporcions de vaixells enfonsats amb productes d'aquest origen.* **Ara bé**, *els estudis en aquest sentit solament permeten arribar a indicar les tendències.* **Amb tot**, *queda clar que la dedicació al vi va ser molt important i les fonts es fan ressò del renom que van tenir els vins tarraconenses.* (CHR12, Prevosti, 128)

'Calculations can also be made of the proportions of shipwrecks with products from there. Ø Studies of this kind only shed light on trends; **however**, it is clear that wine production was of major importance, and the ancient sources report on the fame garnered by the wines from Tarraco'.

The presence of two contrastive markers introducing two contiguous sentences in (11) seems to be the reason why the first one is deleted. The omission prevents processing problems related to the iteration of similar instructions. Repetition does not seem problematic in the source language but the translator has avoided it by omitting the first contrastive DM. In addition, both *ara bé* and *amb tot* are usually translated by *however*, which can have an effect on the strategy.

c) Some deletions are due to a change in the syntactic structure that implies the integration of the DM with another word, as in (12).

(12) *Ens referim,* **per exemple**, *als encapçalats per Ramon Garrabou Segura, Enric Tello Aragay, Rosa Congost Colomer o Armand Alberola Romà, i també als desenvolupats al voltant del Seminari d'Estudis i Recerques Prehistòriques*

de la Universitat de Barcelona i de l'Institut de Ciències de la Terra Jaume Almera (IIGJA), continuador de l'institut de recerca fundat el 1965 per Lluís Solé Sabarís. (CHR12, Martí, 152)
'They include Ø the groups and projects led by Ramon Garrabou Segura, Enric Tello Aragay, Rosa Congost Colomer and Armando Alberola Romà, as well as those conducted around the Seminari d'Estudis i Recerques Prehistòriques of the Universitat de Barcelona and the Institut de Ciències de la Terra Jaume Almera (IIGJA), a continuation of the research institute founded in 1965 by Lluís Solé Sabarís'.

In (12), *ens referim, per exemple, a...* ('we refer, for example, to...') translates as *include*, which integrates the meaning of the discourse action (saying and exemplifiying).

d) The change from inter-sentential to intra-sentential connection can also lead to the omission of a marker.

(13) *No podem oblidar que ambdós autors eren nobles. I ho era especialment sor Isabel de Villena, que es complau a manifestar-se com a tal en la seva Vita Christi.* (CHR11, Ferrando, 134)
'We cannot forget that both authors were nobles, Ø especially Mother Isabel de Villena, who did not hesitate to state this in her Vita Christi'.

In (13), the conjunction *i* ('and') introduces an independent sentence. In the English version, the two sentences are integrated and the conjunction is omitted, thus avoiding a more complex construction including two clauses (coordinated plus relative) instead of one.

Partial omission occurs when one DM in a sequence of combined markers is deleted. The co-occurrence of DMs increases the possibility of deleting one of the DMs, often the first one, which tends to be more general in meaning. This is the case in (14), where the combination *i, tanmateix* ('and yet') is simplified by using a single marker, *yet*.

(14) *En aquest context, les literatures diferents de la castellana i de la francesa difícilment poden gaudir de la consideració i del reconeixement merescuts en l'àmbit internacional, i els seus grans escriptors, com Joanot Martorell, estranyament poden ser reconeguts com a escriptors «clàssics» en el si dels respectius estats.* **I, tanmateix**, *la literatura catalana va ser una de les més importants de l'Europa del segle xv i és avui la més important del món entre les que no tenen al seu darrere un estat (si hi exceptuem Andorra)* (CHR11, Ferrando, 123)

'Within this context, literatures other than Castilian and French can barely eke out the international attention and recognition they deserve, and the major writers, like Joanot Martorell, are rarely considered "classic" writers in their respective states. Ø **Yet** Catalan literature was one of the most important in 15th-century Europe and today is the most important in the world among those with no state behind them (except Andorra)'.

In 11 out of 18 combinations one of the markers has been omitted. However, partial omission in DM sequences is not always the case. Some combinations (7 cases, 38.9%) are maintained (15).

(15) *Finalment, pel que fa a l'estudi específic del canvi climàtic contemporani, en ser-ne la causa l'emissió de gasos d'efecte hivernacle, comparteix mètodes, temes i objectius amb la història de la contaminació.* **I, així,** *l'interès històric per endinsar-s'hi, fonamentalment a través de la documentació d'hemeroteca, també rau en la interpretació dels discursos que no el descriuen.* (CHR12, Martí, 156)

'Finally, in terms of the specific study of contemporary climate change, since the emission of greenhouse gases is its cause, it shares methods, topics and objectives with the history of pollution. **And thus**, the historical interest in examining it, fundamentally through periodical documentation, also entails interpreting the discourses that legislate or describe it'.

To sum up, the meaning of the marker (at the sequential domain), combination and collocational effects, and syntactic changes in the translated text are the general factors that account for the omission of a DM in the corpus analyzed.

4.2 Generalization in the corpus

The generalization of the DM meaning (i.e., a DM translated by a more general one) is almost as frequent as omission (30 cases) and affects contrastive meanings and less frequently additive meanings.

The most frequent cases of generalization involve the DM *however*, used in 93 cases, 25 of which instantiate meaning generalization (83.3% of all generalizations). *However* generalizes the meaning of 8 different contrastive markers in 25 examples: *ara bé* (13 examples), *per contra* (3), *no obstant això* (3), *en canvi* (2); *amb tot, ben al contrari, tot i que, encara que* (1).

(16) *Segons la imatge romàntica preconcebuda que se'n tenia, un cronista així havia de ser noble i un actiu guerrer i havia de formar part de la cort reial des de menut.* **Per contra**, *s'ha pogut confirmar que va néixer en una família de mercaders ben integrada en l'elit burgesa local i en la direcció del municipi (cònsols, batlles, juristes).* (CHR12 Cifuentes, 143)

'According to the preconceived romantic image of him, a chronicler like he must have been a nobleman and an active warrior, and he must have been a member of the royal court from a young age. **However**, it has been confirmed that he was born into a family of merchants who were thoroughly integrated into the local bourgeoisie and town leadership (consuls, bailiffs, jurists)'.

In (16) *per contra* ('instead') expresses the contraposition between two opposing images of a writer, the idealized one and the real one. This instruction is bleached in the English translation by the use of the general contrastive marker *however*.

The DM *however* can be considered a 'literal' counterpart of *però* and *tanmateix*. The source DMs often trigger a more specific instruction, namely, opposition (either strong, *ara bé*, or parallel, *en canvi, per contra*), concession (*no obstant això, amb tot, tot i que, encara que*), refutation (*ben al contrari*) and addition/distribution (*d'altra banda*).[4]

The change from an inter-sentential to an intra-sentential connection may also result in the use of a more general marker, which implies the underspecification of the coherence relation.

(17) *Desapareixia la presència pertorbadora de la mitgera i la superfície del jardí s'aplegaria permetent un ús i un impacte més satisfactoris.* **D'altra banda**, *constituiria la imatge força al voltant de la qual giraria tot el projecte, des de les distribucions interiors fins a les formes i els colors de les façanes.* (CHR12, González, 167)

'The dividing wall as a disturbing presence disappeared, and the garden area was marshalled to yield a more satisfactory use and impact, **and** would become the image and force around which the entire design revolved, from the inside layouts to the shapes and colours of the façades'.

Generalization in our corpus is thus related to the different frequency of the markers in source and target language, as in the case of *however*, which covers the spectrum

---

[4] For a general overview of the meanings of the contrastive DMs in Catalan, see Cuenca, Postolea & Visconti (2019).

occupied by a number of connectives in Catalan, and to the change from inter-sentential connection to intra-sentential connection.

5 Explicitation in DM translation

Explicitation in translation is defined in Vinay and Darbelnet (1958: 8) as "the process of introducing information into the target language which is present only implicitly in the source language, but which can be derived from the context or the situation". More recently, it has been defined as "the verbalization of information that the addressee might be able to infer (e.g. from the preceding discourse) if it were not verbalized" (Becher 2011a: 26). Explicitation of a DM can adopt the form of either addition of a DM or specification of the meaning of an existing DM, i.e. the translation of a general marker into a more specific unit.

Explicitation of connectives has received attention in the literature in relation to the so-called Explicitation Hypothesis, according to which translated texts tend to be more explicit as for cohesive mechanisms than their source texts, regardless of the differences between the linguistic systems of the two languages involved (Blum-Kulka 1986: 19). This hypothesis assumes explicitation as a universal translation strategy. The Explicitation Hypothesis has been critically reviewed by Becher (2011a: 27–28), who argues that it is unmotivated, unparsimonious and vaguely formulated.[5] Becher adheres instead to the Asymmetry Hypothesis (Klaudy and Károly 2005), which points to tendencies in specific pairs of languages:

> explicitations in the L1 → L2 direction are not always counterbalanced by implicitations in the L2 → L1 direction because translators – if they have a choice – prefer to use operations involving explicitation, and often fail to perform optional implicitation.
> (Klaudy and Károly 2005: 14)

Becher (2011b: 219) proposes a revised version of the Asymmetry Hypothesis: "The occurrence of explicitating and implicitating shifts is uniquely determined by (a) lexicogrammatical and (b) pragmatic variables." This implies that there is no universal strategy or subconscious process leading the translator to explicitate, and that the balance between implicitation and explicitation depends on extralinguistic factors:

---

5 For a review of the notion of explicitation, see also Klaudy (2008), Saldanha (2008), Becher (2011b: Section 2.2), Marco (2018: Section 2) or Murtisari (2016), among others.

> Where communicative risk is low and/or translators are willing to take risks, the relationship between explicitation and implicitation is more symmetrical than in cases where risk is high and/or translators are risk-averse. (Becher 2011b: 219)

As for DMs, this implies that the addition of DMs in the L1 → L2 direction is expected to be more frequent than omissions in the L2 → L1 direction.

Becher analyzes the explicitation (and implicitation) of connectives (and in the case of Becher 2011b also other cohesive devices) in a bi-directional English-German corpus of translated business text. His data show that in the English-German direction explicitation (including addition and substitution by a more specific marker, 139 cases) is more frequent than implicitation (including omission and substitution by a more general marker 44 cases). The difference also holds in the German-English direction but it is lower (explicitation: 79 cases; implicitation: 64 cases). These results also indicate a lack of explicitation-implicitation counterbalancing (English into German: explicitation 139, implicitation 44; German into English: explicitation 79, implicitation 64), thus confirming the Asymmetry Hypothesis:

> [...] translators (a) insert cohesive devices – such as connectives – more frequently than they leave them out and (b) insert connectives even in places where there is no specific trigger or motivation to do so [...]. (Becher 2011a: 41)

There are other contributions about explicitation with a more restricted scope, since they focus on one DM or a reduced group of markers. Zufferey and Cartoni (2014) analyze the translation of several causal connectives, mainly used intrasententially, in four languages (French, English, Spanish and Italian) and conclude that two factors have a quantitative influence on explicit marking, namely, the paradigm of connectives in the target language (e.g., *given that* is more frequently used for explicitation than its "counterpart" *étant donné*, which is in competition with *puisque*) and the discourse relation (subjective relations are more frequently explicitated than objective ones).

Not many analyses focus on Catalan DMs. One exception is Marco (2018), who analyzes the use and translation of a group of Catalan connectives indicating concessive contrast (10 markers) and consequence (5 markers) in original literary English texts and their translations into Catalan. Marco's analysis aims at showing to what extent connectives are indicators of explicitation in translated texts. The quantitative analysis shows that there is no significant general difference when comparing original and translated Catalan texts in the case of contrastive connectives, but there is in the case of consequence connectives, which increases in translated texts (normalized frequency per 100,000 words of 49.9 for translations vs. 43.12 for non-translations). This difference is due to a different degree of explicitation: 17.02% of the occurrences of consequence connectives vs. 6.15% for contrast connectives. From a more qualitative perspective, Marco concludes that: (i) some markers are more prone to be added (e.g. *llavors* 'then' 31.8% of addition, *en canvi* 'however' 31%, *per tant* 'therefore' 23.7%, *doncs* 'so, then, therefore' 22.4%), and (ii) the low informative value of the marker as well as subjective/procedural meanings increase the possibility of adding a connective (Marco 2018: 108), which confirms Zufferey and Cartoni's (2014) conclusions.

Finally, specification (i.e., explicitation by substitution) is observed by Becher (2011b: 185) in the case of *and* translated into German as a temporal-causal connective (*gleichzeitig* 'at the same time') and also *but* translated into German as a contrastive connective lacking a concessive reading (*allerdings* 'however'). Bazzanella et al. (2007) discuss the strategies to translate the Italian DM *allora* into French, among which they identify 11 cases out of 109 (10.1%) of 'over-determination', that is, translation by a more specific lexical unit usually translating temporal values (*et ensuite, de nouveau, aussitôt, à ce moment, à cet instant donc, on le pense bien, ah! Mais*). This strategy is lower in frequency than omission (18.3%).

In conclusion, according to the previous contributions, the factors favoring explicitation have to do with the meaning and domain (less frequent when the markers are used at the ideational domain) and the marker, especially when it is underspecified. From the translator's point of view, explicitation processes have to do with the search for naturalness, including avoidance of marked stylistic options and ambiguity, and minimizing the risk of misunderstanding.

5.1 Addition in the corpus

In 34 cases (6.4%) inter-sentential DMs have been added to the target text. The addition of a DM is generally aimed at improving naturalness in the translated text by explicitating a coherence relationship.

a) Considering the general meaning, the most frequently added DMs are those indicating continuity, but also contrast. Continuity markers are added in 20 cases. They generally express a type of additive meaning: *and* (9 cases), *indeed* (3 cases), *in turn* (2 cases) or *in fact* (2 cases).

(18) *Manel Milà i Fontanals, Lluís Domènech i Montaner, Narcís Oller o Àngel Guimerà, entre molts d'altres, van ser ateneistes notables. Ø Alguns d'ells, gràcies a la seva trajectòria ateneística, van fer posteriorment el salt a la política.* (CHR11, Izquierdo, 155)

9 Translating discourse markers: Implicitation and explicitation strategies — 233

'Manel Milà i Fontanals, Lluís Domènech i Montaner, Narcís Oller, Àngel Guimerà and many others were notable athenaeum members. **And** precisely because of their background in athenaeums, some of them were able to take the leap to politics later on'.

Consequence and conclusion markers (*thus, therefore, so, as a result*) are also occasionally added (4 cases).

(19) *Quan, en 1660, la monarquia francesa va crear la imposició de la gabella de la sal a la nova província de Rosselló, immediatament el comerç legal de la sal de Cardona cap al Rosselló es va convertir en comerç il·legal. Veiem Ø com una decisió política repercuteix a les xarxes comercials: el Tractat dels Pirineus significà un canvi estructural per al comerç transpirinenc.* (CHR11, Pojada, 141)
'In 1660, when the French monarchy created the customs gabella on salt in the new province of Roussillon, the legal trade of salt from Cardona to Roussillon immediately became illegal. We **thus** see how a political decision had repercussions on the trade networks: the Treaty of the Pyrenees signalled a structural change in cross-Pyrenees trade'.

As in the case of addition markers, consequence markers are used at the sequential domain, linked to discourse continuity.

Contrastive markers are added 15 times. In fact, *however* is the most frequently added DM (11 cases, 31.4% of all added DMs).

(20) *Les cases les van projectar els ajudants de Gaudí —Francesc Berenguer i Joan Rubió— amb la supervisió del mestre. Ø El projecte de l'església se'l va reservar Gaudí.* (CHR12, González, 174)
'The village houses were designed by Gaudí's assistants – Francesc Brenguer and Joan Rubió – under the master's supervision. **However,** the design of the church was reserved for Gaudí'.

b) The addition of a DM is context-conditioned when it reinforces another particle or word, as in (21), where *however* reinforces the contrastive meaning of *otherwise*.

(21) *En aquella ocasió es va atribuir a una gran nevada el motiu pel qual l'acta electoral es va lliurar amb un retard totalment infonamentat. Ø La realitat se situava en una altra instància.* (CHR12, Rubí, 182)

'At that time, a huge snowstorm was cited as the reason why the report on election results was released with a completely unjustified delay. **However**, the reality of the situation was otherwise'.

c) The change from an intra-sentential to inter-sentential connection can also result in the addition of a DM.

(22)　*Des de la fi del segle xix, amb l'aflaquiment de les relacions de proximitat i la progressió de les llengües d'estat, els Pirineus han esdevingut, a poc a poc, una frontera lingüística entre un occità i un català, ja que els idiomes que parlen s'han considerat llengües diferents, Ø afirmació que varen manifestar els signataris del text aparegut a La Veu de Catalunya [. . .]. (CHR11, Pojada, 140)*
'Since the late 19th century, with a decline in relations of proximity and the spread of the state languages, the Pyrenees have gradually become a linguistic border between Occitan and Catalan, since the languages that are spoken are regarded as different. **In fact**, this claim was expressed by the signatories of the text that appeared in La Veu de Catalunya [. . .]'.

In (22) a complex sentence is divided into two independent units and the second one is prefaced by a DM explicitating a former implicit relation of continuity.

5.2 Specification of DM meaning in the corpus

Another type of explicitation is not based on the addition of a DM but on its translation by a more specific DM (15 cases) or by a lexical expression (4 cases). A more general marker, often a conjunction, can be translated by using a more specific one. This is the case in (23), where an underspecified marker of exemplification (*així* 'thus/so') is translated by a specific one (*for example*).

(23)　*De ben segur, aquestes expedicions punitives no es feien en un sentit únic, sinó que cada banda actuava igual, fet que ocasionava represàlies que justificaven altres represàlies que creaven, d'aquesta manera, un clima de violències i de pillatges fronterers. **Així**, el capità general dels comtats atacà en 1537 uns pobles de les Fenolledes llenguadocianes, incendiant i saquejant Sornià, Sant Pau de Fenollet, Tuixà, Pasiòls i altres llocs d'aquell territori.* (CHR11, Pojada, 139)

'These punitive expeditions most likely occurred in both directions, with each side acting the same, which led to retaliation which in turn justified further retaliation, thus creating a circle of violence and border pillages. **For example**, the General Captaincy of the countships attacked villages in Les Fenolledes of Languedoc in 1537, setting fire to and pillaging Sornià (Sournia), Sant Pau de Fenollet (Saint-Paul-de-Fenouillet), Tuixà (Tuchan), Pasiòls (Paziols) and other sites in that region'.

In (23) the underspecified marker *així* (literally 'so'), which can indicate continuity, consequence and exemplification, is translated by *for example*, a specific transparent DM.

The substitution of a DM in the corpus leads to the specification of several coherence relationships: from pure addition (*i* 'and') to more spedific addition, such as intensification (*furthermore*) or amplification (*indeed, likewise*), from general distribution (*d'una banda* 'on the one hand') to sequencing (*first*), from general contrast (*però* 'but') to concessive contrast (*yet*), from disjunction (*o bé* 'or') to alternative (*alternatively*).

A syntactic context that seems to favor semantic explicitation is when a DM translates a conjunction acting at the intra-sentential level (5 out of 15 cases of specification).

(24) *Al* Conventus Tarraconensis *sembla indicar una situació de prosperitat considerable per part de la població indígena, alliberada de les estructures organitzatives ibèriques, amb facilitat per a vendre els seus excedents agrícoles, amb l'obertura de nous mercats **i** poca competència comercial propiciada per la nova situació de substitució del poder*... (CHR12, Prevosti, 120)
'In the *Conventus Tarraconensis*, evidence seems to indicate a situation of considerable prosperity among the indigenous peoples, who were freed from Iberian organisational structures and could now easily sell their agricultural surpluses with the opening of new markets. **Furthermore**, they had little competition in trade thanks to the new situation of power replacement...'

The compound sentence in (24) is divided into two different sentences and the translator resorts to the insertion of a DM (*furthermore*) in substitution of a general conjunction (*i* 'and').

Explicitation can also be at play when a DM is translated into an equivalent lexical expression. In two cases *ben mirat* is interpreted literally, as a non-fixed unit, and translates as a lexical expression with a similar meaning.

(25) *Dels cinc autors escollits, Roig deu ser l'únic «burgès», però un burgès ben situat econòmicament i socialment.* **Ben mirat**, *no hi hagué una separació absoluta entre una noblesa amb pocs recursos econòmics, que aspirava a obtenir-los, sobretot mitjançant estratègies matrimonials, i una burgesia benestant, que aspirava a ennoblir-se* [...] (CHR11, Ferrando, 124)
'Of the known authors, Roig must have been the only member of the bourgeoisie, but an economically and socially well-situated member. **If we examine the social situation carefully**, there must not have been complete separation between the nobility with scant economic resources who aspired to secure more, especially through marital strategies, and the wealthy bourgeoisie who aspired to nobility [...]'

The lack of a direct correspondence for *ben mirat* in English can be the reason why the DM is translated by a clause.

6 Discussion

The previous analysis of the data shows that DMs are generally translated literally or almost literally. Even though many authors insist that connectives are often added, rephrased or deleted (e.g. Halverson, 2004; Zufferey and Cartoni, 2014; Zufferey 2016), the data discussed here show that this can be an overgeneralization, since in the corpus analyzed literal translation is predominant, even at the inter-sentential level, where DMs are syntactically optional.

The predominance of literal translation is also attested in several papers on the translation of DMs. For example, Halverson (1996) identifies 70% of literal translation of DMs from Norwegian into English, and Denturck (2012) points out that the majority of connectives in her corpus were translated by an equally explicit connective (French translations: 77.5%, Dutch translations: 83.1%).

Our analysis is in agreement with Denturck's (2012) conclusions: "Connectives are most often translated by equivalent markers. Yet, there is also a clear tendency to implicitate" (Denturck 2012: 220), and – we would add in the case of our corpus – also to explicitate, at least in the case of inter-sentential DMs in the Catalan-English direction.

Although literal translation is predominant, implicitation and also explicitation strategies are significant and interesting from a processing perspective.
a) *Implicitation.* Omission is a significant translation strategy (37 examples), even though written academic discourse implies a very limited, almost non-existent, use of pragmatic markers and a high frequency of markers used at

the ideational domain. Generalization of meaning is also frequent (30 examples) and affects additive and also contrastive DMs.
b) *Explicitation*. Addition of markers aims at facilitating discourse processing by explicitating structural functions (sequential domain), when the coherence link between two segments is loose. It is frequent with DMs indicating continuity in discourse, but it is also surprisingly frequent with those indicating contrast, even though they usually imply a propositional load and act at the ideational domain. Specification occurs especially with some DMs used at the sequential domain or when the DM has no direct counterpart.

Becher (2011a; 2011b: chap. 5) lists five factors affecting both the addition and omission of connectives, namely,
1. Complying with the communicative norms of the target language community, e.g., making the target text more explicit, in line with the preferences of the target text readers.
2. Exploiting specific features of the target language system, e.g., including connectives in a specific prosodically integrated slot for that, as in the case of German.
3. Dealing with specific restrictions of the target language system, such as not having a close equivalent in the target language.
4. Avoiding stylistically marked ways of expression, that is, adapting the translated text to the conventions of the target language usage.
5. Optimizing the cohesion of the target text, which is also related to the tendency to avoid stylistic markedness.

Factors 1 to 3 are lexicogrammatical, whereas factors 4 and 5 are (more) pragmatic. In addition, translators seem to follow general processual principles, such as the "general strategy of maximizing explicitness in order to minimize the risk of misunderstanding" (Becher 2011b: 216).

In our corpus, implicitation and explicitation are triggered by common factors:
a) Combination of the DM with another marker or collocational effects with other words.
b) Change from inter-sentential to intra-sentential connection or vice-versa.
c) Meaning and domain of the marker, especially in the case of continuity markers (sequential domain).[6]

---

[6] A similar conclusion is achieved from the field of computation processing (Li et al., this volume, chapter 7). According to Li et al.'s data, the processing of contrastive relations is the most dependent on the presence of a connective.

In addition, the omission of a DM can be associated with:
d) Search for naturalness, including avoidance of marked stylistic options.

Finally, the addition of a DM can be linked to:
e) Minimizing the risk of misunderstanding and optimizing the cohesion of the target text.

A synthesis of the factors identified is shown in Table 2.

Table 2: Factors for implicitation and explicitation strategies.

	Implicitation	**Explicitation**
	Omission (37 cases)	*Addition* (34 cases)
Collocation	Co-occurrence of the DM with another DM, particle or another word partially sharing its meaning	Reinforcing another particle
Scope	Change from inter-sentential to intra-sentential connection	Change from intra-sentential to inter-sentential connection
Meaning/domain	Use at the sequential domain (mainly meaning continuity)	Markers indicating continuity or conclusion (sequential domain) and also contrast
Style/cohesion	Avoiding marked stylistic options	Minimizing the risk of misunderstanding
	Generalization (30 cases)	*Specification* (19 cases)
Scope	Change from inter-sentential to intra-sentential connection	Change from intra-sentential to inter-sentential connection
Meaning/domain	Markers indicating contrast	Markers used at the sequential domain
Style/cohesion	Differences in frequency (the general DM being more frequent than a more direct counterpart)	Translation by a non-connective lexical unit (lack of direct counterpart)

The syntactic and semantic factors have been discussed at length in the previous sections. As for the factors related to style and cohesion, the search for naturalness, including avoidance of stylistically marked ways of expression, accounts for the omission of some DMs. When the meaning of a DM is somehow redundant with respect to another word, as in (26), the DM can be omitted:

(26) En un altre moment, és amb oli que un mercader alvernès instal·lat a Puigcerdà prometé de pagar el mul que acabava de comprar. **A més**, l'oli era també comprat al País de Foix pels mercaders bearnesos que hi anaven a vendre les seves capes de pastors destinades al mercat català. (CHR11, Pojada, 143)
'Another time, a merchant from Auvergne living in Puigcerdà promised to pay for the mule he had just purchased with oil. Ø Oil was also purchased in the Land of Foix by merchants from Béarn who went there to sell their shepherds' capes for the Catalan market'.

The DM *a més* ('moreover') and the adverb *també* ('also') in (26) share a basic meaning of addition, which makes the DM somehow redundant. In general, the English translator seems to avoid redundancy in several cases by integrating in one word the meaning of two semantically related lexical items, as also shown in (11) above, where one of two contrastive DM in contiguous sentences is deleted. These cases, and also the examples of partial omission, can be explained by one of the factors that favor implicitation according to Becher (2011a, 2011b: 217), which is to avoid stylistically marked ways of expression or rather "to avoid stylistic awkwardness".

Style also affects the selection of a marker when there is a large inventory of forms corresponding to the same or a very similar meaning. This observation is made by Becher when comparing German and English:

> The lexicogrammatical system of German favors the use of connectives. One could say that it invites the use of connectives, both by providing a large lexical inventory of connectives and by offering a variety of syntactic slots for accommodating them. (This of course fits in nicely with the observation that the communicative norms of German demand a high degree of cohesive explicitness.) (Becher 2011a: 41–42)

Similarly, previous studies argue that variation in the use of connectives is sought for in academic discourse more frequently in Catalan than in English (Cuenca 2003).

Explicitation can be also accounted for by considering that translators tend to minimize the risk of misunderstanding and optimize the cohesion of the target text (Becher 2011a).

After analysing the data, we can now review the working hypotheses included in Section 1:

(i) Underspecified DMs (such as *and*, *well* or *now* and their Catalan counterparts) are more frequently omitted or added in translation than DMs with a more specific meaning (such as *however*).

The initial hypothesis that omission and addition especially affect underspecified or ambiguous DM is partially confirmed. Whereas "omission is not as frequent for discourse markers with more specific semantics (i.e. less polyfunctional items)" (Crible et al 2019: 145, see also Hoek et al. 2017), the same does not hold for addition or generalization, which also stand out in the case of contrastive DMs. It seems more accurate to conclude that, in our corpus, some general markers, even when they are not polysemous, are more often omitted or added. This is the case, for instance, of the conjunction *i* ('and'), which is deleted 12 times (sometimes in DM combinations) – its counterpart *and* is added 9 times –, and the parenthetical connective *however*, which is added 11 times.

(ii) DMs are more frequently omitted or added when they act at the sequential domain.

This hypothesis is confirmed. Even when a DM has a more specific meaning, omission and addition are linked to a more abstract use, as a sequential linking device. That is, the function remains but the domain changes. So DMs used at the sequential domain increase the possibility of omission or addition, but there are other factors such as combination with DMs or with other words with a similar meaning and change in the syntactic structure that have more impact on the omission or the generalization of a DM in written academic texts as the ones analyzed here. Also stylistic factors – the avoidance of redundancy and ambiguity, minimizing the risk of misunderstanding or search for naturalness related to paradigmatic relations and frequency of use of a DM – seem to be key to account for implicitation and explicitation.

(iii) Similar DMs show different frequencies and contexts of use in different languages.

This hypothesis is confirmed. As already said, *però* and *but*, although being dictionary counterparts, are not discourse counterparts. The counterpart of *però* is not *but*, as a dictionary approach would predict, but *however*. *However* is used in 93 cases in the target text and translates 13 different DMs, namely, *però* (24 cases as a conjunction and 16 cases as a parenthetical connective), *tanmateix* (15 cases), *ara bé* (13 cases), *per contra* (3), *no obstant això* (3), *en canvi* (2), *amb tot* (1), *ben al contrari* (1), *encara que* (1), *tot i que* (1), *d'altra banda* (1). *However* is also added in 11 cases. We can conclude that in the corpus analyzed here *however*, not *but*, is the basic contrastive DM at the text level. In Catalan there are many different markers to express contrast (148 cases expressed by means of 23 different markers), whereas in English the variety is lower: only 15 different markers are used to translate contrast. The most frequently used to link independent sentences is *però* (36 cases), whereas *but* is used only in 9 cases, 2 of which added. This is also related to generalization of meaning and thus implicitation in the Catalan-English direction. The observed relation means that *però* and *but* exhibit different frequencies of use, at least when connecting independent sentences (i.e. inter-sentential use).[7]

7 Conclusions

The analysis of the translation of inter-sentential DMs in a corpus of academic papers in Catalan translated into English has shown that, although literal or almost literal translation is the most frequent translation technique, the techniques associated with implicitation and explicitation are also relevant.

The results point to the following tendencies, corresponding to the research questions presented in Section 1:
1. Implicitation and explicitation of a DM are linked to a variety of factors related to both production and interpretation.
2. Scope (i.e. inter- or intra-sentential connection), collocation and style have an effect on the implicitation and explicitation of DMs in translation.
3. DMs are more frequently omitted or added when they act at the sequential domain.
4. Contrary to expectations, contrastive DM (mainly *however*) are often added and used to generalize the meaning of more specific markers.
5. Cross-linguistic differences (e.g. direct counterparts, paradigmatic relations, frequency of use of a DM, stylistic preferences) account for some cases of implicitation and explicitation.

The approach adopted here is in line with Becher's analysis. First, the corpus includes formal written texts and all connective DMs. Second, the fact that the identification of markers has been made manually and all markers, not only a group of DMs, have been identified both in the source texts and in the translated texts. This procedure broadens the picture with respect to some of the previous

---

7 This kind of asymmetry is observed in other cases. Lewis (2006) compares the French marker *au contraire* (AC) with its English cognate *on the contrary* (OTC), and concludes that "although AC cannot always be translated by OTC, it is hard to find an instance of OTC that cannot be translated by AC. AC would appear, therefore, to have a wider use than OTC" (2006: 143).

contributions to DM implicitation or explicitation, which analyze one DM or a pre-defined group of markers.

The analysis, departing from six translation techniques, has described in detail four of them, namely, omission and generalization (instantiating implicitation) and addition and specification (instantiating explicitation). Several factors favoring DM implicitation or explicitation have been identified and grouped together: scope, meaning, collocation and style. This multi-factorial analysis shows the complexity of the processes underlying decision making in the translation of DMs.

In the light of the approach adopted in the research and the results derived from it, some other general questions remain open to discussion.

a) This study focuses on inter-sentential DMs, which are always syntactically optional. As a consequence, they can be added and deleted without any 'structural' effect, even though the processing of the target text can be affected, since DMs guide discourse interpretation. An analysis considering also intra-sentential DM may lead to different conclusions. Intra-sentential connection is subject to syntactic restrictions (such as verb mode, word order, etc.) that can favor the translation of a DM by another DM and eventually another lexical unit. In any event, the scope of the marker must be taken into account for this can be crucial to account for DM implicitation and explicitation.

b) The omission or addition of a DM is not (always) due to the 'lack of content', 'low information content' or 'high polyfunctionality' of a DM. The semantics/pragmatics is only one factor affecting the implicitation or explicitation of the DM, at least considering the contextual variables of the corpus analyzed here.

c) Implicitation or explicitation of a DM are not 'dangers to be avoided', but ordinary procedures in translation that increase naturality, and avoid ambiguity and stylistic awkwardness.

d) Explicitation does not seem to be always more frequent than implicitation, as some scholars suggest.[8] Contrary to Becher's results, who reports more explicitations than implicitations both in English-German and in German-English translations (139/44 and 79/64, respectively), in the Catalan-English translations in the corpus, implicitation is a little bit more frequent than explicitation (67/53). This may have to do with the fact that we are dealing with inter-sentential DMs, which are always optional and do not establish any kind of syntactic

---

[8] Becher (2010: 17) concludes that "Obligatory, optional and pragmatic explicitations tend to be more frequent than the corresponding implicitations regardless of the SL/TL constellation at hand."

relation between two structures at the sentence level. Since the analysis here is restricted to the Catalan-English direction, a bidirectional comparable corpus should be analysed in order to test the Asymmetry Hypothesis. In any event, the results reported here call for a revision of the hypothesis, since omitting a DM is not always less frequent than adding one.

In conclusion, the factors to implicitate or explicitate a DM in translation are multiple. Some generalizations about the translation of DMs, often repeated in the literature, should be restricted to genres, pairs of languages or specific DMs. The results of the present analysis, although restricted to Catalan inter-sentential DMs translated into English mainly used in the ideational and the sequential domain, challenge some of the assumptions found in the literature. More genres should be analyzed in order to determine the impact of, e.g., interpersonal functions on implicitation and explicitation and other factors may have an influence on the translation strategies.

All in all, corpus analysis of translated texts proves especially relevant to understand why and how inter-sentential DMs are used in discourse production and comprehension and how to cope with them in translation contexts. It also contributes to gain deeper insight into how implicit and explicit coherence relations interplay cross-linguistically.

References

Bazzanella, Carla & Lucia Morra. 2000. Discourse markers and the indeterminacy of translation. In Iørn Korzen & Carla Marello (eds.), *Argomenti per una linguistica della traduzione. Notes pour une linguistique de la traduction. On linguistic aspects of translation*, 149–157. Alessandria: Edizioni dell'Orso.

Bazzanella, Carla et al. 2007. Italian *allora*, French *alors*: Functions, convergences, and divergences. *Catalan Journal of Linguistics* 6. 9–30.

Becher, Viktor. 2010. Abandoning the notion of 'Translation-inherent' explicitation: against a dogma of Translation Studies. *Across Languages and Cultures* 11(1). 1–28.

Becher, Viktor. 2011a. When and why do translators add connectives? *Target* 23(1). 26–47.

Becher, Viktor. 2011b. *Explicitation and implicitation in translation. A corpus-based study of English-German and German-English translations of business texts*. PhD dissertation, University of Hamburg.

Blum-Kulka, Shoshana. 1986. Shifts of cohesion and coherence in translation. In Juliane House & Shoshana Blum-Kulka (eds.) *Interlingual and intercultural communication*, 117–135. Tübingen: Gunter Narr.

Crible, Ludivine, Ágnes Abuczki, Nijolé Burkšaitiené, Péter Furkó, Anna Nedoluzhko, Sigita Rackevičiené, Giedré Oleskeviciene & Šárka Zikánová. 2019. Functions and translations of underspecified discourse markers in TED Talks: a parallel corpus study on five languages. *Journal of Pragmatics* 142. 139–155.

Crible, Ludivine & Liesbeth Degand. 2019. Domains and functions: A two-dimensional account of discourse markers, *Discours* 24, Online: http://journals.openedition.org/discours/9997.

Cuenca, Maria Josep. 2003. Two ways to reformulate: a contrastive analysis of reformulation markers. *Journal of Pragmatics* 3 (7). 1069–1093.

Cuenca, Maria Josep. 2008. Pragmatic markers in contrast: the case of *well*. *Journal of Pragmatics* 40. 1373–1391.

Cuenca, Maria Josep, Sorina Postolea & Jacqueline Visconti. 2019. Contrastive markers in contrast. *Discours* 25. Online: https://journals.openedition.org/discours/10326.

Degand, Liesbeth. 2009. On describing polysemous discourse markers. What does translation add to the picture? In Stef Slembrouck, Miriam Taverniers & Mieke van Herreweghe (eds.), *From Will to Well. Studies in Linguistics offered to Anne-Marie Simon-Vandenbergen*, 173–183. Gent: Academia Press.

Denturck, Kathelijne. 2012. Explicitation vs. implicitation: A bidirectional corpus-based analysis of causal connectives in French and Dutch translations. *Across Languages and Cultures* 13(2). 211–227.

Dupont, Maïté & Sandrine Zufferey. 2017. Methodological issues in the use of directional parallel corpora. *International Journal of Corpus Linguistics* 22(2). 270–297.

Halverson, Sandra. 2004. Connectives as a translation problem. In Harald Kittel et al. (eds.), *An International Encyclopedia of Translation Studies*, 562–572. Berlin: Walter de Gruyter.

Hoek, Jet, Sandrine Zufferey, Jacqueline Evers-Vermeul & Ted J. J. Sanders. 2017. Cognitive complexity and the linguistic marking of coherence relations: a parallel corpus study. *Journal of Pragmatics* 121. 113–131.

Klaudy, Kinga. 2008. Explicitation. In Mona Baker & Gabriela Saldanh (eds.), *Routledge Encyclopedia of Translation Studies*, 80–84. London-New York: Routledge.

Klaudy, Kinga & Krisztina Károly. 2005. Implicitation in translation: Empirical evidence for operational asymmetry in translation. *Across Languages and Cultures* 6(1). 13–28.

Lewis, Diana M. 2006. Contrastive analysis of adversative relational markers, using comparable corpora. In Karin Aijmer & Anne-Marie Simon-Vandenbergen (eds.), *Pragmatic Markers in Contrast*, 139–152. Amsterdam: Elsevier.

Li, Ruiqi, Liesbeth Allein, Damien Sileo & Marie-Francine Moens. this volume. When do discourse markers affect computational sentence understanding?

Marco, Josep 2018. Connectives as indicators of explicitation in literary translation: A study based on a comparable and parallel corpus. *Target* 30(1). 87–111. https://doi.org/10.1075/target.16042.mar

Molina, Lucía & Amparo Hurtado Albir. 2002. Translation techniques revisited. A dynamic and functionalist approach. *Meta* XLVII(4). 498–512.

Murtisari, Elisabet Titik. 2016. Explicitation in translation studies: The journey of an elusive concept. *Translation and Interpreting* 8(2). 64–81.

Saldanha, Gabriela. 2008. Explicitation revisited: Bringing the reader into the picture. *trans-kom* 1(1). 20–35. On-line: http://www.trans-kom.eu/bd01nr01/trans-kom_01_01_03_Saldanha_Explicitation.20080707.pdf

Vinay, Jean-Paul & Jean Darbelnet. 1977 [1958]. *Stylistique comparée du français et de l'anglais*. Paris, Didier.
Zufferey, Sandrine. 2016. Discourse connectives across languages: Factors influencing their explicit or implicit translation. *Languages in Contrast* 16(2). 264–279.
Zufferey, Sandrine & Bruno Cartoni. 2014. A multifactorial analysis of explicitation in translation. *Target* 36. 232–250.

Corpus

Catalan Historical Review, vol. 11 (2018). Online: http://revistes.iec.cat/index.php/CHR/issue/view/9731
Catalan Historical Review, vol. 12 (2019). Online: http://revistes.iec.cat/index.php/CHR/issue/view/9815

Mira Ariel
10 Processing polyfunctional discourse markers: Making sense of Hebrew *harey*

Abstract: This chapter analyzes the polyfunctional Hebrew expression *harey* 'here is', 'hereby', 'after all', focusing mainly on its variety of procedural uses, all of them addressee-oriented. Using *harey*, the speaker instructs the addressee on to how to process the information under its scope, but these processing instructions are remarkably different, even contradictory. Most intriguingly, *harey* introduces both Old information (which introduces a necessary assumption, a justification or even a counter-argument to another speaker) and New information. The information it introduces may be discourse-dominant, but it may be background and non-dominant. These puzzling facts receive a diachronic explanation: The fact that *harey* is a deictic originally accounts for its mobilization into introducing salient, New information, on the one hand, and information already accessible to the interlocutors, on the other hand. Synchronically, different discourse profiles characterize the various *harey* functions, helping the addressee zero in on the relevant function.

Keywords: polyfunctionality, old/new information, background/dominant information, argumentation, grammaticization, Hebrew *harey*

1 Introduction

Mental representations anchored to the "here and now" enjoy a privileged interactional status. They constitute shared information, they are treated as self-evident, and hence as unchallengeable. Surprisingly perhaps, such anchored representations may stand for either New or Old, or Accessible information: Hebrew *harey* 'hereby'/'after all' serves to either confer an immediately Accessible and unchallengeable status on a piece of New information, or to access a piece of information already considered Old/Accessible or shared.[1] Cataphoric *harey*

---

[1] *Harey* here stands for two alternative pronunciations: *harey* and *hare*.

Acknowledgments: The research here reported was supported by an Israel Science Foundation grant (1398/20).

Mira Ariel, Linguistics Dept. and the program of Cognitive Studies of Language and Language Use, Tel Aviv Universtity (emerita), mariel@tauex.tau.ac.il

https://doi.org/10.1515/9783110790351-010

uses (§2) introduce New information into the discourse, with the intention that it instantly function as a privileged, self-evident assumption to be taken for granted by the interlocutors. Anaphoric *harey* uses (§3, by far the majority) introduce information already Accessible and taken for granted by the interlocutors.

As we see below, *harey* is remarkably polyfunctional. Both cataphoric and anaphoric *harey*s carry a number of distinct discourse functions. Such polyfunctionality should all things being equal, cause problems for addressees trying to process the speaker's messages. My goal here is to show how each of these cataphoric or anaphoric functions is associated with a set of grammatical conditions, as well as a unique discourse profile. These facilitate the identification of the specific function intended by the speaker. In addition, some functions are associated (more strongly) with specific genres, which can cue addressees as to which function is more likely. In fact, since there is a marked difference between spoken and written *harey* this chapter is based on two corpora, the spoken Haifa corpus (with 87 usable *harey* tokens) and the written heTenTen corpus (with 268 relevant tokens of *harey* and its variants out of a random sample of 300 tokens).[2] When pertinent, I also cite examples from other sources, which are specified for each example. The analysis below revises and develops my earlier treatment of *harey*, Ariel (1985, 1988, 1998, 1999).[3]

1.1 Cataphoric *harey*s

Cataphoric *harey*s introduce New information into the discourse. What is unique about this specially marked New information is that it is intended to instantly assume the salient status of shared assumptions already previously established. Depending on the nature of the modified information, primarily on the grammatical category it assumes (noun phrase, sentence or utterance) we can distinguish between deictic (2.1), performative (2.2) and main clause (2.3) *harey*s respectively.

---

[2] I thank Yael Maschler for sharing her Haifa Corpus with me, and Elior Elkayam for his help with coding the data here analyzed. Three *harey* utterances in the Maschler corpus were truncated, and are therefore ignored. The written corpus included two types of irrelevant *harey* occurrences, which are here ignored: (1) *harey* is the construct state nominal (see the chapter on the genitive) of *harim* 'mountains'. (2) *Harey* participates in a highly formal and extremely rare idiomatic construction (*lo harey X ke.harey Y*, 'X and Y are quite different from each other'). I use ʃ for the Hebrew post-alveolar voiceless fricative.

[3] Here are two main differences from my previous analyses: First, the current analysis is primarily based on a spoken corpus. Second, the association of each *harey* type with specific discourse profile features is here proposed for the first time.

1.2 Deictic *harey*

Deictic *harey* is best translated as French *voilà*. The closest English counterpart is *here is*, which the speaker prefaces to a noun phrase (NP) when drawing the addressee's attention to a physically present entity, or when introducing a New entity into the discourse. Deictic *harey* is extremely rare, speakers now preferring deictic *hine* 'here is' for this function. Only the written corpus contained such examples, and there were only two of them (0.75%). Note that the modified NP may stand for either a physical entity (flowers in 1a) or an abstract discourse entity (the news in 1b):

(1) a. **harey**   lax   praxim   yerukim
       Here.be for.you flowers   green
       'Here are green flowers for you'. (www.tale.co.il, Jun. 10, 2014).

   b. va-   **harey**   ha-xadaʃot: yonit levi   ʃuv   be-herayon.
      And   here.be   the News: Yonit Levy   again   in-pregnancy.
      'Here is the news: Yonit Levy is pregnant again'. (*Israel Today*, Jul. 16, 2015)

Deictic *harey* points to a discourse entity simultaneously (1a) or immediately later (1b) introduced into the discourse. Since its existence is easily verifiable, the speaker's goal is for this entity to immediately become shared information with the addressee. The information is moreover, focal and highly relevant to the subsequent discourse (i.e., it carries substantial contextual implications). This discourse-prominent status carries over to the two other cataphoric uses of *harey*, which I discuss next.

1.3 Performative *harey*

Performative *harey* modifies a complete utterance. It functions similarly to English *hereby*, which indicates that the speaker is performing a speech act (Austin, 1962). Using a performative *harey*, the speaker's utterance does not describe states of affairs in the world, but rather, brings about some change to it, by establishing a new fact within it. As can be seen in the two examples below, once again, the newly established state of affairs is central to the upcoming discourse, and carries immediate implications. There were no performative *harey* instances in the two corpora here consulted. In fact, Modern Hebrew speakers encounter performative *harey*s mostly when attending the religious Jewish marriage ceremony, where the man traditionally addresses the bride with:

(2) **harey** at mekudeʃet li be-tabaat zu.
    Hereby you consecrated to.me with-ring this.
    'You are hereby consecrated to me with this ring'

Once the rabbi confirms (2), the marriage takes effect.

In a variant performative construction, *harey* is inflected for first person (predominantly), and either governs an infinitival complement or a present tense/ "participle" verbal form. This construction is only found in formal Hebrew, although again, not in the written corpus here examined:

(3) **harey-ni** le-aʃer ki kol ha-pratim ve-ha-uvdot
    Hereby-I to-confirm that all the-details and-the-facts
    hinam Nexonim.
    are Correct.
    'I hereby confirm that all details and facts are correct'.
    (economy.gov.il/services/serviceforms/ishurmaasikshaotavoda2016).

While *harey*less versions of (2) and (3) (the counterparts of English *You are consecrated to me, I confirm that...*) can be used as performative utterances, they do not have to be so used. They can be descriptive assertions. This descriptive use is unavailable when *harey* is included. *Harey* forces a performative interpretation. Performative *harey*'s role is to mark a commissive performative speech act, where the speaker goes on record as undertaking some important commitment upon herself, which carries practical implications. Main clause *harey*, which I examine next, shares this characteristic, and must have evolved out of performative *harey*.

1.4 Main clause *harey* and *harey ʃe*

37 (13.7%) of the written Hebrew *harey*s are main clause *harey*s, where *harey*)or *harey ʃe*- 'harey that') prefaces a noninitial clause within a complex sentence.[4] This subsequent clause constitutes the speaker's Dominant or Prominent assertion (in the sense of Ariel, 2019, Erteschik-Shir and Lappin, 1979, Himmelmann

---

4 Following Even Zohar (1981) these were referred to as VPC (void pragmatic connective) *harey*s in Ariel (1985:2.21).

and Primus, 2015, von Heusinger and Schumacher, 2019), in that it is the part of the utterance that carries its relevance, might be denied or asked about, etc., while the initial clause merely serves as a point of reference for this assertion (Kuzar, 1980). Just like deictic and performative *harey*, main clause *harey* too is restricted to written Hebrew: No such tokens occur in the spoken corpus. About half of the main clause *harey*s (20, 54%) govern *ʃe* 'that', despite the fact that the *harey* clause is not syntactically embedded.[5] In an overwhelming majority of the main clause *harey*s (32, 86.5%) the *harey* assertion follows an explicitly marked conditional antecedent clause (*im* 'if'. . .), and is, thus, part of an *im X harey (ʃe) Y* construction:

(4) im   israel omedet   lifney   ʃoa   **harey ʃe-**
     If   Israel faces   before   catastrophe harey that-
     netanyahu   carix   le-vakeʃ   mi-barak   obama   vizot
     Netanyahu   must   to-ask   from-Barack Obama   visas
     hagira   le-ʃiʃa milyon   yisraelim
     immigration   for-six million   Israelis
     'If Israel is facing a catastrophe, *harey* (that) Netanyahu must ask Obama for immigration visas for six million Israelis'.

Still, despite the surface similarity to a conditional construction, the complex sentence here cannot be equated with a conditional, and *harey (ʃe)* is not synonymous with *az* 'then'. Main clause *harey*s rarely mark the clause they introduce as an implication, which (4) may seem to do. Indeed, *az* 'then' cannot substitute for *harey (ʃe)* not only when the construction is introduced by an expression other than *im* 'if' (see examples 6 and 7 below). And a quarter of the *im* 'if' introduced cases (8/32) cannot accommodate an *az*. The prototypical use of main clause *harey*s is in line with what Sweetser (1990: 5.1.3) called speech-act conditionals, where the speaker construes the performance of the speech act in the consequent (the *harey* modified clause) as enabled by the fulfillment of the antecedent.[6] In

---

[5] Indeed, Hebrew *ʃe-* 'that' is not absolutely restricted to embedded clauses. It is optionally added to *o* 'or' as well, for example.
[6] Sweetser discusses different cases, such as:
Larry: But if you notice,
         there are no registers in here.
(Santa Barbara Corpus of Spoken American English: 029)
where the nonexistence of the registers does not at all follow from the addressee noticing this fact. Rather, the antecedent draws the addressee's attention to the physical surrounding (lacking registers), which provides evidence for the claim in the consequent.

other words, a better analysis for (4) is that the writer's assertion about what Netanyahu should do is made valid on the assumption that the content of the antecedent clause is true (and not because it follows from the antecedent). The examples below will also make this point.

While a conditional antecedent may precede or follow its consequent in all varieties of conditional sentences, speech-act cases included, main clause *hareys* cannot occur sentence-initially. They absolutely must be clause-initial for the subsequent, Dominant clause within the utterance. Reversing the order of the clauses in (4) would create an unacceptable utterance, therefore. Reversing the order, while substituting *harey ʃe* 'harey that' with *harey* does result in an acceptable utterance, but one which is different in meaning, *harey* scoping over the whole utterance, in an anaphoric use (see §3 below). Finally, reversing the ordering while omitting *harey (ʃe)* (after all, speech act conditionals too cannot have an initial *then* consequent) does result in an acceptable sentence, but (a) the effect is different (see below) and (b) large portions of the antecedent must be shifted to the consequent, because it contains a substantial amount of anaphoric reference to the antecedent clause.

These anaphoric references to the antecedent differ from standard conditionals in that in a significant minority of the *im X harey (ʃe) Y* 'if X harey (that) Y' sentences (14 of the 32, 43.7%) the speaker sets out from the assumption that the antecedent clause is actually true, rather than only potentially true:

(5) im   hem   magdirim   et   acmam
     If   they   define   ACC   themselves
     ke-am   **harey ʃe-** hem   am.
     as-nation   harey ʃe-   they   nation,
     'If they define themselves as a nation *harey* they are a nation'

The writer in (5) refers to the Palestinians, who, it is well known, do define themselves as a nation. It therefore seems that the antecedent actually introduces a reference point, a relevant assumption, against which the *harey* clause is to be interpreted, and not a genuinely conditional assumption. Information assumed true is of course a highly appropriate reference point. If conditionality is not necessarily the point for main clause *im X harey (ʃe) Y* 'if X harey (that) Y' then it is also not surprising that in some cases (5, 13.5%) the initial constituent is not a conditional antecedent at all, and is instead introduced by a connective other than *im* 'if'. Note that this initial constituent too introduces a fact, as can be seen in (6):

(6) u-miʃum   ʃe-uxlosiot   ele   gdelot   maher   me-ha-memuca
And-since that-populations these increase faster   than-the-average
harey ʃe-   mispar   ha-miʃpaxot   ʃe.xayot   mi-taxat le-kav
Harey that- the-number.of   the-families that-live below   the-line.of
ha-oni   xayav   li-gdol   midey ʃana.
the-poverty must   to-increase   every year.
'And since these populations increase faster than average *harey* that the number of families living below the poverty line must increase every year.'

Other initial clauses include concessive *be-od ʃe* 'while' and *lamrot ʃe* 'even though'. In two cases, the preceding constituent is not even a clause, but rather a phrase, a complex NP in (7a), a topic announcer PP in (7b):

(7) a. kol   ʃilton   aravi   o   eize   ʃilton   ba-olam   ʃe-eino
        Any   regime   Arab   or   any   regime   in.the-world   that-doesn't
        ʃolet   be-ʃilton   ha-el   ve-dat
        rule   with-the.regime.of the-God   and-the religion.of
        ha-el   **harey ʃe-**   hu   daxuy.
        the-God   harey that-   it   rejected.
        'Any Arab regime or any regime in the world that does not rule in the name of God and God's religion *harey* it is rejected'.

   b.   ba-aʃer   le-ovdey   ha-elilim   **harey ʃe-**   anaxnu
        As   for-worshippers.of   the-idols   harey that-   we
        maskimim   kulanu   ʃe-ein   eloha   Mibaladey elohim.
        agree   all.of.us   that-is no God   except.for God.
        'As for idol worshippers, *harey* that we all agree that there is no god except for God'. The.chabad.org/library/article_cdo/aid/1797347

The mobilization of a conditional antecedent into a construction where it serves as a point of departure for the consequent is not unique to Hebrew. Haiman (1978) has argued that the role of conditional antecedents is precisely that, to provide a background/topic against which some comment is offered. But while standard conditional *im* 'if' constructions *may* function in this manner, main clause *harey* is dedicated specifically to this function. This is why in as many as 7 examples (18.9%) the initial clause merely serves as a foil, for a comparison where the subsequent *harey* clause typically presents a stronger claim:

(8) im   et   mexaot   bil'in   ve-na'alin   lo   hiclixu   ha-hatradot
    If   ACC   protests.of Bilin   and-Naalin   not   managed   the-hassles.of
    u-maacarey   ha-ʃav   ʃel   ha-cava   ve-ha-   ʃabak
    and-the.arrests false   of   the-army   and-the- security services
    li-ʃbor   **Harey ʃe-**   bi-yruʃalaim   ha-ʃita   hoxixa   et   acma.
    to-break   Harey-that   in-Jerusalem   the-method proved   ACC   itself.
    'While the hassles and false arrests of the army and the security services did not succeed in breaking the Bili'n and Na'alin protests, *harey* that in Jerusalem the method proved itself'.

The initial portion preceding main clause *harey*s seems rather long, 8.5 words on average (not counting the introducing connective). Only 5 (13.5%) of them contain less than 4 content words. It seems that main clause *harey (ʃe)* facilitates the processing of these complex sentences, separating out the initial point of departure from the dominant, comment part, whose beginning it marks. Indeed, omitting *harey* in the last example may very well cause processing difficulties, since 'in Jerusalem' might be taken as part of the antecedent rather than the consequent. In light of these distributional findings the fact that main clause *harey* is restricted to written Hebrew, where syntactic structures may be quite complex, is not at all surprising.[7]

But processing ease due to the clear demarcation of the relevant reference point on the one hand and the main assertion processed in relation to it on the other hand within complex utterances is not the only discourse effect associated with main clause *harey*. main clause *harey*-prefaced assertions convey an added stance, absent in standard assertions, not so marked.[8] Consider the subtle difference between the original *harey* utterance in (9a) and the *harey*-less variant I created in (9b):[9]

(9) a. kol   zman   ʃe-hu   roce   le-hagen   al   acmo,   **Harey ʃe-**
         All   Time   that-he wants   to-defend   on   himself, Harey that-
         zohi   zxut-o.
         this.is right-his.
         'As long as he wants to defend himself, *harey* this is his right'.

---

[7] Main clause *harey* shares this function with Mishnaic Hebrew copula *harey* + person agreement, e.g., *harey.hi* 'be.3rd.fem'.
[8] This is the reason for my claim above that even if ordering a *harey*less consequent before the antecedent is acceptable, the interpretation is not identical.
[9] ~ indicates a nonattested example.

b.~ kol   zman ʃe-hu   roce   le-hagen   al   acmo
    All   time that-he wants   to-defend on   himself
    zohi   zxut-o.
    this.is   right-his.
    'As long as he wants to defend himself, this is his right'.

The (9a) speaker *indicates* that s/he is asserting that it is the person's right to defend himself. It can thus be paraphrased with something like 'As long as he wants to defend himself, I hereby assert that this is his right'.[10] This extra effect is missing in (9b), which could be true regardless of the speaker's position. Unlike 9(a), 9(b) is a descriptive statement, more likely. Main clause *harey*s display a self-conscious performativity on the part of the speaker, who goes on record as making a declarative statement, thus underscoring her commitment to the assertion. Main clause *harey* clauses are then more strongly and more subjectively endorsed by the speaker. This can also be clearly seen in (7a), where it is the speaker that declares that such a regime is to be rejected. The connection to performative *harey*, where the speaker performs some commissive speech act is quite clear.

2 Anaphoric *harey*: A low accessibility discourse marker

Most *harey* tokens are not Cataphoric, and do not introduce New information into the discourse. On the contrary, they function as discourse markers whose core meaning marks the information they modify as already Accessible to the addressee. This is the case for all the 87 spoken *harey*s, as well as 228 (85.1%) of the written *harey*s. Anaphoric *harey*s modify whole utterances, the speaker's goal being the activation of a piece of Old information which is Accessible to the addressee although not currently activated. low accessibility anaphoric *harey* has two synonyms in Hebrew: *hen* and *halo*, both virtually absent in spoken Hebrew and quite rare even in written Hebrew.

Consider the following example (10), where the status of Old information is predicated on Svetlana's whole syntactic sentence (not here fully cited) starting with *ki* 'because', and following the *harey*:

---

[10] This is a stronger paraphrase than Sweetser's (1990: 121).

(10) Larissa: az   ex   at   yoda'at   ʃe-hu   mitkaʃer   harbe?
                So   how   you.fm   know.fm   that-he calls   a.lot?
      Svetlana: ki   kʃe-at   mistkaelet   ba-historyat   pniyot
                Because   when-you   look   at-the.history.of   calls
                ʃelo?,   at   ro'a   **harey**,   et   ha-lakoax,   matay
                his?,   you   see   harey,   Acc   the-customer,   when
                hu   hitkaʃer,
                he   called,
                'L: So, how do you know that he calls a lot?
                S: Because when you look at the history of his calls, you see
                harey the customer, when he called. . .'

Now, while every utterance naturally contains some combination of Old and New information (in accordance with the Maxim of Quantity – Grice, 1989), anaphoric *harey* marks the *whole* utterance as a unit as Old information, that is, a representation already available, endorsed or easily endorsable by the speaker and the addressee. Note that the 'Accessibility' condition on anaphoric *harey*s stands in marked contrast to the three *harey* functions considered in §2 above, where the modified information is asserted, and as such tends to be New, and certainly not presupposed to be Old.

The first question that comes to mind with respect to these discourse markers is why they even exist. Even more basically, why do speakers have a use for totally Old information, when discourse norms specify that speakers should be introducing New information (See Grice, 1989, which dictates that speakers must be informative). Indeed, why would a speaker go to the trouble of asserting a piece of information that she assumes is already Accessible to the addressee? The fact that the information is not currently activated is not enough to explain this use, for at any given point in time there is an endless number of pieces of information we store that are not currently activated, but we do not usually have the addressee activate them. The answer is, of course, that these pieces of information are relevant to the ongoing discourse. In other words, while the utterance as a whole is construed as Old information, it is intimately associated with a different discourse segment that is New. The overt marker then draws the addressee's attention to the marked case where the requirement for introducing at least some New information is not met at the utterance level. Incidentally, a language need not dedicate an overt form for this function. The English source for more than half of the *harey* tokens I counted in Hebrew subtitles for TV programs (1979–1981) were marked intonation contours, rather than overt expressions (close to a third of these contained some other Givenness indicator, such as a factive verb). More than a quarter of these "translated" *harey*s occurred in rhetorical questions or tag questions, where again, the answer is self-evident. Another 10% of these *harey*s corresponded to various presuppositional constructions. Only 7% were translations of *course* and *after all*.[11]

How can anaphoric *harey* utterances achieve relevance? There are three predominant ways in which wholly Accessible information *harey* utterances are relevant in an ongoing interaction. A speaker may wish to justify an original claim by relying on Accessible, noncontroversial information (3.1), she may wish to provide the interlocutor with a background assumption needed for the coherence of the discourse (3.2), or she may wish to counter or dispute some salient stance, again relying on some common assumption (3.3). In all these cases the *harey* utterance bears a local relevance (to an adjacent utterance mostly). The information introduced by all anaphoric *harey* utterances is invariably subservient to another, more original speaker contribution, which is discourse-dominant (i.e., relevant to the global discourse topic). In other words, all share a single argumentative goal to support a speaker's claim (be it in support of a salient claim or contra that claim).[12] The fact that it introduces specifically Accessible, noncontroversial information is crucial for the speaker's success in communicating her more original point. 4 discusses the co-occurrence of anaphoric *harey*s with explicit connectives and discourse markers.

2.1 Justification *harey*

Justification *harey* 'after all' introduces a piece of information considered Accessible in order to justify, support or strengthen another, original proposition, typically immediately preceding it. While syntactically independent, these *harey* utterances are pragmatically dependent. They contribute non-prominent propositions, and are not by themselves directly relevant to the topic discussed. Their contribution to the global discourse topic is mediated by the dominant proposition they support. Consider a spoken (11a) and a written (11b) example of justification *harey*:

(11) a. M.T: yediot axronot meʃabeax oto. Vaday.
            Yediot Ahronot praises   him. Of course.
            lama lo.   **harey** iʃto   ovedet ʃama.
            Why not.   After.all wife.his works there.

---

11 I should point out that Hebrew also has an 'after all' expression, *axrey ha.kol*.
12 I thank Yael Ziv for suggesting this unified view of the argumentatitvity of anaphoric *harey*s.

b. u-mi   niz'ak   le-'ezra?   ʃimon peres,   ʃe- hexel   ha-ʃavua
    And-who   hurried   to-help?   Simon Peres   Who-started   this.week
    le-hasbir   le-sarey   ha-xuc   ha-eyropim,   ki   medubar
    to explain To the ministers.of   foreign   the European ki   is-talked
    be-'ecem   be-memʃala   rodefet   ʃalom.   **harey**
    actually   about government   pursuing   peace.   After.all
    netanyahu   eyno   yaxol   li-ʃloax   le-matara   zu   et
    Netanyahu   not   can   to-send   for-goal   this   ACC.
    sar   ha-xuc   ʃelo,   liberman.
    Ministert   he-foreign his   Liberman.
    'And who was quick to help? Shimon Peres, who started explaining to the European foreign ministers this week that we are actually talking about a peace-seeking government. After all, Netanyahu cannot send Foreign Minister Liberman on this mission.'

Using a justification *harey* utterance, M.T in (11a) explains why it is that *Yediot Ahronot* (a Newspaper) praises the man in question: It is because the man's wife works for that paper. The writer in (11b) explains why it is the then President Peres (rather than Liberman, the foreign minister at the time) that was sent to defend the Israeli government to the Europeans: Liberman, an extreme right-wing politician, cannot be sent on such a mission. Both pieces of information are actually digressive with respect to the progression of the discourse. M.T is complaining about the person praised by the paper in (11a), and in (11b) the trouble with the European governments is at issue, not who can defend the Israeli government. The only reason for the introduction of the *harey* prefaced information is to support the speaker's dominant assertion.

Now, I have claimed above that all anaphoric *harey*s, justification ones included, must introduce Accessible information, one taken for granted by the interlocutors. It is important to note that this condition does not simply fall out of the function of justifications in general. Justifications can, but need not present Accessible information. For example:

(12) yeʃ   lexa   et   ha-ʃem +   me'afyeney   ha-korpus
      There.is   to.you   ACC   the-name +   the.characteristics.of the-corpus
      Ha-katuv?   ki   ectarex   le-cayen   zot.
      the.written?   Because   will.need.1st le-cayen   this.
      'You have the name plus the characteristics of the written corpus? Because I will need to indicate this'. (Private e-mail, Feb. 28, 2017)

The writer in (12) explains that the reason for her asking for the information about the corpus is that she will need to provide it in her paper. But this information about the speaker's need cannot be treated as Accessible information, which is why substituting *harey* for *ki* 'because' here would create an incoherent discourse, where the speaker expects her addressee to know something he has no basis for knowing.

The Accessibility condition also explains why the original (13a) *harey* utterance is much more offensive to feminists than the (13b) version, where I substituted *ki* 'because' for *harey*:

(13) a. hen   gormot   nezek   la.naʃim$_j$...   **harey**   hen$_i$
         They   cause   damage   to.the-women$_j$...   **harey**   they$_i$
         crixot   li-hiyot rakot   ve-adinot;   rov   ha-naʃim
         need   to.be   soft   and.delicate;   most   the.women
         rocot   li-hiyot kax...
         want   to-be   so...
         'They [feminists – MA] cause damage to women$_j$... After all, they$_i$ need to be soft and delicate; most women want to be so...' (*Yediot Ahronot*, March 1,1979).

     b.~ hen   gormot   nezek   la.naʃim$_j$...   **ki**   hen$_i$
         They   cause   damage   to.the-women$_j$...   **because** they$_i$
         crixot   li-hiyot rakot   ve-adinot;   rov   ha-naʃim
         need   to.be   soft   and.delicate;   most   the.women
         rocot   li-hiyot kax...
         want   to-be   so...
         'They [feminists – MA] cause damage to women$_j$... Because they$_i$ need to be soft and delicate; most women want to be so...' (*Yediot Ahronot*, March 1,1979).

In both variants in (13) the writer justifies his claim that feminists cause damage to women by asserting that (contra the feminist agenda) women need to be soft and delicate (presupposing that feminism drives women to not be soft and delicate). But the (13a) version *assumes* that this assertion is not original with the writer, but is, rather, Old information, taken for granted by the newspaper readers as well. Hence the different effect.

Interestingly, justification *harey* is not restricted to providing a justification for a previous claim made explicitly. Tal's rhetorical question in (14) strongly implicates that the couple should not have separated. Indeed, it is this implicated inference that the *harey* utterance justifies:

(14) Tal: …*lama hem nifredu, hayu kol kax,*
Why they separated, Were so,
*..haya la-hem kol kax tov be-yaxad, ..**harey**.*
Was to-them so good together, after all.
'Why did they separate, they were so, it was so good for them together, after all'.

And while given their discourse function (accessing an accepted assumption) *harey* utterances are naturally overwhelmingly declarative sentences, here is an interrogative one from the spoken corpus, where once again, it is the implicated content from the rhetorical *harey* question (namely, 'we should not have gotten to the bad situation we are in') that explains the speaker's pain about how government systems don't help people:

(15) MT: *ze ka'av,*
It Hurt,
..ʃe-ani ro'e ʃe-ma'araxot ʃiltoniyot,
When-I see that-systems government,
…ʃe-hayu amurot,
that-were supposed,
..li-hiyot le-cad ha-'am ha-ze,
to-be at-side the-people the-this,
***harey** biʃvil ma higanu le-macavim ka-'ele.*
After.all for what got.1st.pl to-situations like-these.
'It hurt. When I see government systems that were supposed to be on the side of this people, after all, how did we get to such situations?'

Now, note that I term the anaphoric *harey*s in this section "justification" *harey*s. Such *harey* utterances are clearly not strictly 'causal' in meaning, nor do they typically present explanations at the content level in fact. Just like main clause *harey*s operate at the speech act domain, so do justification *harey*s often justify the speaker's speech act, rather than the content of her utterance. In other words, my claim is that the justification *harey* provides a rationale for why the speaker is *saying* something, rather than for why things are the way they are in reality (although, of course, one reason for why the speaker is saying something is that that's how reality is). Consider (16) from the spoken corpus:

(16) Yaffa: ve-tavinu   kama   ima   ʃeli   miskena,
              And-get   how   mother   my   miserable,
              ...meyu'eʃet,   ...**harey** hi   halxa   le-havi
              ...desperate,   After.all,   she   went   to-bring
              li   maimon
              me   Maimon.
              'And get how miserable my mother is, desperate, after all, she tried to get me a Maimon'.

Yaffa's mother is not desperate *because* she tried to get her daughter a Maimon (a Mizrachi Jew). Rather, the fact that she is proposing a nonashkenazi match for her ashkenazi daughter *testifies* to how desperate she is in getting her daughter married. So, the mother's act is the grounds on which Yaffa bases her original evaluation, that her mother is desperate about her.

Justification *harey* has a variant *ʃe.harey* 'that *harey*' form, used roughly for the same function. *ʃe.harey* is restricted to written Hebrew. Consider:

(17) ba-sleng   ha-politi   ʃel.anu   ze   nikra   "medinat   kol
      In.the-slang   the-political   of.1ˢᵗ pl.   it   is.called   "the.state.of all
      ezraxeha" --   hagdara   kimat   absurdit,   **ʃe-harey**
      citizens.poss.3ʳᵈ.pl.fem"   definition   almost   absurd,   that-after.all
      lo   teto'ar   klal   medina   demokratit   ʃe-'eyna
      not   will.be.imagined   at.all state   democratic   that-not
      ʃayexet   le-xol   ezraxeha.
      belong   to-all   citizens.poss.3rd fem.
      'In our political slang it is called "a state of all of its citizens"— an almost absurd definition, since a democratic country that does not belong to all of its citizens is inconceivable'.

But the register difference is not the only difference between the two forms. More interestingly, discourse marker *harey* is free to occur initially, medially or finally.[13] This is not the case for *ʃe.harey*, which is restricted to initial position.

---

[13] In this respect, *harey* is not a prototypical discourse marker according to Maschler's (2009) definition. These tend to occur at the beginning of intonation units (IU). Based on the Haifa corpus, *harey* occurs at IU-initial position (40) or immediately following another connective or discourse marker (8) in more than half of the cases (48, 53.9%). But it occurs in final-IU position in 8 cases (9%) and medially in 32 cases (35.9%). 9 of the tokens (10.1%) occur in a separate IU, which is not turn-initial, and some of these tokens follow a continuing IU. Counts here refer to 89 tokens (truncated cases included). Maschler (2017) notes that what she calls textual discourse markers

Next, ʃe.harey is much more part of the previous clause, which it justifies: It often follows a comma, rather than a period (13/24, 54.2%), which points to its relative integration into the preceding clause. A comparison with the first 24 written justification hareys showed that only a minority of these are similarly integrated to the modified clause (3/24, 12.5%). Finally, whereas harey can cooccur with a connective (such as ki 'because', aval 'but', see 2.4), ʃe.harey cannot (Ariel, 1998). All of these differences stem from a single difference: Unlike harey, ʃe.harey is not a discourse marker, but rather, a causal connective, which has evolved out of discourse marker harey when combined with ʃe 'that/because'.[14] Indeed, ʃe.harey is best rendered by English *since*, rather than by 'after all'. Both similarly restrict the information they modify to "facts", although perhaps not necessarily ones actually known by the addressee. The discourse marker/connective difference can also account for the tone difference between the two forms. *Harey* operates on a subjective, interpersonal level, where the speaker addresses her *harey* utterance argument directly to the addressee.[15] While ʃe.harey is not absolutely an objective causal connective, it is quite close to being so.

2.2 Assumption *harey*

Assumption *harey*, just like justification *harey*, presents a discourse-nonprominent utterance whose relevance to the ongoing discourse is mediated through the dominant utterance(s) it supports. But in this case, the support provided by the *harey* utterance is a background assumption needed for the addressee to follow the dominant argument. Here are two examples from the spoken corpus:[16]

---

are not prototypical. The majority of *harey* tokens (anaphoric *harey*) combine an inter-personal aspect with a textual function.

14 Or perhaps, we should see it as an evolution of causal ʃe once combined with discourse marker *harey* After all'.

15 In Ariel (1985) I noted that written Hebrew justification *harey*s were restricted to relatively interactional contexts. Counts for Anaphoric *harey*s in the daily newspaper *Haaretz*, December 12, 14, 16, 21, 23, 27, 1984 revealed 5 *harey*s in 3 editorial pages, as compared with 2 *harey*s in 9 pages of objective news reporting. But in fact, even these two *harey*s were not part of the news reporting, but rather, quotes from direct speech. Clearly, this interpersonal *harey* has no place in objective reporting.

16 I here leave *harey* in the gloss, for English *after all* is not quite appropriate.

(18) Lilach: e—h, ... axoto—, ʃe-hi   y, ..hu **harey** haxi
             Uh,   sister.his,   who-is y, ..He harey the.most
             katan.   ...hem   arba   ax – im?,
             young.   They   four   brothers?,
             Um, uh, his sister, who is y-- He is *harey* the youngest. They are
             4 siblings.

Lilach breaks off her narrative to add the background assumption that the person in question is the youngest in his family. Nissim's *harey* utterance in (19) provides what he may have perceived to be a missing link which the addressee might wonder about, namely, how come he knew what the President had said:

(19) Nissim: siprati   lo   ma   ʃe-haya,   ...ba-ne'um   ʃel
             Told.1st him   what   that-was,   at.the-speech of
             ha-nasi$_i$.   **harey**   hu$_i$ haya   eclenu,
             the-president$_j$. harey   he$_i$ was   at.our.place,
             be-veit ha-sefer   ha.reali,
             at-the.school   the Reali,
             'I told him what was in the president's speech, *harey* he came to us at the Reali school'.

But note that Nissim's *harey* utterance can also be taken as a justification case, where the speaker provides the *grounds* on which he bases his authority to report on the President's speech. While Lilach's *harey* utterance is an unequivocal assumption *harey*, Nissim's could be either, depending on the speaker's goal. This is not so surprising, given that both justification and assumption *harey* utterances are nonprominent assertions introduced in order to serve another, dominant claim.

Assumption *harey* too modifies information that is already Accessible to the addressee, as can be seen in the following exchange, where S is one of the interlocutors (there was at least one other participant):

(20) R: li   yeʃ   **harey** sinit   ba-bait.   ha-bat
         To.me   there.is   harey   Chinese.fem   at.the-home.   The-daughter
         ʃeli   ve-ha-xatan   ʃeli   lamdu   sinit   ve...
         my   and.the.son.in.law   my   studied Chinese and...
     S: bi-rcinut   lo   yadati.   (Lotan 1990: 17/18).
         In-seriousness   not   I.knew.
     R: 'I have *harey* a Chinese at home. My daughter and
         my son in law studied Chinese and...'
     S: 'Really, I didn't know'.

S's response to R testifies that he expected to receive an Accessible piece of information due to *harey*, and since that was not the case, he comments that he actually did not know that R's daughter was specializing in Chinese. Note the following from the written corpus, where the assumption *harey* utterance is followed by a consequent *az* 'then/so' clause:

(21) Amarti   lo: **harey** ata   yodea   ʃe-haya   naxon   le-hatil
     Told.1st him: Harey   you   know   that-was   right   to-impose
     ma'am   al   yerakot   ve-perot   ve-gam   mas   ha-bacoret   haya
     VAT   on   vegetables and.fruits and.also tax   the.draught   was
     ba-makom,   az   madua   lo   biteta   emdo   nexonot ele?
     in.the-place,   so   why   not   expressed.2nd   positions right   these?
     'I told him: *harey* you know that it was right to impose VAT on vegetables and fruit, and the draught tax was also appropriate, so why didn't you express these correct positions?'

The assumption *harey* utterance sets the relevant background for the question that follows. But even in this seemingly antecedent role within a semi-conditional construction the *harey*-modified information must be Accessible information. Indeed, the comma in (21) could have been a full stop, since there is no syntactic dependency between the *harey* clause and the *az* 'so' clause.[17] Note, then, that *harey* can introduce a starting point assumption (here), as well as a dominant assertion concerning that starting point (in main clause cases). But first, assumption *harey* is restricted to Accessible information, which the initial portion of main clause *harey* is not. Second, main clause *harey* scopes over the main clause only, whereas assumption *harey* scopes over the whole utterance. This precludes their cooccurrence, even when the main clause first part is Accessible, as it is in (6).

---

17 This construction is then quite different from Mishnaic Hebrew initial *harey ʃe*, which introduces a genuine conditional assumption, i.e., not one that must already be Accessible to the addressee, and in addition, must be followed by a syntactic main clause:

harey   ʃe-halax   bno   li-mdinat   ha-yam,   ve-ʃama   ʃe-met
Let's.assume   that.went   son.poss.3rd   to.state.of   the.sea,   and.heard   that-died
bno,   ve-amad,   ve-xatav   nexasav   le-axer   ve-axar   ba
son.poss.3rd   and.stopped   and-wrote   assets.poss.3rd   to-another And-later   came
bno,   matnato   matana.
son.poss.3rd   gift. poss.3rd gift.

'Let's assume that a person's son went away to a state beyond the sea and he heard that his son died and he bequeathed his assets to another, and afterwards his son came back, his gift is a gift (not revocable)'. (Baraitha ב"ב קמו)

2.3 Countering *harey*

Justification and assumption *harey* utterances are auxiliary steps speakers take in order to improve another, dominant argument of theirs. Countering *harey*s stand on their own in that they do not necessarily occur adjacent to a more dominant assertion. They may therefore present discourse-dominant information. Countering *harey*s introduce an argument against some other position already on the table. Consider the following from the written corpus (22):

(22) afilu naniax ʃe-lo hayu piʃey milxama: miʃehu
Even suppose.1ˢᵗ.pl that-not were crimes.of war someone
harey nose lefaxot be-axrayut le- sarbanut
harey bears at.least in-responsibility for- refusal.of
ha-xakira ve-la-dirdur ha-mesukan
the.investigation and-for.the-deterioration the- dangerous
be-ma'amada ʃel isra'el.
of-status.3ʳᵈ.poss.sg.fm of Israel.

'Suppose even that there were no war crimes: someone *harey* is responsible for the refusal to investigation and for the dangerous deterioration in Israel's status'.

The speaker first provisionally adopts the position that no war crimes were committed (the argument on the table). But then s/he counters with 'someone is responsible for refusing to investigate the possibility of war crimes, as well as for the deteriorating status of Israel in the world (the counter-argument). The relation between the first position raised (for the sake of argument) and the *harey* utterance seems to match Anscombre and Ducrot's (1976) characterization of the relation between 'but'-conjoined phrases: *But* conjoins two claims which *support* opposite conclusions. Indeed, in (23) the first claim supports the conclusion that the political leaders have nothing to answer for. The countering *harey* utterance, however, supports the opposite conclusion, namely, that the political leaders have at least two things to answer for.

Nonetheless, countering *harey* is different from the standard, monologic 'but'. Using 'but', the speaker embraces both arguments, despite the fact that they stand in opposition to one another. Consider the following from the written corpus (23):

(23) yadati   ʃe-tihiye   kcat gdola alay,   aval yaxolti   le-vacea
      Knew.1ˢᵗ   that-will.be   a.bit big   on.me   but   could.1ˢᵗ   make
      kama   tikunim.
      a.few   alterations.
      'I knew that it would be a bit too big for me, but I could make a few alterations'.

While the subsequent argument ('I could make some alterations') tends to be the "winning" argument for 'but' conjunctions, the speaker portrays herself as simultaneously entertaining both the argument and the counter-argument (for keeping the dress). Countering *harey*, however, construes the opposing stance as incompatible with the one it counters. Even if both arguments are articulated by one speaker, countering *harey* necessarily involves different voices, holding nonreconcilable stances, where the first one is rejected (and see Zussman, 2013 for similar recent uses of dialogic aval 'but').

The next example (24) makes this point more clearly. Note that here the counter-argument supported by the *harey* utterance is later spelled out (the rhetorical 'That I should commit such a thing? which implicates 'I did not commit this crime', followed by an assertion that the charges are not true):

(24) ba'al   ve-iʃa   xaʃudim   bi-znut   (Newspaper headline)
      Husband   and-wife   suspected   of-prostitution.
      Le.axar ʃa'a   kala   huva   ha-ba'al,   yexezkel,   49,
      After   time   short   was.brought   the-husband Yechezkel,   49,
      le-veyt   ha-miʃpat,   ke-xaʃud   be-ʃidul   iʃto
      to-house   the-court,   as-suspect   of-soliciting   wife.poss.3ʳᵈ.sg.msc
      li-znut.   tguvat   ha-xaʃud   hayta: **harey**   ani
      to-prostitution   the.response.of   the-suspect   was: Harey   I
      saba.   ʃe-ani   e'ese   davar   ka-ze?   ze   lo
      grandfather.   That-I   should.commit   a thing   like-this?   It   not
      naxon!   (*Yediot Ahronot*, Dec. 12, 1979)
      true!
      'Husband and wife suspected of prostitution (Newspaper headline)
      After a while, the husband, Yechezkel, 49 years Old, was brought to court, suspected in soliciting his wife into prostitution. The suspect's reaction was: *Harey* I am a grandfather. That I should commit such a thing?? It is not true!'

Just like we find cases where the *harey* utterance could either be justification or assumption (20), the following excerpt from the spoken corpus, shows two consecutive *harey* utterances. The first one is a countering *harey* case, but the second could be either justification or countering:

(25) MN: tir'e, le-hag-- le-ha'aʃim et va'adat dovrat, ʃe-hi
        Look, To-hag-- to-blame ACC Committee Dovrat, that-it
        lo yarda le-'omek ha-'inyan, axrey arba ʃanim
        not went.down to-depth.of the-matter, after four years
        ʃel avoda, **harey** ha-kalkelan ha-yexidi ʃe-haya ʃama
        of work, harey the.economist the.only who.was there
        ze ʃlomo dovrat, harey yaʃvu ʃam anʃey
        is Shlomo Dovrat, Harey sat there people.of
        xinux.
        education.
        Look, to blag--- to blame the Dovrat Committee that it did not deeply delve into the matter, *harey* the only economist that participated is Shlomo Dovrat, *harey* there were education experts on the committee'.

MN first echoes an accusation against the Dovrat committee, that it did not go deeply into educational matters, presumably because of its focus on financial aspects. MN's first *harey* utterance then counters this echoed argument, stating that Dovrat was the only economist on the committee. This implies that the other members were education experts, which counters the argument that the committee was too much influenced by economists. The speaker then goes on to support her counter-argument with a justification *harey*. She is stating that Dovrat was the *only* economist because there were education specialists on the committee. Alternatively, however, both are countering *harey* utterances, both countering the same position that the committee was too much concerned with financial matters.

Once again, note that as an anaphoric *harey*, countering *harey* shares the 'Accessibility' constraint with justification and assumption *harey*s. In other words, the counter-argument raised must constitute Accessible information. As such, of course, these counter-arguments are especially strong, because they are based on a shared assumption, taken for granted by the interlocutors. This is not necessarily true for all 'but'-prefaced counters, as the following example from the written corpus shows:

(26) txuʃat ha-i-naxat ve-ha-xaʃaʃot ha-nilvim
     The.feeling.of the-dis-satifaction and-the-worries that-accompany
     eleha muvanim, aval yitaxen meod ʃe-hem
     to.it understandable, but likely very that-they

> *mut'im*   mi-ysodam.
> wrong   From-foundation.3ʳᵈ pl.poss.
> 'The feeling of dissatisfaction and the worries that come with it are understandable, but very likely they are fundamentally wrong'.

The statement that the worries are probably wrong most likely is not already Accessible.

Now, one might think that at least this countering *harey* could be classified as a justification *harey*, except that the explicit *harey* proposition here supports the very implicature it generates (the countering stance). Nonetheless, countering *harey* must be recognized as a separate function, because, unlike justification *harey* it cannot be roughly paraphrased by *ki* 'because'. The connective that can replace countering *harey* is utterance-level *aval* 'but'. Moreover, unlike *harey*, English *after all* is not used to counter a stance, but I did find one *but of course* source for a countering *harey*, where *but* provides the countering and *of course* provides the self-evident status of the modified information. Hebrew countering *harey* simultaneously serves both functions.

3 *Harey*, grammar and grammaticization

I have discussed six discourse functions for *harey*, but in terms of conventionally encoded meanings we only have four distinct *harey* meanings: Deictic, performative, main clause and low accessibility (which includes the three anaphoric uses). Cataphoric *hareys* show three distinct uses, where each *harey* is also syntactically distinct (each modifies a different type of syntactic unit). Anaphoric *hareys*, on the other hand, share a single core meaning ('low accessibility'), a single syntactic patterning (all modify complete utterances) and a single overall argumentative role. The different local functions they serve (justification, assumption and countering) are not conventionalized. Rather, they constitute coherence inferences, derived consistently enough based on the fact that the *harey*-modified information is already Accessible, and hence cannot be the speaker's Dominant message. These functions are much more context-dependent, then.

This is why another connective explicitly expressing the coherence relation (of 'justification' etc.) can comfortably co-occur with anaphoric *hareys* without causing any feeling of redundancy. It is precisely the fact that the latter are not encoded for *harey* that accounts for why this co-occurrence is allowed. Note that *aval* 'but' and *ax* 'but', for example, cannot co-occur, and neither can *ki* 'because' and *mipney ʃe* 'because', no doubt because of the redundancy created by repeating the same meaning. Justification *harey* can co-occur with *ki* 'because', and countering *harey* can co-occur with *aval* 'but', however, just because these *harey*s do not encode 'justification' and 'countering' respectively.

A similar percentage of spoken and written *harey*s (11.6%, 13.1% respectively) cooccur with another, preceding connectives: *ve-* 'and' and *ki* 'because' in the spoken corpus, and *aval* 'but' in the written corpus.[18] *Ki* 'because' combines with *harey* only in a small number of the justification cases (22/184, 12%, excluding *ʃe.harey*), as compared with *aval* 'but', which accompanies countering *harey*s in 13/22 (59.1%) of the cases, all of them in the written corpus:

(27) Nachum: hem   hexziru   lo   ribit,   .. ke.ilu,
              They returned   to.him interest   .. like
              .. ki   harey   ze   kesef,
              .. because   harey   this money,
     Omer: k—n
              Y—s
     Nachum: .. ʃe-hem   yaxlu   la-sim ba-bank,
             .. that-they   could   to-put in.the-bank
             .. ve-le-kabel   kesef.
             .. and-to-receive   money.
             'They gave him back interest, like. Because after all, it's money that they could have put in the bank and gotten money (for)'.

Frequent uses of connective + *harey* strings must have made the derivation of such inferences more salient to interlocutors, later in the absence of these connectives (the majority cases) (See Traugott, 2018 on the development of Justification *after all*). Indeed, note that countering *harey* is rather rare, on the one hand, and often accompanied by an overt contrast marker, on the other hand. These two distributional facts point to the relatively new status for this anaphoric *harey*. Most likely, it is the commonly accompanying *aval* 'but' that paved the way for inserting dominant information under countering *harey*, thus diverging from the generally nondominant status of Accessible *harey*-modified information. We note again in this connection that English *after all* is not typically used for the countering function.

The fact that the connectives mark the coherence of the utterance to the surrounding discourse explains why they must precede *harey* (**Harey ki/aval* 'harey

---

18 Not counted here are *ʃe.harey* cases, where *ʃe* 'that/because' has merged into a single connective with *harey* whose meaning is 'since' (see 3.1 above).

because/but'). The latter scopes over a narrower domain, since directly it only pertains to the modified utterance (by marking it 'Accessible information'). The conventional connectives connect (at least) two utterances. Of course, *ki* 'because' and *aval* 'but' encode a much more specific coherence relation than *ve* 'and', and are then restricted to justification and countering *harey*s respectively. *Ve* 'and' cooccurs with all three anaphoric *harey*s.

Now, I have listed 'after all' as the gloss for low accessibility *harey*, but Hebrew does have such an expression as well, *axrey ha.kol* literally, 'after the all'. I suggest that although *harey* and *axrey ha.kol* 'after all' are quite interchangeable, they are not identical. Specifically, *harey* is more grammaticized than *axrey ha.kol* 'after all'. First, there is a difference in the prosody of *harey* and the *axrey ha.kol* 'after all' (in both languages). A prosodic break (marked by a comma in writing) separates *axrey ha.kol* (and English *after all*) from the utterance it modifies, reflecting the looser connection to the utterance it modifies. It also receives nuclear stress. *Harey*'s deeper grammaticization status is reflected by the fact that it is never separated by a comma from the material it modifies in the written corpus (higher integration), and it cannot receive nuclear stress. Only 9 tokens (10.3%) of the spoken *harey*s occur in a separate intonation unit, but these mostly follow a hesitation pause. This prosodic integration of *harey*, not typical of discourse markers (Traugott, 1995), points to a tighter semantic and syntactic connection between modifier *harey* and the information it modifies in comparison to *axrey ha.kol* 'after all'.

I suggest that unlike *harey*, *axrey ha.kol*, just like *after all*, still carries its original meaning, something like 'at the end of the day'. In fact, Halliday and Hasan (1976:270) analyze English *after all* quite literally as "after everything relevant has been considered, what remains is. . .". In other words, the association between *axrey ha.kol* 'after all' and 'Accessibility' may still be transparent. Once everything has played out, everything is known, which is why the following material is presented as factual and Accessible (known) information.[19] Presumably for the same reason, the modified information may be counter to what would be expected, which is a different use of *after all* and *axrey ha.kol*, although one not shared by *harey*.[20]

The association between *harey* (deictic) and Accessible information is more opaque. A more arbitrary convention connects *harey* to 'Accessibility' than *axrey*

---

19 Traugott (2018) argues that it is an argumentative use of an 'in the end' *after all*, especially when accompanied by *because* that served as a bridging context for justification *after all*.
20 Note that, unlike *after all* (and its Hebrew counterpart), *harey* cannot introduce information construed as counter-expectations. See Ariel (1985: 2.221), Halliday and Hasan (1976) and Traugott (2018) on this quite different use of *after all*.

ha.kol. The 'Accessibility' function is not totally conventionalized for the latter yet, which is why it still requires prosodic prominence (separate IU, nuclear stress). It's likely that the relative small size of *harey* (2 syllables, as opposed to 4 syllables for *axrey ha.kol* 'after all') may have facilitated the compact realization of the relation between it and the modified material, but longer expressions can and do reduce phonetically during grammaticization. *Axrey ha.kol* 'after all' is simply not as advanced as *harey* in its grammaticization as a 'low Accessibility' marker.

In fact, this is why *harey* and *axrey ha.kol* 'after all' can cooccur (in this case, either ordering is observed):

(28) **axrey ha.kol, harey** ata ha-menahel.
After all, harey you the-manager.
'After all, *harey* you are the manager'. (www.tam.co.il/22_4_2005/magazin4.htm)

Such co-occurrences may seem surprising at first, for the string seemingly expresses the same 'Accessibility' function twice. Indeed, as mentioned above, *harey* cannot cooccur with its synonymous *hen* and *halo*. The reason for the different co-occurrence restrictions here is the relatively deeper semanticization of *harey* in comparison with *axrey ha.kol* 'after all'. The interpretation of *harey* is never reducible to its etymological (deictic) source. The original meaning of *axrey ha.kol* 'after all' is still available, so that the two expressions are not totally synonymous, which is why they can co-occur.

The conventional combinations of *harey* with *ʃe* 'that', either as *harey ʃe*, roughly 'then', or as *ʃe.harey* 'since' constitute bona fide grammaticized connectives, I have suggested. The former marks a main clause dominant assertion (see again 2.3), the latter has become a subordinate conjunction 'since' (see again 3.1). Indeed, *ʃe.harey* cannot cooccur with *ki* 'because' and *harey ʃe* cannot cooccur with *az* 'then'.

It is not my goal here to provide an actual historical account for how *harey* came to have all of its functions. In line with (inter alia) Hopper and Traugott (1993/2003), Traugott and Dasher (2002), Ariel (2008), Degand (2015) and Brinton (2017), I assume that the evolution of discourse markers is a case of grammaticization, namely it must proceed in small, motivated steps, just like other cases of grammaticization (and semanticization),[21] and that synchronic data can point to

---

[21] There is currently some controversy about the need to distinguish between grammaticization and pragmaticization, the latter specifically applying to discourse markers. While discourse

diachronic development. The polyfunctionality of *harey* is the inevitable result of diachronic change, where old functions do not necessarily disappear due to layering (Hopper, 1991).[22]

Based on the nature of the discourse functions associated with *harey* we can tentatively propose the conceptual grammaticization path for the evolution of *harey* functions in Figure 1. Note that no diachronic claim is here made:

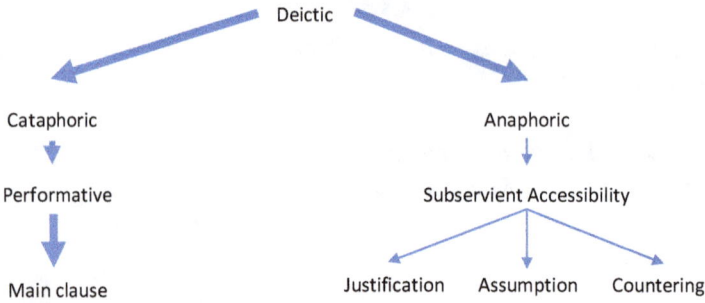

Figure 1: The grammaticization path of *harey*.

Thick arrows stand for fully grammaticized changes, thin arrows stand for discourse-salient realizations of a single encoded meaning.

4 Conclusions

I have discussed the six procedural functions associated with Hebrew *harey* in §2–4, and their potential grammaticization evolution in §5. Now, such rich polysemy, one might think, would result in processing difficulties for the addressee. Surprisingly, however, hardly any cases were found with a potential ambiguity between the functions. This is because each function is associated with a different discourse profile, which addressees can rely on when processing *harey*. Table 1 summarizes the main claims here argued for, and associates each *harey* type with its discourse profile, namely its specific set of grammatical and pragmatic features.

---

markers definitely manifest special features, I am not convinced that these justify viewing the evolutionary changes they undergo as involving a separate mechanism. The same applies to the term lexicalization.
22 A recent theoretical discussion of the rise of discourse markers, as well as case studies from several languages, can be found in Heine et al (2021).

10 Processing polyfunctional discourse markers: Making sense of Hebrew *harey* — 273

Table 1: Summary of the different discourse profiles of the 6 *harey* functions.

	Accessibility status	Modified constituent	Syntactic position	Harey ʃe?	ʃhe.harey?	Hen/halo?	+Overt Connective?	Genre	Discourse status	Frequency (corpora combined)
Deictic	New	NP	Initial	NA	NA	No	NA	Written	Dominant	Rare
Performative	New	Ut	Initial	No	No	No	Yes	Written	Dominant	Rare
Main clause	New	S	Initial	Yes	No	No	No	Written	Dominant	Low
Countering	Old	Ut	Initial/medial	No	No	Yes	Yes (most)	All	Dominant or non-Dominant	Low
Assumption	Old	Ut	Initial/medial	No	No	Yes	Yes ('and')	All	Non-Dominant	High
Justification	Old	Ut	Initial/medial	No	Yes	Yes	Yes	All	Non-Dominant	High

First, each discourse function is associated with an Accessibility status: all cataphoric *harey*s (deictic, performative and main clause) modify New information, whereas all Anaphoric *harey*s (countering, assumption and justification) mark the information they modify as already Accessible to the addressee. Next, note that the different *harey*s modify different syntactic units. Deictic *harey* modifies NPs, main clause *harey* modifies clauses, while the other *harey* types modify whole utterances, which may span over more than one clause. Syntactic position in Table 1 refers to the positioning of *harey* vis a vis the material it modifies. All *harey*s can precede the material they modify, but cataphoric ones must precede it (labeled initial in the table).

Anaphoric *harey*s can occupy all positions, but final *harey*s are quite rare.[23] Only main clause *harey* is substitutable by the derived connective *harey ʃe* 'harey that', and only justification *harey* is (more or less) replaceable by the derived subordinate conjunction *ʃe.harey* 'that harey, since'. Only Anaphoric *harey*s are replaceable by the quite rare synonyms *hen* and *halo*. Of the cataphoric *harey*s, only performative *harey* can cooccur with an additional connective. All Anaphoric *harey*s can cooccur with other connectives. Cataphoric *harey*s are restricted to written discourse, whereas Anaphoric *harey*s are attested in both written and spoken discourse. Information introduced by cataphoric *harey*s is dominant in the discourse, in that it carries the conversation forward, it introduces material which is naturally responded to by the interlocutor. Anaphoric *harey*s mostly introduce nondominant information. These *harey* utterances are directly relevant only to some other, prominent claim, most often an adjacent, explicitly stated assertion. Crucially, such *harey* utterances are subservient to this more original claim in that they provide a rationale for asserting it or an assumption required for processing it. Still, countering *harey* may be dominant (although it does not have to be). Finally, Anaphoric *harey*s are overall far more frequent than *harey*s. At the same time, there are significant differences within the two categories. Deictic and performative *harey*s are extremely rare, whereas main clause *harey* is not infrequent in written discourse. Within Anaphoric *harey*s, assumption and justification *harey*s lead in both genres.

In sum, deictic elements are a well-known source for evolved grammatical morphemes, and *harey*, originally 'here is', is no exception. The evolution of the opposite functions of marking both New information and Accessible information out of a single source is not unique to *harey*. Heine and Kuteva (2002) note

---

[23] 6/84 (7.1%) of assumption and justification *harey*s follow the information they modify. Assumption *harey*s are equally divided between initial and medial position. Justification *harey*s are far more frequent in initial position. These findings are true for both the spoken and the written corpora.

the frequent development of demonstrative expressions into both focus markers (New information) and to definite articles (Accessible information). But *harey* is especially interesting given its variety of functions within each sub-category, namely New information deictic, performative and main clause, and Accessible information *harey*s, routinely mobilized for introducing auxiliary assumptions in support of a discourse prominent assertion (justification, assumption and countering). While now responsible for diverse discourse functions, it is reasonable to hypothesize that their evolution followed small, motivated inferential steps. Still, although inferencing is certainly involved in distinguishing between the different *harey* functions currently, addressees can reliably use the discourse profile cues summarized in Table 1 to zero in on the speaker-intended *harey* function. Such an analysis of polyfunctional procedural expressions as distinguishable according to their different discourse profiles and genres explains how come language users can tolerate so much ambiguity. I hope future research focusses (also) on this processing perspective when analyzing polyfunctional linguistic expressions.

References

Anscombre, Jean-Claude & Oswald Ducrot. 1976. L'argumentation dans la langue. *Langages* 42. 5–27.
Ariel, Mira. 1985. *Givenness marking*. Tel Aviv, Israel: Tel Aviv University PhD dissertation.
Ariel, Mira. 1988. Retrieving propositions from context: why and how. *Journal of Pragmatics* 12. 567–600.
Ariel, Mira. 1998. Discourse markers and form-function correlations. In Andreas H. Jucker & Yael Ziv (eds.), *Discourse markers: Descriptions and theory*, 223–259. (Pragmatics and Beyond New Series 57). Amsterdam: John Benjamins.
Ariel, Mira. 1999. Mapping so-called 'pragmatic' phenomena according to a 'linguistic-extralinguistic' distinction: The case of propositions marked 'accessible'. In Michael Darnell, Edith A. Moravcsik, Frederick J. Newmeyer, Michael Noonan & Kathleen M. Wheatley (eds.), *Functionalism and formalism in linguistics*, vol. II: Case studies, 11–38. (Studies in Language Companion Series 41). Amsterdam: John Benjamins.
Ariel, Mira. 2008. *Pragmatics and grammar*. Cambridge: Cambridge University Press.
Ariel, Mira. 2019. Different prominences for different inferences. *Journal of Pragmatics* 154. 103–116.
Austin, John L. 1962. *How to do things with words*. Oxford: Clarendon Press.
Brinton, Laurel J. 2017. *The evolution of pragmatic markers in English: Pathways of change*. Cambridge: Cambridge University Press.
Degand, Liesbeth & Jacqueline Evers-Vermeul. 2015. Grammaticalization or pragmaticalization of discourse markers?: More than a terminological issue. *Journal of Historical Pragmatics* 16. 59–85.
Erteschik-Shir, Nomi & Shalom Lappin. 1979. Dominance and the functional explanation of island phenomena. *Theoretical Linguistics* 6. 41–85.

Even-Zohar, Itamar. 1981. Russian VPC's in Hebrew literary language. *Slavica Hierosolymitana* VI-VI: 413–417.
Grice, H. Paul. 1989. *Studies in the way of words*. Cambridge, Mass.: Harvard University Press.
Haiman, John. 1978. Conditionals are topics. *Language* 54. 564–589.
Halliday, M. A. K. & Ruqaiya Hasan. 1976. *Cohesion in English*. London: Longman.
Heine, Bernd & Tania Kuteva. 2002. *World lexicon of grammaticalization*. Cambridge: Cambridge University Press.
Heine, Bernd, Gunther Kaltenböck, Tanya Kuteva & Haiping Long. 2021. *The rise of discourse markers*. Cambridge: Cambridge University Press.
Himmelmann, Nikolaus P. & Beatrice Primus. 2015. Prominence beyond prosody – a first approximation. In Amedeo De Dominicis, ed., *Prominences in Linguistics, Proceedings of the pS-prominenceS International Conference University of Tuscia*. Viterbo: DISUCOM Press, 38–58.
Hopper, Paul J. 1991. On some principles of grammaticization. In Elizabeth Closs Traugott & Bernd Heine (eds.), *Approaches to grammaticalization*. Vol. 1: Focus on theoretical and methodological issues, 17–35. (Typological Studies in Language 19.1). Amsterdam: John Benjamins.
Hopper, Paul J. & Elizabeth Closs Traugott. 1993/2003. *Grammaticalization*. Cambridge: Cambridge University Press.
Kuzar, Ron. 1980. On the linguistic marker *harey*. *Machbarot le-sifrut, xhevra u-vikoreet* 1.
Maschler, Yael. 2009. *Metalanguage in Interaction: Hebrew Discourse Markers*. Amsterdam John Benjamins.
Maschler, Yael. 2017. The emergence of Hebrew *loydea/loydat* ('I dunno MASC/FEM') from interaction: Blurring the boundaries between discourse marker, pragmatic marker, and modal particle. In Andrea Sansò & Chiara Fedriani (eds.), *Pragmatic Markers, Discourse Markers and Modal Particles: New Perspectives*, 37–69. Amsterdam/Philadelphia: John Benjamins.
Sweetser, Eve. 1990. *From etymology to pragmatics: Metaphorical and cultural aspects of semantic structure*. (Cambridge Studies in Linguistics 54). Cambridge: Cambridge University Press.
Traugott, Elizabeth Closs. 1995. The role and development of discourse markers in a theory of grammaticalization. Paper presented at The *International Conference of Historical Linguistics* XII, Manchester.
Traugott, Elizabeth Closs. 2018. Modeling language change with constructional networks. In Pons Bordería, Salvador & Oscar Loureda (eds.), *Beyond Grammaticalization and Discourse Markers: New Issues in the Study of Language Change*. Leiden: Brill.
Traugott, Elizabeth Closs & Richard B. Dasher. 2002. *Regularity in semantic change*. (Cambridge Studies in Linguistics 97). Cambridge: Cambridge University Press.
von Heusinger, Klaus & Petra Schumacher (eds.). 2019. *Special issue: Prominence in discourse*. *Journal of Pragmatics* 154.
Zussman, Ofir. 2013. Grammaticization paths of concessive constructions. Tel Aviv, Israel: Tel Aviv University PhD dissertation.

Index

abductive 51, 53–54
academic background 78
– higher 79
acceptability 45, 53–54, 58–59
acceptability of sentences 53
acceptability scores 55, 58–59, 61
accessibility function 271
accessibility status 273–74
accessible information 247, 257–59, 264, 267, 270, 274–75
accuracy 8, 168, 175
acquisition 74, 78, 89, 116
addition 34, 74, 80, 134–35, 147, 149
addition of a DM 215–16, 218–19, 222, 230–35, 238–40, 242
additive relations 74, 146, 167
adversative 8, 167, 173, 176–78, 181
adversative connectives 8, 167, 177–79, 183
adversative relations 167, 179
allocentric 7–8, 121–22, 125–26, 128, 132, 136, 138–40, 142–45, 147
allocentric condition 7, 125–27, 142, 146, 148, 151
allocentric orientation 142, 145–46, 149
allocentric task 7, 126, 128, 132, 135–41, 145–46, 148, 151–52
annotation 133–34, 141, 191, 196–98, 201
Asymmetry Hypothesis 216, 230–31, 243
Author Recognition Test 6, 73, 76, 81, 84

backchannels 197, 202
BERT 162, 169, 171, 175

Catalan 11, 215, 217, 229–31, 234, 239–41
cataphoric 11, 247–49, 255, 268, 272, 274
causal connectives 5, 45–47, 60, 62–63, 91, 167, 177, 231
causality 34, 54, 97, 116
causal relations 23, 28, 45, 48–49, 58, 62, 74–75, 90, 94–95, 97, 113–14
cognitive complexity 6, 74–76, 78, 81
cognitive effort 27, 34–35, 92
cognitive load 2, 7, 12, 121, 125, 127–28, 132, 138–41, 143, 151, 153

coherence relations 2, 6–7, 9, 89–96, 98, 104, 106, 113–16, 123, 215, 218, 268, 270
computational dialogue systems 9, 193–210
computational language processing 2, 178, 183
computational language understanding 9, 160, 183
computational models 8, 161–62, 178–79, 181, 183
conceptual meaning 18–19, 40, 71
concessive relations 74, 90, 95–97, 112, 114, 148
consequence 75, 80, 83, 92, 96, 109–10, 114, 134–36, 146–47, 231, 235, 242
continuation 194, 204, 222, 227
continuity 28, 36, 89, 94, 222, 234–35
contrast 7, 9, 18, 21, 126, 134–35, 147, 222, 232, 238, 240–41
corpus
– spoken 248, 251, 260, 262, 266, 269
– written 248–50, 264–65, 267, 269–70
corpus analyses 124, 161, 243
corpus data 6, 11, 49, 60, 69, 76–77, 80–81, 192
counter-argument 247, 265–67
cross-linguistic studies 96
crowdsourcing experiment 4, 47, 52, 56–57
C-units 198

DART scheme 198
deictic 247–49, 251, 268, 270–74
dialogue 85, 155, 191–92, 194, 201, 211
dialogue acts 3, 9, 13, 191–95, 197–99, 201, 206–7, 209–10
discontinuous relations 23, 96
discourse comprehension 11, 70, 161, 168
discourse connectives 57, 62, 69, 89–90, 92–93, 96, 159–62, 165–68, 173–76, 179, 183
discourse functions 11, 126, 134, 146–47, 199, 260, 268, 272, 274–75
discourse marker use 2–3, 7, 121, 127, 143
discourse relations 19, 34, 71, 81, 133, 146–48, 161–62, 166–68, 177, 181, 183

discourse segmentation 193
discourse segments 4, 20, 30–31, 34–36, 39, 70–71, 133, 206, 256
domains 1, 10, 14, 70–72, 134–35, 143, 145, 155, 211, 215–17, 232, 237–38, 244
– ideational 134–35, 144–147, 152, 216–17, 232, 237–38
– interpersonal 134, 144–46, 152, 217
– rhetorical 135, 144–45, 217
– sequential 7, 134, 144–48, 167, 216, 222, 228, 233, 238, 240–41, 243
– speech act 47–48, 260
domains and functions 134–35, 143, 211
dominant information 247, 265, 269, 274

effect of connective omission/removal 168, 179, 223
effect of discourse connectives/discourse markers 8, 23, 25, 29, 34–38, 92, 112, 161, 168, 183
effect
– cognitive 28, 31–32, 36, 40–45, 75–76, 121, 128, 134
– disruptive 113, 115
egocentric 2, 7, 121, 125, 127–28, 132, 136, 139–40, 142–45, 148, 152
egocentric orientation 146, 149–50
egocentric task 7, 126, 128, 132, 135–41, 144–49, 151–52
English 3, 10, 11, 19, 22, 24, 74–75, 160, 162, 215–17, 231, 236, 239–41, 243, 249–50, 268–70
epistemic 25, 32, 47–48, 50–51, 61, 63, 134
exemplification 234–35
experimental approach 2–3, 17, 118
experimental design 73, 127, 152
experimental studies 5, 22, 26, 45–46, 51, 61–62
explicitation 10, 12, 179, 215–16, 218–19, 222, 224, 230–43
explicitation and implicitation 224, 231
Explicitation Hypothesis 216, 230
explicitation strategies 217, 222
exposure to print 2, 5–6, 12, 69–70, 72–73, 76–78, 80, 83–84
eye-tracking 41–43, 95

filler 7, 57, 134, 152, 209
fluency 14, 124, 127
– reading 6, 89, 92, 94–95, 97, 99, 114–15
focus 12–13, 69, 71, 91, 113, 128, 162, 174, 181, 231
focus operators 23–24, 30
French 2, 4, 45, 47–49, 52, 54, 56, 60, 63, 74, 76–77, 78, 80–81, 84, 89–90, 95–100, 104, 106, 112, 114, 115, 223–224
frequency 6, 46, 60, 74–76, 78, 81–82, 84, 136, 138–41, 151, 153, 215, 217, 238, 240–41
frequency bands 139–41, 143, 151, 153
frequency effects 84, 151

generalization of meaning 218–19, 222, 228–30, 237–38, 240–243
genre 1, 225, 243, 248, 273–75
German 19, 23–24, 115, 223, 239, 242–243
grammaticalization 13, 23, 39, 134
grammaticization 247, 268, 271

Hebrew 11, 247–76, 257, 268, 270, 272

ideational, *see* domain
illocutionary force 9, 18, 21, 191, 199–200, 205, 207–8, 210
implicature 21–22, 268
implicit marking 103–4, 107
implicitation 10, 215–17, 219, 222–25, 230–31, 236, 238–39, 241–42
incoherence 76, 97, 106, 108, 111–13, 115, 168
individual differences 2, 5, 69–70, 72, 76, 78, 80, 83, 115
instructional meaning 18, 21
interpersonal, *See* domain
intonation 9, 201–2, 210
intonation units (IU) 261
intra-sentential connection 225, 227, 229–30, 237–38, 241–42
Italian 19, 23

language acquisition 34, 72
language comprehension 12, 158
language development 70
language processing 8, 71–72, 123, 125

language proficiency 12, 81, 91–92, 95, 98, 100, 107, 113, 115–16
learner 6, 69, 72–73, 80–83, 91, 93, 95, 115
lexical cue 89–90, 106, 114–15
lexical item 71, 239
lexical unit 218–19, 222, 232, 242
Lextale scores 98, 100, 108, 113
Lextale task 100
low accessibility 268, 270
low cognitive load condition 127–28, 132, 140, 153

measures of language proficiency 81
modal particle 18, 20
monosemy 141–43
multifunctionality 1, 123, 134

native and non-native readers 6, 89, 96–97, 100–102, 104–7, 110–12, 114
natural language inference (NLI) 161, 171
natural language processing (NLP) 3, 159–61
new information 11, 47, 197, 224, 247–48, 255–56, 274–75
non-literal translation 218–19, 221–22
non-native readers 6–7, 89–97, 100–116

objective relation 5, 45, 48–49, 53–56, 58–62
objectivisation 62–63
older speakers 46, 62
omission 9, 179, 215–16, 218–20, 225–28, 231–32, 236–38, 240, 242
– partial 220, 227–28, 239
– total 220, 225
online-processing 6, 12, 74, 93, 95, 97

paradigmatic relations 10, 240–41
paraphrase detection 161–62, 172–73, 178
parenthetical connective 217, 240
pause 9, 132, 192, 201–2, 210
performative 248–51, 255, 268, 272, 274–75
polarity 34, 74
polyfunctional 75, 92–93, 115, 248, 275
polyfunctionality 75–76, 115, 123, 215, 247–48, 272
polysemous 126–27, 138, 142–43, 148
polysemy 7, 123, 126–27, 141–42, 151, 272

position 18, 173, 183, 215, 222, 274
– utterance-initial 204, 210
positive sentiment 172–73
pragmatic markers 133, 167, 236
Principles of discourse marking 2–3, 17–40
print exposure 83
procedural meaning 11, 17–21, 30, 32, 40, 71, 124, 167
proficiency 80, 91–92, 160

Qualtrics 57, 100

reading comprehension 70, 72
reading experiments 2–3, 23, 94, 96, 114
reading times 36, 95, 97, 100–103, 105, 107, 110–12, 167, 181
reanalysis 4, 17, 26, 35, 37–39
reason 21, 50–51
redundancy 239–40, 268
reformulation 126, 147–48
rhetorical *See* domain

scope 215, 238, 241–42
second language acquisition 2, 13, 80, 89
second language learner 5–6, 12, 80, 83
self-paced reading task 104
sense 27, 199
sentence processing 9
sentence processing models 161
sentential adverb 17–18, 25, 32–33
sentiment 172–73
sentiment classification 165, 172–73, 181
sequential, *See* domain
signal 106, 114, 125, 127, 167–68, 195, 203
Slovene 9, 11, 191, 193–96, 198, 200, 203, 208–9
social media 12, 46, 56, 62–63
source text 216–17, 224, 230, 241
Spanish 11, 19, 22–24, 28, 30, 95–96, 114, 223, 231
speaker orientation 2, 7, 121, 127, 138–40, 142–49, 151
specification 7, 9, 126, 134–35, 147–49
specification of meaning 215–16, 218–19, 222, 230, 232, 235, 237–38, 242
specification relation 148
speech act 47–48, 191–92, 249, 251

speech act theory 192, 196
spoken interaction 13, 121, 193
students 5, 52–53, 61, 63, 73, 77–79
subjective 56, 65, 262
subjective relation 45–46, 48–49, 51–56, 58–61, 231
subjectivity 5, 45, 49, 51
subject of consciousness 50–51

target 60–61
target area 25–26
target language 223–24, 229–31, 237
target text 222, 232, 237–40, 242
task 35, 37, 57, 79–81, 84, 98, 100, 128–32, 136, 151–52, 160–61, 169, 172–75, 178
taxonomy 20, 147–48
teenager 6, 69, 72, 75, 77–80, 82–84
temporal relation 75, 134–135, 146–47, 224
text comprehension 83, 91–92, 166
Title Recognition Test (TRT) 83
translated text 10, 216–17, 220–21, 226, 228, 230–32, 237, 241, 243
translation process 10, 12, 215, 217, 225
translation technique 218–22
TTR (type-token ratio) 136–38
turn 194, 197, 200, 204–7, 210
type-token ratio, *See* TTR

under-determinacy 28, 30–31, 34, 39
underspecification 124, 215, 229
university student 4–6, 45–47, 53, 55–56, 59–62, 72–73, 77–78
unmarked utterance 25, 27, 29–33, 36–39

variability 72, 76–77
variable 7, 12, 23, 72, 98, 125, 127, 141

WO-aware models 175–76, 178, 181
word order 164, 169, 173, 175, 178, 242
working memory 71, 128, 130, 138, 152
written mode 6, 46, 69–72, 74–78, 80–83

younger speakers 5, 12, 46, 49, 62, 63, 83, 129

www.ingramcontent.com/pod-product-compliance
Lightning Source LLC
Chambersburg PA
CBHW050518170426
43201CB00013B/2004